ACCESS TO WESTERN ESOTERICISM

SUNY Series in Western Esoteric Traditions
Edited by David Appelbaum

ACCESS
TO
WESTERN
ESOTERICISM

Antoine Faivre

STATE UNIVERSITY OF NEW YORK PRESS

Articles of Book II originally published in journals :

"Foi et savoir chez Franz von Baader et dans la gnose moderne," pp. 137–156, in *Les Études Philosophiques*, Paris, P.U.F., 1977, n° 1.

"Église Intérieure et Jérusalem céleste," pp. 77–91, in *Cahiers de l'Université Saint-Jean de Jérusalem*, Paris, Berg International, 1976, n° 2.

"Le Temple de Salomon dans la théosophie maçonnique," pp. 274–289, in *Australian Journal of French Studies*, Melbourne, The Hawthorne Press, septembre 1972, vol. IX, n° 3.

"Les Noces chymiques de Christian Rosencreutz comme pèlerinage de l'Âme," pp. 139–153, in *Cahiers de l'Université Saint-Jean de Jérusalem*, Paris, Berg International, 1978, n° 4.

"Miles redivivus (Aspects de l'Imaginaire chevaleresque au XVIII° siècle)," pp. 98–124, in *ibid.*, 1984, n° 10.

"Les Métamorphoses d'Hermès : Cosmologies néo-gnostiques et Gnose traditionnelle," pp. 95–120, in *ibid.*, 1979, n° 5.

Published by
State University of New York Press, Albany

For information, address State University of New York Press, :
90 State Street, Suite 700, Albany, NY 12207

Production by Cathleen Collins
Marketing by Nancy Farrell

Library of Congress in Publication Data

Faivre, Antoine, 1934–
    [Accès de l'ésotérisme occidental. English]
    Access to Western esotericism / Antoine Faivre.
        p.   cm. — (SUNY series in Western esoteric traditions)
    Includes bibliographic references and index.
    ISBN 0–7914–2177–5. — ISBN 0–7914–2178–3
    1. Occultism—History.   I. Title.   II. Series.
BF1412.F313   1994
133'.09—dc20   94–2064
                                                                  CIP

10 9 8 7 6 5 4 3 2

FOR ROBERT SALMON

BY THE SAME AUTHOR

Kirchberger et l'Illuminisme du XVIIIè siècle. Den Hag: Martinus Nijhoff, series International Archives for the History of Ideas, nr. 16. 1966.

Eckartshausen et la théosophie chrétienne. Paris: C. Klincksieck, 1969.

L'Esotérisme au XVIIIè siècle en France et en Allemagne. Paris: Seghers-Laffont, series La Table d'Emeraude, 1973. Spanish edition: *El Esoterismo en el siglo XVIII.* Madrid: EDAF, 1976.

Mystiques, Théosophes et Illuminés au siècle des Lumières. Hildesheim: Georg Olms, series Studien und Materialien zur Geschichte der Philosophie (Band 20), 1977.

Les Contes de Grimm (Mythe et Initiation), Paris: Les Lettres Modernes, series Circé (Cahiers de Recherche sur l'Imaginaire), nr. 10-11, 1978.

Accès de l'Esotérisme occidental. Paris: Gallimard, series Bibliothèque des Sciences Humaines, 1986, Revised and translated into English for the present volume.

Toison d'Or et Alchimie. Paris-Milan: Archè Edidit, 1990. English edition: *The Golden Fleece and Alchemy.* Albany: State University of New York Press, Suny Series in Western Esoteric Traditions, 1993.

L'Esotérisme. Paris: Presses Universitaires de France, series "Que Sais-Je?," nr. 1031, 1992, new ed. 1993. Italian edition: *L'Esoterismo, storia e significati.* Milan: SugarCo, 1992. Translated into English for the present volume.

The Eternal Hermes. Grand Rapids (Mich.): Phanes Press. Forthcoming (1995).

Physica Sacra (Etudes sur Franz von Baader et les Philosophes de la Nature). Paris: Albin Michel, series Idées. Forthcoming (1995).

CONTENTS

BOOK TWO
STUDIES IN ESOTERICISM

A BIBLIOGRAPHICAL GUIDE TO RESEARCH

PREFACE TO THE PRESENT EDITION

Since the Academy, by definition, is curious about everything, it could have long ago established both a curriculum and a research program devoted exclusively to esotericism. At least two obstacles stood in the way.

First of all, the transdisciplinary character of esotericism is hardly compatible with the separation of the disciplines, which resemble well labeled jars lining a pharmacy shelf. In the past few years, it is true, the use of communicating vessels has somewhat modified the situation, although genuine transdisciplinarity is still often confused with casual pluri- or interdisciplinarity. The second reason relates to the first. Vast areas of our Western cultural history, obscured a priori by theological or epistemological positions, were deliberately omitted, abandoned to the curiosity of eccentrics or even cranks and to capricious handling, which only increased the distrust of serious, albeit somewhat prejudiced investigators and established thinkers vis-à-vis this peripheral domain. The distrust is so pervasive that many scholars are still wondering what esotericism is or whether it truly merits study.

Today, to be sure, neither the partitions nor the distrust have completely disappeared, but they are in part compensated for by the desire to leave nothing unexplored. This is why historical research bearing on precise points of esotericism (i.e., on specific works and certain authors) is multiplying, chiefly in France, Italy, England, and the United States. While for centuries Germany was the repository of traditional science in Europe, for nearly forty years now the Germans have preferred to keep anything considered "irrational" at a distance. This means they have sacrificed the best for fear of the worst, discarding both the wheat and the chaff.

In 1965 the chair in the History of Western Esotericism (under the title: "History of Christian Esotericism") was established in the Religious Studies section of the Ecole Pratique des Hautes Etudes at the Sorbonne. The first holder was François Secret, a specialist in the Christian Kabbalah. Thus, for the first time, esotericism took its place in the official curriculum, no longer a peripheral inclusion of an author tolerated by chance or exception in a program of study. To my knowledge, no other establishment in France or elsewhere has followed that example yet, and that despite the proliferation of sections and departments of Religious Studies. We should, however, cite the creation of a Hermetic Academy in the United States by Professor Robert McDermott in 1980. This academy has presently assembled around 150 researchers, mostly university based. The latter also belong to the Esotericism and Perennialism Group, formed in 1986 within the very large American Academy of Religion.

When I assumed François Secret's chair in 1979, the name of the directorship became "History of Esoteric and Mystical Currents in Modern and Contemporary Europe." Some time earlier, encouraged by my colleagues Pierre Nora and Jacques Le Goff, directors of prestigious collections at Editions Gallimard, I conceived the ambitious project of writing a massive *History of Esotericism in the West*. But on reflection I was soon persuaded that such an enterprise would be premature for what I could do, since I could not imagine such a work as a simple catalog. Suspecting that the work in question would never see the light of day, Nora then suggested that I submit for his series a collection of studies that would be timely as well as reflective, which would constitute so many "approaches" or "means of access" to Western esotericism. This book appeared in 1986, followed by a little book called *L'Esotérisme* in 1992.

The present work is the translation of these two volumes of unequal length, originally published in French. The first (*Accès de l'ésotérisme occidental*, Paris, Gallimard, 1986) contains a long general introduction, seven focused essays, and an extensive bibliography. The second (*L'Esotérisme*, Paris, P.U.F., coll. "*Que Sais-Je?*" 1992) contains a methodological introduction and a brief account of the types of Western esotericism. Book I of the present work includes the introduction of the latter book as "Methodology," as well as a good part of the introduction to *Accès* as "Keyword Definitions." Book I includes also the historical summary from *L'Esotérisme* as "a short History of Western Esoteric currents (Essay on periodization)." Book II contains six of the seven articles of the 1986 French edition. The essay missing here was published in English as "Ancient and Medieval Roots of Modern Esoteric Movements" in *Modern Esoteric Spirituality* (New York, Crossroads Series in *World Spirituality: An Encyclopedic of History the Religious Quest*, vol. 21, 1992). In view of the English translation of elements presented here, I made, of course, a number of revisions and corrections to the original French text. Moreover, I made an effort to highlight the bibliography at the end. The latter represents the spirit of the entire work, conceived as a conjunction of clarifications, orientations, approaches.

I wish to thank William D. Eastman and David Appelbaum for our fruitful interactions and for their spontaneous interest in the project I submitted to them. Thanks to them, the present work has been realized. For helpful suggestions concerning Renaissance esotericism I am indebted to Jean-Pierre Brach, and for friendly editorial assistance, to Karen Claire Voss.

Antoine Faivre
Paris, July 1993

BOOK ONE

APPROACHES TO WESTERN
ESOTERIC CURRENTS

Part One

Methodology and Reflexions

I) METHODOLOGY

The key word in this book for which general consensus on meaning has not yet been established covers a loosely defined concept. However, if we judge on the basis of bookstore offerings as well as on media discourse and imagery, there is a great deal of interest in it. Under the heading of esotericism, merchants and journalists group together for convenience such diverse topics as astrology, parapsychology, Tarot and yoga side by side with Freemasonry, theosophy, and alchemy. It would be difficult to prepare an exhaustive inventory, while too many articles, added by the whims of fashion, would make the whole an incongruous display. Let us recognize from the outset that the meaning of "esotericism," never a precise term, has begun to overflow its boundaries on all sides.

Three possible paths present themselves to anyone who wants to see into the matter clearly. The first would consist of making an inventory, lumping together any and everything that has been termed "esotericism." This might be the method of a sociologist who, easily satisfied, could interpret the results as showing the need our contemporaries feel for the irrational. The second way would be to decide on the basis of value criteria what deserves to be called "esotericism," which might, of course, entail throwing a few babies out with the bath water. One can guess where that might lead. If we renounce taking inventory of the stands at the fair and donning the garb of the guru, there still remains a third possibility: A careful study of the material. There we see harmonies and contrasts appear before us. (If we are to see beyond the panes of glass surrounding us, we must do some looking in libraries and museums.)

To be sure, academic recognition of esotericism as a special field of study already exists, in France where there is a chair for "esoteric currents" as in other countries where related programs are in operation (cf. *supra* in "Preface"). But up to now there has hardly been any critical questioning of this specialization, although each discipline must define its own purview. The proposed system of criteria in the present introduction bears on these esoteric "currents." It does not pretend to be more than a methodological tool, subject to refinement and correction. The historical survey that follows stems directly from these methodological propositions. For reasons to be taken up later, this system of criteria treats essentially the modern period of Western esotericism.

A) Overly Restricted Definitions of "Esotericism"

The lexical content of the word "esotericism" is slight.* ("Eso" means "inside" and "ter" implies an opposition.) Like any word rather empty of meaning in itself, "esotericism" has shown it can be inflated, permeated, and semantically overdetermined. Still, it is by no means its etymology that must be queried but rather its function, which calls forth a bundle of attitudes and an ensemble of discourses. The question for us is whether these attitudes and these discourses permit the observer, i.e., the esoterologist, to circumscribe a possible field of study. Above all, we do not want to start with what "esotericism" would be "in itself," we doubt that such a thing exists. Nor is this even a domain in the sense we would use in speaking of the domain of painting, philosophy, or chemistry.

Rather than a specific genre, it is a form of thought, the nature of which we have to try to capture on the basis of the currents which exemplify it. Thus the adjective appeared long before the noun, which dates only from the beginning of the nineteenth century. In fact, it would be advantageous, wherever possible, to use the adjective, and the plural form of the noun. (Likewise, it might be preferable to use words like "astrology" or "alchemy" in the plural.) Moreover, how could an abstract definition avoid an a priori assumption about what it ought to be, its "real" nature, i.e., finally basing itself on a philosophical or ideological presupposition? It appears more fruitful to start with its variable usages within diverse discourses and to query what observable realities these usages stem from; then to take as material for study, the appearance of fields that explicitly present themselves as esoteric as well as those discourses that may implicitly present themselves as esoteric. Finally, to ask what guiding criteria could be used to determine if a discourse or a work is esoteric, whether it is considered to be already or not.

---

* I would like to express my gratitude to the Crossroad Publishing Company for permission to use here (pages 11 to 15) part of the material presented in my "Introduction" to *Modern Esoteric Spirituality* (Volume 21 of "World Spirituality, An Encyclopedic History of the Religious Quest", New York, 1992, pages XI to XXI).

These empirical reflections start with a threefold interrogation. What implicit criteria are used by university programs that treat materials that are explicitly qualified as esoteric? What does the noun "esotericism" seem to cover since it came into use at the beginning of the nineteenth century? Especially, what does it cover among words used more or less synonymously, notably since the Renaissance? What would be the basic characteristics which, taken as a whole, could serve as a methodological base, even provisionally, for a history of Western esoteric currents?

"Esotericism" conjures up chiefly the idea of something "secret," of a "discipline of the arcane," of restricted realms of knowledge. It is certain that mystery inspires reverie, confers a dimension of depth on the world and that things too familiar easily lose their attraction. Thus esotericists knowingly cultivate mystery. Certainly it is not a question here of considering the use of the word "esotericism" illegitimate for secret, "restricted" teachings. But we want only to note that it is not especially operative, because it is much too exclusive. A large part of alchemy, for example, is not secret, when one considers the fact that since the sixteenth century, an abundant literature on alchemy has been continuously disseminated. The same is true of theosophy. Boehme's writings, so very representative, were destined to circulate in various milieus. These examples could be multiplied. And when secrets do exist, they are generally open secrets. The etymology of "esotericism" clarifies the idea of secret by suggesting that we can access understanding of a symbol, myth, or reality only by a personal effort of progressive elucidation through several successive levels, i.e., by a form of hermeneutics. There is no ultimate secret once we determine that everything, in the end, conceals a secret. Let us note also that peripherally, "esoteric" is sometimes used to qualify the hidden God (as in Franz von Baader).

"Esotericism" has a second, very widespread meaning. Here it serves to designate a type of knowledge, emanating from a spiritual center to be attained after transcending the prescribed ways and techniques—quite diverse considering the schools or the currents—that can lead to it. This spiritual locus, this higher level of "knowledge" would overarch all particular traditions and initiations, which are only so many means of access. It is identical to all who achieve it; experience of its attainment is the proof or guarantee of the "transcendent unity of religions." Let us note also that in this context, "esotericism" means as much the ways that lead to this "center" as the "center" itself. Esotericists who speak of esotericism in this second sense (oftentimes they speak of "esoterism") tend, just like mystics, to maintain a discourse marked by subjectivity. And if they wish to escape this trait, they tend towards a form of normative or doctrinal discourse. In any event, this second sense is too restricted for us to be limited by it.

To use the word in these two different but contiguous meanings is quite legitimate. Unfortunately, the notion of "esotericism" is often confused with other notions, already in general use and with which it is has become identified. One example is the general notion of "initiation." However there exist all sorts of initiations, the goal and significance of which vary enormously according to context, whether the initiation is conferred individually (from master to disciple) or collectively. Moreover, is not initiation itself a substantial part of most religious traditions? Finally let us mention the confusion, incurred by ignorance or an inquisitorial spirit between esotericism and religious marginality. This confusion leads to contradictions that various sectarianisms exploit, thereby making any serious approach impossible. Esoteric currents could not, except by intellectual dishonesty, be defined as by nature marginal to the churches. Specifically, the doctrinal elements that can be found in esotericism are not the same as those that identify them as esoteric. Therefore, to start with doctrinal elements only perpetuates the misunderstandings. By means of bits and pieces of theology or metaphysics plucked from here and there, we can build up a heresy that does not exist, just for the pleasure of criticizing it later. Thus, above all else, esotericism involves a form of thought. Following this mode of thought does not mean denying or adopting any dogma whatsoever, and the fact that esotericism often happens to be accompanied by heretical propositions is in no way what defines it as esoteric. Just as there is no lack of esotericists at the very heart of Catholicism, without being heretical for all that. This said, the status of esoteric currents cannot be defined except as a function of their relationships to the dominant religions. In the Latin West, these relationships have been and remain difficult with the Catholic and Protestant churches.

B) The Formation of a Referential Esoteric Corpus in the Renaissance

We are speaking now of "esotericism" in a sense both more general and more precise: a third sense that is neither that of a "secret" nor that of a "spiritual center to be attained." This sense is more general, in allowing to cover entire areas of material presenting common elements: a kind of unity of fact. And it is more precise since it does not lose sight of the aspects of the imaginary it calls forth—and which, as we shall see, considerably overflow the entirely too restrictive usages alluded to earlier—aspects that are united under the same heading *by the West.* To be sure, words also exist in the East that some have tried to make correspond more or less to esotericism. But these words are loaded with different connotations. They refer to meanings that are too diverse, conceptually too restricted, or anthropologically too vast to be applied to the field that concerns us here. In the Far East and in other cultural terrains, esotericism does not even have its own status, whereas in the West it does. To be perfectly clear, it would be difficult to understand what a "universal esotericism" might be.

What we mean by the West is the vast Greco-Roman ensemble, both medieval and modern in which the Jewish and Christian religions have cohabited with Islam for several centuries. The present reflections involve essentially the modern esoteric currents, i.e., the Latin West since the end of the fifteenth century. It is only then at the beginning of the Renaissance, it would appear, that we see emerging a will to bring together a variety of ancient materials of the kind we are concerned with here, and that it was believed then that these materials could constitute a homogeneous whole. Certain among them were found linked from the beginning of our era to forms of Hellenistic religiosity (Stoicism, Gnosticism, Hermetism, Neopythagoreanism) and later to the three Abrahamic religions. But in the Renaissance came the idea of considering them as mutually complementary and looking for their common denominators (cf. Marsilio Ficino, Pico della Mirandola, *et alia*). Thus, especially after 1492, the Jewish Kabbalah penetrated Christian milieus and celebrated surprising nuptials with neo-Alexandrian Hermetism in a light of analogy and a climate of universal harmonies. The more or less explicit project consisted in placing these traditions in a diapason, arranged into consonances. Then the *prisca theologia* of the Middle Ages underwent a transformation. It became *philosophia occulta* and *philosophia perennis*, terms that were not interchangeable, but that were applied to a nebula endowed with relative autonomy in the mental universe of the epoch, and detached from theology properly speaking. The representatives of *philosophia perennis*, real or mythical, constituted links in a chain. Their names are Moses, Zoroaster, Hermes Trismegistus, Plato, Orpheus, the Sibyls, and many more. It already constitutes, give or take a few nuances, of course, what some would call the "Tradition." The work of the historian is not a matter of wondering whether a similar tradition really existed as such before the Renaissance, invisible and hidden behind the veil of eventual history, but of trying to seize the emergence of this idea in imagery and discourse, i.e., through the forms it could have taken on up to that point.

This autonomization of a body of knowledge, increasingly considered "exoteric" in relation to the official religion is truly in the sixteenth century, the point of departure for what can be called "esotericism" in this third sense of the word. In the Middle Ages, such an autonomization was not necessary because this same body of knowledge had bearing on the forms of the imaginary in which it was inscribed, which were generally in phase with theology. When the latter unburdened this part of itself, a vast abandoned field was soon recuperated, reinterpreted from the outside (i.e., outside the field of theology). Esotericism became the object of a body of knowledge where access no longer happened by itself, but needed specific new approaches. Whoever said "esotericism" said "go to what is more *interior*," an "interior" that became such because now believers were on the "exterior." In the Middle Ages, that "more interior" did not exist, since a believer was always "inside." We cannot overemphasize the importance of the role played by humanist scholars in the genesis of modern esotericism. Reacting to the appropriation of philosophy by the Scholastics, the humanists professionalized such esoteric sciences as Hermetism or Kabbalah, practicing a monopoly of another sort themselves! At that time, esotericism was basically a matter for specialists, but while theologians addressed listeners who could understand, these specialists were more likely to address the cognoscenti, who by necessity, were other scholars.

And what does this body of knowledge bear upon? Essentially on the articulation between metaphysical principles and cosmology. This articulation did not create a problem as long as the cosmological domain (that of "second causes") remained subordinate to metaphysics. The very idea of esotericism was hardly traceable. But when the sciences of Nature freed themselves from theology, they began to be cultivated for themselves (a process that in Christianity and Islam took hold in the twelfeth century). Henceforth the esoteric field could be constituted, which in the Renaissance began to deal with the interface between metaphysics and cosmology, i.e., to function as an extratheological modality for linking the universal to the particular. However, it filled the interface with speculations that were much more cosmological than metaphysical. There is little metaphysics in Giordano Bruno, and the alchemists began to think divinity alchemically rather than think alchemy divinely.

From then until the present, a vast field is constituted, comprised of fundamental characteristics (or components) selected from a multiform historical corpus. Before presenting the components, let us recall what formed the corpus. On the one hand, are presented three rivers, the three "traditional sciences," which do not seem to belong to any epoch in particular: alchemy, astrology, magic (in the Renaissance sense of *magia*), generally linked to some kind of arithmosophy (or science of numbers, to which are attached, of course, various forms of musical esotericism). Still active in our own times, they maintain close interconnections. On the other hand, there are a certain number of streams that have hollowed out their bed at relatively determinable moments (often starting with a founder's text). These are in no way alien to the three large rivers because all this is intermingled. From the end of the fifteenth century on, these streams are the Christian Kabbalah (an adaptation of the Jewish Kabbalah), neo-Alexandrian Hermetism, discourses inspired by the idea of *philosophia perennis* and of the "primordial Tradition," the philosophy of nature of the Paracelsian variety, then the Romantic (partly German) *Naturphilosophie*; from the seventeenth century on, theosophy and Rosicrucianism (both Germanic at first), as well as the later associations (initiatory societies more or less inscribed in the wake of the former).

We might have believed that these rivers and streams would disappear after the Renaissance. But when the great epistemological break of the seventeenth century occurred, they survived, and the scientism of the nineteenth century did not cause them to dry up. Today esotericisms are more present than ever before. Their tenacious permanence appears in modern times as a counterpart of our scientific and secularized vision of the world. But it would be simplistic and erroneous to reduce this longevity to a need to react against the imaginary and *epistémè* in place. More than a reaction we could be dealing with the possible forms that one of the two poles of the human soul, i.e., mythic capacity, dons for actualization. (The other pole is the so-called rational thought, which in the West is modeled on a kind of Aristotelian logic.)

Here we confront a heteroclite body that must be studied in the relations its parts maintain among themselves and vis-à-vis the diverse religious, political, and cultural contexts with which it is associated. A considerable corpus, complex contexts, all the more so since what belongs to esotericism does not always bear the name. There are those who are like Molière's Monsieur Jourdain (who had realized that he had always spoken prose); in reverse, there are people who label themselves esotericists but whose activity does not go beyond that of fortune tellers or who use the word to baptize their own doctrine. Now esoteric currents are not identified by a word but by guideposts, just as for us today gods are less identifiable by proper names than by their attributes. None of the signs or components that will be presented later is doctrinal. Nor can esotericism be defined simply on the basis of the various ways esoterists themselves define it. Neither, as we have seen, on the basis of sectarian presuppositions bearing on what it "ought" to be, contrary to what certain others do today who claim it for themselves, intending to place their little parish above all the rest. On the other hand, if we approach esotericism phenomenologically as a form of thought, an ensemble of tendencies to be described, we can avoid doing violence to historical data.

It would not be doing too much violence to this data to look for guiding notions that at first glance would be esoteric because esoterists have considered them to be so. An example would be the *magia naturalis* (so-called natural magic) or sophiology (discourse on the Sophia of the Old Testament, the marriage of our soul with Sophia). But this would assuredly not be the best way to approach the question. In truth, if the idea of *magia naturalis* may be tinged with esoteric coloration, it may just as well not be, depending on the authors who discuss it. Moreover, in the Latin West, divine Wisdom (the Sophia) belongs to theology almost as much as to theosophic tradition.

Nor would we be doing violence to historical data in cataloging the preferred images, symbols and motifs that esoteric literature uses—occasionally to the point of satiety. Among these are found the androgyne, the Fall, the philosopher's stone, the "subtle body," the *Anima mundi*, the geography of the sacred (e.g., subterranean cavern, mandala design, or labyrinth), the book of magic, and such dramatis personae as Hermes or Orpheus. One could easily cite scores more. But motifs hardly serve to circumscribe the nature of the esoteric terrain, given that the majority of these motifs are found nearly everywhere in various disguises. Any motif returns in the end to an archety-pology such as that of C.G. Jung, i.e., an anthropology. That esoterologists are called on to take an interest in the archetypes is self-evident, but if their field merely coincides with that of anthropologists or psychologists, what would be their *raison d'être* and why continue to speak of esotericism or eso-teric currents? Reciprocally, if the esoteric terrain concerns anthropologists of the imaginary, it is no less evident that the mere presence in a work of a theme of more or less universal dimension need not categorize that work as esoteric. It is an issue that concerns not only the dissolution, always to be feared, of the field we are studying into other fields of study, but also the very status of its historical position in general vis-à-vis anthropology and vice versa. Between one and the other, the relationships that ought to arise from complementarity are sometimes made difficult by virtue of reductionist, dila-tory historicism on the part of the former and a tendency to amalgamate on the part of the latter.

C) The Components of Esotericism Considered as a Form of Thought

In the modern West what we may call "esotericism" is a form of thought identifiable by the presence of six fundamental characteristics or components, distributed in varying proportions inside its vast, concrete, historical context. Four are "intrinsic," meaning that they must all be present for a given mater-ial to be classified under the rubric of esotericism. By nature they are more or less inseparable, as we shall see, but methodologically it is important to distin-guish them. To them two more components are added that we shall call sec-ondary, i.e., not fundamental, but frequently found in conjunction with the others.

Here are the four fundamental elements:

1) Correspondences. Symbolic and real correspondences (there is no room for abstractions here!) are said to exist among all parts of the universe, both seen and unseen. ("As above so below.") We find again here the ancient idea of microcosm and macrocosm or, if preferred, the principle of universal interdependence. These correspondences, considered more or less veiled at first sight, are, therefore, intended to be read and deciphered. The entire uni-verse is a huge theater of mirrors, an ensemble of hieroglyphs to be decoded. Everything is a sign; everything conceals and exudes mystery; every object hides a secret. The principles of noncontradiction and excluded middle of lin-ear causality are replaced here by those of the included middle and syn-chronicity. We can distinguish two kinds of correspondences. First, those that exist in nature, seen and unseen, e.g., between the seven metals and the seven planets, between the planets and the parts of the human body or character (or of society). This is the basis of astrology—correspondence between the natural world and the invisible departments of the celestial and supercelestial world, etc. Next there are correspondences between Nature (the cosmos) or even history and revealed texts. Here we find the Kabbalah, whether Jewish or Christian, and various varieties of *physica sacra*. According to this form of inspired concordism, scripture (the Bible, for example) and Nature are in harmony, the knowledge of one aiding in the knowledge of the other. Ultimately, the world stage is a linguistic phenomenon. But neither correspondences nor concordism necessarily mean "esotericism." Such are found present also in many a philosophical or religious current where each more or less delimits the nature of its own networks of analogy and similitude. This principle is equally at work in the procedures of divination, poetry, and sorcery, but the latter, nonetheless, are not synonymous.

    2) Living Nature. The cosmos is complex, plural, hierarchical—as we have just seen with the idea of correspondence. Accordingly, Nature occupies an essential place. Multilayered, rich in potential revelations of every kind, it must be read like a book. The word *magia*, so important in the Renaissance imaginary, truly calls forth that idea of a Nature, seen, known, and experienced as essentially alive in all its parts, often inhabited and traversed by a light or a hidden fire circulating through it. Thus understood, the "magic" is simultaneously the knowledge of the networks of sympathies or antipathies that link the things of Nature and the concrete operation of these bodies of knowledge. (Let us think of the astral powers that the magus brings to talismans, Orphism in all its forms, especially musical forms, the use of stones, metals, plants favorable to reestablishing physical or psychological harmony that had been disturbed.) Inscribed in this perspective, Paracelsism represents a vast current with multiple ramifications, from animal magnetism to homeopathy, by way of all the forms of *magia naturalis* (a complex notion at the crossroads of magic and science). More than the practices, properly speaking, it is knowledge—in the sense of "gnosis"—which seems to contribute to establishing the notion of the esoteric attitude. This is knowledge in the sense Goethe meant when he had Faust say that he burns with desire to "know the world/in its intimate context/to contemplate the active forces and the first elements." To this is often added, fraught with implications for alchemy and for a *Naturphilosophie* of esoteric character, an interpretation of a teaching of Saint Paul (Rom. 8:12–22), according to which suffering Nature, subjected to exile and vanity, also waits to take part in salvation. Thus are established a science of Nature, a gnosis laden with soteriological elements, a theosophy which labors over the triad of "God–Humanity–Nature" from whence the theosopher brings forth dramaturgical correspondences, complementary and forever new.

However, we must note that since the beginning of the twentieth century, in the wake of an ontologically dualist metaphysics—and a theology, which since the nineteenth century has neglected Nature by letting science take over the universe—the emergence of a form of monist spiritualism in which Nature (the created world) is neglected, even denied in its reality through the influence of Oriental, especially Hindu, doctrines. This is a current that grants Nature only a quite inferior place at best and rejects modernity, including the sciences stemming from it. For the observer of present-day tendencies, this is an interesting phenomenon and for the historian, an off-course current.

3) *Imagination and Mediations.* The two notions are linked and complementary. The idea of correspondence presumes already a form of imagination inclined to reveal and use mediations of all kinds, such as rituals, symbolic images, mandalas, intermediary spirits. From whence the importance of angelology in this context, but likewise of the "transmitter" in the sense of "initiator," of "guru" (cf. also *infra*, apropos of the sixth element). Perhaps it is especially this notion of mediation that makes the difference between the mystical and the esoteric. In somewhat oversimplified terms, we could say that the mystic—in the strictly classical sense—aspires to the more or less complete suppression of images and intermediaries because for him they become obstacles to the union with God. While the esoterist appears to take more interest in the intermediaries revealed to his inner eye through the power of his creative imagination than to extend himself essentially toward the union with the divine. He prefers to sojourn on Jacob's ladder where angels (and doubtless other entities as well) climb up and down, rather than to climb to the top and beyond. The distinction is merely a practical one. Indeed, there is sometimes a great deal of esotericism in a mystic like Saint Hildegard, and we note an acute mystical tendency in many an theosopher, e.g., Louis-Claude de Saint-Martin.

It is the imagination that allows the use of these intermediaries, symbols, and images to develop a gnosis, to penetrate the hieroglyphs of Nature, to put the theory of correspondences into active practice and to uncover, to see, and to know the mediating entities between Nature and the divine world. It would be instructive to trace the history of the imagination in the West, i.e., its status. We would thus shed light on its importance for it is in no way, as in Kant, the simple, restrained psychological faculty between perception and concept, or "the mad woman in the attic," mistress of error and delusion whose victims are those who flee the world but remain trapped in their own inner universe. But rather it is a kind of organ of the soul, thanks to which humanity can establish a cognitive and visionary relationship with an intermediary world, with a mesocosm—what Henry Corbin proposed calling a *mundus imaginalis*. Arabic influence (Avicenna, Sohravardhi, Ibn Arabi) was able to exert a determinative influence here in the West, but independently Paracelsism found very comparable categories. And it is especially under the inspiration of the *Corpus Hermeticum* rediscovered in the fifteenth century that memory and imagination are associated to the extent of blending together. After all, a part of the teaching of Hermes Trismegistus consisted of "interiorizing" the world in our *mens*, from whence the "arts of memory" cultivated in the light of magic, during and after the Renaissance.

Understood thus, imagination (*imaginatio* is related to *magnet, magia, imago*) is the tool for knowledge of self, world, Myth. The eye of fire pierces the bark of appearances to call forth significations, "rapports" to render the invisible visible, the "*mundus imaginalis*" to which the eye of the flesh alone cannot provide access, and to retrieve there a treasure contributing to an enlargement of our prosaic vision. The accent is placed on vision and certainty, rather than on belief and faith. This imagination founded a visionary philosophy. Such especially energizes theosophical discourse in which it is exercised and deployed on the basis of verses of the revealed Book, both in the Jewish Kabbalah with the *Zohar* or in the great Western theosophical current which takes flight in Germany at the beginning of the seventeenth century.

4) Experience of Transmutation. If we did not consider the experience of transmutation as an essential component, what is discussed here would hardly exceed the limits of a form of speculative spirituality. Now we know the importance of initiation rituals in what on the most popular plane is called to mind by words like "esotericism," "gnosis," and "alchemy." Transformation would hardly be an adequate term because it does not necessarily signify the passage from one plane to another, nor the modification of the subject in its very nature. "Transmutation," a term borrowed from alchemy in our context, seems more appropriate. It should be understood also as "metamorphosis." It consists in allowing no separation between knowledge (gnosis) and inner experience, or intellectual activity and active imagination if we want to turn lead into silver or silver into gold. What modern Western esoteric currents often call "gnosis" in the current modern sense of the term is that illuminated knowledge that favors the "second birth"—a capital notion here, especially in theosophy. It seems that an important part of the alchemical corpus, especially since the beginning of the seventeenth century, had as its object less the description of laboratory experiments than the figurative presentation of this transmutation according to a marked path: *nigredo* (death, decapitation of the first matter or the old man), *albedo* (work in white), *rubedo* (work in red, the philosopher's stone). The rapprochement could have been suggested with the three phases of the traditional mystic's way: purgation; illumination; unification. It is often implied in such contexts that transmutation can just as well occur in a portion of Nature as in the experimenter himself.

Such would be the four basic components upon which the methodological approach proposed here for modern Western esotericism rests. Two more might be added, "relative" insofar as they are not indispensable to the defini-

tion. To present them as two new necessary conditions would limit the
exploratory field too much. These two "relative" elements deserve to be considered nevertheless in their specificity because they frequently occur with
the four others. On the one hand we could call this the practice of the concordance and on the other hand the transmission.

5) The Praxis of the Concordance. What is designated thus is not a property of Western esotericism throughout but marks most particularly the
beginning of modern times (end of the fifteenth through the sixteenth century; cf. *supra*, concerning *philosophia perennis*) to reappear at the end of the
nineteenth century in a different and triumphant form. This shows up in a
consistent tendency to try to establish common denominators between two
different traditions or even more, among all traditions, in the hope of obtaining an illumination, a gnosis, of superior quality.

To be sure, there exists a practice of concordance that could be called
"external." This is based solely on the recognition or simple respect for all
established religions that must then be investigated for points of convergence
capable of bringing together men of good will in a spirit of indifferent or
active tolerance. The type of concordance meant here is of another nature. It
tries to be more creative; it concerns individual at least as much as collective
illumination and manifests the will not only to eliminate some differences or
to uncover harmonies among diverse religious traditions, but to acquire
above all a *gnosis* embracing diverse traditions and melding them in a single
crucible. This would give the "Man of desire"* an X-ray plate image of the
living and hidden trunk behind and beneath the visible branches of the dis-
crete traditions. Starting with the nineteenth century this tendency really
stands out, as a result of a better knowledge of the East, then thanks to the
influence of "comparative religion," a new academic discipline. This reaches
the point where the proponents of traditionalism, those called the *perennialists*
in English, go so far as to postulate and teach that a "primordial Tradition"
exists, overarching all the other religious or esoteric traditions of humanity.

6) Transmission. Emphasis on transmission implies that an esoteric
teaching can or must be transmitted from master to disciple following a
preestablished channel, respecting a previously marked path. The "second
birth" comes at that price. Two notions follow from this: a) the validity of
knowledge transmitted by an affiliation of unimpeachable authenticity or
"regularity" (the believer must be attached to a tradition considered as an

---

* "Homme de Désir": a human being inspired by the desire to deserve the love of God and to
know His secrets. The expression comes from the Vulgate ("vir desideriorum," see Book of
Daniel, IX, 23; X, 11; X, 19) and was widely used by Louis-Claude de Saint-Martin (see his
book *L'Homme de Désir*, Lyons, 1790), by his master Martines de Pasqually and by several
authors thereafter. Arthur E. Waite translates : "Man of Aspiration".

organic and integral ensemble deserving respect); b) the initiation, that is generally effected from master to disciple. (A person cannot initiate himself, any way he chooses, but must go through the hands of an initiator). We know the importance of these conditions in the genesis and development of secret, initiation societies in the West.

Just as there exists a form of thought of the esoteric type, so there exists one of a scientific, theological, or utopian type. The specificity of each consists in the simultaneous presence of a certain number of fundamental characteristics or components. Obviously the same component could belong to several forms of thought. Each puts into operation its own activities and procedures, its diverse ways of arranging and articulating its components. In this way, each constitutes for itself a body of references, a culture. There are references common to several forms of thought, e.g., "mystical" and "esoteric." With the latter, the "scientific" maintains complex and ambiguous relations where certain philosophies of Nature are at stake. It is especially interesting to note the oppositions and rejections. They are not caused uniquely by incompatible components among two forms of thought but can result also from an epistemological break inside one of them. Thus, inasmuch as the "theological" was presented in the form of a symbolic theology (e.g., the early Fathers, in the School of Chartres, or in St. Bonaventure), it was rather close to esotericism (without the two blending together for all that), but with appearance of Scholasticism in the thirteenth century such theology was increasingly in opposition to esotericism.

Therefore, to study the history of Western currents of esotericism would be first of all to identify the simultaneous presence of the six components in the works and discourses where they are found. These components can be positioned quite unequally. On the other hand, they are as identifiable in music, art, and literature as in explicitly esoteric works. We can no longer keep up with the Shakespeare studies devoted to that aspect of his dramas.

D) Advantages of the Empirical Approach

Far from sending us to doctrinal contents, the six components serve as receptacles into which various types of experiences or imaginaries* are distributed. We can enter there as many hierarchical views of the Neoplatonist type (like: the high is placed hierarchically above the below) as non-hierarchical views of

---

* "The (an) imaginary": In the sense that it has recently acquired in Humanities, mostly in France ("l'imaginaire"), this substantive refers to the images, symbols, myths, which consciously or not underlie and/or permeate a discourse, a conversation, a literary or artistic work, a current of thought, an artistic or political trend.

the hermetic type (like: God can be found just as well in a grain of sand as anywhere else; heliocentrism changes nothing essential). In the same way "transformation" can cover very different theological aspects depending upon whether or not belief in the existence of "subtle bodies" is present. A theosophy can be "emanationist," or "creationist." It can admit or reject reincarnation just as easily without having its esoteric character questioned. The question is in fact less one of believing than of knowing or of seeing. . . . It would appear, thus, advantageous to seek out similar constitutive elements having value as receptacles of the imaginary, rather that to try to find what would stem from separate explicit beliefs or professions of faith. The advantage is two-fold .

The first advantage is facilitating the sketch of a possible boundary around the field. A boundary, happily quite fluid, favoring and respecting its transdisciplinary character which considerably overflows into art, politics, literature, history of ideas. (Concerning the history of ideas one of the more interesting aspects of contemporary esotericism is the manner in which some of its representatives adapt to modernity, even postmodernity, which others reject.) A thoroughly understood transdisciplinarity respects the specificity of disciplines in order to keep any from being absorbed by neighboring disciplines of expansionist or encroaching tendencies. This implies that each define its scope in a sense that is not too "universalizing" to keep from being dissolved in a nearby ocean.

Thus the project of constituting a domain that would be "universal" esotericism appears somewhat unsuited to seat the status of our specialization on a solid basis. To be sure, there is perhaps "some esotericism" in other cultural terrains (e.g., ancient Egypt, Far East, Amerindian civilizations, etc.), and the temptation to apprehend a "universal" esotericism, to seek out its probable invariants is understandable. In a recent work (*L'Esotérisme*, Paris, R. Laffont, 1990, pp. 311–364), Pierre A. Riffard tried to present such invariants. These would be, according to this scholar, the impersonality of the authors, the opposition between the profane and the initiated, the subtle, correspondences, numbers, occult sciences, occult arts, and initiation. Riffard examined the text of the *Emerald Tablet* and found his eight invariants there. (Let us note in passing that we also find in the *Emerald Tablet* our four component-conditions, plus the second of our relative components.) This proves that his taxonomy can be utilized, at least in certain cases. Nevertheless, if we can establish an agreement on the subject of correspondences, indeed on initiation (which would closely correspond to our "transmission" and "transmutation"), that is not the case for the six other invariants. Thus, Riffard's proposition is different from ours. He means to find his eight universals from the beginning of the history of civilization, a bold and stimulating undertaking, but which appears rather more able to serve as an instrument for investigating vast terrains, already so constituted, such as the history of philosophy (so long as it takes up the universal history of philosophy), the works on the imaginary (those which for nearly twenty-five years have detailed their method), or anthropology in the broad sense. Methodologically, it appears more valid to start from the empirical perspective that esotericism is a Western notion. And that the latter goes back to an ensemble of materials already sufficiently varied and thorny for it to be preferable to study them inside their context. Thus esotericism, according to Riffard, escapes what the present proposal attempts to enclose through research, not of invariants, but of elements that would be found together: a) in a given historical period or geographical domain; b) from the moment when names are sought to designate them as a whole. It is a more circumscribed enterprise, but one which allow us to avoid anachronisms like the following.

Today and for the last three centuries there are enthusiasts who see in the religion of ancient Egypt an esotericism, present in the form of mysteries, symbols, initiations, and information hidden from the profane. Now, even presuming that the enthusiasts are correct, what they describe would never be but a form of religiosity shared by many other religious systems, and it is hard to see why that should be termed "esotericism." It appears more pertinent and legitimate to study forms of egyptomania and egyptophilia proper to Western esotericists themselves, because if there is an Egyptian esotericism, it exists first of all in our modern imaginary. Whether or not the latter since the seventeenth century, reflects what ancient Egypt really was concerns the historian of Western esoteric currents only very indirectly.

Limiting the scope of the field means likewise not unduly extending it to nearby sectors despite actual overlappings and obvious proximities. A phenomenon like the New Age, so interesting today for the sociologist, psychologist, and historian of religions, comes under the rubric of New Religious Movements (NRM) rather than esoteric currents properly speaking. (The domain of the NRM has an importance which the university is only now beginning to fully appreciate. It will require special chairs.) In the same way parapsychology and witchcraft, sectors with often obvious connections to modern esoteric currents, do not for all that form an integral part of them. There are likewise some institutions like Freemasonry that come under the heading of esotericism only in certain aspects. (There are forms of Freemasonry almost completely devoid of esotericism.)

If the first advantage of the approach seems to be that it lets us sketch in the borders, the second is that it lets us distance ourselves from each esoterist speaking in that capacity—seeing that often, in our century, thoughts or schools tend to present themselves as esotericism-in-itself, as *the* way, *the* true Tradition, in opposition to other approaches. Some of the former present the postulate that all religious traditions in the world, all expressions of the sacred join together beyond their differences in a higher unity, with the result that we no longer know whether it is still a question of esotericism or of the sacred in general under all its forms, of the Myth, of religion *sub specie aeternitatis*. This tendency is often accompanied by a dogmatic attitude and confers henceforth to the uttering voice a militant, partisan, even fundamentalist coloration.

Still some of these currents (e.g., the neo-Guénonian or traditionalist and the Frithjof Schuon school in its continuation), derivative as they may be, appear quite respectable on an intellectual level. It is not the same for many a suspect or hodgepodge discourse proffered in our days by people convinced they hold the truth, who co-opt a shameless appropriation of the word "esotericism." We thus witness a perversion in a caricatural or paranoid vein of the most humanely valuable legacies of the esoteric traditions. How can we then be astonished when serious minds, somewhat uninformed on the complexity of these problems, have trouble assessing the situation and are often inclined to view the objects of our discipline with suspicion or irony?

Not only the delirious, alas, are available to sow confusion (and furnish weighty arguments to the traditionalists). We now see appear, in impressive numbers, more serious students, indeed specialists of one discipline or another, who get involved speaking authoritatively on esotericism when they have no particular competence. The reason for this phenomenon is twofold. On the one hand, this vast terrain, until now badly beaconed, still little attended to by universities, represents a choice prey for imperialist projects. On the other hand, above all, in our times where the book market is intensely active and where for lack of specialists in sufficiently large number (and this is a euphemism) editors of Western countries lack touchstones when they must decide to whom to assign texts (popularizing essays, summaries, dictionary entries, etc.) on esotericism in general. Now the fact that someone deals with mystics, religious symbolism, or psychology does not necessarily qualify him to write such texts—but he or she receives the assignment for lack of someone better. The result is that today almost anybody thinks he has rights to esotericism; almost anybody speaks of almost anything with impunity, with the complicity of the editors and the public.

A situation like this arouses in other serious minds—and not the least of these—an understandably negative reaction. If one has to write on a subject that an esoterologist would consider as pertaining to esotericism—e.g., a study (a book, journal article, dictionary entry) on Swedenborg or alchemy in seventeenth-century England—there is no need there to examine the notion of esotericism (suspect in their eyes) nor even to bring it up. It suffices to have studied properly what is going to be discussed. In fact, we observe (and there is nothing surprising about this) that it is not the esoterologists who do the studies the most scientifically satisfactory on the authors or these currents but specialists engaged in focussed research (e.g., in the Jewish or Christian Kabbalah, philosophy in the Renaissance, the history of science at such and such a time). The result is that instead of the recuperating perspectives already mentioned, the attitude of many these specialists is rejection pure and simple. Rejection of a notion of esotericism understood as scientifically operative and distrust of any enterprise tending to circumscribe a specific corpus—operative also—of esotericism because for them this corpus can only overlap those, already extant, of philosophy, literature, art, etc. But a similar suspicion as well as the homogenizing "confusion" constitute, no doubt, a stimulant indispensable for the growth and autonomy of our new discipline.

Therefore it behooves us to use the word "esotericism" wisely. We should not consider it a bearer of a spiritual or semantic value that it does not contain in itself. We should not make it designate a landscape in which by virtue of some intention or other, all cats would be gray. We should extricate it, if possible from the recuperators, scholarly or otherwise. We should consider it a frame of mind, a style of imaginary, through which circulates a tincture permeating diverse materials to give them a specific hue. The approach proposed here translates thus a twofold concern. On the one hand, to have differences respected; on the other hand, to carry empirical research, without ideological apriori, of transversal pathways and converging byways. Thus we can in the future make a clearing into many other hitherto unexplored gardens. Let us preserve this term so suitable for denoting an ensemble of cultural and religious realities, which a family resemblance seems to bind together sufficiently to authorize our making them a field of study. The official disciplines or specializations which so willingly marginalize these realities are themselves never more than the expression of one form of the imaginary among others.

II) SOME KEY CONCEPTS: GNOSIS, THEOSOPHY, SECRECY, OCCULTISM, HERMETICISM.

A) Gnosis

Gnosis (from the Greek, *Gnosis*, "*knowing, knowledge*") is a spiritual and intellectual activity that can accede to a special mode of knowledge. Unlike scientific or "rational" knowledge (which, moreover, gnosis does not exclude but uses), gnosis is an integrating knowledge, a grasp of fundamental relations including the least apparent that exist among the various levels of reality, e.g., among God, humanity, and the universe. Gnosis is either this knowing in itself or the intuition and the certainty of possessing a method permitting access to such knowledge. This project is more inclusive than Aristotelian metaphysics because it aims at integrating the self and the relationship of the subject to the self, as well as to that of the entire external world, in a unitary vision of reality. To a static metaphysics of being, gnosis thus opposes a dynamic and genetic metaphysics. The gnosis of esoteric currents possesses two very characteristic traits. On the one hand, it abolishes the distinction between faith and knowledge. (From the moment a person "knows," faith is no longer necessary.) On the other hand, this gnosis is presumed to possess a soteriological function, i.e., it contributes to the individual salvation of the person who practices it. The word "gnosis" serves to denote as much the spiritual and intellectual attitude itself as the referent corpus that illustrates it. Part of that corpus constitutes a very specific ensemble, Gnosticism, a religious system appearing along side Christianity in the first centuries of our era (with Basilides, Valentinus, Marcion, etc.). An original feature of this system is absolute ontological dualism (rejection of the created world, considered as evil), professed by numerous representatives and that the gnoses of later western esotericisms would rarely retain—but which would reappear later in religious movements not specifically esoteric like Bulgarian Bogomilism and Catharism. "Gnosis" in the singular is often used as a synonym of "gnosticism," so that the mistake is sometimes made of identifying gnosis in general with this particular system.

Besides the etymology referred to earlier, for "esotericism" the following is occasionally proposed: "eso-thodos," method—or way—toward the interior ("eiso-theo"—I make enter). This means "entry into the self." This is why it is sometimes called "interiorism": a knowledge that passes through a gnosis to reach a form of individual illumination and salvation. A knowledge of the relationship uniting us to God or to the divine world, or even the knowledge of the mysteries inherent in God. (In that case gnosis is theosophy in the strict sense.) To learn these relationships, the individual enters or descends into him- or herself: therefore "interiorism," but without any romanticized or intimist connotation, which would neglect an engaged resonance with the world and with God to the advantage of introspection alone. By the same token we do not enter into our self any way we choose, but according to an initiatory process. (*Initium*, initiation, beginning, are kindred notions.) Here it is important to "recognize" the guideposts because the way is marked by a series of intermediaries. According to the forms that the esoteric tradition takes, these are simply states of being (esotericism is then the study of and experimentation with the inner twilight realms), but more generally, angels, or entities called "*intellectus agens*" or "*animae coelestes*," more or less numerous, more or less personalized, but which are always in a certain way connatural to us—without which relationships could not be established. In order to travel felicitously along our initiatory path, it is less a matter of inciting them to intercede in our favor than of coming to know them.

We follow this path by committing ourselves to it, either alone, helped by appropriate texts, which hide the mysteries while revealing their keys, or with the help of an initiator, who can be an isolated master or a member of an initiatory school. The initiation serves to regenerate our consciousness, thanks to a process that lets us reappropriate the knowing we have lost—the theme of Lost Word, the exile caused by the original sin, etc.—and thanks to which we refashion the experience of our relationships to the sacred and the universe. Whether or not a disciple has a master, he has to access a knowing—or a form of nonknowing—transmittable by the word and, thanks to that, to advance in the knowledge of the connections uniting the disciple to higher entities (theosophy *strictu sensu*) and to cosmic forces, to living Nature (theosophy *lato sensu*).

To succeed it is necessary to practice what is traditionally called "active imagination," the essential component of esotericism, as we have seen. This imagination lets the disciple escape both from the sterility of a purely discursive logic, and from the rule-free extravagances of fantasy or sentimentality. This imagination is what prevails against the dangers of the essentially psychic lower imagination, source of error and untruth. The imagination, true organ of the soul, puts us in contact with the *mundus imaginalis* or the "*imaginal*" world. (Henry Corbin coined that appropriate adjective.) The imaginal world is the space of intermediary beings, a mesocosm possessing its own geography, thoroughly real, perceptible to each of us as a function of our respective cultural imagery. From this point on we will use "gnosis" in a general sense. The Greek root (*gnosis*), the same as in Sanskrit (*jnana*)—likewise for "knowledge, "*Erkenntnis* or "*connaissance*"—means simultaneously "to know" and "sapient wisdom." Late Greek thought, then patristic Christianity, as a result of distinguishing between "*gnosis*" and "*épistème*," introduced a separation between knowledge and its sacred source, while the root *Kn*, apparent in *genesis*, implies simultaneously knowledge and the coming to being. Franz von Baader, the most important German theosopher of the nineteenth century, was thus able to devote a part of his work to the ontological identity of learning and engendering. In bringing us to birth, or rather rebirth, gnosis unifies and liberates us. To know is to be liberated. It does not suffice to utter symbols or dogmas, it is necessary still to be engendered by them in the very place where spiritual traditions really are fulfilled, a space accessible only to those who succeed in penetrating into the time and space proper to the imaginal.

Gnosis indeed is not knowledge by itself; between believing and knowing there is a third term: the imaginal. Islamic gnosis establishes the division clearly: intellective knowing, knowledge of the traditional givens that are the object of faith, and knowledge or internal vision, intuitive revelation. It is the latter that opens the imaginal for us: "Gnosis" is inner vision. Its mode of expression is narrative; it is a *recital*. It believes only to the extent it knows. It is wisdom and faith. It is *Pistis Sophia*" (Henry Corbin). "Gnosis" must therefore be understood here in its first sense of higher knowledge, which is added to the common truths of objective Revelation, or "the deepening of that Revelation rendered possible by a special grace," according to Pierre Deghaye's elegant definition. A divine science par excellence, which the eighteenth-century theosopher Friedrich Christoph Oetinger called *philosophia sacra*. Sacred philosophy, bringing salvation, soteriological because it has the virtue of effecting metamorphoses, the inner mutation of human beings, thanks not to discursive thought but to a narrative revelation of hidden things, a salvific light bringing life and joy, which effects and assures salvation. To know what we are and whence we came is already, in a certain way, to be saved. Knowledge that is not theoretical but operative, and which for that reason transforms the knowing subject, just as alchemy, besides material transmutation is the transformation of the adept himself.

Shiite esotericism and the Jewish Kabbalah both represent a spiritual attitude essentially comparable to that of Christian esotericism. By nature Islam lent itself to the flowering of esotericism. According to the Koran tradition, the Koran possesses seven esoteric senses, to which a *hadith* of the prophet alludes: "I plunged into the Koran's ocean of secrets, and I pulled out the pearls of its subtleties. I raised the veils of sounds and letters covering its true realities, the secret meanings that are kept there far from the eyes of men." The gnostic practices the *ta'wil*, i.e. a spiritual interpretation. The letter is only the *zâhir* (back) of a *bâtin* (cavern, matrix) or hidden reality. More than the other branches of Islam, such as Sunnism, Shiism conceived of divine revelation in the light of prophecy never finished in time and a permanent interpreter of that very revelation. This does not mean replacing already existing divine law by another law, but it means uncovering its plenary sense ever better and more fully. Such conceptions are in no way incompatible with the purest Christianity, even if the official theologies have had a tendency to smother them. The reason, or pretext, of that obscuring is due in part to the emphasis in official catacheses on the absolute transcendence of God with respect to the creature, lest the gulf separating them be filled. Now "*trans*" does not only mean a frontier. It has two meanings, depending on whether it is envisaged as verb-prefix or a preposition. In the first case there is continuity, passage as in "*transeunt Rhenum*"; in the second there is discontinuity (*incolunt trans Rhenum*). Despite the presence of a negative theology proper to the majority of Western esotericisms, as to what constitutes divinity itself, the latter always insist on the procession of stages and of entities mediating between God and His creatures.

Therefore, esotericism permits access to a higher level of intelligence, where dualities of all kind are transcended in a unity that is in no respect passivity. It is a unity not under the jurisdiction of an identific schema or regime, but subject to a "dualitude" operating in a dynamic, or rather, in an energetic fashion. To designate that active state various words have been proposed: the inner man (St. Paul), the supramental (Sri Aurobindo), illuminative intuition (René Guénon), the transcendental Ego (Husserl), enstasis (Mircea Eliade). There is also the "infusion" of Raymond Abellio, who has also drawn up a list of these terms and spoken in this regard about "concrete and permanent participation in universal interdependence" in view of the fulfillment in man and woman of the mystery of incarnation. Enstasis aspires to be expressed, to be diffused, to communicate, not in the form of effusions—whence the word "infusion"—but of transmission, oral or written, through a veil of symbols and in anonymity or at least with a concern to recreate and rediscover rather than to seek originality at any price. Humility, therefore, but intellectual and not sentimental. Love, as well, but which to find or preserve its strength keeps from being sentimental and is not merely desire or sensuous attraction. Desire for infinity? More likely, as Frithjof Schuon emphasized, the logical and ontological tendency of this love toward its own transcendental essence.

Gnosis calls forth the mystical, just as anything mystical always contains some gnosis. Mysticism, more nocturnal, would willingly cultivate renunciation; gnosis, more solar, would observe detachment and would practice systematization, although the mystic occasionally finds in his own path the same intermediary entities as the gnostic does. But while the gnostic first seeks illuminating and salvific knowledge, the mystic limits the number of intermediaries as much as he can and aspires above all to unite with his God—a union that, in the three Abrahamic religions maintains the ontological separation between God and Man. To esotericism thus understood are attached procedures or rituals that aim at eliciting the concrete manifestation of particular entities. Such is theurgy.

The esoteric attitude in the sense of "gnostic" is thus a mystical experience in which intelligence and memory participate, both being expressed in a symbolic form that reflects diverse levels of reality. Gnosis, according to a remark by theosopher Valentin Tomberg, would be the expression of a form of intelligence and memory that had effected a passage through a mystical experience. A gnostic would therefore be a mystic capable of communicating to someone else his own experiences in a manner that would retain the impression of revelations received in passing through the different levels of the "mirror." An example of a mystic proposition would be "God is love; he who dwells in love dwells in God and God in him;" or "my Father and I are one." An example of a first-level gnostic proposition would be "God is a Trinity: Father, Son, and Holy Ghost" or "In my Father's house there are many mansions."

B) Theosophy

Theosophy is a gnosis that has a bearing not only on the salvific relations the individual maintains with the divine world, but also on the nature of God Himself, or of divine persons, and on the natural universe, the origin of that universe, the hidden structures that constitute it in its actual state, its relationship to mankind, and its final ends. It is in this general sense that we speak of theosophy traditionally. Theosophy, in the sense we are using it, confers on esotericism this cosmic, or rather cosmosophic dimension, thereby introducing the idea of an intentionality in the world, that keeps esotericism from succumbing to solipsism. Theosophy opens esotericism to the entire universe and by the same token renders possible a philosophy of nature.

"*Theosophia*" etymologically is "wisdom of God." The word is used by several Church Fathers, both Greek and Latin, as a synonym for "theology," quite naturally since "*sophia*" means at once knowledge, doctrine, and wisdom. The *sophos* is a "wiseman." The "*theosophoi*" are "those knowing divine things," and that, however, does not necessarily mean theologians! It would be interesting to systematically trace the use of this word by religious authors from the beginning of Christianity until the Renaissance. We would see that it occasionally differs from the sense of its synonym "theology" such as we understand it today. Theosophy is distinguished from theology to suggest more or less the existence of knowledge of a gnostic type. It is in this sense, for example, that Pseudo-Dionysus tends to use it in the sixth century, as well as, though somewhat less clearly in the thirteenth century the author of the astonishing *Summa Philosophiae*, who is perhaps not Robert Grosseteste, but who in any case, came from the same milieu as he did: theosophers are only authors inspired by the holy books, and theologians (like Pseudo-Dionysus or Origen) are those who have the task of explaining theosophy. We see that the terms are the opposite of the present-day meaning. We must wait until the Renaissance for more frequent usage but it is still synonymous, sometimes, with theology or philosophy. Johannes Reuchlin, who at the beginning of the sixteenth century did much to promote the Christian Kabbalah, speaks of "*theosophistae*" to designate decadent scholastics as does Cornelius Agrippa when both could have used the label in its present meaning. Du Cange instructs on the use, at the time, of "theosophy" for "theology" (*Glossarium ad scriptores mediae et infimae latinitatis*, 1733/1736). From 1540 to 1553, Johannes Arboreus (Alabri) published a *Theosophia* in several volumes, but hardly touches on esotericism.

The meaning of the word becomes clearly defined at the end of the sixteenth century, probably under the influence of the *Arbatel*, a book of white magic that appeared undated, but around 1550 or 1560, followed by numerous reprintings. Here, theosophy has already almost its present meaning. It begins to be used in this esoteric meaning by Henrich Khunrath at the very end of the sixteenth century. Boehme's theosophy always starts with Nature, which he conceives as essentially celestial and divine. Contemporary also is the title under which Valentin Weigel's *Libellus Theosophiae (Ein Büchlein der göttlichen Weisheit)* first appeared at Neustadt in 1618. This is not the author's title—he died thirty years earlier—but it is the one used for publication. We see from these examples that the meaning of the word becomes more precise at the same time that the notion receives its definitive elaboration in Germany from several contemporaneous authors, and its features are subsequently retained. This moment when theosophy acquires its patent of nobility corresponds to the apogee of German baroque literature as well as to the birth of the "Rosicrucian" movement (ca. 1610–1620). Henceforth the word will be used often, e.g., by Johann Georg Gichtel and Gottfried Arnold. It is already accompanied by a kindred term, fashionable with Rosicrucians and Paracelsians, first used by the Platonic and Hermetist philosopher Francesco Patrizi: "Pansophy." This term combines two notions of theosophy, Wisdom by divine illumination and Light from Nature. In 1596, Bartholomäus Scleus opposed particularist or sectarian theologians with his "*Mystica Theologia Universalis und Pansophia*," which for him was the same as "*Magia coelestis*" or celestial magic. It is more customary to mean by "Pansophy," as it was defined a little later by Jan Amos Comenius, a system of universal knowledge, all things being ordered and classified by God according to analogical relationships. Or, if you prefer, a knowledge of divine things acquired via the concrete world, i.e., the entire universe, in which the "signatures" or hieroglyphics must first be deciphered. In other words, the Book of Nature helps us understand better Holy Scripture and God Himself. This would reserve the term theosophy for the reverse procedure, knowing the universe thanks to our knowledge of God. But, practically speaking, especially from the eighteenth century onward, "theosophy" is generally used to designate the Pansophic progression as well.

In the eighteenth century, the word and concept "theosophy" enter the philosophical vocabulary and become widespread. The two most important theosophical works at the beginning of the century are also German. They have wide-ranging repercussions, and their titles are explicit: *Theophilosophia theoretica et practica* (1710) by Sincerus Renatus and *Opus mago-cabalisticum et theosophicum* (1721) by George von Welling. It is in this sense once more that Franciscus Buddeus uses the word in his *Isagoge* (Leipzig, 1727). But especially pastor Jacob Brucker devotes a long chapter to theosophy in his *Kurze Fragen aus der Philosophischen Historie* (Ulm, 1735) in German, followed by his monumental *Historia critica Philosophiae* in Latin (Leipzig, 1741). All theosophers are represented there. We have the impression that he has left out none. It is the official consecration in the world of letters, so much so that Brucker will remain through the Enlightenment the obligatory reference in the history of philosophy. Few authors, even among the esotericists, will have contributed as much as he to promote theosophy, which he himself did not find congenial!

At the same time, the word is missing from most of the major French dictionaries during the Enlightenment. We do not find it in Furetière, nor in either the *Dictionnaire de l'Académie* or Bayle's *Dictionnaire*. In Trévoux' dictionary there is a brief, though inoffensive, mention. But Denis Diderot, makes up for lost time. In a long article in his great *Encyclopaedia*, entitled "Theosophers," which he himself wrote, he repeats entire passages of Brucker's texts in French without citing his source, while committing some misinterpretations, which free translation does not altogether excuse. His

French is indeed more elegant and charming than the cumbersome Latin of its model, but the content is superficial also. Diderot meanwhile wavers between sympathy and disdain. At any rate, despite an attraction for the representatives of this form of esotericism, he himself does not have a theosophical cast of mind. At any rate he contributed to spread the use of the word in France. It will continue to be used occasionally in other senses. For example, Kant calls "theosophism" the system of philosophers who like Malbranche believe they can see everything in God, and Antonio Rosmini uses "theosophy" to designate the general metaphysics of being (in *Teosofia*, 1859). But even with somewhat vague connotations, it is almost always the esoteric sense that prevails from then on. Thus, Friedrich Schiller titles one of his first texts *Theosophie des Julius*, which appeared in *Thalia* in 1787. Some confusion is introduced in 1875 when Madame Blavatsky founds the "Theosophical Society," which took its highly syncretist teachings chiefly from the East.*

By "theosophy" as by "esotericism, " we mean then first a hermeneutic, i.e., an interpretation of divine instruction, e.g., from a revealed Book, founded both on an intellectual and speculative operation and upon a revelation caused by an illumination. (The mode of thought here is analogic and homologic, with both the human being and the universe considered as symbols of God.) In the case of theosophy, properly speaking, this interpretation of divine teaching has bearing on the inner mysteries of the Divinity itself (theosophy *strictu sensu*) or of the entire universe (theosophy *lato sensu*, as used here).

The theosopher starts with a revealed given, his myth—for example, the narrative of Creation in the Book of Genesis—from which he evokes symbolic resonances by virtue of his active imagination. Understood as a way of individual salvation, gnosis implied already an idea of "penetration." But this time that means going down not only into the depths of self. This catabasis or anabasis is presumed to be effected also in the depths of Nature and of the divine itself. Nature aspires to a deliverance the key to which is held by Man. Since the Alexandrian *Corpus Hermeticum*, Western esotericism has tended to hold the principle of the divine origin of the human *mens*, which makes it contain also the organization of the universe. Our *mens* has a nature identical to that of the stellar governors of the universe described in the *Poimandres*. Therefore it is identical to that of the reflections and projections of those in the more concrete world that surrounds us. And the Deity that "rests in itself" as Boehme says, i.e., dwelling in its absolute transcendence, at the same time

---

* On the history of the word *theosophy*, and of the movement of that name, see my article "Le courant théosophique (fin XVIè–XVIIè siècles): essai de périodisation", in *Politica Hermetica*, nr. VI, 1993 (Lausanne: L'Age d'Homme), pp. 6–41. Forthcoming translation in *Theosophical History* (journal published by the California State University, Fullerton).

comes from itself. God is a hidden treasure who aspires to be known. He lets himself be partially revealed by halving himself at the heart of an ontological sphere, situated between our created world and the unknowable which is allegedly the place of encounter between Him and the creature. Thus transcendence and immanence are reconciled.

"Imagination and mediation": this category of esotericism, cited earlier, represents an essential aspect of theosophy. Indeed, no more so in the Abrahamic theosophies than in the others, truth is not manifested in abstract ideas but takes on visible forms and envelopes. In itself Divinity is immutable, and yet it makes itself manifest. There is the paradox! We know Divinity but only by living images of its manifestation. The infinite is "fixed" in limits. (*"Der Urgrund fasst sich im Grund,"* says Boehme.) But the creature losing itself through dedication to the infinite, going beyond limits to the infinite, means going to an evil infinite, as happened to Lucifer.

Let us cite Boehme once more for he is characteristic of this form, this current of thought, while at the same time he is a model, at least in a poetic mode, for modern theosophy. He tells us that Nature is one of the specific modes of Revelation. By starting from our most concrete nature in order to raise ourselves to the science of higher Nature, we practice a gnosis that is specifically theosophic because this gnosis is not only abstract knowledge but is accompanied by a transformation of ourself. Earlier we recalled that theosophic discourses are partially tributaries of the cultural milieus in which they flourish. This is something we must keep in mind whenever we study such a discourse. Thus, Boehme's theosophy is an amalgam between the medieval mystical tradition (that of fourteenth-century Germany) and the *Natur-philosophie* inspired by Paracelsus. What Boehme retains from German mysticism, in a properly theosophic turn of mind, is the theme of the second birth, which for him is equivalent to the alchemists' *Great Work*. It is the birth of the Christ in Man through the Holy Spirit and the Father. But with Boehme a philosophy of Nature serves to materialize in some respect that notion of the second birth through meditation on symbols to achieve the "fixing" of Holy Spirit in the body of light. We see the relationship to mysticism. However, the theosopher does not limit himself to describing the itinerary he has followed through torments and joys, as does, for example, St. John of the Cross. The theosopher starts with a personal event, which he subsequently objectifies in his own way, projecting it backwards on a macrocosmic soul in the image of celestial totality, and practices thus a form of exemplariness in reverse. The difference with mysticism appears especially, of course, in the fact that the contemplative claims to abolish images, while for Boehme and theosophers generally, the image is, on the contrary, the fulfillment.

In this respect we could call theosophy a theology of Revelation, if we realize that this Revelation is that of God in the interior of a creature at the same time it is the Revelation of God to Himself. Theosophy would thus be, at least in this cultural context a theology of the image, since the latter, far from being a simple reflection, truly represents the ultimate reality to the extent that the finality of each being is to produce its image, which in the last analysis is the best of itself. In realizing our perfection, or rather our integrality, we incarnate ourselves. Each being possesses a finality of perfection, which passes through the image and its incarnation. (In the seventeenth century, *Bild* still signified both "image" and "body.") Thus the letter of Holy Scripture is the very body in which God is manifest and, consequently, Christian theosophers are almost all "*bibelfest*": they want to be "scriptuary" like the Jewish Kabbalists.

We understand better the success of theosophy and pansophy in the intellectual and spiritual climate of the late Renaissance, if we juxtapose it with the need, found in so many men in the seventeenth century, to seek the explanation of the structure of the universe and its cohesion. Both theological and scientific thought tried to define the relationship of the microcosm and the macrocosm, i.e., of Man and the world, and to integrate everything in a general harmony according to perspective of synthesis truly able to favor a solidarity of spirit. This is why pansophy, total science, as its name indicates, appears as a branch of theosophy, indeed, as its synonym. On the other hand, the Reformation included, undoubtedly in embryo, if not theosophic elements, never discernable in the thought of its founders—at least a disposition to encourage its presence by virtue of an original or constitutive mixture of the mysticism and rationalism in Protestantism. Moreover, the recommended reading of Scripture, enlightened by the Holy Spirit, could only favor bold and individual speculations, especially arising at the moment men began to see in their Lutheranism more a moralizing catechism than a teaching for life.

Behind the complexity of the real, the theosopher seeks the hidden meanings of the ciphers and hieroglyphics of Nature. A quest inseparable from an intuitive plunge into the myth to which he belongs through faith, where his active imagination sends forth resonances appropriate for being gathered into a bouquet of meanings. At the same time that he starts from a reflection on things in order to understand God, so he tries to seize the becoming of the divine world—his question is not "*an sit Deus*," but "*quid sit Deus*"—in order to understand the world at the same time and to possess thereby the intimate vision of the principle of the reality of the universe and its becoming. The aspects of myth he emphasizes are quite naturally those that the established churches have tended to neglect or ignore: the nature of the fall of Lucifer and of Adam, androgyny, sophiology, arithmosophy. . . . He believes in a permanent revelation directed to him, and his discourse always gives the impression that he receives knowledge and inspiration simultaneously. He inserts each concrete observation into an integral system that is not the least totalitarian but is indefinitely open, always based on the triptych of origin, present state, and ultimate ends, i.e., his system is based on a cosmogony (bound to a theogony and an anthropogony), a cosmology, and an eschatology. St. Paul himself would have justified in advance this active and operative quest, affirming that "the Spirit searches everything, even the depths of God" (I Cor. 2:10). The theosopher, like the gnostic generally, accompanies the acquisition of deep insight with a change in being, a felicitously inevitable process as soon as he *plays the part* in theogonic and cosmic dramas or seeks, like Boehme, to achieve a "second birth." His discourse, akin to a recital or recitative, gives the impression of being less his work than that of a spirit speaking through him. It is only in his choice of images, in the form of his discourse, that we can discover each time his own originality. Moreover the essential for him is not so much to invent or to be original, as to remember, or to devote his energy to rediscovering the living articulation of all things visible and invisible, by scrutinizing both the Divine and observed Nature often in its most infinitesimal details, and becoming the hermeneut of theosophers who have scrutinized these details before him.

In the archaic epoch of Greece, *mythos* and *logos*—which together make up mythology—did not contradict each other but called forth a sacred narrative of gods and heroes. Little by little, *logos* took precedence over *mythos*, philosophy over mythology, to the detriment of metonymy and meaningful displacements of sense. Recent contemporary hermeneutics has at least recovered the plurality of meaning, but though "plural," it does not have the same ends as the theosophic project. By nature the latter avoids impasses because, instead of juxtaposing the translations of the senses, theosophy practices advancing a discourse that does not pretend to speak about anything other than itself. The revealed narrative of myth, on which it rests is there to be relived, under penalty of dissipating in abstract notions. Thus theosophy has often, albeit tacitly, supported theology, revitalizing it when it risked sinking into the conceptual. The conceptual, for Boehme, Oetinger, Baader, and other theosophers, always waits for its reinterpretation in and through a *mythos–logos* wherein the concept, bereft of its privileged status, retains at best the status of a provisional, methodological tool. Because, much more than recourse to abstraction, it is the experience of the symbol that assures the grasp of the mythic experience. Any myth to the extent it is complete, i.e., consists of the triptych mentioned earlier, is presented by the same stroke as a narrative of origins. It reports on events happening *in illo tempore*, as Mircea Eliade has so pertinently noted, which establish ritual acts and theosophic discourses.

The theosopher exploits thoroughly the exploratory range of the mythic narrative in unveiling the infinite richness of its symbolic function—the "natural tableau of relationships uniting God, Man and the universe," as expressed in the title of a splendid work (1782) of Louis-Claude de Saint-Martin. This richness gives us the means to live in our world as in a Baudelairean "forest of symbols." Symbols, not allegories, because it is not a matter of extracting from the images clothing the revealed narrative a sense other than the narrative itself and that could be expressed—or reduced—by another kind of discourse. Permanent renewal in the latent sense of the Book, a sense that the Book only allows us to approach with the help of the Spirit, theosophy ties together the origin and the end, i.e., the theogony, indeed the anthropogony, and the eschatology. But, of course, a "complete" theosophy adds to these dimensions that of cosmology or, rather cosmosophy, endless reflection on the different material and natural levels, a gnosis perpetually nourished by the discovery and explanation of analogies. Thus, human existence is apprehended as a totality wherein our life finds its East and its Meaning.

Comparable in this to prophesy, although by different modes, theosophy is an "*ex–plicatio*" of Revelation. Christianity especially lends itself to such an "amplification." Does not the Gospel of Luke (1:1–13) begin with these words: "Inasmuch as many have undertaken to compile a narrative of the things which have been accomplished among us just as they were delivered to us by those who from the beginning were eyewitnesses of the Word . . ." In Judaic tradition, the function of *midrash* is to actualize Revelation by interpreting it as a function of the present. Christianity keeps, as a need inherent in its basic nature, this necessity of a continuous Revelation because, although definitive for the essential (Heb. 10:12–14), it remains necessarily veiled in part, apophatic. On the theophany of Jesus, Origen and Gregory of Nyssa explain that His glory was made manifest in the mist. This means that Revelation remains until the last day, the object of prophetic elucidation, theosophy raising the value of the mist itself. In both cases entering into an increasingly profound understanding of the "mystery" is neither an insoluble enigma nor problem but a message proposed, support for endless meditation.

We could say that two forms of theology exist. First of all, teaching by various denominational churches of what revealed Truth is. But there is also another form of theology that corresponds to the attempt to acquire knowledge (*gnosis*) of the immense domain of reality deep within which occurs the working of salvation. A knowledge that bears on the structure of the physical and spiritual worlds, on the forces operative within time, the relationships among these forces, both micro- and macrocosmic, the history of their transformations, the relation between God, humanity, and the universe; a domain which in itself deserves exploration for the glory of God and the good of fellow men; an exploration that also responds to the demands of talents made fruitful (Mat. 25:14–30). In Christianity there have been theologians, like St. Bonaventure, who devoted themselves to a theosophic approach to Nature because deciphering the "signature of things" constitutes one of the two complementary directions of theology, the theosopher being a theologian of that Holy Scripture we call the universe.

We can distinguish with Valentin Tomberg, two modes of that theosophic approach based on the idea of universal correspondences. First of all there is a theosophy bearing on temporal relationships, what he calls a "mythological symbolism" where the mythological symbols express the correspondences among the archetypes in the past and their manifestation in time. For example, the nature of Adam's sin, the Fall of Adam and Eve, and their glorious original state are the object of a theosophic projection on the nature of man as such, the task he must accomplish, notably the redemptive work he must effect on Nature. A myth of this type is the expression of an "eternal idea" emerging from time and history. On the other hand, there is a theosophy bearing on space, the structure of space, and what Tomberg calls a "typological symbolism." The latter concerns essentially the central panel of the "complete" theosophic triptych mentioned earlier (theogony and cosmogony, cosmosophy, eschatology). This time we are dealing with symbols that link their prototypes on high to their manifestations down below. Ezekiel's vision, for example, expresses a typological symbolism that implies a universal cosmological revelation. The *Merkaba* or the mystic way of the Chariot, which comes out of the Jewish Kabbalah, is based entirely on that vision of Ezekiel. The author of the *Zohar* sees in the living creatures and wheels Ezekiel describes a complex of symbolic images interpretable as a key to cosmic knowledge. Of course, the two modes of approach (mythological symbolism and typological symbolism) usually coexist in the same discourse.

The revelations thus described evidently give the impression of "objectifying in a macrocosm what passes in the individual *psyche* out of touch with God." This is the reason, Pierre Deghaye recalls, that the German philosopher Ludwig Feuerbach reduced theosophy to the status of "esoteric psychology." Deghaye prefers to see, notably in Jacob Boehme whom he has studied especially, "a veritable psychology of depths," but without taking a stand on the objective reality of what Boehme's revelations purvey to us, i.e., without reducing these revelations to a single dimension that would be of a purely psychological order. To be sure, we have quickly detected in theosophers the alliance of desire and concept, so much so that mystics could find theosophy nourished on Nature speculations too scientific, and that those holding a purely objective rationality tend to consider Nature philosophers—in the Romantic sense of *Naturphilosophie*—too mystical, in any case like people whose discourse, at best, reveals nothing other than the movements at work in their unconscious. It seems that there would be more people today to take theosophy seriously because our epoch considers ever more seriously the possibility of a connaturality of our spirit and the universe. In other words, we do not exclude the possibility that some of our images reflect hidden structures of this universe and that the great founding myths correspond to them. . . . Thus it remains that the theosophic glance can be extraordinarily fecund, counterbalancing dualisms and ideologies of all kinds. Indeed, theosophy does not pretend that we must go beyond Man in order to transform him into something else. Theosophy only reminds humanity of what our true powers were and tries to give them back to us. It teaches that nothing is gained, finally, in wanting to scale heaven in contempt of earth or in wanting to be satisfied with the descent of the gods without trying to visit Olympus with them: anabasis and catabasis, like Castor and Pollux, are inseparable and complementary. Thanks to theosophy also, the fragmented, splintered "multiverse" becomes the universe once more, a world bearing meaning and composed of living pluralities.

C) Secrecy

Are all esotericisms necessarily bound to the notion of secrecy? Do they contain elements that must not be disclosed in contrast with exotericisms whose discourse is meant for the public forum? Let us be careful not to reduce esotericism, to *disciplina arcani*, as we have seen might happen. Limiting esotericism to that single dimension proceeds often from bad faith, ignorance, or even intellectual sloth—it is less difficult to restrict one's field to simple questions of vocabulary! Most of the time there is no desire for "secrecy" in the conventional sense of the term. A secret needs no one to protect it. In fact, we may speak of confidential teaching Jesus allegedly gave his disciples or of teaching kept jealously at the heart of initiatory societies. *Disciplina arcani* means chiefly this: the mysteries of religion, the ultimate nature of reality, hidden forces in the cosmic order, hieroglyphs of the visible world—none of which lends itself to literal understanding. Neither do such lend themselves to a univocal explanation but rather must be the object of progressive multi-leveled penetration.

In an essay published in 1906, Georg Simmel gave a statement on the sociology of secrecy, showing that even apart from esotericism, a secret is a component of the structure of social interaction. Thus secrecy does not seem to us a component of esotericism qua esotericism. A so-called "secret" society is not created in view of some kind of hocus-pocus, but—as Raymond Abellio has put it so well—to give a small group of people transparency because the world itself is globally opaque. And generally it is not a doctrine that the initiate is supposed to keep hidden, but at most the details of a ritual. Nevertheless, nearly all those of Freemasonry have been published for a long time and this is hardly considered as a breach of "Masonic secrecy"! If a Freemason or a member of any esoteric society whatsoever must conceal the name of his affiliated brothers, that is at most a measure of discretion. In the Hellenist religions, the situation was comparable. What an initiator was to keep to himself did not deal with an ineffable religious instruction, comprehensible to him alone anyway, but a ritual in its purely material aspect. Indeed, if we take the sacred seriously, we must always put up a slight partition, simply theoretical really, between the sacred and the profane, precisely in order not to profane what is held dear, what has been obtained with difficulty in undergoing diverse trials.

This paradox is illustrated best, in my opinion, in a beautiful engraving by Achilles Bocchi. His *Symbolicae quaestiones* (1555) presents a Hermes (symbol LXII) holding in his left hand a seven-branched candelabra while his right index finger seals his lips. By this gesture Bocchi wanted to attribute to this god of language, discourse, and exchange, the same gesture as Harpocrates makes! A hermeneutic tension is established between veiling and unveiling, silence and speech, hiding and revealing, by the device of a pregnant image that no conceptual explanation could equal.

On an individual level, we could establish a rapprochement between silence or secrecy, and the famous "melancholic" humor so ubiquitous in the hermeticism of Marsilio Ficino, Pico della Mirandola or Cornelius Agrippa, bound also to the alchemical *nigredo*, first stage presided over by Saturn of the alchemical path. This is an introversion, comparable to a dryness retaining light, exemplified by crystals, and which can remain only provisional. How to carry on discourse, indeed, while applying laboriously, even painfully, the precept from the *Emerald Tablet*: "Separate the subtle from the gross"? The incandescent melancholy mentioned by Aristotle hardly furthers interchange, while the *furor divinus* of Plato would encourage communication. But one and the other are partly bound. When subjected to them, it is better to live them, not as a contradiction, but as a paradox inscribed in our nature for it is in that of gods as well.

By the same token, we can juxtapose esotericism and exotericism. What is reserved for an elite versus what is addressed to all. A valuable and fruitful distinction, so long as we avoid considering this a case of incompatibility. We must remember that there exists an esotericism of exotericism and an exotericism of esotericism, as if each of them were understood only as a function of the other or represented the other side of the same medal. I can attempt to penetrate a teaching open to all, e.g., an elementary catechism, by trying to uncover the spirit hidden behind the letter; on the other hand, a text, obscure for those not prepared to read it and addressed to readers familiar with the difficult arcana it contains, can be the object of a unilateral, moral, utilitarian reading. Basically it is a question of different levels of reading. The exoteric corresponds to the literal or moral level, the esoteric to the anagogic level, the allegorical and symbolic situated in between. But the problem of relationship between esotericism and exotericism is posed today in a more interesting way, especially of the notion of Tradition (cf. below).

D) Occultism

In a broad sense, occultism is a dimension of esotericism. Indeed, once esotericism integrates the whole universe into its spiritual praxis, i.e., Nature entire, visible and invisible, it is not surprising to see it take up very concrete practices. Each has its own method, but the laws establishing them rest on an identical principle, just as the branches of a tree are nourished by the same sap. Essentially this is the homo-analogical principle matching like to like, and this means one of the two can act on the other. This occurs by virtue of "correspondences" that unite all visible things and likewise unite the latter with invisible realities. Experimental science is hardly capable of accounting for them.

Among these practices it is conventional to arrange all forms of "mancies" with astrology at the head of the list. But it must be realized that on the most elevated plane, the esoteric, astrology is less a science of divination than a body of knowledge—a gnosis—of invisible relationships between the stars and men. Likewise, alchemy is a gnosis. To the extent that the Adept undertakes to direct a parcel of matter, and by that act, himself as well, to its glorious state "before the Fall," it is magic in the noblest sense. But when its project is limited to metallic transmutation alone, or to spagyria, we would say it is occultism. Let us mention also occult medicine, which rests on the properties of certain stones or plants gathered at a propitious moment and, more generally, magic in all its forms, white or black. For example, theurgy or the practice of invoking intermediate entities, generally angelic, is a form of white magic. (In this respect, we speak of *evocations* apropos of occultism, and more appropriately of *invocations* in a traditional theosophic context.) All these branches of occultism rest on the doctrine of correspondences, or the law of universal interdependence, which expresses a living and dynamic reality. They truly make sense only when directed by the active imagination, which like a catalyst or a chemical indicator puts into action networks of cosmic and divine analogies and homologies. In the most noble sense, an occultist is simultaneously an esotericist, or a theosopher.

The distinction between esotericism and occultism did not really enter the vocabulary until the middle of the nineteenth century, a time when a need was felt to create this second substantive, which coincided precisely with the appearance of a trivial esotericism. Moreover, esotericism has its practical dimension also. It is not pure speculation to the extent that active knowledge, illumination, and imagination which compose it, correspond to a form of praxis—just as occultism brings back necessarily to a form of universality. The problem in terminology is complicated by the fact that "occultism" is sometimes used in the sense of "esotericism."

Eliphas Lévi (1810–1875) is credited with the coining of this term. He derived it from *"philosophia occulta,"* in the sense promulgated by Henricus Cornelius Agrippa in *De Occulta philosophia* (1533), to designate a group of investigations and practices having to do with such "sciences" as astrology, magic, alchemy, and the Kabbalah. "Occultism" is used in these two meanings: a) any practice dealing with these "sciences." If esotericism is a form of thought, occultism would instead be a group of practices or a form of action that would derive its legitimacy from esotericism. Thus "occultism" is sometimes a synonym of "esotericism" (e.g., Robert Amadou, *L'Occultisme: esquisse d'un monde vivant*, 1950), but "esotericism" serves more generally today to designate the type of thought that informs these "sciences." b) A current appearing in the second half of the nineteenth century with Eliphas Lévi and reaching its apogee at the turn of the century (cf. *infra*, *History of Esoteric Currents*, II, 3).

Hermeticism, Hermetism, Hermesism

In English, the word "hermeticism" (adjective "hermetic") designates: a) the Alexandrian Greek texts and teachings (called *Hermetica*) from the beginning of our era, associated with the name of Hermes Trismegistus, as well as works and currents directly inspired by the *Hermetica*, chiefly from the sixteenth century onwards; b) Alchemy; c) Both a) and b) simultaneously and in a general manner most of the forms taken by modern esotericism (e.g., Christian Kabbalism, Paracelsism, Rosicrucianism, Theosophy).

Nevertheless, to designate a), the word "hermetism" is much more appropriate. This is the word that is now used in this sense by most scholars to avoid confusion.

I have suggested using "hermesism" (adjective "hermesian") to designate a frame of mind placed under the sign of Hermes, the god with the caduceus. The "hermesian" attitude thus refers more generally to Hermes Mercury than to Hermes Trismegistus alone. (Cf. also *infra*, apropos of the "three ways" that I distinguish in present-day esotericism.)

III) REFLECTIONS ON "TRADITION," OR THE THREE PATHS OF ESOTERICISM TODAY

The word "Tradition" with a capital "T" became dominant in the West at the end of the last century. In the Middle Ages, there was occasionally the need to draw up lists of initiates, or alchemists, serving as a reference, hence authorities, e.g., in the famous text called *Turba Philosophorum* (thirteenth century). At the beginning of the Renaissance we see emerging a chronology of divine envoys and men through whom "true philosophy," in the "traditional" sense of the term, was expressed, or so it was believed. The most commonly recognized chain of initiates at that time included Enoch, Abraham, Noah, Zoroaster, Moses, Hermes Trismegistus, the Brahmins, the Druids, David, Orpheus, Pythagoras, Plato, and the Sibyls. From this arose the expression "*Philosophia perennis*," proposed by Augustino Steuco in 1540, in his book by the same name, borrowed by Leibniz in a philosophical sense that extended way beyond its use in esotericism. The extreme interest shown in this succes-

Table of Basic Concepts

		ESOTERICISM/HERMETICISM (Broadly Defined)		OCCULTISM
	REVELATION	GNOSIS	PRACTICES	PRACTICES
Plan Divine	* Revealed Books * Mystical Experience, as personal union with the divine * PROPHETISM as direct revelation	ESOTERICISM (restricted meaning): illumination & salvation via a knowledge of links between men & intermediary or Divine THEOSOPHY (restricted meaning): emphasis on nature of God, hidden mysteries of the Divinity. Broadly defined: active imagination applied to myth (theogony, anthropogony, cosmology, eschatology).	White magic, including THEURGY: evocation of angelic spirits, ritual reintegration ALCHEMY, in its spiritual & soteriological aspect	Black magic Necromancy Sorcery
Natural	Signatura rerum Astra, Naturalia, Mirabilia "hieroglyphs" of Nature	PANSOPHY: aspect of theosophy broadly defined, emphasis on cosmology. From the concrete world to the divine (the Book of Nature helps understand the Scriptures and God). PHILOSOPHY OF NATURE "RATIO HERMETICA"	* Natural magic (hermetic medicine and concrete use of signatures Hermesian arts astrology & all "mancies" Emblems, Art of Memory Initiatic societies & their rituals	

sion of proper names declines towards the middle of the seventeenth century. It is maintained in the eighteenth century by theosopher Friedrich Christoph Oetinger, who extensively used the concepts of *"Philosophia sacra"* and "philosophy of the Ancients." Later, from the end of the nineteenth century up until today, this idea returned in full force under a new name: "Tradition." Esotericists and initiatory societies of diverse inspiration laid claim to the word so that a certain confusion surrounds it. Let us propose a three-part methodological distinction. It seems to us that to discover Tradition or rather to rediscover it, we have more or less a choice among three possibilities: 1) the "severe or purist" path, 2) the "historical" path, and 3) the "humanist or alchemist" path.

A) The "Purist" Path

Representatives of the "purist" path posit the existence of a "primordial" Tradition—which should not be taken in an historical or chronological sense—defined by René Guénon, the incontestable master of this pathway in the twentieth century, as of "non-human" origin. This treasury of wisdom and gnosis once belonged to humanity, which allowed it to be dispersed and diluted. To find the true esoteric way again, we must seek it there where alone it exists; i.e., beyond the exoteric foundations that are the religions, simply branches of a transcendent unity. Thus Frithjof Schuon is thereby justified in titling one of his works *The Transcendent Unity of Religions*. In Catholicism and Freemasonry Guénon sees the depositories of one part, and one part only, of this legacy, which, moreover, is found nowhere better preserved than in certain forms of Hindu metaphysics. However, at the same time and quite correctly, he notes that Westerners have little to gain in uprooting themselves culturally and metaphysically, i.e., in abandoning one of the three Abrahamic religions (Jewish, Christian, Muslim) in exchange for the light of the East.

   In Guénon's perspective, the difficulty in finding the primordial Tradition again, even partially, implies great rigor in selecting an initiation. Initiation must be regular, therefore inscribed in an authentic affiliation, ancient and uninterrupted. "Tradition" means approximately the same thing as the Hebrew word "Kabbalah" (as a common noun, more than a theosophic *corpus*), i.e., "transmission." The regularity of these transmissions must be scrupulously guarded so that they may be effected directly from master to disciple, or by the channel of a group's internal initiations. As a corollary, we note in Guénon and his followers a lack of interest in theosophic currents, which play, nevertheless, an integrating role in Western esotericism in its best and most authentic aspect, especially the German *Naturphilosophie* and theosophy. Thus they are closed to what is essential in the history of esotericism in the modern West. Having made this choice, they show little curiosity in various modes of emergence of the Tradition or traditions. And if they happen to leave their own domain, it is often only to declare other domains anathema. On the other hand, they consider our present world, increasingly fallen, as belonging to the *Kali Yuga*, a term borrowed from Hindu cosmology: a dark age from which nothing more can be expected either in the arts, literature, society, nor science. To such an extent modernity is a disaster for human society. However, let us not confuse Guénon with his followers, often much more "purist" than he.

Dualism that goes back to an identic regime: from René Guénon to Julius Evola or to Georges Vallin, it is always "*the*" metaphysical perspective that is proposed to us: *Unity* in the singular—a fusion in the Same, through mysticism or a gnostic consciousness. Various forms of Neoplotinian thought encourage such a fusion because in identifying with the Self, the soul reconstitutes the plenitude of pure Being, restores the primacy of the Same, of the always identical. This form of esotericism presents itself as *the* guardian of *the* Tradition; it is, above all, an intellectual mysticism, opening like the Vedic conception on an atonic, flat, amorphous vision of the World: a mysticism quite removed from the spiritually concrete, because of its rigidity.

For René Guénon, the "hermetic tradition" concerns a knowledge that is "not metaphysical" but rather "cosmological" (micro-macrocosm relationships). The hermetic teachings, as specialized bodies of knowledge, are only derived and secondary, with respect to principles. They pertain to the Royal Art, not the Sacerdotal Art (cf. his article "Hermès" in *Le Voile d'Isis*, April 1932). This restriction certainly highlights a fundamental aspect of the "purist" path. On one side there are the "principles," and on the other the "specialties," the second merely follow from the first. We could object that the principles are accessible to us only by a praxis passing through the Myth. Now, the Myth, being both the departure and arrival points of any esoteric hermeneutics, the endeavor to transform it into principles causes it to lose its specificity whether it changes level by becoming theology or by becoming degraded into ideology.

B) The "Historical" Path

To follow the path I have called "historical," would mean, as the word implies, less to emphasize the existence of an originary and primordial Tradition and to rediscover it after difficulties, than to grasp its modes of emergence through the traditions and, in a deliberately syncretist spirit, to follow the latter through history as they can be seen in religious rites, transcendentally inspired arts, and, of course, in the various forms of esotericism properly speaking. The Tradition, they say, is "one," but it is recognized as having branched out in a varied and complex manner. There would be an architecture, an arithmology, a sacred music in opposition to all that stands out in profane or secularized domains. In this path little attention is paid to the variety of doctrinal elements: reference to a metaphysical "East," not necessarily geographic, suffices to orient a quest, to unify an investigation, despite the diversity or simultaneity of the modes of approach. To be sure, the true Sage belongs to *one* tradition, but it is recognized that before choosing one's own tradition—before becoming a Sage—it is not bad to try out several, especially when one did not grow up receiving from one's parents or teachers religious instruction that could subsequently be enriched. Those who hold to this path flit happily here and there in a process comparable to American students "shopping around" at the beginning of the academic year, spending a fair amount of time sitting in on often very different classes before making a choice. The difference is that souls seeking a Tradition in this second path generally remain gleefully "shopping around." This path is much more popular than the first since it favors the cultural enrichment of its representatives when they are persons of breadth. In France, the *Atlantis* and *La Nouvelle Acropole* Associations, with their magazines, different as they are from each other, illustrate rather well this sociocultural and neoreligious current.

Towards the end of the nineteenth century diverse factors could have contributed to encourage this frame of mind, which is so widespread today. Among other significant events of this complicated period so full of intense curiosity when ardent seekers had to struggle against a gross official scientism, let us record Helena Petrovna Blavatsky's creation of the Theosophical Society in 1875, which lit a syncretist bonfire that is still shooting sparks, and the World Parliament of Religions at the Columbian Exposition in 1893—the first international congress of comparative religion. The subsequent development of the latter in universities, the increase of exchanges among countries, the Western avidity for oriental religions (especially since the dawn of Romanticism), and the expansion of information media (reproductions and encyclopedias), all facilitated a more or less global grasp of the spiritual treasury of humanity. Esoteric societies that bring together a large number of members profit from these possibilities by filtering, each in its own way, this heritage to acquire a specific teaching, and they practice a rather broad syncretism, even when they pretend to hold a message that is theirs alone; e.g., AMORC (Rosicrucians) and the Theosophical Society with their branches throughout the world. If, as is the case with these two large organizations, they reach a vast public, we see them also hold a prudent openness to modernity. But generally, the adherents of the Tradition, even those of this second pathway, intend to oppose their conception of esotericism to all that does not come explicitly under the traditions they uphold.

C) The "Humanist" Path

Openness to modernity makes possible a third path, which we shall call "humanist" by virtue of the expanded field of research and activity it permits, or "alchemist" to the extent that it touches upon a transmutation of ourselves and the world. Recently two American scholars, Sheldon R. Isenberg and Gene R. Thursby, have proposed isolating within contemporary *philosophia perennis* an "evolutionary" current and a "*devolutionary*" current, the dividing line coming precisely between their respective stands on modernity. The second would correspond approximately to our first two pathways, the first to our third. Besides Guénon and Schuon, devolutionaries would be Seyyed H. Nasr, Marco Pallis, Titus Burckhardt, and Huston Smith. Oscar Ichazo, G.I. Gurdjieff, and Jacob Needleman would represent the evolutionary current. This distinction is useful and convenient, but a three-way distinction perhaps allows the complexity of the problem to emerge even more clearly, despite the admitted risk of disagreement in attributing any given philosopher or school to one of these three ways. Nevertheless, it is chiefly between the first two that the demarcation appears least evident.

The point here is not to reconcile Hermes and Darwin, contrary to what seemed possible to nineteenth-century occultism, for the cleavage between evolutionist anthropocentric humanism and evolutionary hermetist humanism is unbridgeable. Nevertheless without abandoning the possibilities offered by the first two nor being limited to them either, with the third pathway it is a question of taking the world for *prima materia*, that entire world that Guénon disdained as a product of the *Kali Yuga*. To be sure, in the majority of Western esoteric currents, especially of the Christian variety, Nature has always been the object of such attention, due to the "signatures" it bears, and its possible transfiguration by humanity. But the crux here is to allow in this third pathway, besides the natural universe, the world of culture and science, i.e., the entire first floor and basement of the house where the traditions, properly speaking, occupy the second floor. Why, for example, does what the apostle Paul say about Nature (Rom. 8:19–22) not apply just as well to this profane world? Why would he not also aspire to leave behind the exile and vanity, not by its destruction but by a new "adoption" and "redemption" of it? This frame of mind presumes generally an approach to the divine different from that of the first two pathways. This approach is difficult to reconcile with the dualism of creationist theologies or with the monism of undifferentiated Unity, because the project in question goes well beyond simple recognition of the fact that vices or constraints of present-day society can favor a higher consciousness of the Tradition itself. More radically than Nicholas of Cusa, Jacob Boehme sees in God not only the coincidence of opposites but the essential form of contradiction. Even in Nature, he does not consider contradictions as different aspects of a unique or identical action, but as a constitutive opposition of all reality in all of its floors. From whence an interest, among Boehme's followers, and more generally among Western theosophers, in the highly ramified domains of knowledge and consequently their eclecticism.

This eclectic tendency was obviously reinforced by the Renaissance, but it was already present in many writings in the *Hermetica*. We find a trace of it in the great medieval *Summae* (Vincent de Beauvais, Bartholomew of England). In contemporary esotericism, the human sciences (psychology, anthropology) and the exact sciences (biology, microphysics) can serve as grounds to be explored for those on the third pathway. They cheerfully admit the existence of a collective unconscious, even to the point of conferring upon it a properly esoteric dimension (which Jung had not tried to), that of a transconsciousness branching out upon an imaginal world. The comparative study of folk tales and myths of all lands can only, they say, enrich with new dimensions a comprehensive hermeneutics. They love to study what can be known of the structures of matter, such as what microphysics brings to light, in order to find the figurative terms of comparison with arithmological intuitions of the past and in order to read new signatures therein. Instead of Tradition, they are more likely to speak of a traditional spirit, composed of intense and focused curiosity, such as the need to create bridges between departments of learning. This, in the best of cases, opens onto *Naturphilosophie* in the theosophic sense of the term. They are well aware that modernity is not free from danger, but they do not consider such danger inevitable. With them the concept of Tradition refers less to an immutable deposit than to a perpetual renewal.

This third path is that of Hermes, who teaches us how to see the myth and mystery in our lives (even in our most profane existence), and how to place these in our range of knowledge. But the gathering up of modernity to place it in the athanor presumes that we are familiar with the athanor and with modernity as well. This twofold requirement can only be satisfied by acquiring a level of culture that must encompass more than the esoteric. "We are condemned," notes Mircea Eliade, "to learn about the life of the spirit and be awakened to it through books." Erudition is "baptism by Intellect." Even more, therefore, are we condemned to that in a domain as interdisciplinary as esotericism where our cultural acquirement can even less afford to be limited to narrow specialization. How can we put ourselves within range of a theosopher, a ritual, a book of alchemy, without having questions about the landscape: the neighboring fields, the common borders, the philosophical, literary, and sociological contexts? Certainly not to break and splinter selected objects, nor to strike them with insignificance by reduction, but rather to return to them after we have taken on this supplementary knowledge, to question them all the better, then, on their specific, irreducible content, since we are at that point, more capable of making the prism of their uncoercible kernel sparkle and shine through our hermeneutics now enriched with new tools.

Today, the absence of erudition, as much as the lack of rigor, is more exasperating than ever, in this crossroads domain so open to entry. People come in and out as in a mill: lax or chimerical minds, halfhearted or nonexistent documentation, repackaging of old errors and tenacious swarms of counterfeits, absence of scientific accouterments in reprintings of old works, here is the daily parade of disappointments that await the serious amateur. There are also counterfeits presented by authors who construct their success on a reduction of the content of religious myths to trivial or "scientific" historical events. To be sure, euhemerism has existed through time, but it takes on evermore promiscuously the colors of current fashion. For example, in *Chariots of the Gods*, Erich von Daeniken interprets biblical hierophanies as traces of a visit from extraterrestrial beings. These new forms of euhemerism adorn themselves with a science fiction that proves less a servant of the imaginary than an ally of gross reductionism. It is the work of what, to borrow an image furnished by Athenian events in B.C. 415, we should happily call *hermocopides* or "Hermes mutilators." We should also call hermocopides those people who present alchemy as a process that produces energy for a utilitarian purpose. Today, instead, there seems to be a need for reverse euhemerism! The reversal of planes is manifested also by the habit of confusing the simple and legitimate need for psychic integration with an initiatory course understood as an authentic pathway to esoteric realization. The sudden compulsion for initiations, occult fairs, the jungle of movements and groups springing up nearly everywhere, but especially in the geographic Far West, sometimes keeps us from discerning between the occasional expression of an authentic aspiration and what translates only into a need for individual or collective therapy. A profusion of pseudo-initiatory discourses, visited and orchestrated by the media, increases the confusion between the fantastic and the esoteric, and between destructuring fragmentation and formative or creative integration. The ideals of communal effervescence that a number of "new religious movements" espouse are attached to a vague mysticism-fusing, monist, thus identific—and, as a consequence, only slightly hermesian. On the other side, anomic pluralisms have not only given rise to schools of thought but also to life attitudes based on a savage plurality, a taste for the unheard of, and for the unexpected—as formerly in Surrealism—a diversity cultivated for itself and where are found retrieved, though out of context, some shreds of esotericism.

Whether this savage imaginary is inflationist or monist, it bears witness, in spite of everything, to the need to escape the "official" regime of the imaginary, the schizomorphic regime in our societies for which our pedagogies and epistemologies show their inadequacy. Timidly, as constrained by internal needs, the exact sciences begin to propose models more apt to respond to the complexity of the real. We thus see effected a rapprochement of the two modes of thought, which during the late Renaissance seemed definitively divorced. Esotericism would once more be able to nurture scientific thought, and the latter could stimulate hermesian, theosophic reflections. The point would not be to encourage a confusion of levels, but rather to specify evermore precisely the dynamic elements capable of enriching scientific thought as well as the human sciences, with esotericism cultivating, on its part, more rigorous standards through contact with these sciences. Such elements could be a mode of plural reading and a more-generalized practice of a *ratio hermetica*.

Western hermetists, especially those of the Renaissance, believed that reading of the myth is the key to understanding art, poetry, science, and technology—and not the reverse. The need for a remythification of the cosmos and humanity was felt, and this meant not creating anew false—totalitarian or fragmentary—myths, but refusing them by demystifying them; not adoring the ancient or recent idols but ceasing to idolize history or to succumb to philosophies of history as to any other form of ideology. To rediscover the reading of myth, whether it be within the framework of an established religion or outside it, is also to learn to read again the book of the world, of Man, and of certain theophanies. It means understanding that language, as Gilbert Durand puts it, passes first through reading, so much so that writing—so highly exalted by formal linguistics as the first datum to be deciphered—is only secondary. "The Art of Memory," such as practiced in the Renaissance (a manner of reading the world by interiorizing it and subsequently writing it from inside the self), could just as well as certain other "ancient sciences," reorient us toward an anagogic hermeneutic of Nature, human activities, and texts, thanks to modes of reading suitable for revealing the metalanguages or living structures of signs and correspondences. Reading in this way means seeking the depth of things in the right place, not in socio-economic infrastructures, nor in latent contents of the unconscious, but beyond them, in Nature itself.

This is a reading that is necessarily plural, which is itself the expression of an ethic of plural totality—in the active manner of being and having—an ethic which refuses to flatten the soul by objectifying the problems of the spirit under the form of reductive or abstract concepts. This is an ethic that transcends the illusion of the banal and finds meaning in the concrete again, at a time when the denial of meaning calls to mind the gesture of a Prometheus who would blind us with a torch of artificial light. This is an ethic that refuses the agnostic impasse of those who indulge in pure abstractionism, of those who flee meaning by identifying it with formal relations, with the exchange of empty signs, by slipping it into the trapdoor of a linguistics devoid of external reference, without heuristics. Solipsism, atomization, incommunicability form the ransom of formal, identific, or dualist modes of reading, while the sciences of Hermes mark the pathways of alterity, living diversity, and the communication of souls. These are guides to closure or alterity in our arts and literatures, depending on whether Narcissus, Dionysus, and Prometheus each reign as absolute master or whether Hermes, on the contrary, stimulates living relationships among them.

Increasingly we see signs prophesying a new reading of myths and a different approach in the human sciences, through the work of those who help install a planetary dialogue by deprovincializing ethnology and religious studies. Thus, Mircea Eliade shows how the profane itself reflects the mythic and by integrating a poetics into his scientific project he makes felt the nature and exigencies of a quest that can aptly be called traditional. More explicitly a traditionalist, Seyyed H. Nasr, succeeds in showing what the great historic avenues of gnosis and the sacred have in common and what differentiates them.

The exegeses of Ananda Coomaraswamy, Mircea Eliade, Henry Corbin, and Seyyed H. Nasr always start with the notion of *philosophia— theosophia— perennis*, and it is to this that their hermeneutics always returns. But not one of them neglects erudition, critical apparatus, or the historical and philosophical tools that constitute a specific aspect of modernity. With them, university scholarship becomes the aid, today indispensable, of Tradition, which they approach both as savants and philosophers.

But we see also, on a parallel track, put into place an *epistémè* that recognizes the possible coexistence of several regimes of rationality, including *ratio hermetica* as Gilbert Durand has called it and, which he himself, and after him, Jean-Jacques Wunenburger, have defined by its terms and modalities. A *ratio hermetica* whose abandonment to the exclusive advantages of a strict identific Aristotelian-type philosophy appears to have been at the origin of the crisis of our human sciences. Guarantor of the cosmic order and unification of the subject, this *ratio* bears in addition the promise of exchanges between esotericism and the human or exact sciences. This guarantor, as a "Higher Science" of a Paracelsian type, as a repository of knowledge of concrete facts, of "mirabilia," is always able to profit better from the contributions of "objective" science without losing sight of what the latter neglects. On the other hand, this official science can be enriched by not rejecting, even in an exploratory guise, the hermetic principle of similitude, the notion of participation of entity-forces, nor the idea that Nature is composed of concrete pluralisms: elements of the *ratio hermetica* where "dualitude" would almost be the common denominator. The notion of "dualitude," present throughout Hermeticism (the word itself is recent but the traditions spoke of syzygies), calls to mind a grid of polar forces in antagonistic positions. The notion excludes a unitary concept based on a single principle of identity and also excludes a dualist conception that basically only reverts back to identity. It excludes likewise a dialectic of the Hegelian-Marxist variety, which is never more than a conjunction of monism and dualism. It is precisely the ubiquity of these identific schemes that dualitude questions. From Aristotle to Marx or to Lévi-Strauss, we see reinforced a simple order of things making up an economy of structural antagonisms, however, at work everywhere. On the other side, among the systems proposed up until now in the periphery of hermetic currents, we believe Stéphane Lupasco's is the most apt to break the hold of the identific hydra because he has developed a science of the energetic and the complex that rejoins alchemy by raising the logic of dualitude to a law, universal in every manifestation. The energetic, the master key to any complex logic (see J.-J. Wunenburger, *La raison contraductoire*, Paris, 1990) is affected too presumptuously by the scientific ideology of the last century to the advantage of structural and information concepts, which never cease blocking the way to a nonidentific thought such as that of the *ratio hermetica*.

To think in terms of dualitude, e.g., Wunenburger's beautiful image of the bow and its cord, is to refuse to put the psychic universe in opposition to the physical universe, but to think of them instead as two sides of the same Whole. It is to refuse to put the metaphysics of Being in opposition to that of Knowing. It is to refer one and the other to a principled homogeneity. It is to substitute a metaphysics of Becoming for this opposition. It does not mean placing Being and Becoming back to back, the simple and the complex, the One and the multiple, nor giving in to the dialectics of dualizing and reabsorbing, like the Neoplatonic schemas and German idealism or its materialist sequels, but to think that everything, as Western esotericism has always known, takes place in an ensemble of forces opposed in a living tension. We find this even in God according to Jacob Boehme, associated by this theosopher with the essential form of contradiction and not only in a coexistence of contraries. It is understandable, moreover, that contemporary scientific rationality has some trouble following Boehme or Baader into the bold but grounded uses they make of contradiction and paradox. On the other hand, an esoteric form of thought, comfortable with modern and contemporary science, would be, more than in the past, capable of giving rise to a new philosophy of Nature, comparable through its orientation to that of German Romanticism, but this time better adapted to the concrete, spiritual exigencies of our time. Now, it does not yet exist, so to speak, because ardent seekers have failed to position myth in the field of scientific knowledge.

In fact, the scientific and spiritual openness permitted by the third path must not serve only to enlarge the field of our epistémè or to succor spirits weary of identific monism and schizophrenic dualism. This opening should serve even more to nurture esotericism on two planes: the elaboration of a *Naturphilosophie*, and an ongoing resumption of the alchemical work of the self. We would be almost tempted to speak of a fourth path, if the third, being esoteric also, did not simultaneously bring with it certain specific requirements. Indeed, we risk forgetting these as we proceed along the third path. The attraction of intellectual ludism and the joyous satisfaction in an enlarged scope of knowledge, are the siren songs that we have to learn how to hear, recognize, and to move beyond. In poeticizing the world by a multilayered reading of it, always both new and traditional, we risk forgetting that *poïein* means first of all "to create." Having occupied ourselves with their retrieval and having remained mere spectators, we may be tempted to euphemize the myths and their scenarios instead of returning, better actors each time, upon the stage where they are playing. Basically, the danger consists in giving in to the temptation of euphemizing that which in esotericism is necessarily dramatic.

A horizontal universalism, syncretist in the best sense, must be supported by a metaphysical perspective to avert disintegration, especially in our contemporary world of spiritual debacle and alienation. It is not enough to rethink the imaginary while recognizing that all our representations and activities—our societies, arts, technologies, etc.—never do more than express one. Still we must wonder about the backdrop of this imaginary. Does it rest upon a "groundlessness" as Cornelius Castoriadis thinks? More likely on a Paradise, as Marc Beigbeder suspects, but a Paradise that it is incumbent upon the esoteric project to rediscover, to explore, and then to bring back to emergence.

If a hermesian reading of the world nurtures its children better than residual formal or abstract signaling, it is not by itself sufficient to transform us. Reading is not doing, the *gai savoir* is not yet praxis. If astrology, like beams from headlights on a highway, neither eliminates the ditches nor determines our choice of itinerary, our seeing in the light of analogy the networks of correspondences between microcosm and macrocosm does not appreciably diminish the disorder of the world and humanity, and does not suffice to lead them back to their original harmony. Attached to every gnosis is an effort of work. Our knowing better how to consult the maps of our anthropological and cosmic geography does not imply that we shall be capable of transporting ourselves appropriately armed to the field of operations. Likewise the circulation and exchange of goods, however much it be Hermes' domain, cannot be confused with palingenesis.

Thus, more than "humanist," our third pathway should be called "alchemist," because this adjective evokes the exigencies of the *nigredo* (work in the black, first stage in the course of the work) that simple aesthetic jubilation would risk losing sight of. *Nigredo, albedo, rubedo,* correspond to a three-stage path that can be undertaken without our having to consider ourselves alchemists. Thus we would not hesitate to recognize those three stages in the works of some people who do not claim to be "esoteric" or "alchemist," but who, more so than others who do make such claims, give evidence of a concrete involvement in an operative pathway which, one may legitimately claim, ends in the Great Work, the Philosopher's Stone. This is what Françoise Bonardel has recently shown convincingly, through the example of a large number of modernist authors and creators, while guarding against diverse forms and risks of euphemization (*Philosophie de l'Alchimie: Grand Oeuvre et Modernité,* Paris, 1993). Any esoteric way passes necessarily through an alchemist ascesis, to be distinguished from asceticism, source of our technological progress but not necessarily a model to follow for someone who wants to experience Wholeness. To consider reading as a mode of initiation, to take a book as instrument of discovery in the *Nigredo,* can arouse in us the appearance of that "incandescent melancholia" that the Renaissance esotericists knew well.

The ascesis required here fully assumes the dramatic. I see it composed of salvific tensions between contradictory poles—this does not necessarily mean anguish—of paradoxes surmounted and maintained, of transforming and installing stages of living polarities. In the first place, ascesis means mounting the blade of a cutting edge and is thus dangerous in itself as well as flanked by perilous gulfs on either side. To avoid the latter means resisting on the one hand the temptation of absolute idealism or an equally intransigent dualism, both homogenizing, and on the other hand immersion in the heterogenizing multiple. But since staying in a state of immobility on the blade can wound our high-wire imaginary, we must find what movement to carry out, in order to escape this third danger while advancing. Contradictorial movement that will be salvific, while contradictional (to use terminology dear to Stéphane Lupasco) would be mortal. Movement that is not the simple result of opposing forces nor equilibration obtained once and for all—and that must correspond to an individuation in C.G. Jung's usage of the word—but ongoing reprise and recreation. In the lineage of Jacob Boehme, Franz von Baader or Stéphane Lupasco—but it was also that of Heraclitus—all that is, or is constituted, takes place as a whole in an ensemble of opposing forces in living tension, ternary or quaternary. These forces are keys to genuine transmutations, as opposed to simple metamorphoses.

The guide Hermes-Mercury does not have the responsibility of accompanying us as far as that, although for purposes of discussion we have used "hermesism" and "esotericism" as synonyms. But what accompanies us are the *traces* of Hermes, like the pebbles dropped by Tom Thumb. Among all the gods, he is perhaps the one who can be left alone to play in us with the fewest risks. But it would be a mistake to be content with his presence alone. Hermes waits for us to come deliver him so that he may help us undertake the task, to choose our other gods, to make good use of our myths. But after that, it is up to Hermes Trismegistus to take the baton. The Alexandrian writings placed under the sign of the Thrice Great—are on the one hand, of a rather pessimistic inspiration, recalling our first pathway (the so-called "purist" Tradition), and on the other hand, under the jurisdiction of a comprehensive esotericism capable of welcoming all the beauty and complexity in the world. Should we see in this double attitude a contradiction in thought due to a variety of authors, like the best historians of these texts sometimes do? Let us, rather, acknowledge instead a hermeneutic tension inciting us to surmount this constitutive antagonism of our era, thanks to an unceasing work of an ongoing and creative back-and-forth between the VIth and VIIth Major Arcana Tarot cards of Marseilles (*The Lovers* and *The Chariot*). Work without which the mystery of Hermetic tension would not open upon a palingenesis, and would risk degenerating each time into a simple model of thought.

Part Two

A Short History of Western Esoteric Currents

CHAPTER ONE

ANCIENT AND MEDIEVAL SOURCES OF
MODERN ESOTERIC CURRENTS

I) ESOTERIC CURRENTS IN THE FIRST ELEVEN CENTURIES

A) Alexandrian Hermetism

The heterogeneous corpus called the *Hermetica* is composed of a few scattered works—lost for the most part—written in the Greek of the Alexandria region at the dawn of our era, and edited and revised over several centuries. It treats astrology, alchemy, *Naturphilosophie*, theosophy, and theurgy. One collection, compiled at a late date, stands out: the *Corpus Hermeticum*, which brings together texts drafted in the second and third centuries A.D. They are fifteen in number, to which were added the *Asclepius* and the *Fragments of Stobeus*. Their author or legendary inspiration is Hermes Trismegistus, the "Thrice Great," whom numerous and contradictory genealogies associate with the Egyptian god Thoth, called "Hermes" by the Greeks. He is alleged to have lived in the time of Moses. The Egyptians, one believed, owed their laws and knowledge to him. The Middle Ages did not know the *Corpus Hermeticum*, rediscovered in the Renaissance, only the *Asclepius*. Despite the speculative nature of the *Corpus Hermeticum*, we should not look for a unified doctrine there. As we move from one text to the next, we find contradictions because it is the work of many authors. The most celebrated treatise is the *Poimandres*, the theosophic discourse that opens the *Corpus Hermeticum*, which develops a cosmology and an anthropogony in a mode of illumination and revelation. Among the themes emerging from this discourse, we find that of the Fall and reintegration, and that of memory in its relations with the active imagination.

If the *Corpus Hermeticum* itself does not take up alchemy, almost everything we know about Western alchemy is found assembled in the writing belonging to this group. It would appear to have been unknown in Pharaonic Egypt and to have developed as a prolongation of Hermetic astrology based in the notion of a sympathy linking each planet to its corresponding metal. Until the second century B.C. alchemy remained a technique associated with the praxis of goldsmithing. With Bolos of Mendes in the second century B.C. it takes a philosophic turn and presents itself more and more often as a revealed science. Zosimos of Panopolis (third century or beginning of the fourth) whose twenty-eight books have been preserved, developed visionary alchemy; he is followed in this by Synesius (fourth century), Olympiodorus (sixth century) and Stephanos of Alexandria (seventh century), all of whom consider alchemy a spiritual exercise.

B) Esotericism in Other Non-Christian Traditions

Four other non-Christian currents are important in the genesis of modern esotericism. First, the Neopythagoreanism of the first two centuries A.D. will continue to reappear as various forms of arithmosophy. Second, Stoicism, which extends over nearly two centuries and includes esoteric elements, as is apparent from its emphasis on knowledge of the concrete universe and on an organic totality guaranteeing harmony between things terrestrial and celestial. Third, Neoplatonism from Plotinus (205–270) to Damascius (480 ff.) taught methods for accessing a suprasensible reality and for constructing or describing that reality in its structure and articulations. Porphyry (273–305), Iamblichus (*The Mysteries of Egypt*, ca. 300), and Proclus (412–485) figure among the most visible Neoplatonists in later esoteric literature. Finally, the Jewish Kabbalah, a theosophy. In the fifth or sixth century a cosmosophic text of some pages is drawn up: the *Sepher Yetzirah* (*Book of Creation*), which prefigures what will become the Kabbalah properly speaking. Along with all that comes intense Arabic intellectual activity linked to the rapid expansion of Islam. The Arab *Epistles* of the Sincere Brethren (ninth century) are filled with cosmogonic esoteric speculations. From the ninth century onwards, Neoplatonic and Hermetic texts are translated into Arabic and inspire original works: *Theology of Aristotle*, ninth century; *Picatrix*, a tenth-century encyclopedia of magic, partly of Greek origin; *Assembly of Pythagoras* (*Turba Philosophorum*), a compilation of statements on alchemy; *De causis*, ca. A.D. 825 where we find the first version of the famous text called the *Emerald Tablet*.

C) Esoteric Aspects in Christian Thought of the First Eleven Centuries

Whether or not there existed a primitive Christian esotericism and whether or not it was essentially Jewish are topics still debated today. Clement of Alexandria (160–215), whose Hellenist Christianity is colored with Jewish esotericism, emphasizes in his *Stromata* ("Miscellanies") the importance of gnosis, i.e., a knowledge that upholds faith and transcends it. Origen (185–254) recommends a constant effort to interpret the Scriptures on several levels in order to pass from faith to gnosis. On the periphery of more or less "official" Christianity, which both represent, Gnosticism is a theosophy with varying forms having a common theme: deliverance from evil through the destruction of our universe and the election of our soul above and beyond it. Unlike Basilides and Valentinus, other gnostics of the second century like Marcion teach a dualist conception of Man and the world that is found again in the Manichean current issuing from Mani in the third century. (Evil is ontologically equal to Good.) Metaphysical pessimism marks the theosophy, albeit very rich and filled with inspiring images, of the Gnosticism that stems from Bulgarian Bogomilism in the tenth century, and, hence Catharism. In the following period three great names stand out. First, Pseudo-Dionysius who, inspired by Proclus, wrote in Greek in the sixth century (*Mystical Theology, Divine Names, Celestial Hierarchy*) and drew from the Scriptures a theosophy of mediation "imagining" a triple triad of angelic entities. Around a century later, Maximos the Confessor wrote commentaries on Pseudo-Dionysus. Finally in the ninth century, John Scottus Eriugena, an Irish monk, wrote *Periphiseon* ("Divisions of Nature"), one of the most important intellectual monuments of the Middle Ages.

II) ESOTERICISM IN MEDIEVAL THOUGHT

A) A Theology of Esoteric Cast

The twelfth century discovered Nature illuminated by analogy. Arabic science, which had recently become accessible to the West, favored such integration in the world. In the School of Chartres, especially Bernard Silvester (*De mundi universitate*, 1147) and William of Conches (ca. 1080–1145) there is no hiatus yet between metaphysical and cosmological principles. But that is not the only such group. The era sees also the masterwork of Alain of Lille's (1128–1203) *De planctu naturae*, the brilliantly illustrated, mystico-theosophic texts of Hildegard of Bingen (1099–1180), notably her *Scivias*. Appearing also are Honorius Augustodunensis's *Clavis Phisicae* and *Elucidarium* as well as many other similar creations. If this Roman period favors esotericism because of the importance of correspondences, imagination, mediations, Nature, and pathways of spiritual transformation, the Franciscan spirit in the thirteenth century reinforces this tendency through its love of Nature. The Oxford School contributed much as well: Robert Grosseteste's theosophy of light, Roger Bacon's alchemy and astrology, etc. By the time that the infiltration of Arabic texts into Latinity is nearly completed, around 1300, we witness in Christian theology the triumph of Latin Averroism (i.e., the Arab Averroes, 1026–1098, interpreter of Aristotle) to the detriment of the influence of Avicenna, a Persian (980–1037). In the. West, Averroism supplants

Avicennism, thereby ushering into theology, a near total eclipse of the *mundus imaginalis* and its intermediaries, sacrificing as well the active imagination to a rationalism that in the end will become the distinct property of the Western spirit. On the other hand, the Christian and Islamic twelfth century will develop increasingly a theology of "second causes" (especially cosmology), which will problematize the articulation between metaphysical principles and cosmology. This disappearance and this problematization will favor the emergence of esotericism as it is usually understood.

B) Summae *and Universal Syntheses.*

Numerous *summae* are compendia of prodigies or primarily records of the powers at work in the four realms. They foreshadow the *Philosophia occulta* of the Renaissance. This is the case for example of Vincent de Beauvais' *Speculum naturale* (1245) or Bartholomew of England's *De proprietatibus rerum* (ca. 1230). But there are also "*summae*" which are systems of thought, grand philosophical syntheses. (Not all are under the sway of esotericism, that of St. Thomas is far from it!) The Calabrian abbot Joachim da Fiore (ca. 1135–1202), who distinguishes three great periods of Universal History (the reign of the Father, that of the Son, and—still to come—that of the Holy Spirit) was to have a considerable vogue in modern times, but less because of theosophical speculations about the "Third Age" or the future spiritual guides of humanity, than because of its usefulness to philosophers of history. Let us cite also the *Ars Magna* of Raymond Lull (1235–1316), a combining "art" with universal pretensions, marked by medieval Neoplatonism as transmitted by John Scottus Eriugena, i.e., a dynamic Platonism, close to the Jewish Kabbalah then flourishing in Spain. At the very end of the Middle Ages, Nicholas of Cusa (1401–1464), who perhaps cannot be labeled an esotericist, foretold Renaissance Hermetism by his idea of the fundamental unity of religions (*De pace fidei*, 1453), and proposed a world system, a theory of "opposites" wherein the infinitely large coincides with the infinitely small—a "total" science encompassing astrology as well.

C) Hermetism, Astrology, and Alchemy

Numerous works on magic have an esoteric character like the *Picatrix* (of Arabic origin, as we have seen, known now through Latin translations and adaptations) or those coming under *ars notoria*, art of calling angels. The *Corpus Hermeticum* was lost until the Renaissance, but the *Asclepius* in Latin was available, and other hermetist texts circulated. (*Liber XXI philosophorum*, one of the best known, dates from the twelfth century.) The names of Roger of Hereford and John of Spain stand out in twelfth-century astrology, but this science is not essential in a world still traversed by the Divine. Dante places two famous astrologers of the thirteenth century in hell: Michael Scotus and Guido Bonatti. At the beginning of the fourteenth century Lull makes a large place for astrology in his *Ars Magna*, as does Pietro of Abano in his *Conciliator*. Cecco d'Ascoli (1269–1327), another astrologer with flair, died at the stake in Florence. As for alchemy, it is hardly known in Europe before the twelfth century. Islam introduced it through Spain. Circulating at the end of the thirteenth century are two Latin alchemical texts that proved influential: *Turba Philosophorum* (cf. *supra* for its Arabic origin), which gave dialogues of bygone alchemists; the *Summa*, a compilation of writings attributed to Geber, an Arab. *Aurora consurgens* is attributed by legend to St. Thomas Aquinas. Let us mention also works attributed to the Catalonian Arnald of Villanova (ca. 1235–1311), notably the *Rosarium Philosophorum*, and, starting with the fourteenth century (when alchemical literature can be truly said to soar, staying plentiful up to the end of the eighteenth century), authors like John Dastin, Petrus Bonus (*Pretiosa margarita novella*, ca. 1330), Nicholas Flamel (1330–1417), with whom lovely legends are connected, which still cause much ink to flow, George Ripley (*The Compound of Alchemy*, 1470, and *Medulla alchimiae*, 1476), and Bernard of Treves (1406–1490). Just as in the late Hellenist period, medieval alchemy tended to be deployed on two planes, operative and spiritual.

III. INITIATORY QUESTS AND ESOTERIC ARTS

A) The Jewish Kabbalah

Clearly the Kabbalah represents the essential of Jewish esotericism. Its influence in Latinity is considerable, especially from the Renaissance onwards. Following the *Sepher Yetsirah* (cf. *supra*), a compilation of Kabbalistic materials carried out in Provence in the twelfth century makes up the first exposé of the Kabbalah properly so-called. This is the *Bahir*, which orients the Kabbalah in the double direction of a gnosis of Eastern origin and a Neoplatonism. Numbers and letters of the Old Testament are the object of a hermeneutics effecting a knowledge of relationships between God and the world, thanks to a knowledge of intermediary chains and according to an interpretive method seeing in each word and letter of the Torah a meaning with multiple ramifications. The Kabbalah was next enriched by what has remained its most important book, the *Sepher ha Zohar* or *Book of Splendor*, appearing in Spain after 1275. An agreeable compilation due probably to Moses de León, it represents the summit of the Jewish Kabbalah, i.e., a speculative mysticism applied to the knowledge and description of the Divinity's mysterious works. The Zohar considerably prolonged the Talmudic dimension relative to the tasks or rites for developing a mythology of Nature, a cosmic valorization from which Renaissance thought profited. Finally the great mystic Abraham Abulafia (1240–1291), born in Saragossa, taught a meditation technique of interest to esotericism in its initiatory and symbolic aspect but calling on physical techniques also.

B) Chivalry and Initiatory Societies

The art of church building was transmitted to the workshops from which modern Freemasonry is derived. Masons' obligations constitute the "Old Charges" wherein the texts which have come down to us go back to the end of the fourteenth century. (These are the *Regius*, ca. 1390, and the *Cooke*, ca. 1410, which discuss geometry as a script of God that arose simultaneous with the origin of the world.) Chivalry is also initiatory in some of its aspects. (The Templar sites of Tomar, Portugal, for example, bear traces of certain forms of esotericism within that knightly order.) But let us take care not to confuse history and literature! The destruction of the Order of the Temple in 1312 has given rise to a Templar myth that barely corresponds to the facts. Likewise the Albigensian Crusade undertaken in 1207 has given rise to legends concerning their alleged "esotericism." When there was esotericism, it was generally less in those orders or movements properly speaking than in much later discourses they inspired, especially since the beginning of modern times. Thus the symbols of the Order of the Golden Fleece, founded by Philip the Good in 1429, served to launch once more the myth of Jason into the Western imaginary, notably in alchemical literature and esoteric Freemasonry. We find a more obvious esotericism in Amaury de Bène's "Frères du Libre Esprit" ("Brothers of the Free Spirit," 1206) or, even more, in the *Gottesfreunde* ("Friends of God"), gathered around laic Rulman Merswin (1307–1382) in their Alsatian cloister called *Ile Verte* ("Green Island").

C) Esotericism in the Arts

In the twelfth and thirteenth centuries, churches and cathedrals made use of a visionary theology filled with theophanies and metamorphoses. Their repertoire of symbols was founded on a subtle knowledge of the relationships uniting God, humanity, and the universe. But we should not attribute to their architects and builders more esoteric intentions than they had, despite some possible references to alchemy (e.g., the bas-reliefs on the central portal of Notre Dame in Paris) or astrology (Sun and Moon Tower of Chartres Cathedral, zodiac signs on the cathedral of Antwerp, etc.). It is once again alchemy that in the fourteenth century appeared in beautiful illuminated manuscripts e.g., Constantinus or at the beginning of the fifteenth century, *Aurora consurgens*, the *Book of the Holy Trinity*, while in architecture the palace of Jacques Coeur (1395–1456) at Bourges has been interpreted by some alchemists as a "philosophical dwelling." Astrology is present in art in the very widespread form of engravings showing the "children of the planets." Playing cards, appearing around 1375, began from the early fifteenth century to be symbolic repositories for the gods and the planets.

Initiation, secrecy, love, and illuminated knowledge blend together in a chivalric imaginary wherein an immense literature surrounds the legendary King Arthur. This is the *Matière de Bretagne* ("Brittany material") with heroes like Arthur, Perceval, Lancelot, and the Fisher King. Initiatory scenarios and symbols characterize even more the specifically Grail literature. This appears around 1180 when the books of Chrétien de Troyes and Robert de Boron associate Western traditions of chivalric and Celtic type (notably the Druidic traditions, cf. the *Vita Merlini* in the twelfth century) with an esotericism linked to Christianity, especially to the powers of the blood of Christ, collected by Joseph of Arimathea. Then, between 1200 and 1210, Wolfram von Eschenbach devoted his *Parzival* to the Grail and chivalry, in which some alchemical and hermetist elements might be identified. Without always being alchemical, though always at least initiatory, the quest of the Grail, recalled in *Der Junge Titurel* by Albrecht von Schwarzenberg, a long epic written a little after 1260, contains a striking evocation of the Imago Templi, the Temple of Solomon, and the Heavenly Jerusalem. The science of Hermes is also present in *Le Roman de la Rose* begun by Guillaume de Lorris and continued by Jean de Meung. (This editing was carried out from 1230 to 1285.) We see there a rich symbolic universe that miniatures and illuminated pages would soon embellish further.

CHAPTER TWO

ESOTERICISM AT THE HEART OF THE
RENAISSANCE AND IN THE FLAMES
OF THE BAROQUE

I) *PHILOSOPHIA PERENNIS*, A DISCOVERY OF HUMANISM

A) Re-emergence and Success of the Corpus Hermeticum

Around the year 1450 in Florence, Cosimo de' Medici entrusted Marsilio
Ficino (1433–1499) with the creation of a Platonic Academy and about twelve
years later asked him to translate, even before any of the works of Plato, the
texts of the *Corpus Hermeticum*, which had just been rediscovered in
Macedonia. This Latin translation appeared in 1471 and went through no less
than twenty-five editions before 1641, to which were added other translations
as well. One thing common to all these commentaries—beginning with those
of Ficino himself—was that these texts and their "author," Hermes Trismegistus, were believed to belong to a far distant past, to the age of Moses. In
these texts they perceived a foreshadowing of Christianity; also the presence
of a teaching that revealed the *philosophia perennis* or "eternal philosophy" of
which this Hermes was one link in a supposed chain of well-known figures.
This Renaissance search for a *Prisca theologia* represents one way in which
Western esotericism focused its obsessive quest for origins (cf. above).
Neoalexandrian Hermetism, i.e., the rediscovered Hermetism of the ancient
Greeks, helped give birth to a form of religious universalism similar to that
previously espoused by Nicholas of Cusa. It also tended to flourish under
conditions of tolerance. In England it was stifled during the Puritan period
under Edward VI and Mary. In Germanic countries its reception was long
hindered for yet another reason since Lutheranism did not look favorably on
all forms of humanism.

Among the sixteenth century exegetes and publishers of the *Corpus Hermeticum* we find, in addition to Ficino, the names of Ludovico Lazarelli (1507/1549), Foix de Candale (*Pimandre*, 1579), and Hannibal Rossel (*Pymander* 1585/1590). Other authors whose work bore the stamp of this brand of esotericism were Symphorien Champier (*Liber de quadruplici vita*, 1507), Francesco Giorgi of Venice (*De Harmonia mundi*, 1525, translated into French by Guy Lefèvre de la Boderie in 1579), Henricus Cornelius Agrippa (*De occulta philosophia*, 1533), and Francesco Patrizzi who, like Bruno, tried to reestablish a real religion based on Hermetic writings and Zoroastrian oracles (*Nova de Universis philosophia*, 1591). It also colored the work of John Dee (1527–1608) and of Giordano Bruno (1548–1600). In 1614 a Genevan Protestant named Isaac Casaubon demonstrated that the texts of the *Corpus Hermeticum* did not go back any further than the early centuries of the Christian era. Some Hermetists deliberately ignored this discovery; others only slowly took notice of it, but because it was now suspected of being much less ancient than previously believed, it attracted fewer and fewer admirers and commentators. There were enough, however, to prompt a landmark English translation (by John Everard, 1650 and 1657) and to continue to attract the interest of several noteworthy persons. Robert Fludd made it one of the foundations of his theosophy (*Utriusque cosmi historia*, 1617/1621), while Robert Cudworth (*The True Intellectual System of the Universe*, 1678) and Henry More (1614–1687) used it to support their metaphysical ideas. Athanasius Kircher, who studied the relationship of Hermetism to ancient egyptian thought, contributed more than anyone to the inauguration of the wave of egyptomania that marked the Early Modern period. Finally, this Hermetism also found its way into several realms of discourse outside the bounds of esotericism proper; for example, in the sciences with Copernicus (who mentioned Trismegistus in his *De Revolutionibus* of 1543) and with Kepler (*Harmonices Mundi*, 1619); and in humanism with Robert Burton (*Anatomy of Melancholy*, 1621).

B) *The Christian Kabbalah*

The ancient Jewish Kabbalah put a greater emphasis on theogony and cosmogony than on salvation history or messianism, however, after the 1492 diaspora the latter tendencies began to overtake the former. Isaac Luria (1534–1572) redirected the reading of the Kabbalah in these new directions, which were to become a distinct school within the Jewish tradition and also, in eighteenth-century Christianity with Fr. Chr. Oetinger. The 1492 decree expelling the Jews from Spain had a second effect. It brought on a cultural exodus directed mostly toward Italy, which helped to make the Jewish Kabbalah known and thus stimulated the development of its Christian variant. The Christian Kabbalah did not literally begin with Pico della Mirandola (1463–1494), but it is with him that it really took hold. His aim was not a Christian interpretation of Jewish theogony, but rather a Christian hermeneutic that utilized the methods of the Jewish commentators to discover the truths hidden in the sacred texts. Thus, his "theses" (ninety *Conclusiones* presented in 1486) marked the beginning of this particular intellectual current. In them he asserted that esoteric Judaism was in accord with Christianity and that "no science proved the divinity of Christ better than did the Kabbalah and magic."

It was during this period (between 1492 and 1494) that Jacques Lefèvre d'Etaples wrote *De magia naturali*, which dealt with magic and the Kabbalah, Johannes Reuchlin wrote *De Verbo mirifico* (1494, followed by his *De arte cabbalistica* in 1517), and the converted Jew Paul Ricius offered his Latin translations of Hebrew texts (*Porta lucis*, 1515) to those interested in arithmosophy, theosophic exegesis, and divine nomenclature. Kabbalah, magic, Hermetism and alchemy were more or less interwoven in the bold synthesis of Henricus Cornelius Agrippa, *De occulta philosophia*, written sometime after 1510 and published in 1533. The *De arcanis catholicae veritatis* (1518) by the Franciscan Pietro Galatino was widely circulated in the sixteenth century. Other Franciscans who delved into the Christian Kabbalah were Jehan Thenaud, whose writings were undertaken at the request of Francis I, and especially Francesco Giorgi of Venice who dedicated his *De harmonia mundi* (1525, followed by his *Problemata* in 1536) to Clement VII. This monument of esotericism should not, however, make us forget the writings of Cardinal Egidio of Viterbo, a genius of truly universal learning (*Libellus*, 1517; *Scechinah*, 1530). The most famous representative of this esoteric current was Guillaume Postel (1510-1581), who was expelled from the Company of Jesus in 1545. In 1553 he made a translation with commentary of the Zohar followed in 1548 by an *Interprétation du candélabre de Moyse*, but many other books, including the first Latin translation of the *Sepher Yetzirah*, were the product of this fruitful talent as well. This Christian esotericism took root in England primarily in the seventeenth century with James Bonaventure Hepburn (*Virga aurea*, 1616), Robert Fludd (*Summum bonum*, 1629), and Henry More the Cambridge Neoplatonist. In his refutations of Giorgi of Venice, Fludd, Postel, and Jacques Gaffarel, Father Marin Mersenne tried (*Observationes*, 1632) to combat what had practically become the fashionable way of thinking and which, despite his efforts, was to remain so for a long time to come. Finally the *Cabala denudata* (1677/1684), by Knorr von Rosenroth (which contained a Latin translation of part of the Zohar) was full of theosophical ideas and texts, took up the torch of Reuchlin, Postel and their followers, and became an obligatory reference point for later theosophers.

C) Homo Universalis: *Activity, Dignity, Synthesis*

Thanks to men like Pico and Ficino new horizons such as Hermetism and the Jewish Kabbalah were opened up to the early Renaissance. Not only were they a means of stepping back from the cultural and spiritual fields inherited from the Middle Ages, but the *philosophia perennis* and Christian Kabbalah were also expressions of the need to construct a "concordance" among the various traditions and fostered speculation on, and construction of, interrelationships among different levels of reality. This was accompanied by an exaltation of human labor and human activity. In Ficino's work Hermetism and Platonism served to underscore the grandeur of humanity and to present a theosophic vision of the cosmos (*Theologia Platonica*, 1469/1474; *De vita coelitus comparanda*, 1489). The multitalented polymath Pico tried to bring Plato, Aristotle, and Christianity into one harmonious synthesis, but he also sought a reinterpretation of Christianity using "the Kabbalah and magic." Whereas the Kabbalah deals with initial causes, "*magia,*" which deals with intermediate causes such as stars, links the natural with the religious and brings the separate branches of scientific knowledge and religion back to their common trunk. (Pico's curiosity did not really extend to the philosophy of Nature or to mathematics, however, in spite of the magnificent, visionary cosmology set forth in his *Heptaplus*.) His spirited critique of determinist astrology reasserted the freedom of the individual person. In his *Oratio de dignitate hominis* he extolled the idea of freedom. Man is not merely a microcosm, a reflection of the macrocosm; but rather he possesses the faculty to decide both his own destiny and his place in the hierarchy of being. With their emphasis on the active role and efficacy of the will, on the search for the transmutation of what was originally interior and exterior to our own being by virtue of vital, living interconnections, and finally on a never-ending and eclectic curiosity and search for knowledge, Ficino and Pico showed themselves to be part of a family of kindred spirits characteristic of modern Western esotericism.

II) THE GERMANIC CONTRIBUTION: *NATURPHILOSOPHIE* AND THEOSOPHY

A) Paracelsism

During the sixteenth century Lutheranism tended to impede the acceptance of Neoplatonism, neo-Alexandrian Hermetism, and the Kabbalah in Germanic lands. Nothing really comparable to the Florentine Academy existed there. In its place we find a form of theosophy whose original stem was Paracelsism, and whose main offshoots were such intellectual currents as Boehmenism or Rosicrucianism. The Swiss Theophrastus Bombastus von Hohenheim, called Paracelsus (1493–1541), spent an itinerant life of healing and writing across Europe. Appointed professor at the Academy of Medicine in Basel in 1527, he did not remain there long because of official displeasure at his reformist ideas. He used the German vernacular instead of Latin and, most importantly, he attacked the authority of the ancients (such as Galen), for which he wanted to substitute experimentation. At his death he left a considerable body of work (*Opus paramirum, Philosophia Sagax* and many other titles) of which only small number were published during his lifetime. (Not until Huser's edition of 1589 did the majority of his writings get into print.)

Whereas in the Neoplatonic tradition one passed from the divine first principle to physical matter through a series of stages, with Paracelsus, Nature emanated directly from the omnipotence of the Almighty. Nature was epiphany. But he resembled the Neoplatonists Plotinus and Proclus in his qualitative conception of time, "which proceeds by a thousand paths," every individual thing having its own unique, alchemical-like rhythm. Furthermore, with Paracelsus Western alchemy reached a turning point. No longer just a means of gaining knowledge about the world, about mankind, and about the Creator Himself, it became an all-encompassing vision. Everything, including the stars, was created "chemically" and continues to evolve in a "chemical" manner. At the same time, the "science of Hermes" became organically linked to astrology, which Paracelsus regarded not as a science of influences or blind determinism but as a blueprint or representation of the interdependencies of the universe, where the stars are at least as much "within" Man as they are outside of him. An element of our mind, a part of our own soul, called the "Light of Nature," reveals to us the *magnalia Dei* or mutual relationships and interconnections between humanity, the earth, and the stars on the one hand, and the stars and metals or chemical elements on the other. Just as our physical bodies draw nourishment from the elements, so do our invisible sidereal bodies nourish themselves by allowing the "*Gestirn*" (the spirit of the stars) to work within and act upon them. Not only the physician, but also Man in general, must learn to welcome into his own being this "Light of Nature." Paracelsus, as well as Pico and Ficino, understood human existence dynamically as an ongoing process of fulfillment. Here the emphasis on the individual is unmistakeable, whereas the thinking of the Middle Ages enfolded man within a preordained community.

This way of thinking became widely dispersed. It radiated throughout various branches of knowledge, especially from the end of the century on. Esotericism was not the only area affected. Chemistry, in its modern guise, also was, as was medicine, despite numerous and strong opposition (Thomas Erast, *Disputationes*, 1572/1573, for example). Most of the major figures who continued this line of thought kept the Paracelsian idea of the complementarity of those two books called the Bible and Nature (Peter Severinus, 1540–1602; Gerhard Dorn, between 1565 and 1585). Among those who followed in his wake were Johann Baptist Van Helmont (1577–1644) and Oswald Croll (*Basilica chymica*, 1609).

B) Boehmenist Theosophy

Because of the emphasis it placed on this "Light of Nature" Paracelsism was more an esoteric philosophy of Nature than a theosophy proper, but it was from this well that German theosophy would draw its inspiration. The sixteenth century was not lacking in theosophists even outside of Germany. To the names of Giorgi of Venice and Guillaume Postel, who have already been mentioned, we might add others, like Lambert Daneau (*Physice christiana*, 1571). But again it was in Germany that another great strain of theosophy emerged with Jacob Boehme (1575–1624). Even before Boehme arrived, Valentin Weigel (1533-1588), a pastor from the vicinity of Chemnitz, effected a fusion of the Rhinish—Flemish mystical tradition with the down-to-earth thinking of Paracelsus. Originally a shoemaker from Goerlitz in Silesia, Boehme had a visionary experience in 1610 that was brought on by contemplation of a pewter vessel, an experience that determined his spiritual vocation as well as his vocation as author. *Aurora* (1612), the first book to emerge from this enlightenment, circulated in manuscript and caused him trouble with the Protestant authorities. Later works had the same result. (Only *Der Weg zu Christo* appeared during his lifetime, in 1624.) Out of his abundant production, one of the most astonishing in Baroque German prose, I would mention *De tribus Principiis* (1619), *De signatura rerum* (1621), *Mysterium Magnum* (1623), only the titles of which are in Latin.

Boehme was not a humanist, and if one were to seek influences on him they would be Paracelsus, alchemy, and probably the Kabbalah. In contrast to the medieval and even the Neoplatonic concept of the Divine, Boehme did not see it as static but rather envisaged it as a passionate struggle of opposing principles. Before Being there was the *Ungrund*, a primordial freedom "without cause." It was not Reason but rather an irrational principle, the Will, that was the basis of Being. Accordingly, Boehme did not recognize a Supreme Being in the manner of Eckhart's *deitas*, which was outside all becoming, but rather a Heraclitean-like fire, a God who is never *in esse* but always *in fieri*; a Supreme Being who "sees" in His living mirror, in the Divine Wisdom or Sophia, the potential world. Once created by this vision, the divine image then wills, magically engenders, the temporal image into being. Sophiology, an intellectual discourse inspired by the personification of Wisdom that appears in the Old Testament, had not yet become the object of much speculation in the West. (But the *Amphitheatrum* of Khunrath, which appeared in 1595, could have set Boehme on this path.) The theme of Sophia leads into the major intellectual avenues of Boehme's works, which are built up like a great Baroque cathedral: the fall of Lucifer and Adam, the spiritual corporeality of the angels, the idea that all exterior form is language or *Figur*, the seven "spirit-sources" existing from all eternity, etc. This "prince of Christian theosophy" contributed in large measure to the formation of a spiritual conscience in the general turmoil of seventeenth-century Germany. Animated by his spirit and thinking, theosophy continued to flourish in other countries as well, with Angelus Silesius (*Cherubinischer Wandersmann*, 1657), Johann Georg Gichtel (1638–1710), Gottfried Arnold (1665–1714), Pierre Poiret (1646–1719), Antoinette Bourignon (1616–1680), John Pordage (1608–1681), and Jane Leade (1623–1704). Although somewhat distinct from theosophy strictly speaking, the so-called Cambridge School of Neoplatonism (Henry More and Ralph Cudworth), as well as several schools and authors, were intrigued and influenced by Boehme and Paracelsus in whose names both faith and knowledge would be so often combined.

C) *The First Rosy-Cross*

The first known printed texts dealing with the Rosy-Cross appeared at the beginning of the seventeenth century. It all began in 1614 at Cassel with a small, anonymous, 38-page manifesto in German, the *Fama Fraternitatis* "of the praiseworthy order of the Rose Cross," addressed "to all the learned of Europe." On the one hand, it contained a critique of the spiritual state of Europe, accompanied by ideas on a possible redemption that would result not through the churches but by means of a universal spiritual science in which heart and mind are united. On the other hand, there were traces of the Christian Kabbalah, Pythagorism, and a strong dose of Paracelsism. To all this was added the biography of a mythical character, C. R. C., a great traveler who was supposed to have lived in Arabia, in Egypt, and then to have returned to Germany to found this Fraternity. In 1604, one hundred and twenty years after his supposed death, it was claimed that his tomb had been found and that it contained magic formulas and secrets of life. In 1615 the *Fama* was republished in Frankfurt together with another work, the *Confessio Fraternitatis*, whose anonymous authors declared that the world had entered the age of Mercury, the "lord of the Word." They claimed to be on the verge of unveiling some of the Adamic language with which the hidden secrets of the Bible and also of creation itself could be discovered since the Holy Scriptures were "the Compendium and the quintessence of the whole world." The third proto-Rosicrucian writing (*Chymische Hochzeit Christiani Rosencreutz Anno 1459*, 1616), also anonymous, was an initiatory novel whose hero, Christian Rosencreutz, undertook a journey expressing in alchemical metaphors the holy and mystical marriage of Christ with His Church, of God with His creation. This wonderful Baroque novel continues to inspire works of exegesis.

The first two of these three texts were written during the time of crisis at the beginning of the Thirty Years' War. Among their authors were Tobias

Hess (1568–1614) and Johann Valentin Andreae (1586–1654). The former was known as a doctor and esotericist; the latter, who belonged to an important Lutheran dynasty in Swabia, was unquestionably the author of the 1616 novel. Andreae left a considerable body of work at his death. During his lifetime he was exposed to recurring troubles with the Protestant authorities who rightly suspected him of being at the root of this Rosicrucian myth, which, from the moment publication of the two original manifestoes, experienced an immediate and lasting success. Numerous publications both for and against the Rosicrucian texts appeared in several countries (more than 200 between 1614 and 1620, and about 900 up to the beginning of the nineteenth century!). Among the most important authors who helped spread Rosicrucian ideas were Robert Fludd (1574–1637), Julius Sperber (?–1619), Elias Ashmole (1617–1692), Michael Maier (ca. 1566–1622), Samuel Hartlib (1595–1662), Jan Amos Comenius (1592–1670), John Heydon (*The Holy Guide*, 1662), and Theophilus Schweighardt (*Speculum sophicum—Rhodo-Stauricum*, 1618), all of whom took up the seeds planted in the Rosicrucian fiction. In Comenius especially, the pacifist program of Andreae, which was limited to Germany and the Lutheran confession, "took on a planetary dimension and looked forward to the humanitarianism of Freemasonry" (R. Edighoffer). In fact, the ideas sown by Comenius took shape in 1660 with the founding of the Royal Society of London. (The English, too, showed themselves more receptive to the introduction of Rosicrucian ideas than the French.) This Rosicrucian development had two main consequences. First, it strengthened the interest of that era in theosophical speculations about Nature in the Paracelsian tradition (which should be called pansophism since theosophy, *strictu sensu*, has more to do with "intra-divine" processes so to speak). Second, the belief that a Rosicrucian society actually did lie behind these manifestoes caused real societies to spring up. The explosion of initiatory societies in the Western world from the seventeenth century onward was a direct result of this.

These three proto-Rosicrucian writings were part of a theosophical context, which itself was not much older and to which they were in part connected. This context is represented by the works of Aegidius Guttman (whose *Offenbarung göttlicher Majestät*, published in 1619, had circulated in manuscript ever since it had been written, probably around 1575), Simon Studion (whose *Naometria* dating from the same period has never been published but which also circulated in manuscript), and especially Johann Arndt . In his *Vier Bücher vom wahren Christenthum* (and primarily in the last of these four volumes which appeared in 1610), Arndt worked out and defined what in his own terms would be known as "mystical theology"; that is, an attempt to integrate medieval mysticism, the neo-Paracelsian inheritance and alchemy with theology. If this integration were to be possible, it would be through the individual's ability to achieve a "second birth." This was understood as being the acquisition of a new body in the soul of the Elect. This mystical theology should probably be seen as a subtle link between the Roscicrucian Manifestoes and the "Alchemical Wedding" of J.V. Andreae.

III) READING THE WORLD AND MYTH

A) *"Philosophia Occulta"*

From the end of the fifteenth to the end of the seventeenth century, all the currents that have been mentioned until now concerned the *Philosophia occulta*, a magical vision of the world in which everything acts upon and reflects everything else analogically. Witchcraft and its spells, black magic, pacts with the Devil, and incantations are not directly linked to the concept of esotericism as we have defined it, but represent the black side of *Philosophia occulta* and an important part of the collective imaginary of the time. There was here a great deal of *magia naturalis*, a premodern type of natural science. *Magia naturalis* is the knowledge and use of occult powers and properties that are considered "natural" because they are objectively present in nature (cf. for example, *Magiae naturalis libri viginti*, 1589, by Giovanni della Porta). This type of magic is hardly distinguishable from the tentative beginnings of modern science and often looked like a form of naturalism colored by atheism. But this ambiguous expression could also refer to *magia* in the esoteric sense, seen as an attempt to unify Nature and religion (notably in the search for an alternative to the Aristotelianism condemned by the church). To *Magia* belongs white magic or theurgy, which uses names, rites, and incantations with the aim of establishing a personal link with entities that are not part of the world of physical creation. These two aspects of *magia naturalis* (the naturalist type and white magic) sometimes mingle, as in "celestial" or "astronomical" magic, where the stars can in fact be considered simultaneously from the point of view of the influence they are supposed to exert physically and of the influence exerted by their "will" (cf. *De vita coelitus comparanda*, 1489, by Marsilio Ficino; *De occulta philosophia*, 1533, by Henricus Cornelius Agrippa).

Five other names should be added to these major figures in "occult philosophy" (besides Fludd, Paracelsus, and others mentioned previously who are naturally connected with it): Johannes Trithemius (1462–1516), abbot of Sponheim, whose *Steganographia* remained unpublished until 1606, and whose *De Septem Secundeis* (1522) dealt with the seven deities or intellects that animate the celestial orbs and the history of the world. Jacques Gohory (alias Leo Suavius, ca. 1520–1576), a musicologist, neo-Paracelsian, and author of *De usu et mysteriis notarum liber* (1550), among other works. The Elizabethan seer, John Dee (1527–1608), who incorporated the speculations on angels in the Kabbalah with the Pseudo-Dionysian hierarchies, was the author of the famous *Monas hieroglyphica* (1564), a key to understanding the symbols of different interconnections between God, humanity, and the universe. Giordano

Bruno (1548–1600) was a Copernican influenced by Alexandrian Hermetism and a champion of religious tolerance. In his occult philosophy of Nature, Bruno did not give much place to the world of angels; and it was not his magic books (*Sigilla sigillorum*, 1583; *De Imaginum (. . .) compositione*, 1591, etc.) that got him burned at the stake by the Inquisition, but rather his anti-Trinitarian opinions. Finally, we have the Dominican Thomas Campanella (1568–1639), the last of the great Renaissance philosophers in the tradition of Ficino (*De sensu rerum et magia*, 1620).

A kind of celestial arithmetic and music is a constant underpinning to this universalist magic. Henceforth, and more than ever, astrology should take on the role of "queen of sciences." This role suits it extremely well under its Paracelsian aspect, characterized as it is by acausal relationships. But during the seventeenth century astrology began to take on another aspect that distanced it from esotericism. The two most important theoreticians of the century, Placido Titi (*Physiomathematica*, 1650) and Jean-Baptiste Morin (*Astrologia Gallica*, 1661) sought to bring astrology into complete accord with the cosmologies of Aristotle and Ptolemy at the very time when their own theoretical foundations were being definitively undermined by discoveries in astronomy and by the new celestial mechanics.

Notwithstanding, in the sixteenth and seventeenth centuries intermediate spirits, stars, the things of this Earth, were still seen as "corresponding" in the sense of the interconnections that Ficino, for example, saw taking place by means of the "spiritus mundi," a vehicle of stellar influx. It was not the medieval world of the *Picatrix* that changed, but rather the role of Man that was perceived differently, as being less passive. The chief of our active faculties by which we penetrate the world of these "correspondences" is the imagination, the *vis imaginativa*. This can have a physical effect on our own bodies or even beyond them, but it is equally an instrument of knowledge or gnosis. Connected to this idea was the celebrated "art of memory," successor to the methods of medieval mnemotechnics and primarily derived from Alexandrian Hermetism. This consisted in bringing all human history, all Nature—all knowledge—into our *mens*, by associating mental images with mythological and planetary referents (cf., especially Giulio Camillo, *L'idea del teatro*, 1550, and various works of Bruno and Fludd). Neopythagorean numerology almost always figured as part of this process. Arithmology was itself the object of a study by Josse Clichtowe (*De mystica numerorum significatione*, 1513), a disciple of Lefèvre d'Etaples. The latter was also the teacher of the arithmosophists Charles Bovelles and Germain de Ganay. Another work on numerology was that of Petrus Bungus (*Numerorum mysteria*, 1588). Numerology also played a role in the cosmology of Johannes Kepler himself (*Mysterium cosmographicum*, 1596), who was also an astrologer. For Fludd, numbers and mathematics were a special tool that enabled him to study the entire structure of the visible and invisible universe in its totality. In his mind they were closely related to music, just as they had been for Giorgi of Venice (cf. supra) and Fabio Paolini (*Hebdomades*, 1589), and later for Michael Maier in his *Atalanta fugiens* (1618).

The sixteenth century also witnessed the appearance of certain historical figures whom posterity would endow with an aura of mystery, such as Michel de Nostre-Dame (alias Nostradamus, 1503–1566), for example, who practiced theurgy and who wrote "prognostications" in verse about the course of future history. (His *Centuries* and *Prophéties* have been republished many, many times), and Georg Faust, who lived from about 1480 to 1540 and was supposed to have signed a pact with the Devil. His sulphurous story, told in a German *Volksbuch* printed in 1587, was the basis for innumerable works of fiction. Finally, we should note that the universities of the seventeenth century (probably in Germany more than elsewhere) witnessed a lively interest in the occult in the form of "dissertations" and "disputations." In Spain and Portugal too, a strong Islamic influence created fertile ground for interest in the *philosophia occulta* (to mention only the works of the physician Ioavo Bravo Chamisso—*De medendis cororis malis*, 1605—and the Cordoban jurist Francisco Torreblanca—*Demonologia sive de magia*, 1623).

B) Alchemy: the Science of Man, Nature and Myths

Alchemical texts were still circulating primarily in manuscript at the beginning of the sixteenth century. One such work was a treatise by Ludovico Lazarelli; another was the *De Auro* by Giovanni Francesco Pico della Mirandola (written in 1527 and published in 1586). Among the most well-known works were the poem *Chrysopoeia* (1515) by G. A. Augurello, *Ars transmutationis* (1518) by J. A. Pantheus, *Coelum philosophorum* (1525) by Philip Ulstad. In addition to these individual works, treatises such as the *De Alchemia* of 1541 or those put together by Gulielmo Gratarolo (especially the one entitled *Verae alchemiae . . .* , 1561), circulated in collected format. In the wake of Paracelsus's work a great deal of alchemical literature began to appear, starting at the end of the sixteenth century under the rubric of theosophy, or rather pansophism (Thomas Vaughan, *Magia adamica*, 1650). This is particularly true in the case of Elias Ashmole, one of the founders of the Royal Society, and also in that of the Englishman Samuel Hartlib whose Invisible College sought to bring together all chemical and alchemical knowledge. Besides this pansophist inclination, there were three other characteristics evident during the seventeenth century: 1) an interest in mythology as an allegorical system behind which are hidden the keys to the secrets of the "Opus Magnum" (cf. Clovis Hesteau de Nuysement's *Traictez du vray Sel*, 1621; or Guillaume Mennens' *Aurei Velleris libri tres*, 1604; this train of thought went back to the High Middle Ages); 2) a partiality for elaborate illustrations (cf. *infra*); 3) the publication of encyclopedic works and compendia: *Theatrum*

Chemicum Britannicum edited by Elias Ashmole (1652); *Theatrum Chemicum* (6 vol., 1659/1661); *Musaeum Hermeticum*, 1678; *Bibliotheca chemica curiosa*, by J.J. Manget (1702, 2 in–fol.).

Alchemy was patronized by several German emperors (notably Rudolph II in Prague, as well as Ferdinand II) and by many German princes. The learned creators of modern science themselves did not disdain it. Isaac Newton (1642–1727) devoted considerable time to it (about half of his alchemical writings date from the seven or eight years following the publication of his *Principia* in 1686).

C) A Hermetic-Emblematic Art

There existed a hermetist type of art in Renaissance Italy, whether in the appearance of the figure of Trismegistus in certain designs (as in the 1488 pavement of Siena's cathedral), or in the intermingling of the signs of the zodiac with mythical characters and hermetist symbols in frescos and paintings (the Borgia apartments of the Vatican, the 1478 "Primavera" by Botticelli, etc.). In the plates of the *De Mundi aetatibus imagines* (1545/1573) by the Portuguese Francesco de Holanda we immediately recognize a brilliant precursor of Boehme and W. Blake. For a period of thirty years, beginning with the end of the sixteenth century, there was a profusion of works whose engravings have as much, if not more, importance than the text. Primarily works of alchemy, they followed the emblematic tradition that had only recently begun with Alciati. Among these works were *Cabala* (1616) by Steffan Michelspacher, the *Opus medico-chymicus* and *Philosophia reformata* (1622) by J.D. Mylius, *De lapide philosophico* by Lampsprinck (1625), the collection by Ashmole cited previously, the *Mutus liber* (1677, without text), and especially the celebrated *Atalanta fugiens* (1618) by Michael Maier, whose fifty plates of emblems were each accompanied by a text and a musical score. The wonderfully illustrated works of Heinrich Khunrath (*Amphitheatrum Sapientiae Aeternae*, 1595) and of Robert Fludd (*Utriusque Cosmi historia*, 1617/1621) were not so much alchemical as they were theosophical. The same is true of the 1682 Amsterdam edition of the complete works of Boehme brought out under the direction of J.G. Gichtel.

Literature too carried on a fruitful relationship with esotericism. The *Hypnerotomachia* (or *Dream of Poliphilus*, 1499) by Francesco Colonna, the *Cinquième Livre* (1564) of François Rabelais, and the *Voyage des Princes fortunés* (1610) by Beroald de Verville, all arose from a type of literary esotericism similar to the Rosicrucian novel (1616) of Andreae discussed above. Mannerism and occult science got along very well together in the works of Maurice Scève (*Microcosme*, 1562), Guy Lefèvre de la Boderie (*La Galliade*, 1578), Fabio Paolini (*Hebdomades*, 1589), Edmund Spenser (*The Fairie Queene*, 1596), Torquato Tasso (*Mondo creato*, 1607), and Gianbattista

Marino (*Dicerie Sacre*, 1614). Dramatists transported this same science onto the Elizabethan stage in plays that were either wholly imbued with it (William Shakespeare, *The Tempest*, 1610) or which ridiculed it (Ben Jonson, *The Alchemist*, 1610). The list of works is too numerous to mention, from the Baroque Boehme-like poetry of Johannes Scheffler's (alias Angelus Silesius) *Cherubinischer Wandersmann* (1675), to the extremely popular *Comte de Gabalis ou entretiens sur les sciences secrètes* (1670) of Montfaucon de Villars to the explicitly alchemist theatre of Knorr von Rosenroth (*Conjugium Phoebis et Palladis*, 1677).

In painting, the canvases of Hieronymus Bosch (ca. 1450–1516; "The Garden of Delights," ca. 1510) and of Pieter Bruegel the Elder (ca. 1520–1569; "Dulle Griet," 1562) have to this very day not yet revealed all their secrets. Two seventeenth-century pictoral representations deserve special comment. The anonymous painting called "The Virgin Alchemist" in the church of Saint-Maurice in Rheims, which probably dates from the beginning of the seventeenth century, can be viewed with both hermetist and numerological interpretations. Secondly, there is the kabbalistic altarpiece "Turris Antonia" (or *Didactic Painting of Princess Antonia of Würtemberg*) painted at Bad-Teinach (1663/1673). Both these paintings are still found in their original locations. Besides, some books which are not explicitly esoteric sometimes contain illustrations inspired by these traditions; for example, in the *Icones Biblicae* (1627) of Matthieu Merian a picture (reprinted in the Lutherian Bible of Strasburg, 1630) represents the Wedding at Cana in a setting alluding to the Rosicrucian teachings and the Philosophical transmutation.

CHAPTER THREE

ESOTERICISM IN THE SHADOW
OF THE ENLIGHTENMENT

I) SUNBURST OF THEOSOPHY

A) At the Dawn of Illuminism

Translated into German in 1706, the *Corpus Hermeticum* is treated as a subject for scholarly presentations in late-Germanic humanism (See *Bibliotheca Graeca* by J.A. Fabricius, 1708/1727). Shortly before, Gottfried Arnold, himself a theosopher and sophiologist, had produced a copious review from the more or less "heretical" mystics and esotericists (*Kirchen- und Ketzerhistorie*, 1699/1700); he was followed by lengthier and more critical developments, devoted to the Kabbalah, Pythagoreanism and Theosophy by Jacob Brucker *Historia critica philosophiae*, vol. II and IV, 1743). Thanks to editions or exegeses of Boehme's works by J.G. Gichtel and J.W. Ueberfeld in Germany and by D.A. Freher and William Law in England, the Boehmian movement is thereby passed on into the eighteenth century. The "Bible of Berlebourg" (1726/1742) contributes to disseminating it within the pietist milieu which is poised to accept it. It is also in Berlebourg that Hector de Saint-Georges de Marsais publishes his theosophic works (*Explication de la Genèse*, 1738) which were influenced by that "Bible," by Boehme, Madame Guyon and Pierre Poiret. Due to an inspiration which is simultaneously pietist and alchemical, *Le mystère de la Croix* (1732) by Douzetemps at times had comparable tones. However, on the fringe of this theosophy with mystical leanings there appears another, in the wake of what is at once Boehmian and Paracelsian, closer to the occult sciences. The initiatory societies will be considerably influenced by this theosophy oriented towards magic. It is represented especially by three major works in German: *Theo-Philosophia Theoretico-practica* (1711) by Samuel Richter (alias Sincerus Renatus); *Aurea catena Homeri* (1723) by A.J. Kirchweger; and *Opus mago-cabbalisticum et theosophicum* (1735) by Georg von

Welling (alias Salwigt), which we know was to influence Goethe. Finally, about 1730, modern Freemasonry, called speculative and born in London in 1717, introduces the myth of the death and resurrection of Hiram into its rituals; hence this is a discourse that will fall in with the esoteric interpretations. Thus, in the thirties there appear, mainly on the continent, systems or "Rites" (rituals) consisting of High Degrees (i. e., degrees which are superior to the three standard degrees of Apprentice, Fellow Craftsman and Master Mason and which constitute what is called "blue" Masonry or "Craftmasonry") very propitious to accepting an esotericism with connotations that are sometimes chivalric or Christian, sometimes "Egyptian" or neopagan.

B) The Great Theosophers

The years between 1770–1815 correspond to what is apropriately called in French "Illuminisme" (in the esoteric sense of the word). Let us consider here those whose lives or works are completed before the end of the First Empire, a time when theosophy shines with all its fire. In 1745, the Swede Emmanuel Swedenborg (1688–1772), a celebrated scientist and inventor, interrupts his specifically scientific activities as a result of dreams that arrive suddenly transforming his inner life. He immerses himself in study of the Scriptures and composes his *Arcana coelestia* (1747/1758) followed by numerous works. Swedenborg presents his visions using images and figures, intended to formulate a kind of descriptive geography of celestial spheres and spiritual worlds. His work contributes much to spreading to a wide public the idea of universal relationships, ranging from Nature to Man and from Man to God, which are presented as a complete series of hierarchical levels; in the natural world, every object, even the most minuscule, "corresponds" to something in the spiritual world, without solution of continuity. His colorful but somewhat rough style is off-putting to many readers (e.g., Kant criticizes Swedenborg on philosophical grounds in *Träume eines Geistersehers*, 1776), yet no other theosopher has exerted more conspicuous influence on nineteenth-century literature. During the seventies, his writings began to be transmitted widely, through translations and synopses. The majority of other great theosophers place little value on Swedenborg, whose Christology seems questionable, but Swedenborgianism inspired some Masonic rites, and in 1787 prompted Anglican ecclesiastics to create a religious sect called the New Church, which is still flourishing today.

Encouraged by his reading of Boehme and the Kabbalah, the Swabian Friedrich Christoph Oetinger (1702–1782), a Lutheran pastor, philosopher of Nature, and alchemist, makes himself the exegete of Swedenborg, from whom he distances himself. Oetinger represents eclectic scholarly esotericism. For him, *magia*, the loftiest of sciences, is a method used to study the relationship between earthly and heavenly forms. Everything is "physical" ("Corporeality is the end, the goal, of God's works."), but only a "superior physics," linked to an ongoing hermeneutic of Nature and the Scriptures, provides us with the keys of knowledge regarding the way in which the Divine and Nature interpenetrate (*Biblisches und emblematisches Wörterbuch*, 1776; *Oeffentliches Denckmahl der Prinzessin Antonia*, 1763). By means of an exposé on the Kabbalah of Isaac Luria, Oetinger makes Hasidism, which is spiritually close to pietism, known to the German pietists. Less a physicist and kabbalist, Michael Hahn (1758–1819) is still a great theosopher along the lines of Boehme, and his works on the androgyne and the Sophia remain classics of the genre. Not very mystical, barely influenced by Boehme and more popular through his writings, Karl von Eckartshausen (1752–1803) of Munich hardly owes anything to these Germans. His exceedingly rich work (of which *Zahlenlehre de Natur*, 1794, and *Die Wolke über dem Heiligthum*, 1802, are a part), frequently translated and reproduced in numerous languages, even today continues to touch varied readers and alchemists. The Alsatian Friedrich-Rudolf Saltzmann also published a theosophical work in German in the early years of the nineteenth century, but this enjoyed a more limited reception (*Es wird alles neu werden*, 1802/1810).

In France, Martines de Pasqually (1727–1774), founder of the theurgical Order of the "Elected Cohens," is the author of the *Traité de la réintégration des êtres*, one of the masterpieces of modern theosophy. Under his influence, Louis-Claude de Saint-Martin (1743–1803), the so-called Unknown Philosopher, writes *Des erreurs et de la verité* (1775), *Tableau naturel* (1781), followed by *L'Homme de désir* (1790), *Le Nouvel homme* and *Ecce Homo* (1792). During a trip to Strasbourg (1788/1791) he strikes up a friendship with Saltzmann, who reveals Boehme to him. Other works of theosophy permeated with Boehmism follow (*Le Ministère de l'Homme-Esprit* and *De l'Esprit des choses*, 1802). Saint-Martin is not only an emulator but also undoubtedly a great French writer, and the most important Christian esotericist of his time, whose influence, directly and indirectly, has never ceased to spread. He has left behind interesting correspondence not only with Masons, but also with Elected Cohens, such as J.B. Willermoz (cf. *infra*) and with people spiritually closer to him like the Bernese Niklaus Anton Kirchberger (1739–1799). Also taking his place in the gallery of famous theosophers is Jean-Philippe Dutoit-Membrini (1721–1793), the author of *La Philosophie divine* (1793), and a thinker who owes nothing to Saint-Martin. Finally, in the last years of the century and the Empire period we see a philosophy of Nature of the esoteric type (cf. *infra*), especially in Germany.

C) Faces of Illuminism

Completing this gallery are other figures won over to theosophy, but marked by forms of devotional esotericism or notable peculiarities. First we have the engaging Johann Caspar Lavater (1741–1801). A pastor in Zurich, curious about supernatural phenomena, he does not disregard theurgy. When the opportunity presents itself, he practices mesmerism and develops ideas characterized by a naturalist christology (*Aussichten in die Ewigkeit*, 1768/1778), but he is especially remembered as the great modern theorist of physiognomy (*Physiognomische Fragmente*, 1775/1778). Certainly no other German language thinker since Luther maintained a correspondence as monumental as his. Johann Heinrich Jung-Stilling (1740–1817) resembles him because of the importance of his correspondence and his interest in parapsychological phenomena (*Theorie der Geisterkunde*, 1807). Communication with the spirit world is also a focal point for Johann Friedrich Oberlin (1740–1826), a pastor of Steinthal in Alsace. In Russia, Ivan Vladimir Lopuchin (1765–1815) left behind a small pearl of theosophic literature (*Quelques traits de l'Eglise intérieure*, 1791), translated and republished several times and close to hesychasm because of the techniques regarding posture which he teaches in it. A translator of Boehme, Swedenborg, Eckartshausen, and Jung-Stilling, Lopouchine is also the founder of a journal, *Le Messager de Sion* (1807/1817), which is inspired by the teachings of the Russian Martinist Freemason, Nikolai Novikov (1744–1718).

Beyond these avenues of esoteric Christian spirituality, Illuminism contains others of somewhat neopagan direction. If Antoine Fabre d'Olivet (1767–1825) writes *La Langue hébraïque restituée* (1810, published in 1816/1817), it is not out of Judeo-Christian zeal, but rather out of concern to discover the origin of language; his *Vers dorés de Pythagore* (1813) attempts to show the existence of a lost universal Tradition. Less philosophical and markedly encyclopedic in nature is the survey produced by Court de Gébelin (1725–1784), *Le Monde primitif* (1773/1784), which is one of the first attempts to rediscover through various well-known traditions what will later be called the primordial Tradition. Finally, Egyptology furnishes both the initiatory framework and the settings for numerous discourses and esoteric practices, from the novel by the Abbot Jean Terrasson (*Sethos*, 1731) to the *Nouvelles recherches sur l'origine et la destination des pyramides d'Egypte* (1812) by A.P.J. de Vismes, and works devoted to "Egyptian" forms of Masonry (cf. *infra*), *The Magic Flute* (the opera by Mozart, 1791), and *Kostis Reise* (1795) by Eckartshausen.

II) FROM THE ARTS OF READING TO THE ART OF SUBTLE FLUIDS

A) Permanence of Occult Sciences

Thanks to a few erudite treatises, the Christian Kabbalah survived in the first half of the century. Initiated by the Christian Kabbalist Christian Fende and the Jewish Kabbalist Koppel Hecht, Oetinger writes his famous "didactic picture" of 1763, an interpretation of the esoteric altar that was painted during the preceding century and preserved in the church of Bad-Teinach (cf., *supra).* Pythagorism and Hermetism continued their course without ever really being interrupted (numerous Neopythagorean writings, as we see in works such as *Les Voyages de Pythagore en Egypte* by Sylvain Maréchal in 1799, and the new German translation of the *Pimander* in 1781). In the popular context of the salons and of the "carrefours," the period of Illuminism (the name given to the theosophically oriented trend of the time) favors the reign of individuals expert in the exploitation of a taste for the supernatural, like the Count de Saint-Germain (1701–1784) and Joseph Balsamo (*alias* Cagliostro, 1743–1795). The powers that gullible contemporaries attribute to them reflect a general craze for the occult sciences, borne out in particular by the numerous editions of the *Grand* and the *Petit Albert,* by copious literature on vampirism, which was especially widespread from 1732 until the *Traité sur les apparitions* (1746) by Dom Calmet, and by the numerous debates on sorcery. When one does not believe in the supernatural, one likes to entertain colorful illusions, hence the appreciation for robots and for entertaining experiments of physics. One captivating and unsettling individual personifies the diverse forms of this state of mind on the eve of the Revolution: the Frenchman Alliette (*alias* Etteilla), who is a combination of charlatan and theosopher as well as alchemist (*Les sept nuances de l'oeuvre philosophique,* 1786), one of whose claims to fame is having contributed to making known the divinatory Tarot. A little later, even more in the domain of Agrippa, a compilation destined to be a great success heralds the occult literature to come: *The Magus* (1801) by Francis Barrett (alongside whom we can cite Karl Joseph Windischmann, *Untersuchungen über Astrologie, Alchemie und Magie,* 1813).

In France especially, music becomes the object of esoteric speculation, and results in printed works, and also as in the "pianos of colors," described by Father Castel in 1740 and by Eckartshausen in 1788. Saint-Martin is the only one in the century to perfectly integrate a speculation developed on music in a theosophical treatise (*Des erreurs,* 1775, and *De l'Esprit des choses,* 1802), but one must forget neither A.P.J. de Vismes (*Essai sur l'homme, ou l'homme microcosme,* 1805) nor the first research done by Fabre d'Olivet. Finally, it is a time of intense activity for illuminated prophets: during the Revolution, Suzette Labrousse, Catherine Théot; at the close of the Empire, Mademoiselle Le Normand; in England, Richard Brothers; in Germany, Thomas Pöschl; elsewhere, a great many others.

B) *Alchemy, the Dark Side of the Enlightenment and the Light Side of Mythology*

The advance of chemistry, which definitively acquires its status as a scientific discipline, already foreshadows the irremediable decline of operative alchemy, but interest remains alive and literature remains plentiful, even after the publication of Lavoisier's works (1787/1789). In Diderot's *Encyclopédie,* the articles "Alchemy" and "The Alchemist" by Maloin are quite favorable.

The fact is that some scientists presume to see in it a realm of poorly explored investigation; common people see it as a source of immediate wealth; and ardent rationalists consider it to be the practice of charlatans. For part of the general public alchemy has a supernatural aspect which primarily concerns the manufacturing of gold, i.e., "operative" alchemy. As before, it is often difficult to distinguish this from "spiritual" alchemy, which presents itself as a form of gnosis. From out of a very significant editorial production (albeit one from which the tradition of fine illustrations has disappeared), let us consider three aspects. The first concerns the fashion of enjoying collections of treatises. After those by J. J. Manget (cf. *supra*) there appear, this time in the vernacular, the *Deutsches Theatrum Chemicum* (1728) by Friedrich Roth-Scholtz, the *Neue Alchymistische Bibliothek* (1772) by F.J.W. Schröder, and still others. Added to this production, we now find the need to discuss alchemy in terms of historiography (Nicolas Lenglet-Dufresnoy, *Histoire de la philosophie hermétique*, 1742), detailed bibliographies (Roth-Scholtz, *Bibliotheca chemica*, 1727) and dictionaries (Dom Pernety, *Dictionnaire myth-hermétique*, 1758). A second aspect is the production of an alchemical reading of narratives of Greek and Egyptian mythology, either by reducing the ancient "Fables" to an allegorical discourse whose sole intention was to provide a coded description of the processes of transmutation (typical in this regard are the *Fables égyptiennes et grecques dévoilées*, 1758, by Dom Pernéty), or by interpreting this mythology on several levels in a nonreductionist way, by following a hermeneutic of a theosophical character (for example Hermann Fictuld, *Aureum Vellus*, 1749, and Ehrd de Naxagoras, *Aureum Vellus*, 1753, both in German and Anselmo Caetano's *Ennoea*, 1732/33, in Portugese). These two types of exegesis have their precursors (Michael Maier especially). Theosophers like Saint-Martin (for whom the heuristic value of alchemy does not exceed the material level) approve of the second no more than the first. A third aspect of alchemy in the time of the Enlightenment is its diffuse but obvious presence among scientists and philosophers of Nature, who are more or less won over to Paracelsism, such as Herman Boerhaave, J.R. Spielmann, Johann Juncker and, of course, Oetinger. This connection foreshadows the Romantic *Naturphilosophie*.

C) Animal Magnetism

According to one of the most widespread ideas in alchemical thought, matter contains a light or an invisible spark whose nature is that of the Word, of the Creator of light on the first day. This fiery principle of universal character, halfway between the natural and the supernatural, is of great importance in western cosmologic conception. It has assisted interpretation of the Platonic idea of the Soul of the World in several directions and has become diversified in innumerable themes and motifs. Widespread in the eighteenth century, the tendency to mix experimental research and speculative thought now fosters its reappearance under two new forms. During the previous century, researchers (Rudolf Gockel and Athanasius Kircher among them) became enthusiastic about phenomena of magnetic and electric nature. During the time of the Enlightenment, certain philosophers of Nature close to Oetinger develop a "theology of electricity." They are, in particular, J. L. Fricker, G.F. Rösler, and Prokop Divisch (*Theorie der meteorologischen Elektrizität*, 1765). If the theosophic character of their speculations is evident, it does not apply completely in the same way as those of the Swabian doctor Franz Anton Mesmer (1734–1815), and yet during his lifetime, mesmerism left no esotericist indifferent.

In order to research the cause of universal gravitation, Mesmer postulates (from his doctoral thesis *De influxu planetarum in corpus humanum*, 1766) the existence of an invisible fluid that flows everywhere and that serves as a vehicle for mutual influence among heavenly bodies, Earth, and living things. After having first treated with the application of magnets (a procedure done again later by Charcot), then with palpation, he spells out a therapy that consists of having people sit next to each other around a tub filled with water, iron filings, and sand. They communicate with the tub by means of iron rods or ropes and thus form "chains": the "magnetism" is thus made to pass from one or several healthy people also seated around the tub into the ill person or persons. Settling in Paris in 1778, Mesmer enjoys quick success, but he at the same time clashes with a lack of understanding on the part of official medicine. Magnetism takes hold in the provinces while becoming tinged with occultism: in Strasbourg with A.M.J. de Puységur, in Lyon with J.B. Willermoz, in Bordeaux with Doctor Mocet, in Turin with Doctor Giraud whose friend, Nicolas Bergasse, clarifies the doctrine in a *Théorie du monde et des êtres organisés* (1784). Mesmer also bestows an initiatory character on his activities by creating a "Society of Harmony" in 1783 whose numerous symbols are drawn from the Masonic tradition. In 1785 he writes: "We are endowed with an internal sense which is in relation to the entire universe"; an idea which will have repercussions among the German Romantics; all the more pronounced since the internal "sense" of Kant looks impoverished when compared with what, in Mesmer's domain, signifies an unfolding of the possibilities of Being. Animal magnetism is not only a fashion or an isolated episode with no future, but one of the vivid events of culture at the twilight of the Enlightenment, in the subsequent *Naturphilosophie*, in literature, and in the history of dynamic psychiatry up to and including Freud.

III) A CENTURY OF INITIATIONS

A) Templar Strict Observance and Rectified Scottish Rite

It is obviously the high degree rites that contain the most esoteric content, therefore Anglo-Saxon Freemasonry is less esoteric in character. Let us review the most important of these rites, without stopping to ask ourselves each time whether or not they have "Masonic legality" in the eyes of English authority (a complex question that extends beyond the current framework). We begin with two of the most studied rites. The first is the system created by Baron Karl von Hund around 1750, called Templar Strict Observance. It claims to be a filiation of the Order of the Temple disbanded by Philip the Fair. This Strict Observance will remain the most important Masonic system in Germany until the eighties. In France beginning in 1754, Martinès de Pasqually (cf. *supra*) established a distinctive Rite called the Elect Cohens, which was not Masonic *per se*, whose vocation was theurgical and whose ritual was operative-magical. Pasqually created "temples" for his rite in several cities in France and in the sixties he conferred the Cohen initiation upon Jean-Baptiste Willermoz (1730–1824), a native of Lyon, who was also initiated into the Strict Observance. He himself with the help of other Masons of Lyon, began in 1777/1778 to develop a Masonic rite whose symbolic system was largely dependent on Martinesist "Cohen" philosophy, although its calling was not theurgical. The result of this work was the Order of Beneficient Knights of the Holy City (the sixth and final rank of the Rite), the ensemble of the six grades that form the Rectified Scottish Rite. At its inception, it was linked to the Strict Observance and it rapidly created Lodges in France, Italy, Switzerland, and Russia. At the end of the seventies, two of the leading personalities of the Strict Observance, Duke Ferdinand of Brunswick and Prince Charles of Hesse Cassel, passionately interested in esoteric science, decided to call together representatives of the Strict Observance to a large Masonic Convention for the purpose of reflecting upon the origin, nature, and aim of Freemasonry. Ferdinand sent circulars to several individuals to prepare the ground (Joseph de Maistre, initiated into the Rectified Scottish Rite, responded to it with his famous *Mémoire* of 1780). The Convention met at Wilhelmsbad in July and August of 1782. There they abandoned the myth of Templar filiation, and the Willermoz system received worldwide acceptance. This Convention was important event because on this battlefield could be seen two categories of Masons confronting each other: one group directed towards various forms of esotericism, the other—also numerous in the Strict Observance—taking their inspiration from the rationalism of the Enlightenment. Under the name of "Martinism" the Rectified Scottish Rite quickly won adherents in Russia, where the Gold- und Rosenkreutz (Golden Rosy-Cross) Order also made its way, and where Nicolai Novikov (1744–1818) is a central figure in this double movement.

B) Other Masonic (and Para-Masonic) Systems

We must distinguish between Christian or Western rites (to which the Rectified Scottish Rite and the Strict Observance belong), of a medieval and chivalric type, whose referential "Orient" is the Holy Land, Jerusalem; and the somewhat neopagan Egyptian Rites, although sometimes the boundaries are blurred, and, of course, a person may belong simultaneously to several of these Rites. In 1777, the order called the "Golden Rosy-Cross" which was formed in the seventies in Germany, creates a merger among all its Lodges or "Circles" while assuming the name "Golden Rosy-Cross of the Ancient System" and granting nine high degrees, each marked by an alchemical symbolism. With the accession to the throne of Frederick William II (1786), who was a member, the order entered a period of dormancy without ever actually being banned. Its editorial activities mark the esoterism of the end of this century (cf. for example, the *Geheime Figuren der Rosenkreuzer*, 1785/1788, a collection of very beautiful engravings and texts).

The Benedictine Antoine Joseph Pernety (1716-1796) managed to become acquainted with the Golden Rosy-Cross in Berlin, where he became established from 1767–1782 in his capacity as librarian of the Royal Library of Frederick William II: the small sect of "Illuminés" that he led then devoted itself to oracular practices entailing questioning the "*Sainte Parole*" ("Holy Word"), a kind of hypostasis of the Supreme Intelligence. Pernety left Berlin in 1783 and settled in Avignon, moving his society to a mountain not far from there, called "Thabor." The Polish starost Thaddeus Grabianka, who had been a member of this for several years, formed a dissident group in Avignon called The New Israel, with Octavio Capelli, the "Man-God," as leader, who received communication from the archangel Raphael. The French Revolution dispersed the Illuminés of Avignon; a large number of important personalities in Europe will become members of this.

Let us cite nine initiatory societies that fall under the jurisdiction of this first category: the "Swedish System," founded around 1750 by Karl Friedrich Eckleff; the Order of the "Blazing Star," whose founder is Théodore Henri de Tschoudy (1766); the System of Johann Wilhelm Zinnendorf (1770), inspired by the Swedish System; the Cléricat, a creation of Johann August Starck around 1767; the Philalèthes, beginning in 1773, the first Masonic institute for research of an esoteric character (Savalette de Langes, its most important figure, formed in 1785 and 1787 in Paris an international interallegiant Lodge destined to share all possible knowledge dealing with esotericism and Masonry). Then we have the Brothers of the Cross, a Rite founded by C.A.H. Haugwitz around 1777; the Asiatic Brethern, for Austria and especially the south of Germany (a creation of Heinrich von Ecker-und-Eckhoffen around 1779); the Primitive Rite of the Philadelphians, founded by F.A. de Chefdebien in 1780; and the Illuminated Theosophers, patterned after Swedenborgianism, important in England and the United States (a Rite born via the impetus of Bénédict Chastanier around 1783). Finally, we have the Ancient and Accepted Scottish Rite, established in France in 1801; and the Order of the Orient, founded in 1804 and organized in 1806 by B.R. Fabré-Palaprat under the denomination the Johannine Church of Primitive Christians, which is a neo-Templar Order. Counting the three systems cited in the preceding heading (Strict Observance, the Elect Cohens and the Rectified Scottish Rite), we find no less than fourteen that pertain completely to esotericism. This is also the case of six others of "Egyptian" character, which are: the African Architects, a creation by Friedrich von Köppen around 1767; the Hermetic Rite, established around 1770, inspired explicitly by the teachings of Hermes Trismegistus; and Cagliostro's Egyptian Rite, which dates from 1784. The dawn of the Empire in Italy sees the appearance of the Rite of Misraïm (albeit not very "Egyptian"), brought to France by the Bédarride brothers, followed in 1815 by the rite of Memphis, to which one must add the Mages of Memphis, created at the end of the eighteenth century. But these twenty rites do not represent a complete list. . . .

C) Initiation in Art

Literature fosters fertile ties with Illuminism, which are sources (among others) of the literary genre labeled "the fantastic" (in this respect *Le Diable Amoureux* of Jacques Cazotte, 1772, marks a turning point). The century abounds with fictional works of an occult or supernatural nature: bearing witness to which are new editions and translations of the *Comte de Gabalis*, or a collection of imposing dimension such as *Voyages imaginaires*. Some of these works are humorous or parodic (Mouhy, *Lamekis*, 1737; T.G. von Hippel *Kreuz- und Querzüge*, 1793). This output, stimulated by *Séthos* (1731, cf. *supra*), exploits initiatory themes. Sometimes it is serious and pertains to esotericism, especially when the purifying experience is stressed (the *Relation du Monde de Mercure*, in Volume XIV of the *Voyages imaginaires*, and the *Confessions du comte de C[agliostro]*, 1787, can be categorized as being half-way in between), a characteristic of a number of novels and stories beginning in the latter part of the eighteenth century, mostly in Germany: Jean Paul, *Die unsichtbare Loge*, 1793; J.H. Jung-Stilling, *Heimweh*, 1794; Eckartshausen, *Kostis Reise*, 1795; Goethe, *Das Märchen* or *The Green Serpent*, 1795 (his magnificent poem *Die Geheimnisse*, of Rosicrucian inspiration, dates from 1785); Saint-Martin, *Le Crocodile*, 1799; Novalis, *Heinrich von Ofterdingen* and *Die Lehrlinge zu Sais*, 1802; E.T.A. Hoffmann, *Der goldene Topf*, 1813. In the Masonic stream, Mozart's opera *The Magic Flute* (1791) and Zacharias Werner's play *Die Söhne des Thals* (1802/1804) are two of the best-known works.

    William Blake (1757–1827), poet, engraver and bard of creative imagination (*The Marriage of Heaven and Earth*, 1793; *Visions of the Daughter of*

Albion, 1793) burns in the alchemic furnace of his genius contributions from Hermetism, Swedenborg, and the philosophy of Berkeley, transmutes them into a dazzling hermesian work, which really falls under the heading of esotericism, but which, at the same time, defies any possible classification. We could cite many more authors in the English domain, such as James Thomson, author of *The Seasons* (1726/1730) whose works are marked by Hermetism. More than anyone else in the tradition of German Romanticism, painter Philipp Otto Runge is the closest to theosophy, especially to Boehmenism (cf. his painting "Der kleine Morgen," 1808). Lastly in Italy we are indebted to Prince Raimondo di Sangro di San Severo (1710–1777), from whom Cagliostro received instruction, for the astonishing "Hermetic monument," the San Severo Chapel in Neaple.

CHAPTER FOUR

FROM ROMANTIC KNOWLEDGE TO
PROGRAMMATIC OCCULTISM

I) THE ERA OF *NATURPHILOSOPHIE* AND THE GREAT SYNTHESES

A) *"Nature" Philosophers During Romanticism (1790–1815)*

A new way to approach the study of Nature appeared during the last decade of the eighteenth century—a unique trend that would dominate for some fifty years. This was the *Naturphilosophie* which, broadly speaking, was particularly a component of German Romanticism. In several of its representatives it takes a form that relates directly to esotericism. In its most general form it was, according to F.J.W. Schelling (1775–1854), a temptation to bring to light what had been continuously repressed in Christianity: to wit, Nature. Various factors contributed to this breakthrough. First of all the persistence of *magia* among physicist-philosophers (like Oetinger), more generally that of esotericism throughout the course of the eighteenth century. Then came the influence of French naturalism (e.g., Buffon, D'Alembert), which was not devoid of speculation on the life of matter or on the Anima Mundi. There was the work of Kant in which some thought they found a universe produced by the imagination through the synthesizing and spontaneous activity of the mind. There was also the new popularity of Spinozism, which tended to consider Nature as something spiritual and the Spirit, hearth of energy, as the source of the whole of the finite universe. Finally, there was the climate proper to the pre-Romantic period: on the one hand, infatuation with everything relating to magnetism, galvanism, electricity (Galvani's experiments in 1789, Volta's battery in 1800); on the other hand, bold syntheses, tinged with esotericism, in important *Kultur*-philosophers like J.G. Herder (1741–1804), one of the forerunners of the movement.

Here are the three common denominators or essential characteristics of *Naturphilosophie*. 1) A conception of Nature as a text to decipher by correspondences. Nature is filled with symbolic implications; its signification resides outside itself, so much so that rigorous science is only a necessary point of departure for an inclusive grasp of invisible processes, i.e., a "nature naturing." 2) A taste for the living concrete and for a plural universe. *Natur*-philosophers are all more or less specialists (chemists, physicists, geologists, engineers, physicians), but specialists whose thought rises to eclectic syntheses and tries to embrace a polymorphic world comprised of different levels of reality in its complexity. The compartmentalization of Nature into separate categories, characteristic of a mechanist imaginary, gives way to the attempt to grasp the whole animated by dynamic polarities. 3) The identity of Spirit and Nature, considered as two seeds of a common root (matter and Nature rest on a spiritual principle, for Spirit inhabits them). By the same token, knowledge of Nature and knowledge of oneself go hand in hand. A scientific fact is perceived as a sign, the signs correspond, concepts borrowed from chemistry are transposed into astronomy or human feelings. We can understand why animal magnetism was the object of passionate interest.

To be sure, not all *Natur*-philosophers could be labeled esotericists. The epithet could only be partially applied to Schelling (*Weltseele*, 1798), who was, nonetheless, the most famous representative of this current. There is also esotericism when *Naturphilosophie* incorporates, exploits in a theosophic mode, a founding myth that is more or less still that of the "savior saved." It is the story of a captive light captured, so to speak, so that another light, remaining free all the while, comes in some way as an awakener. The knot of this theosophico-romantic narrative is there and is presented as an opposition between "light" and "heaviness," in which the latter is understood as a product in which primitive energies have been engulfed. The relationship to alchemy is obvious, so much so that Schelling's *Naturphilosophie* appeared from the beginning as an attempt to bring together the traditional givens of pansophy (cf., *supra*) and the spirit of Kantian philosophy.

Franz von Baader (1765–1841), a theosopher of Munich, towers over Romantic esotericism, and no doubt also over that of the entire nineteenth century. Although he is one of those who brought about German *Naturphilosophie* (*Beiträge zur Elementarphysiologie*, 1797; *Über das pythagoräische Quadrat in der Natur*, 1798), this represents only one aspect of his work. It is an important aspect since he was as far removed from Schelling's "naturalism" as from Hegel's "idealism," and therefore Baader never stopped affirming a position between the two which was rich in fruitful philosophical tensions. Called "Böhmius redivivus," Baader takes his place among the great hermeneuts of Boehme's writings, but his own extremely speculative discourse is devoid of the prophetic, brilliant inspiration so characteristic of Baroque theosophers and still discernible in Saint-Martin. Baader comments at length on Saint-Martin's work and finds inspiration in it, keeping his distance all the while because of the importance Baader gives to Nature and alchemy. Themes like the androgyne, Sophia, the successive Falls, magnetism, and love are subjects to which he gives original, yet traditional, treatment representing a *summum* of everything essential in Christian esotericism (cf. e.g., *Fermenta cognitionis*, 1822/1825). Baader is not just an armchair philosopher. He is a mineralogist, and with Madame de Krüdener, is one of the propagators of the Holy Alliance during the period when Alexander I tended toward mysticism and esotericism. Baader's voice was heard in Europe in the liberal Catholic milieus.

Let us cite among several important representatives of this tradition those most attached to esotericism. First of all A.K.A. Eschenmayer (1770–1852), Friedrich von Hardenberg (alias Novalis, 1772–1801), and Johann Wilhelm Ritter (1776-1810). Then come G.H. von Schubert (*Ahndungen einer allgemeinen Geschichte des Lebens*, 1806; *Symbolik des Traums*, 1814), I.P.V. Troxler (*Blick in das Wesen des Menschen*, 1812), Carl Gustav Carus (*Psyche*, 1848). Goethe is connected by and large to this tradition because of his scientific works on the metamorphoses of plants (1790) and colors (*Zur Farbenlehre*, 1810). The major contribution of *Naturphilosophie* to nineteenth-century science is the discovery of the unconscious (especially with Schubert and Carus). This is the Romanticism in which psychoanalysis plants its roots, and also the climate in which modern homeopathy was born with Friedrich Hahnemann (1775–1843).

B) *Esotericism on the periphery of Naturphilosophie (1815–1847)*

In Germany, translations of Saint-Martin (one by G.H. Schubert) were widely read in these milieus. Impressed by the influence of animal magnetism, Johann Friedrich von Meyer (1772–1849), a Frankfurt theosopher, whose own works were discreet and protean, and who was the first to translate into German the *Sepher Yetzirah*, touches on almost all of the occult sciences. His journal *Blätter für höhere Wahrheit* (1818/1832) is one of the most interesting documents of the period. Along with von Meyer, the poet Justinus Kerner (1786–1862) assures his glorious place in the history of metapsychia with the publication of *Die Seherin von Prevorst* (1830). In Germany three more works summarize and synthesize the history of "magic": *Zauberbibliothek* (1821/1826) by George Konrad Horst, *Christliche Mystik* (1836/42) by Joseph Görres, *Geschichte der Magie* (1822 and 1866) by Joseph Ennemoser. In France, Fabre d'Olivet pursued his work from a pagan perspective (*Histoire philosophique du genre humain*, 1822/1824, a grandiose fresco highly esteemed by occultists at the end of the century). After *La Clef de l'infini* (1814) by Höné Wronski, seekers of the universal keys, such as Giovanni Malfatti di Montereggio (*Anarchie und Hierarchie des Wissens*, 1845), were not lacking.

Simultaneously a man of the right and a person sympathetic to utopian socialisms, Pierre-Simon Ballanche (1776–1847) was somewhat isolated, and he could have become a great theosopher. Among the French a magnificent figure of a Christian Hermetist stands out: Paul-François-Gaspard Lacuria (1808–1890), an abbot who wrote *Harmonies de l'Etre exprimées par les nombres* (1847), and who found in theosophy the key to music and arithmology. In the wake of Agrippa, Hortensius Flamel (*Le Livre d'or* and *Le Livre rouge*, 1842), probably a pseudonym of Eliphas Lévi, succeeded in combining Fourierism and esotericism. Swedenborgian theosophy is represented by Jean-Jacques Bernard, author of *Opuscules théosophiques* (1822), which is an attempt to fuse Martinism and Swedenborgianism. Edouard Richer and especially J.F.E. Le Boys des Guays (1794–1864) actively propagated the teaching of the Swedish master. Esoteric Messianism, brought from Poland by Adam Mickiewicz and André Towianki in the 1840s, greatly influenced Eliphas Lévi, as did another Pole, Höné Wronski (*Messianisme*, 1847). We note that in the period up to 1847, alchemy seems moribund despite *Hermès dévoilé* (1832) by Cyliani and the *Cours de philosophie hermétique* (1843) by Cambriel.

C) *Esotericism in Art (1815–1847)*

A natural complicity had formed between the Baroque imaginary and the esoteric frame of mind. The same happened with Romanticism, although the relationship was more obvious in Germanic countries than elsewhere. If the taste for synthesis and sorrowful sentiment on the limitations of the human condition are two major traits of European Romanticism and gnoses, it is the same for the myth of the Fall and the reintegration, an obsessive theme that traverses this Romanticism from one end to the other and all theosophical discourses. In France, Charles Nodier's particularly fantastic viewpoint, which brings together haphazardly the most diverse motifs, contributed to maintaining the public's appetite for a kind of Illuminism. Less of a dilettante, Balzac was inspired by Saint-Martin and Swedenborg (*Louis Lambert*, 1832, *Séraphita* and *Le Livre Mystique*, 1835). Esotericism in its most initiatory form was the subject of George Sand's *Consuelo* (1845). It is didactic and explicit in other novels, among which the best known are Alphonse Esquiros' *Le Magicien* (1836), and Sir Edward Bulwer-Lytton's very rosicrucian *Zanoni* (1842). In the 1820s esotericism represents a significant part of Friedrich Schlegel's critical work. In the year preceding his death in 1831, Goethe wrote *Über die Spiraltendenz* and finished *Faust*. Theosophy colors, in an occasionally deep way, the *Carnets* of Joseph Joubert (1754–1824), which he kept assiduously from 1786 until his death. The posthumous writings (1840/1841) of the painter Philipp Otto Runge testify to the presence of esotericism within what was one of the most profound reflections on art. To be sure, magnetism was the object of numerous reflections on art and the subject of numerous literary adaptations but these tended to fall under the jurisdiction of the fantastic (E.T.A. Hoffmann, *Der Magnetiseur*, 1817; Edgar Allan Poe, *Mesmeric Revelation*, 1844).

II) UNIVERSAL TRADITION AND OCCULTISM

A) *From the Romantic Orient to the India of the Theosophical Society*

At the end of the eighteenth century, images of India penetrated the Western imaginary. Above all, the Orient is one of the discoveries of Romanticism: Joseph Görres's writing on Asian myths (*Mythengeschichte der asiatischen Welt*, 1810), Friedrich Schlegel's on India (*Über die Sprache und Weisheit der Inder*, 1808). These were not about esotericism, and yet it is true that these works attest not only to the general interest in European myths, tales, and legends, but also fall under the spell of the Romantic pursuit of the One, a quest that will relaunch the idea of *perennial philosophy*, which is now extended to all traditions worldwide, and no longer focused only upon those of the Mediterranean world. The word "Tradition" appears in the German title of a landmark book by F.J. Molitor on the Kabbalah (*Philosophie der Geschichte oder über die Tradition*, 1827), followed by Adolphe Frank's *La Kabbale* (1843). In another scholarly work, Jacques Matter's *Histoire du gnosticisme* (1828), we find the first use of "ésotérisme" which has been located to date (by Jean-Pierre Laurant, 1990).To this corpus were added two further obsessive themes: the great pyramid (John Taylor's *The Great Pyramid*, 1858) and that of Druidism as the mother religion of humanity. A return to the hermetist current followed the speculations on the great pyramid. In 1866 Louis Ménard produced a *Hermès Trismégiste* (the French translation of major texts of the *Corpus Hermeticum* preceded by a landmark introduction). This book inspired new translations and glosses, works written for the most part by personalities affiliated with the Theosophical Society or with Rosicrucian Orders. Hermetist literature went naturally with the vogue for "tradition" which it either encouraged or stemmed from. Founded in 1875, the Theosophical Society favored the success of this idea of universal Tradition, which was increasingly termed "primordial," the better to define it as the mother of all other traditions. The founder (cf. *infra*) of the Theosophical Society contributed a great deal to it through her own works, which guaranteed this movement a great success (*Isis Unveiled*, 1877; *The Secret Doctrine*, 1888). At the end of the century the appearance of a science of comparative religion and the convocation of a large "Parliament of Religions" at Chicago (1893) encouraged the growth of believers in the Universal Tradition. It took the form of a best-seller in 1889 with the publication of Edouard Schuré's much translated and reissued *Les Grands Initiés*. There we find again five of the ancient "sages" of *perennial philosophy* as the Renaissance knew them but now flanked by more exotic names. Schuré's list includes Rama, Krishna, Hermes, Moses, Orpheus, Pythagoras, Plato, and Jesus.

B) Appearance of Spiritualism and Occultism (1840–1860)

During the first half of the century animal magnetism was prodigiously popular and prolonged its existence by engendering different currents. As early as the end of the eighteenth century one of the original forms that magnetism took was to pose questions bearing on the supernatural to subjects who had been put in a state of magnetic sleep ("crisiacs" of J.B. Willermoz and the Chevalier of Barberin; later, practiced by J. Kerner, cf. *supra*). In 1848 a year after Andrew Jackson Davis's *The Principles of Revelation* (a great classic of mesmerist literature in the United States), spiritualism arose. The Fox sisters at Hydesville, also in the United States, questioned spirits through the intermediary of mediums, but these were no longer intermediary entities like angels, but spirits of the dead who respond, this time by the mechanical gimmick of tapping on a table in a preestablished code. Spiritualism had arrived, it conquered Europe and could now count millions of sympathizers. Its first important theoretician was H.L. Rivail (alias Allan Kardec, *Le Monde des Esprits*, 1857) who transformed it into a religion tinged with sentimentalism and rationalism. Coming on the scene at the same time as "classic" Anglo-Saxon fantasy literature and Marxism, the spiritualist movement does not belong to the history of esotericism properly speaking, but would be closely associated with it because of its wide influence and because of the problems it raised. Elevated by Kardec to the rank of a veritable dogma, the idea of reincarnation—rarely adopted by Anglo-Saxons—was in harmony with the egalitarian and utopian tendencies of the period.

There were some ambiguous relationships established between esotericism and the more picturesque socialist utopias. Perceptible in Alphonse Esquiros (*De la vie future du point de vue socialiste*, 1850) and in the Druidism of Jean Reynaud (*Terre et Ciel*, 1854), they appear clearly in Charles Fourier (1772–1837; *La Théorie des quatre mouvements* came out in 1807, but its real success came much later). It was the form, not the content of his discourse that brought Fourier, the "Ariosto of the Utopianists" close to the visionary theories of Swedenborg, or at least it sounded like a praiseworthy, albeit inadvertent, parody of the latter. After 1848, even more than before, Swedenborgianism itself was colored by humanitarian prophetism. The names of Hortensius Flamel (cf. *supra*) and Eliphas Lévi form a link between illuminated socialism and the esotericism represented by Louis Lucas (*Une révolution dans la musique*, 1849), J.-M. Ragon (*Orthodoxie maçonnique* and *Maçonnerie occulte*, 1853) and Henri Delaage (*Le Monde occulte*, 1851). These years were also highlighted by substantial alchemical essays by Mary Ann Atwood (*A Suggestive Enquiry into the Hermetic Mystery*, 1850), by a lovely

book by Frédéric Portal on *Les Couleurs symboliques* (1857) as well as by the
first large anthology of theosophic texts, assembled by Julius Hamberger, a
close disciple of Baader (*Stimmen aus dem Heiligthum der christlichen
Theosophie*, 1851). This was also the period when Masonic literature made
general use of the word "esotericism" (cf., e.g., E.-U. Marconis de Nègre, *Le
Sanctuaire de Memphis ou Hèrmes*, 1849).

With Alphonse–Louis Constant (alias Eliphas Lévi, 1810–1875) appears
the occultist current properly so-called. Levi's youth was devoted to utopian
and humanitarian ideas leading to his imprisonment as a revolutionary. In
1852 he met Wronski and in 1854 with Bulwer-Lytton he evoked up the
spirit of Apollonius of Tyana. He then became the principal exponent of esotericism in Europe and the United States. Awkward as a compiler, but
admired as a synthetizer by many esotericists, this magus inspired conviction
and came along at the right time (*Dogme et rituel de Haute magie*, 1854–1856;
Histoire de la magie, 1860; *La Clef des Grands Mystères*, 1861). The year 1860 is
an important date, because in addition to the publication of the *Histoire de la
magie* Louis Figuier published *L'Histoire de le merveilleux* and Alfred Maury,
La Magie et l'astrologie.

C) Rise of Occultism in the Era of Scientism and the Permanence of Theosophy (1860–1914)

One of the aspects assumed by the *philosophia occulta* in the course of its history
is the occultist current. It is more a counter-current to the extent that vis-à-vis
the triumph of scientism, it presents itself as an alternative solution.
Generally occultists do not condemn scientific progress or modernity.
Rather, they try to integrate it within a global vision that will serve to make
the vacuousness of materialism more apparent. We recognize here an echo of
the pansophic program and *Naturphilosophie*, but the new orientation differed
because of its penchant for phenomena and demonstration as well as its
attraction for the picturesque and fantastic, often cultivated for their own
sake. The world had definitely become disenchanted. This said, we are not
dealing with a homogeneous movement, but only a prolongation of the occult
sciences before 1860, now confronting materialist positivism and now being
linked by affinity to the Symbolist current.

Some strong personalities dominated a rather heteroclite crowd. In
France, Dr. Gérard Encausse (alias Papus, 1865–1915), nicknamed the Balzac
of occultism because of his voluminous work, put himself forward simply as a
physician, investigator, and experimenter. His *Traité de science occulte* was published in 1888, the same year as the first issue of his journal *L'Initiation*. This
was a watershed year that saw the founding of the "Society for Psychical
Research" in London and several important initiatory associations (cf. *infra*).
Papus with his friend from Lyons L.-N.-A. Philippe (1849–1905, called

"Maître Philippe") went to St. Petersburg on several occasions at the request of Nicholas II whom they initiated into Martinism. The man whom Papus called his spiritual master was Alexandre Saint-Yves d'Alveydre (1842–1909) who around 1900 invented a magical"Archeometer," a key to universal correspondences and authored penetrating studies on musical esotericism. Along with them let us also cite Stanislas de Guaïta and the Sâr Joséphin Péladan (1858–1918), who represent a somewhat literary occultism. Albert de Rochas (1837–1914), Charles Henry (1859–1926), and Albert Faucheux (alias François–Charles Barlet, 1838–1921) were more oriented toward philosophical or scientific speculation.

In Prague several centers of occultism were active around 1900. In Holland, occultism was well represented by Frederic Van Eden (*Het Hypnotisme en de Wonderen*, 1887); in Germany by Carl du Prel (*Studien aus dem Gebiete der Geheimwissenschaften*, 1894/1895) and especially Franz Hartmann (1838–1912). Moreover, most of these names are found associated with the history of contemporary initiatory societies (cf. *infra*), especially in Anglo-Saxon countries where association activities and erudition characterize the most impressive occultists. Among these we should remember at least three names: G.R.S Mead (1853–1933, editor of the *Corpus Hermeticum* 1906), William W. Westcott (1848-1925), Sir Arthur Edward Waite (1857–1942). In Russia Piotr D. Ouspensky (1878–1947) had already written almost all of his work (*Tertium Organum*, Russian edition in 1911, English in 1920; *A New Model of the Universe*, a series of essays published separately in Russian in 1914, collected in English in 1931). In these we find occultism, a very interesting *Naturphilosophie*, considerations on the Tarot, dreams, etc. To all this we should add that astrology was fashionable again from 1880 to 1914, as can be seen from its enlarged place in occultist literature, by the appearance of numerous specialized works and by the work of extraordinarily well-known esoteric astrologers like William F. Allan (alias Alan Leo, 1860–1917).

Between occultists and theosophers the border is sometimes fluid because the greatest among the occultists, e.g., Barlet are theosophers as well, and theosophers like Rudolf Steiner, not prone to ignore the occultist current, integrate it in their own way. This was not the case with Vladimir Soloviev (1853–1900), *Natur*-philosopher and sophiologist (*Conférences sur la théantropie*, 1877/1881; *La Beauté de la Nature*, 1889; *Le Sens de l'Amour*, 1892/1894). If that Russian theosopher distanced himself from occultism, that is less the case with the Austrian Rudolf Steiner (1861–1925), polyvalent theosopher and *Natur*-philosopher. During his student years in Vienna, he was busy with the sciences in the wake of Goethe whose scientific works he edited (1883/1897). After that he continued to reflect on the esoteric import of the teachings of the genius of Weimar (*Goethe als Theosoph*, 1904; essays on *Faust* and the *Märchen* date from 1918). His voluminous production includes drama, innumerable lectures, essays, and treatises (*Theosophie*, 1904; *Die Geheimwissenschaft im Umriss*, 1910). According to the Christocentric evolutionism that characterizes his thought, he intended to fully assume the acquisitions of the Western spiritual history with a view to their transmutation. He did not mean to return to a primordial Tradition where manifestations in the form of new divine avatars are passionately awaited. (That is why the Theosophical Society's presentation of young Krishnamurti as a Christ come back to earth in 1913 brought about Steiner's break with that society.) Humanity in its forward movement must always work at finding its balance between two poles: the cosmic forces of expansion (dilation of the being, aspiration toward the heights, but also egocentrism) and the forces of concentration (hardening, materialization). Reincarnation and "karma" function as instruments of liberation. Steiner called his system "Anthroposophy" to distinguish it from the teaching of the Theosophical Society, and gave that name to the Society he founded in 1913 (the *Anthroposophische Gesellschaft*).

III) ESOTERICISM IN INITIATORY SOCIETIES AND IN ART (1848–1914)

A) Masonic or Para-Masonic Societies

As we have seen, with the Masons it is especially in the higher degrees that esoteric tendencies can be expressed. Now, after the French Revolution most of the Masonic systems disappeared. The Rectified Scottish Rite, nevertheless, continued in Switzerland; the Ancient and Accepted Scottish Rite also stayed active, as did a section of "Egyptian" Masonry, chiefly because of the Rites of Memphis and Misraïm. But at the end of the nineteenth century, after this long period of latency "in sleep," we see the same phenomenon as a hundred years earlier, i.e., the creation and propagation of new societies of this type. In 1868 Paschal Beverly Randolph (1825–1875) founded the oldest Rosicrucian group in the United States, the Fraternitas Rosae Crucis. Somewhat later, in 1876, the Swedenborgian Rite of the "Illuminated Theosophists" (cf. *supra*) returned to Europe from America and spawned numerous Lodges. The Societas Rosicruciana in Anglia with a clearly Christian orientation and grafted on regular Masonry included high degrees inspired by those of the eighteenth-century Gold- und Rosenkreuz. Founded in London in 1867, this order was created by scholarly esotericists and occultists: Robert W. Little (1840–1918) and Kenneth R.H. Mackenzie (1833–1886). Bulwer-Lytton and Eliphas Lévi were honorary members, and W. W. Westcott was the Supremus Magus from 1891–1925.

In France, Guaïta and Péladan founded the Rose-Croix Kabbalistique in 1888 (it was to have many an explosion and fragmentation), and in 1891

Papus established a mixed *Ordre Martiniste*. (The adjective refers to Saint-Martin.) We saw that Nicholas II, open to occultism like the last Romanovs, became a member. In 1888 also, in Germany, there was the Esoteric Rosy-Cross of Franz Hartmann, in England the Order of the Golden Dawn (a neo-Masonic adaptation admitting women). Created by W.W. Westcott, W. R. Woodman, and S.L. MacGregor Mathers, the Golden Dawn found inspiration in the Kabbalah as well as the Tarot and gave a large place to ceremonial magic (which was not the case with the Societas Rosicruciana in Anglia). Mathers' translation of *The Sacred Magic of Abra-Melin the Mage* (theurgic ritual of the seventeenth century) was not published until 1939. It is a ritual often practiced by the members of the Golden Dawn notably Aleister Crowley (1875–1947) who joined in 1898 and stayed in for two and a half years. Writer William Butler Yeats (1865–1939), who was initiated in 1888, directed it for several months. A. E. Waite joined in 1891. *The Stella Matutina* was a branch founded in 1903. Around 1901, Viennese occultist Carl Kellner (1850–1905) installed a *Ordo Templi Orientis*, a secret science research Lodge where Theodor Reuss (1855–1923) and Aleister Crowley also held leadership roles. Crowley's organization of the rituals gave them a sexual and anti-Christian cast. He himself created the parallel *Astrum Argentinum* in 1910, which was integrated into the *Ordo Templi Orientis* in 1912. Rudolf Steiner affiliated with *Ordo Templi Orientis* around 1905 and led the German branch, but left in 1914 to create his own Anthroposophical Society at Dornach, near Basel; his organization is devoid of Masonry (cf. *supra* and *infra*). Another important organization is the Rosicrucian Fellowship, established in 1907 by Carl Louis von Grasshof (alias Max Heindel, 1865–1919), with its large world center in Oceanside, California.

There were also circles, associations, and movements more or less independent of the initiatory groups properly so-called. Such is the Mouvement Cosmique, founded around 1900 by Max Théon. It was the continuation of a so-called Hermetic Brotherhood of Luxor, and started publishing in 1903 an enormous work called *Tradition cosmique* dedicated to the "primitive tradition." Some of these movements bring together Christian esotericists; this is the case with Anna Kingsford's Hermetic Academy (cf. *infra*), but it was chiefly a French phenomenon: Yvon Leloup (alias Paul Sédir, 1871–1926), a Papus collaborator, led the group called *Les Amitiés spirituelles*; Paul Vulliaud (1875–1950) founded the journal *Les Entretiens idéalistes* in 1906, as well as an artistic and literary movement of the same name; Jesuit Victor Drevon (1820–1880) and Alexis de Sarachaga (1840–1918) created the "Hiéron," a study center at Paray-le-Monial in 1873.

Obviously this is only a partial listing. It does not include properly constituted sects which would distract us from our purpose (despite the ritualistic

and esoteric aspect of at least one of them, the *Eglise Gnostique*, founded by
Jules Doinel in 1890).

B) The Theosophical Society

Founded in 1875 in New York by Helena Petrovna Blavatsky (known as
H.P.B., 1831–1891), Henry Steel Olcott (1832–1907) and William Quan
Judge (1851–1896), the Theosophical Society—having nothing to do with
Freemasonry—has undergone variations in form and ramifications throughout its history. However, the latter have conserved the same common denominators: they do not propose any degrees or ranks of initiation; they teach no
doctrine (despite the title of the book *The Secret Doctrine*, 1888); and H.P.B.'s
books serve as reference (besides the above mentioned, there is also *Isis
Unveiled*, 1877). When it was founded, the Theosophical Society established a
threefold goal, respected by all branches that developed from it: a) to form the
nucleus of a universal fraternity; b) to encourage the study of all religions,
philosophy, and science; c) to study the laws of Nature as well as the psychic
and spiritual powers of Man. Through its content and inspiration, it is largely
an offshoot of Oriental spiritualities, especially Hindu, reflecting the cultural
climate in which it was born. It was the wish of H.P.B. and her society to
always show the unity of all religions in their esoteric foundations, and to
develop the ability to become theosophers in those who so desired. The
Theosophical Society, especially in the beginning, dedicated a large part of its
activities to the psychic or metapsychic fields, so popular at that time.

H.P.B. left for India in 1878, founded her journal *The Theosophist* there
in 1879, and installed the official headquarters of the Theosophical Society at
Adyar, near Madras, in 1883. She was well-thought of by the natives of the
country, who had little trouble detecting a very tolerant mind behind this
movement. H.P.B. returned to Europe in 1885. After her death, the history of
the Theosophical Society's branches became complex (the most interesting
case probably being that of the United Lodge of Theosophists, founded in
1909 by Robert Crosbie). The diffusion of this movement is widespread on an
international scale (it is now rooted in most Western countries) and favored
by three factors. First, there is the presence of such remarkable personalities
as Annie Besant (1847–1933) who became president in 1907, Franz Hartmann
(founder of the German branch in 1886), and Rudolf Steiner (Secretary
General of the German section in 1902). Just as he left the Ordo Templi
Orienti, Steiner broke away from the Theosophical Society (cf. *supra*) in
1913, claiming that the inclination toward Oriental traditions did not seem to
be quite compatible with the Christian, Western character of his own theosophy. Before him, Anna Bonus Kingsford (1846–1888)—an outstanding figure
in the feminine, Christian esotericism of the seventies and eighties—made
the separation for the same reason, and permeated her newly founded

Hermetic Society with Christianity (cf. her wonderful book *The Perfect Way*, 1881). By creating their own organizations, figures such as Steiner and to a lesser degree, Anna Kingsford actually helped contribute to the extension of the mother society's teachings, even though under a modified form.The second factor are the numerous links that the various branches maintained with most of the other esoteric societies; the International Spiritualist and Spirit Conference (1889) and the Masonic and Spiritualist Conference (1908) which met in Paris both represent and are good examples of these crossroads of ideas and tendencies (the divisions between most of the movements are not tight, and opposition and fulminating excommunications arise mainly within each group).The third factor is obviously the high percentage of artists who are known to have felt the influence of the Theosophical Society.

C) *Esoteric Arts and Literature*

Among the great French writers, Gérard de Nerval is the one who integrated the largest number of esoteric elements in his writings (*Voyage en Orient*, 1851; *Les Illuminés*, 1852; *Les Chimères*, 1854).The sonnet of Charles Baudelaire (*Correspondances*, c. 1857) became a kind of poetic "Emerald Tablet," and his texts on the creative imagination are akin to some of the most classical esoteric texts. The literature of Victor Hugo (1854) in *Les Contemplations* at times becomes that of a visionary theosopher (that same year Hugo's spirit is said to have conversed with the spirit of Shakespeare). In France, occultism found its best fiction writer in the person of Villiers de l'Isle-Adam (*Isis*, 1862; *Axël*, 1888), and some presence in Saint-Pol-Roux (1861–1940) (*Les Reposoirs de la Procession*, 1893). It inspired the spectacular saga of J. Péladan (L'Ethopée, 1886/1907). The exhibitions of the Salons of the Rosy-Cross, tied to the order founded by Péladan, correspond to one of the most aesthetically fertile periods of the occultist movement. Works by Félicien Rops and Georges Rouault were admired there from 1893 to 1898, and Erik Satie was present too. In Germany between 1843 and 1882, the work of Richard Wagner, which incorporated into the Belle Epoque the idea of music elevated to the heights of religion, always had (text and score) a privileged hermeneutical place for esotericists; however, if there is any esotericism, it is most often found in their interpretations. This remark can be applied just as well to the painter Arnold Böcklin (1827-1901) or to Gustave Moreau (1828–1898). Esotericism, however, is explicit in the architectual undertakings of Rudolf Steiner who, like Wagner in Bayreuth, created a *Gesamtkunstwerk* ("total artistic work," a very Germanic idea) in Dornach (in the vicinity of Basel). Construction of the building, the Goetheanum, began in 1913. Steiner's four dramas (1910/1913, *Die Pforte der Einweihung, ein Rosenkreuzermysterium* in 1910) are performed there, along with some of Edouard Schurés plays. Another example of *Gesamtkunstwerk* is the project done by the composer Alexander Scriabine (1872–1915), a grandiose "mystery," which would have surpassed by far even the greatest ambitions of Wagner. He was unable to finish the work, but there is esoteric sensitivity throughout the remainder of his musical pieces. In Russia we have the poems of Alexander Biely (*Petersburg*, 1914), and in Sweden, August Strindberg's plays (*Inferno*, 1897). More so than in other places, especially during the Symbolist period, England and the United States had many who were writer and "magus" as well: A. Crowley, P.B. Randolph, A.E. Waite, Arthur Machen, and of course the great William B. Yeats, and Arthur Symonds (*Images of Good and Evil*, 1899).

CHAPTER FIVE

TWENTIETH-CENTURY
ESOTERICISMS

I) GNOSES IN THE WAKE OF THE WESTERN TRADITION

A) Success of the "Traditional" Sciences

The traditional sciences (astrology, alchemy, and magic) remain very much alive, directly touching a vast public. Their activities, as much speculative as operative, have been practiced within innumerable initiatory associations and by individuals. The most popular is clearly astrology, queen of the arts of divination. What book store does not dedicate shelves to astrology taking over a large part of the section devoted to "esotericism" or "occultism"? Is there a newspaper that does not have its special columns of daily or weekly advice? This is because despite its most widespread aspect—predictions that are simplistic, clichéd, commonplace, utilitarian, or "astroflash"—astrology still responds to a more or less conscious need to find once more in our uncentered and fragmented world the *Unus mundus*, the unity of mankind and the universe, through an integral language based on the principle of similitude. When this need is conscious, when it opens out upon a reflection—on a veritable hermeneutics of "signs"—which integrates a praxis and a gnosis, then we may speak of "esoteric" astrology. After Alan Leo, numerous twentieth-century astrologers from Karl Brandler-Pracht (1864–1945) to André Barbault, including Daniel Chennevière (alias Dane Rudhyar, 1895–1985) deserve this adjective. Thanks to them, astrology is on its way to obtaining its own status at the heart of the humanities.

In the other occult sciences we observe this duality. The Tarot, a specific art since Eliphas Lévi, is the subject of an extensive literature, both scholarly and popular, and increasingly suffuses our culture. It has always served to tell fortunes, but through a hermeneutic of situations and characters, it also opens out upon a gnosis and occasionally integrates the Kabbalah and astrology. (e.g., A. Crowley, *Ambrosi magi hortus rosarum*, 1928; Marc Haven, *Le Tarot*, 1946; Paul Marteau, *Le Tarot de Marseille*, 1949; Valentin Tomberg, *Meditationen*, 1972, cited *infra*) .

In the same way the field of alchemy is divided between mere "spagyrists"with no pretension to gnosis (like the "hyperchemists," operative or not) and the alchemists who are *Natur*-philosophers Some of these occasionally have organizations; the Paracelsus Research Society of Salt Lake City, directed by Albert Riedel (alias Frater Albertus, d. 1984), is a typical example, but there are many other circles of that type, often neo-Paracelsian like that of Alexander von Bernus (1880–1965) in Germany. Outside of such associations, the practice of alchemy is more likely to keep the character of a private religion as it has always tended to do. Rare ineeed are the genuine "Philosophers" who have left an interesting written work—so customary in previous centuries. This explains the success of an alchemist like Eugène Canseliet (1899–1982; *Alchimie*, 1964) whose fame also owes much to the mystery that surrounds his master Fulcanelli. Among other publications this master left *Mystère des Cathédrales* (1925), and the disciple Canseliet *Deux logis alchimiques* (1945/1979) wherein they give more attention to deciphering esoteric signatures on the stones of certain edifices than to looking for the Philosopher's Stone themselves. Other authors, engaged in the alchemical tradition evoke its spiritual or initiatory aspects without claiming to be operatives themselves (e.g., Julius Evola, *La Tradizione ermetica*, 1931). Thanks to easily available facsimile reproductions (texts and images), appearing especially in the 1970s and 1980s and also to the works dedicated to it by researchers in the humanities and the philosophical interest it aroused (cf. *infra*), alchemy enjoys good standing in Western culture.

Magic as a practice comes under the jurisdiction of esotericism if it is inscribed in a gnostic vision of the world. Thus defined, it is extremely widespread in our century, but it is especially thanks to various societies and groups that we can have an idea of the forms it takes—because they are rarely much of a secret. For methodological reasons it is appropriate to separate ceremonial magic from initiatory magic, as Massimo Introvigne (cf. *infra*) has recently suggested. Ceremonial magic emphasizes knowledge and/or power and the efficacy of ritual. The second emphasizes the legitimacy of initiatory filiation, as the condition of an authentic transformation of the receiver. Both kinds of magic are practiced in the hothouses of esoteric societies. In principle these are quite discreet; however, taken as a whole, they produce an abundant literature. Several works cited in this chapter stem from them.

If the current of the Christian Kabbalah dried up long ago, that of the Jewish Kabbalah still flows to inspire esotericists with a presumed key to gnosis, but which they often cut away from its Hebrew roots and soil, to use its *sephiroth* as tools of thought. Such is the case of Raymond Abellio

(1907–1986) in *La Bible document chiffré* (1950) and other writings. For those not reared in the Jewish tradition, the corpus of Greek and Latin references lends itself better to a hermeneutic. For that matter, there is an ongoing esoteric exegesis of the *Corpus Hermeticum* (e.g., Shrine of Wisdom editions, 1923; Duncan Greenless, *The Gospel of Hermes*, 1949; and Jan Van Rijckenborgh, *De Egyptische oer-gnosis*, 1960/1965).

B) Presence of Christian Theosophy

The chief representatives of a genuinely Christian theosophy are French, German, and Russian. Rudolf Steiner continued his personal work in *Mein Lebensgang*, his autobiography, appearing in 1925 and his study of Andreae's *Chymische Hochzeit*, in 1917/1918. The influence of the other great figure in German theosophy, Leopold Ziegler (1881–1958) is more discreet. This sedentary sage on the banks of Lake Constance shared with Réne Guénon the idea of a primordial Tradition fragmented, hidden, forgotten, but if he scrutinized the myths and studied religions, it was more as a disciple of Boehme and Baader, as a theosopher attentive to the symbolism of phases of alchemical transmutation. Thus he placed Sophia at the very heart of his gnosis, associating her with a *Naturphilosophie* inseparable from a philosophy of history—history itself grasped in its entirety, as much biological as spiritual. (Cf. *Ueberlieferung and Menschwerdung*, 1948 and *Gestaltwandel der Götter*, 1922).

Can we speak of theosophy amid the Russian sophiologists? The Orthodox Church dedicated two temples to Sophia, the Saint-Sophia Churches of Constantinople and Kiev. The Russian Church made this personage a real, central figure, contrary to what happened in Western Christianity where she is present mostly in esotericism. As a religious theme and object of belief, Sophia does not by herself come under the jurisdiction of esotericism, but she occupies a large place in theosophic discourse. The publications of Paul Florensky (1882–1943) remain on the side of this discourse (*La Colonne et le fondement de la vérité*, 1914) as do those of Sergei Bulgakov (1877–1945: *The Wisdom of God*, 1937, *Du Verbe incarné*, 1943, and *Le Paraclet*, 1946). Tommasio Palamidessi (1915–1983), inspired not only by V. Soloviev, but by Florensky also, founded in 1948 an initiatory Order "Loto + Croce," which became the *Associazione Archeosofica* in 1968. Philosopher Nicholai Berdyaev (1874–1948) was closer to Germanic theosophy than Florensky or Bulgakov: *Le Sens de la création*, 1930; *Esprit et réalité*, 1937; *Etudes sur Jacob Boehme*, 1930 and 1946. A great admirer of Boehme ("A summit in the visionary strength of man") and Baader, but critical of occultism—whose "great meaning" is however "to be already turned toward the cosmic secret and toward man's part in it"—Berdyaev attacks the teachings of the Theosophical Society and Steiner because of their evolutionism, and sees in them "a serious symptom of the decomposition of the physical plane of the being" (cf., *Le Sens de la création*).

If esotericism is only one aspect of Berdyaev's work, that of Boris Muraviev (1890–1966; *Gnôsis, étude et commentaire sur la tradition ésotérique de l'orthodoxie orientale*, 1961/1965, written in French), is entirely dedicated to it. This *summum* of psychosophy, anthroposophy, historiosophy, presented in the form of a course planned for the illumination and transformation of the reader, is the work of a very independent theosopher (in spite of the fact that he is influenced by Gurdjieff). There are virtually no references to the Western corpus, a lacuna that makes it no less profound and stimulating. The Center for Christian Esoteric Studies, created by Muraviev in 1961, has had some success, but the finest and most instructive Western esoteric book in the twentieth century is by a Russian of Baltic German origin Valentin Tomberg (1901–1973), a professor of law who ended his career in London: It is the anonymous *Méditations sur les 22 Arcanes majeurs du Tarot*, written in French, first published in German (1972) and then in other languages. There is perhaps no better introduction to Christian theosophy, to occultism, to any reflection on esotericism than this magisterial work, not that of a historian but of an inspired theosopher and—a rather rare occurrence—one who is careful to respect history. Let us note that, despite its title, it is hardly a treatise devoted to the Tarot. (The Arcana serve only as a point of departure, support, and reflection).

In France Auguste-Edouard Chauvet (1885–1955) continued the work of Fabre d'Olivet and SainteYves d'Alveydre, examining the books of Moses. He starts with the work of his two predecessors but enriches their contribution with new perspectives. He is the author of *Esotérisme de la Genèse* (1946/1948), which is one of the most authentic works of Christian theosophy in the twentieth century. Chauvet's disciple and commentator is Robert Amadou, who is not only a historian of the first rank for Western esotericism (cf. *infra*), but a theosopher also, chiefly in the wake of Saint-Martin. His personal stand until now is expressed in essays (from *L'Occultisme, esquisse d' un monde vivant*, 1950 to *Occident Orient: parcours d'une tradition*, 1987), far too few, considering their quality.

The work of Henry Corbin (1903–1978) does not come under the purview of Christian theosophy, but any serious reflection on it is henceforth enriched by a new and fecond recontextualizing in the three great "religions of the Book" (Jewish, Christian, and Muslim). A translator and commentator of Iranian and Islamic philosophical texts, this university scholar knew how to join scientific rigor to personal engagement (a theosophy whose Christian component has a docetist hue). This combination allowed him to apprehend the specificity of his subjects both from inside and the outside. Thanks to Corbin, the intrinsic relations that linked Christian theosophers (e.g., Swedenborg and Oetinger) to their Shiite Islamic homologues were clearly visible. He was the first to expose a theory of the *mundus imaginalis* (or the "imaginal"), a specific, intermediary mesocosmos, situated between the sensible and intelligible worlds, there where spirits corporealize and bodies spiritualize themselves. The Sophia and the world of angels therefore have a large place in this voluminous work. (Let us cite only *L'Imagination créatrice dans le soufisme d'Ibn' Arabi, 1958; Terre céleste et corps de résurrection,* 1960; *En Islam iranien,* 1971/1972).

C) Gnosis and Science: Towards a New Pansophy

The occultist movement had demonstrated its powerlessness to call forth a new *Naturphilosophie* comparable to that of German Romanticism. Similarly, the twentieth century was to have no current like that. To be sure, we can consider as *Naturphilosohie* some important features in the work of names already discussed (e.g., R. Steiner, A. von Bernus or B. Muraviev). But other esotericists who take on the task of building a *Naturphilosophie* no longer show a unified front. Moreover, their influence has to compete with speculations of a new type which, despite a somewhat esoteric style, are in no respect esoteric.

These speculations stem from one of the actual orientations of physics, astrophysics, and the life sciences that increasingly tend to propose models of the universe and see themselves obliged to suggest hypotheses of meaning. The problem of origins of the cosmos and the problem of the relationship between Spirit and Nature are thus currently the subject of impassioned debates in which the old representatives of theosophy, pansophy, or *Naturphilosophie* are sometimes invoked but almost always with a view to proposing a vision of the world resting on scientific considerations. Even if a new science emerges, thanks to shattering, epistemological breakthroughs, freed from the scientistic ghetto, the neognosis still is not a gnosis in the esoteric sense of the term, whether we are dealing with Raymond Ruyer's *La Gnose de Princeton* (1974), Fritjof Capra's *The Tao of Physics* (1975), or Jean Charon's *L'Esprit cet inconnu* (1977). We are in no way intending to imply that orientation is in itself less important or less interesting than an esoteric *Naturphilosophie*, nor to deny that between them a fruitful circulation could be established. It is only a question of not confusing the planes. There is no gnosis properly so-called without prior adherence to a narrative of origins (a founding myth) unrolled through symbols, which a spiritual hermeneutics has the task of forever probing thanks to the glance of fire of the Spirit, which as the Apostle says, (I Cor.) "searches everything, even the depths of God." Scientific neognosis resembles gnosis only in borrowing what is on the surface. The neognosis can only describe actions, while the gnosis accounts for the acts. As Jean-Louis Vieillard-Baron, one of the most authoritative voices pleading in favor of such a *Naturphilosophie* today, so aptly recalls: "philosophy of Nature is the redemption of Nature by human thought, which alone reintegrates her into the absolute." This being said, a *Naturphilosophie* could not do without all the contributions that the new scientific spirit has made possible.

Along with the other esotericists already mentioned, we should make room for some others who are among the most representative of a *Naturphilosophie*. For G.I. Gurdjieff (1877 or 1866–1949), as for Boehme, Nature has a double nature, a creational nature and an eternal nature, a duality that is embodied in the appearance of a considerable number of levels of materiality (a distinction whose pertinence is revealed by the discovery of the quantum world), and that is inscribed within a network of universal interdependence. Structured by a numerology both traditional and original, this cosmology or cosmosophy, rich and complex, is inseparable from a pedagogy spoken of as "awakening." The practice of awakening profoundly marked Gurdjieff's disciples. He himself explained a part of his *Naturphilosophie* in *Beelzebub's Tales to His Grandson*, published in 1950. Settled in France in 1922, he founded his "Priory at Avon" and in 1933 settled definitively in Paris. In 1915 Ouspensky (cf. *infra*) met Gurdjieff, and we owe to him a rigorous report of the master's propositions as well as of the "work" carried out in the groups (*In Search of the Miraculous: Fragments of an Unknown Teaching*, 1949, which contains a complete teaching of *Naturphilosophie*).

Currently we see being elaborated a serious and promising reflection around this idea taken in its sense of gnosis. And that, from esotericists as different as Raymond Abellio, already mentioned (*La Structure absolue*, 1965) and Seyyed Hossein Nasr (*Man and Nature*, 1968), from scholars such as microphysicist Basarab Nicolescu (*Nous, la particule et le monde*, 1985; *Science, Meaning and Evolution: The Cosmology of Jacob Boehme*, 1992) or philosophers such as Michel Cazenave (*La Science et l'Ame du Monde*, 1983).

II) THE FOUR WINDS OF THE TRADITION

A) *Guénonism, a New Phenomenon*

To counteract the proliferation of initiatory orders linked to the occultist current and the latter's sometime suspect aspects on the spiritual plane, Frenchman René Guénon (1886–1951) undertook a work of reformation under the sign of the Tradition. He knew these Orders well because he had been a member of several in his youth. He had even flirted with spiritualism around 1908. In 1914 he was initiated into the Great Lodge of France. At the heart of the Gnostic Church he had frequented, men like Léon Champrenaud and Albert de Pourvourville influenced him; to their influence was added that of certain Orientals whom he met in 1908 and 1909. Thus, his vocation as reformer was formed. In 1921 Guénon published his *Introduction générale à l'étude des doctrines hindoues* in which he explains the essential elements of his metaphysics. In *Le Théosophisme, histoire d'une pseudo-religion*, published the same year to attack the Theosophical Society, he demonstrated his biting, polemical turn of mind, which also animated *L'Erreur spirite* (1923), another poisoned arrow, aimed now at spiritualism. We find in almost all his subsequent works this will to cleanse and purify, which bears not only on esoteric or occultist currents but also on Western philosophers (*Orient et Occident*, 1924) throughout. In 1927 *Le Roi du Monde* affirmed the existence of a spiritual center or "geometric space," guarantor of the orthodoxy of different traditions, and *La Crise du Monde moderne* situated our present civilization with respect to the Hindu theosophy of cosmic cycles, identifying our era with the epoch called *Kali-Yuga*, a dark period of degeneration coming at the end of one of the great cycles or *manvantaras*. In 1930 Guénon went to Egypt where he lived until his death, which occurred in his home in Cairo. He wrote *Le Symbolisme de la Croix* (1931), *Les Etats multiples de l'Etre* (1932), *Le Règne de la quantité et les signes des temps* (1945), *La Grande Triade* (1946). His voluminous bibliography is not limited to these titles, since Guénon was always an indefatigable correspondent, a polemicist with an acid pen, and a prolific writer of articles.

Guénon held a complex metaphysical doctrine of Hindu origin, bearing on Non-Being (Brahma, the Absolute) and on Being—its manifestation—in "multiple states" to which men and women are bound. His metaphysics in itself is no more "esoteric" than any other, thus, it is his metaphysics that has earned him a place in the foreground of contemporary esotericisms. Three other reasons for his prominence may be adduced. First, his numerous public stands; he attracted much attention by making pronouncements. Second, his insistence on a "primordial Tradition," and, with regard to initiation, the need for authentic affiliation. Third, the quality of inspiration in his works dedicated to symbolism (for example, *Le Symbolisme de la Croix* and *La Grande Triade*).

To oppose the proliferating initiations that he considered for the most part false, Guénon proposed the initiatory regularity of the Freemasons or of the Catholic Church. The latter, however, is only an initiatory channel. Christianity itself must be transcended for any religion qua religion is only a form, a limiting aspect of the "supreme intellectuality" or an avatar of the primordial Tradition. He found this notion in his heritage from the Renaissance, from Romanticism, and from the Theosophical Society, and he hypostasized it as no one before him had done. A solitary figure stubbornly clutching his rocky cliff of wisdom, Guénon represents an impressive voice of intellectual asceticism. None better than he warned against the confusion of the psychic and the spiritual, against sentimentality where spirituality is called for. It remains, nevertheless, that this Descartes of esotericism, whose power of synthesis, rigor of thought, and power of argument can only be admired, cheerfully threw out several babies with the bath water. By refusing Western philosophy, he virtually ignored German theosophy (the Germanic world was alien to him). Through distrust of adulteration, he kept nothing—or nearly nothing—of the Western hermetico-alchemical tradition. He located the great divorce from metaphysics (with Guénon, "esotericism"—or better: "esoterism"—takes on the sense of "metaphysical principles," "exotericism" covering everything individual) in the Renaissance. Through ignorance of the epistemological breakthroughs of his own times, he had a false—because outdated—idea of science. (It is true that he himself was neither a man of science, a scholar, nor a historian.) He rejected science, just as he condemned modernity in all its aspects, and he proudly ignored Nature. There was no place here for any *Naturphilosophie*. (The "world of manifestation," i.e., the palpable world, he liked to say, has even less reality than our shadow on a wall.)

Because of this lack of interest in Nature and the greater part of traditions found in Western esotericism, in the history of the latter, Guénonism is truly a new phenomenon: but one possessing great breadth, which today touches minds in all milieus, charmed by the clarity, indeed, the simplifying nature of his thought, which no doubt encourages too readily the abandoning of complex realities, cultural richness, esoteric or otherwise, for the benefit of metaphysical certitudes having the value of dogma. The word "perennialist" from the Latin *philosophia perennis* fits this religious philosophy, which emphasizes the primordial Tradition, mother of all others, understood in Guénon's own particular way. His principal respresentative today is Frithjof Schuon, a Swiss living in the United States, whose influence reaches a very extensive public, especially among intellectuals. (*De l'Unité transcendante des religions*, 1948; *L'Esotérisme comme principe et comme voie*, 1978; *Sur les traces de la religion pérenne*, 1981, etc.) In the wake of Guénon and Schuon (who should be kept distinct because of the differences between them), several striking personalities stand out. In France, Constant Chevillon (1880–1944, who could not have known Schuon), an important figure in Martinism and Masonry (*La Tradition universelle*, 1946), Léo Schaya (*La Création en Dieu*, 1983), philosophers Georges Vallin and Jean Borella: In Italy, Julius Evola (1898–1974), a philosopher of the political extreme right, already mentioned above apropos of alchemy. In Germany, Titus Burckhardt (1908–1984). In England, Martin Lings (*The Eleventh Hour*, 1987), who was Guénon's personal secretary. In the United States, Ananda K. Coomaraswamy (1877–1947), Seyyed Hossein Nasr (*Knowledge and the Sacred*, 1981), Huston Smith (*The Religions of Ma*n, 1958; *Forgotten Truth*, 1976; *Beyond the Post-Modern Mind*, 1982). Among these persons exist differences of perspective that this brief presentation could not take into account but that distinguish them from the two leaders. (For example, we note a genuine *Naturphilosophie* in S.H. Nasr and an authentic Christianity in Jean Borella.)

B. Initiatory Societies

Among the Masonic rites already discussed the Rectified Scottish Rite, the Ancient and Accepted Scottish Rite, and Memphis-Misraïm have been quite active since World War I. In the para-Masonic domain, Martinism fragmented into several orders with a complex history and in which, depending on the branch, ritual from the time of Papus or the theurgy of the Elected-Cohens is still practiced. The brethren of the Societas Rosicruciana in Anglia, limited to regular Masons, pursue initiatory work of a Rosicrucian type behind the discreet cover of their lodges or "Colleges." The Golden Dawn, which, as we saw, came from the Societas Rosicruciana in Anglia, disappeared in its original form at the beginning of the century. The Order of the "Builders of the Adytum," founded by Paul Foster Case (1884–1954) was a kind of prolongation; Hermetism, the Kabbalah, and the Tarot were among its objects of study. The Ordo Templis Orientis (cf. *supra*) saw much development in the United States, especially, with an important center in California.

The symbol of the rose and cross is the object of considerable interest largely overflowing the boundaries of para-masonry. Created in 1915 by Harvey Spencer Lewis (1883–1939), AMORC (Antiquus Mysticus Ordo Rosae Crucis) already had several million members at the time of his death. It is the first mass movement in the history of Western esotericism. Open to the external world and to modernity, it brings to its members both an initiatory path and a culture (numerous conferences, visits to sites, libraries, etc.). The world headquarters in the large A.M.O.R.C. center in San José, California, moved to Omonville, France in 1990. The Lectorium Rosicrucianum (or Golden Rosy Cross) founded at Haarlem, in the Netherlands in 1924 by Jean Leene (alias Jan Van Rijckenborgh, 1896–1968) with an important center at Ussat-les-Bains, France is quite different. This order does much less proselytizing than AMORC. Its teaching is of a type both gnostic (in the sense of ancient gnosticism) and Cathar, rather difficult to blend with traditional Rosicrucianism of the seventeenth century, which is a pansophic current. That is, however, precisely what the thinkers of the Lectorium are trying to do. Among the numerous neoRosicrucians, let us cite also the Italian *Fraternità Terapeutica Magica di Miriam*, created by Ciro Formisano (alias Giuliano Kremmerz, 1861–1930). It has therapeutic aims that join Rosicrucianism and Egyptomania and has had some success since its founder's death. (His *Corpus Philosophorum totius Magiae* was published in 1988/1989.) Many other Rosicrucian Orders exist besides these. (The most complete repertory is found in Massimo Introvigne's book *Il Cappello del Mago*, Milan, 1990.)

The Anthroposophic Society, which in 1923 became the *Allgemeine Anthroposophische Gesellschaft*, has maintained an intense activity that its founder's death did not diminish. As before, Dornach remains a place of rich culture and an illustrious center favored by the success of Steiner schools for children. (The first *Freie Waldorfschule* was established at Stuttgart in 1919.) The same is true for the Theosophical Society whose centers remain very active in the countries where it has taken hold. Its branches, however, are varied. Some of them separated themselves from it to constitute original organizations, such as the Loge Mystique Chrétienne of the Theosophical Society (cf. *supra*), close in spirit to Anna Kingsford and founded by psychoanalyst Violet Mary Firth (alias Dion Fortune, 1890–1946, who belonged to the Golden Dawn). In 1928 it became the Society of the Inner Light, where various forms of sexual and evocatory magic are practiced.

Besides formally constituted associations, there are Fraternities and study associations of every variety. Such is the Grande Fraternité Universelle of Serge Raynaud de la Ferrière (1916–1962), originating in 1947 and especially active in Central and South America; very eclectic, it combines "Precolumbian" teaching with speculations on the Age of Aquarius. It is a mass movement, as is The New Acropolis, founded in the 1950s by the Argentine Angel Livraga (1930–1991). Installed in numerous countries (by Fernand Schwarz in France), The New Acropolis gives courses and edits journals dedicated to the diverse religious traditions of humanity, notably their artistic attributes. In 1952, Colombian Samael Aun Weor (1917–1977) founded the Gnostic Association for Anthropological and Cultural Studies. It too is very eclectic, mixing Buddhism, Tantrism, Steinerian anthroposophy, sexual alchemy, and the teachings of Gurdjieff. Let us cite in conclusion the Atlantis Association and its journal by the same name, founded in 1927 by Paul Le Cour (1871–1954), one of the first to launch the idea of the Age of Aquarius, characterized by Christian esotericism of an eclectic sort, where the myth of Atlantis holds an important place. Still very active, the Atlantis movement is presently led in France by esotericist Jacques d'Arès.

C) *Tradition: A Multifaceted Notion*

To the associations just discussed we could add others, most of which would fall within the purview of New Religious Movements (NRM). Numerous in fact among the NRM—a phenomenon that has broadened considerably in the twentieth century—are those whose teaching or doctrine contains elements of the esoteric type (e.g., the Fraternité Blanche Universelle of Peter Deunov and Mikhael Aïvanhov.) The same is true of the "new therapies" and of the "channeling" or "branching" of entities from beyond (a recent form taken by spiritualism). These diverse orientations belong to the New Age, a diffuse movement that appeared in the 1970s in California, originating in part with Alice Bailey (1880–1949), founder of the Arcane School in 1923. New Age adherents proclaim the coming of a new era, that of Aquarius, characterized by progress under the sign of a rediscovered harmony and an enlarged consciousness.

On the shores of this oceanic landscape, esotericism loses its contours. They dissolve in the fairs of occultism. The "Kohoutek Celebration of Consciousness" at San Francisco in January 1974, was a veritable marketplace filled with unbelievable and improbable bric-a-brac, where all imaginable sciences could be found cheek by jowl, in stands and booths. This was only one of the first manifestations of its type, on a grand scale, in a long series, still ongoing. But the positive aspect of this kind of event, is on one hand, the felt need for "transformation" that motivates its participants, and on the other hand, the opportunity for anyone capable of winnowing to discern the good grain beneath the chaff.

The world of publishing provides group fairs of another type. *Le Matin des magiciens* (1958) by Louis Pauwels and Jacques Bergier, which quickly appeared in several languages, is a typical example. It is a masterpiece of confusionism, an adroit commercial undertaking, successfully supported by the journal *Planète* (1961/1968), whose program consists in presenting metaphysical and religious mysteries as scientific enigma and vice-versa. Even there it is possible on balance to be positive, for the project attracted attention to esoteric aspects of culture and spirituality far too neglected until then. Something else that misleads the public is the political cooption of esoteric themes. It has been proven that theoreticians in or close to Nazism used such themes; they did so in a limited way that has subsequently been exaggerated (cf. the seminal work of Nicholas Goodrick-Clarke, *The Occult Roots of Nazism*, 1985). It is also true, to paraphrase an oft-cited expression, that Nazism was a matter of "esoteric truths gone mad." The meaning of myths can always be subverted. Nevertheless, it should be recognized that there is a natural affinity between some representatives of the Tradition (in its restricted, pure sense) and some movements of the extreme right, but that phenomenon is as new as traditionalism itself, and we saw that in the last century the political orientation of many an esotericist was pointed in the opposite direction.

III) ARTS AND HUMANITIES

A) Esoteric Arts and Literature

In the twentieth century as earlier the presence of esotericism in art and literature is not always the expression of a personal engagement. (It is the same with the fantastic; a good author does not necessarily believe in his or her phantoms). From a vast selection, we list only a few characteristic works, limiting ourselves mainly to explicit esotericism. We see it in three German novelists. Gustav Meyrink (*Der Golem*, 1915; *Das grüne Gesicht*, 1916, etc.) for whom literature served as a platform, has been accorded the triple title of great initiate, excellent fantasy writer, and true novelist. Occultism and *Naturphilosophie* permeate more discreetly several narratives of Hermann Hesse (*Das Glasperlenspiel*, 1943). Magic, occultism, and *Naturphilosophie* are present in *Tödliche Anstösse* by Herbert Kessler (1983). The Anglo-Saxon area is especially rich in the fantastic, with a novel like Lafferty's *Four Mansions*

(1969) as well as the majority of the work of H.P. Lovecraft (1890–1937). In France there are few novels to mention, but of course there are Frédérick Tristan's *L'Homme sans nom*, 1980, and *Les Tribulations de Balthasar Kober*, 1980. It is possible that the Italian Umberto Eco (*Pendolo di Foucault*, 1988) has resuscitated a fictional genre in which occultist esotericism is a privileged reservoir of themes. Here the book is a work of art, a ludic space. It does not pretend to deliver messages. There are also novels that are not in the esoterist purview in which authors like Raymond Abellio and Mircea Eliade have inserted initiatory messages.

Oscar Venceslas Milosz's prose and poetry (*Ars Magna*, 1924; *Les Arcanes*, 1927) display the work of a great initiate and an immense artist. (Along with William Butler Yeats, he is perhaps the most authentically esoteric among the great authors). The Russian writer Alexander Blok (*The Rose and the Cross*, 1915) is close to him in more ways than one. Surrealists have delved into occult sciences (André Breton, *Arcane 17*, 1947; *L'Art magique*, 1957), but the engagement is far more serious in the case of the younger authors of the "Grand Jeu" (René Daumal, *Le Mont Analogue*, 1952). Portuguese Fernando Pessoa's poems and prose pieces are often imbued with esotericism (e.g., *A hora do diabo*, 1931/1932).

In the plastic arts the influence of the Theosophical Society proved deep and lasting (cf. the good retrospective *The Spiritual in Art: Abstract Painting 1890–1985*, 1986). In the work of the German Joseph Anton Schneider-franken (alias Bo-Yin-Râ, 1876–1943), poet, spiritual master (*Das Buch der Gespräche*, 1920), still influential, painting and writing found their inspiration in an esotericism of an Oriental cast. The paintings of Lima de Freitas's latest period give the impression through their figurative character of being surrealistic, but in fact they are distinguished from surrealism by their elaborately developed Neopythagoreanism and their explicit references to esoteric themes of a pervasive spiritual meaning ("Calmo na falsa morte," 1985; "O Jardim dos Hesperides," and "O Túmulo de Christian Rosenkreutz," 1985, etc.) In architecture, let us recall that the Goetheanum, near Basel (cf. *supra*) was rebuilt after its fire in 1922 and that its stained glass windows, inspired by a very anthroposophic symbolism are marvelous. Among the numerous Tarot decks from this century, several demonstrate an attempt of figurative renewal in the fin-de-siècle occultist fashion ("Cartomancia Lusso"; Pamela Coleman Smith's "Rider-Waite Trot," Frieda Harris's "Thot Tarot," 1940, inspired by A. Crowley.) The quite figurative art in color plates and illustrations for Anglo-Saxon books on esotericism feature an original combination of modern style with Neo-Romanticism and deserve study (e.g., Manly Hall's *The Secret Teaching of All Ages*, 1928).

Musical esotericism is difficult to discuss other than with respect to theories expounded by the composers, but when such theories exist, we can expect to find them in the works. This is the case with Cyril Scott (*Music: Its*

Secret Influence Throughout the Ages, 1933) or Karlheinz Stockhausen (*Texte zur Musik*, 1970/1977). In cinema there would be little to say, except considering the esoteric exegeses the films can inspire. Explicit esotericism is relatively rare. In 1920 Henrik Galeen used the theme that had just inspired Meyrink in *Der Golem*, but the film dealt chiefly with the fantastic, more than with the novel or the Jewish esoteric tradition of the Golem. Cinema can represent explicit occultism, but it is ill-suited to the expression of the esoteric form of thought, except by the use of oblique means, e.g., filming some initiatory projects as in Peter Brook's *Meetings with Remarkable Men*, 1978. Nevertheless, the titles of four fine works with strong alchemical connotations blend in other references of an esoteric cast: Stanley Kubrick's *2001. A Space Odyssey*, 1968; John Boorman's *Excalibur*, 1983; Russel Mulcahy's *Highlander*, 1986; George Lucas' celebrated *Star Wars*, 1977, and its sequels.

B) Psychology and Humanities

Some of Freud's thinking is rooted in Romantic *Naturphilosophie*, which discovered the unconscious, but it goes to Hermann Silberer to have been the first to give a psychoanalytic reading to alchemical texts in *Probleme der Mystik und ihrer Symbolik*, 1914. However, it was Carl Gustav Jung (1875–1961) who was the great explorer of the psychological treasures of the esoteric corpus, especially the alchemical corpus (*Psychologie und Alchemie*, 1926/1952; *Mysterium Conjunctionis*, 1955/1956, etc.). His nonreductionist turn of thought allowed him to discover how alchemical transmutation and the symbolism of its marked course correspond to a highly positive work—because transformative—of the psyche in search of its own edification or harmonization and of its *individuation*. Moreover, his theory of archetypes—or primordial images universally present and belonging to our species as a whole—which led him to posit the existence of a *collective unconscious*, also universal, has revealed the isomorphy of images and symbols whose linkage had scarcely been noted before. Putting these common denominators into perspective in this way allowed the form of thought that is esotericism to be situated in an anthropological context that transcends it and thereby demarcates its specificity all the better.

An admirer of Jung and Bachelard, Gilbert Durand selects, like them, from the repertory of esotericism (although not from there alone) something to nourish his reflections on the "anthropological structures of the imaginary" (to recall the title of his book of 1960). At the same time he goes further than Jung and Bachelard by positing the imaginary—and the mythic—as the first irreducible element capable of accounting for the diverse forms of our mind's activity, the rational being only one among others. Few university faculty have contributed so much to bringing the esoteric corpus out of its ghetto and giving it keys to the city of the humanities. (Jung had brought it into the immense field of psychology.) In this enterprise, G. Durand is served by a personal engagement with the "traditional" type (though not in the sense of "perennialist") and by a vast breadth of culture (*Sciences de l'Homme et Tradition*, 1975; *Figures mythiques et visages de l'oeuvre*, 1979; *Beaux-Arts et archétypes*, 1989, etc.)

Some philosophers are pursuing a somewhat similar path by introducing the esoteric corpus into their field of reflection, either to lead philosophy back to its vocation of spiritual exigency and the transmuting practice of our being (François Bonardel, *L'Hermétisme*, 1985; *Philosophie de l'Alchimie*, 1993), or to open classical logics to new approaches (Jean-Jacques Wunenburger, *La Raison contradictoire*, 1990), or to link metaphysics and psychology (Robert J.W. Evans, *Imaginal Body*, 1982; *The New Gnosis*, 1984). It is not an accident, moreover, if in our times psychology and esotericism keep close ties. At the heart of a universe for a long time bereft of consciousness and a human community deprived of ideologies, even ideals, modern man and woman must confront their individuality alone. In this sense we can be said to live in a "psychological" epoch. Esoteric traditions bring to the knowledge of self an approach that does not depend on prior adherence to a belief system or an ethical system but one which is able to confer meaning on the universe and on our lives. This is how esotericism now indirectly penetrates the contemporary public on a large scale through therapy. From whence the success of gurus such as Gurdjieff or those who know how to translate his jargon into clear language (e.g., John G. Bennett, *Gurdieff: Meeting a New World*, 1973).

It is no accident either if human sciences like anthropology, history of religions, etc., are open to esotericism and vice versa. Pico della Mirandola's *Discourse* on human "dignity" has once more become an actuality. It is incumbent on humanity to engage in continuous redefinition to discover or rediscover its place within Nature and within a universal culture and society. The magisterial work of Mircea Eliade (1907–1986), anthropologist and historian of religions, responds well to this double demand of culture and universality. According to him the first demand represents today the indispensable detour for entering into any "initiation" worthy of the name. The second, understood as the intelligence of differences as much as resemblances, is as removed from narrow historicism as from artificial universalism, abstract or disincarnate. No exclusivism either, in that corpus, which gives to esoteric currents the place they deserve (*Histoire des croyances et des idées religieuses*, 1976/1983; *Occultism. Witchcraft and Cultural Fashion*, 1976, etc.).

C) *Historians of Esotericism*

This aspect of Eliade's corpus represents the bridge that connects anthropology and history. No doubt this was a unique enterprise in its ambition and its breadth, but increasingly general histories and encyclopedias devote a specific chapter or specific entries to esotericism. Although we often find in them the details we seek for a given author or current (cf. *supra*), their mediocrity is often evinced in their lack of clear discernment of their subject. Let us note also the existence of collections and series which, while not specializing in esotericism, properly speaking, nevertheless contain mines of information and references, like the *Eranos Jahrbücher* (1933/1988) or the *Cahiers de l'Université de Saint-Jean de Jérusalem* (1975/1988) .

There are important specialized journals also. For alchemy we have the very scientific *Ambix* (England, 1937—), *Cauda Pavonis* (U.S.A., 1974—), *Chrysopoeia* (France, 1987—), *The Hermetic Journal* (England, 1978—); *La Tourbe des Philosophes* (France, 1977—) devoted partly to operative alchemy; and *Le Fil d'Ariane*, Belgium, 1977—). The French university journal *Politica Hermetica* and the Association of the same name (1984—) are devoted to the history of relationships between esotericism and politics. In France, likewise, the goal of the journal *A.R.I.E.S.* (1985—) is to report on research, recently completed or in progress. The German journal *Hermetika* (1983—) specializes in translations and exegeses of hermetic and hermetist texts.

Among historians, there are specialists for one author or current and generalists. Among the specialists, Auguste Viatte did a pioneer work in weeding the garden of Illuminism (*Les Sources occultes du Romantisme*, 1928). After the very focused works of André-Jean Festugière on hermetic texts (*La Révélation d'Hermès Trismégiste*, 1949/1954) and his scientific presentation of the *Corpus Hermeticum* (1954/1960), the modern hermetist tradition has been studied in the seminal works of scholars like Frances A. Yates (*Giordano Bruno and the Hermetic Tradition*, 1964), Daniel P. Walker (*Spiritual and Demonic Magic*, 1969), Cesare Vasoli, Eugenio Garin, and others, not to mention the works of Rolf Christian Zimmermann on Goethe's hermeticism (1969/1979). Robert Halleux's works on ancient alchemy presently are stimulating several investigators more specialized in the modern period. The monumental work of Gershom Scholem has opened horizons that go beyond the Jewish Kabbalah strictly speaking, a domain in which the main scholar today is Moshe Idel. François Secret has devoted some of his work, which is voluminous and of the highest scientific quality, to the Christian Kabbalists (*Les kabbalistes chrétiens de la Renaissance*, 1962). Paracelsus and Paracelsism are now much better known thanks to Walter Pagel and Kurt Goldammer, as well as to Allen Debus (*The Chemical Philosophy*, 1977). The Rosicrucian current of the seventeenth century is better known thanks to Roland Edighoffer (*Rose-Croix et société idéale*, 1982/1987) and Carlos Gilly, and one cannot forget the penetrating studies of Ernst Benz, Bernard Gorceix, Pierre Deghaye, Jacques Fabry, and Jules Keller on many aspects of Germanic theosophy. Guénonism likewise was the object of a historico-critical examination (cf. Jean-Pierre Laurant's works especially since 1975). Finally, the list of all those who work on the relations between esotericism and literature or art would be long (Jean

Richer, Alain Mercier, James Dauphiné, Yves Vadé, Charles Nicholl, Lyndy Abraham, etc.), or of all those who edit texts and documents (like Stuart R. Kaplan, *The Encyclopedia of Tarot*, 1978/1990).

Among the works of generalists many of whom of course are specialists also, we find the monumental encyclopedia established by Lynn Thorndike (*A History of Magic and Experimental Science*, 1933/1958, 8 vols.), which remains an indispensable research tool despite its outdated rationalism. More focused, but also encyclopedic, are the trilogies of Karl R.H. Frick (*Licht und Finsternis* and *Die Erleuchteten*, I, II, 1973/1978), devoted especially to esoteric societies, and James Webb (*The Occult Underground*, 1974; *The Occult Establishment*, 1976; *The Harmonious Circle*, 1980) on currents of the past 150 years. J. Gordon Melton has established detailed bibliographies on magico-religious currents in the U.S., but with him especially we arrive on the shores of the continent of New Religious Movements. If this domain sometimes blends with the esoteric field, we have seen that it is also distinct from it. However, NRM specialist Massimo Introvigne has just brought out the finest study devoted to all magic currents and societies of the West since 1850 (*Il Cappello del Mago*, 1990). One of the most eminent university scholars in our discipline, Joscelyn Godwin, pursues with equal felicitousness, a two-pronged research program. A specialist in musical esotericism, he covers a period spread out over several centuries in this domain (*Harmonies of Heaven and Earth*, 1987; *L'Esotérisme musical en France*, 1991, etc.), devotes himself also to authors and currents of diverse epochs (numerous publications, notably on Robert Fludd, Athanasius Kircher, fin-de-siècle esotericism, etc.).

Among the generalists are found likewise esoterologists anxious to grant status to their discipline. First of all, Robert Amadou (already cited), a great scholar of this material, a specialist in Saint-Martin, and an indefatigable archivist. Next is Gerhard Wehr, an author who through a series of high-quality monographs tries to harmonize R. Steiner, C.G. Jung, Novalis, and Boehme, and knows how to sketch on occasion an interesting tableau of Christian esotericism (*Esoterisches Christentum*, 1975). Finally Pierre A. Riffard (*L'Esotérisme*, 1990), is the first to have seriously attempted a coherent methodological approach to the notion of esotericism (cf. *supra*, *Methodology*). Students are aided by excellent libraries. Besides the already important collections in the world's largest libraries, they have specialized collections available also, among which the Bibliotheca Philosophica Hermetica of Joseph R. Ritman in Amsterdam merits special mention. Now open to investigators, it brings together some 15,000 titles (from the fifteenth to the beginning of the twentieth centuries), divided into five large sections: Alchemy, Hermetism, Kabbalah, Theosophy, and Rosicrucianism.

BOOK TWO

STUDIES IN ESOTERICISM

.

FAITH AND KNOWLEDGE IN
FRANZ VON BAADER AND
IN MODERN GNOSIS*

Faith and knowledge. *Glaube und Wissen.* . . . There are kindred spirits for whom the two notions are indissociable. All the Gnostic thinkers belong to this group, in the larger sense, although there also exists a form of gnosis without faith. Among the "Gnostics," those who are called "theosophers" in our modern Christianity link closely together faith and knowledge, belief and understanding.

THE STAKES

St. Paul juxtaposes these two notions: "Now faith is the assurance (*substantia*) of things hoped for, the conviction (*argumentum*) of things not seen. . . . By faith we understand (*intellegimus*) that the world was created by the word of God, so that what is seen was made out of things that do not appear." (Heb. XI:1–3)[1] And the *Dictionnaire de Théologie Catholique* defines "faith" as an intellectual assent, although produced through the influence of the will. But then, in what does one have faith? In the risen Christ, according to the revealed writings; from that point on, there is no faith without a certain conventional teaching, simple though it may be, to which we give our assent, therefore without "knowledge." But "knowledge" is focused on what? On the relationship between that event (the Incarnation, the Resurrection) and myself, but also between it and the world and, consequently, on the henceforth quite peculiar nature of the relationship between myself and the world.

---

* Paper presented at the Conference of the "Centre d'Etudes Supérieures de la Renaissance" in Tours, May 1976.
1. Holy Bible, Revised Standard Version.

According to my temperament, I feel myself from then on fundamentally implicated, either on the moral plane (works) or on that of understanding, or on both planes at once. For many believers, faith can only make knowledge desirable, for they aspire to understand what they love and, at the same time, their love is a means of understanding. What is it that will ever allow them to understand better? The teaching received, reflection, and illumination. The degree to which each of these three means of understanding is present gives each believer a unique religious position, all the more specific in that the apprenticeship of understanding or (and) the skill—the ability to act, whether one is speaking of social commitment or of theurgy—are, for certain individuals, inseparable from understanding itself. That is why faith, which does not go without involvement of the being often appears as "knowledge" in movement, that is, as an ever deeper comprehension of Holy Writ, which is at once the object and the instrument of understanding.

First, one has faith; next, one reads the texts. But that is not always true and the reverse is perhaps often true. No matter: what is essential for the flowering of faith in and through the knowledge to which the text invites us is the practice of reading at different levels: the literal, the allegorical, the anagogical. The theosopher is mostly interested in the third level, in the attempt to trace backward, to take the scriptural datum back to its original meaning, to originate it thanks to inner illumination and to speculation based on homologies—*imaginatio vera*, which is presented as the hermeneutic par excellence, that *tâ'wil* that Henry Corbin mentions with respect to the Shiite theosophers. That is why Christian theosophy tends so much to identify understanding and salvation, remembering that St. Paul himself seems to excuse his own daring: "the mind scrutinizes everything, even the depths of divinity. . . ."

The theologian and the theosopher, those two men who may have the same faith, do not resemble each other completely. The dissimilarity has to do with the nature of knowing and the methods that lead to it. The theologian tries to define faith, and he reasons on the data of belief, their implications in men's lives. He tries to specify, to delimit, to circumscribe. The theosopher does not distinguish himself from the object of his study; for him, every increase in knowledge is accompanied by a change in his being. He proceeds by identification; he plays in cosmic dramas. The discourse that he offers, the "recitative" that he entones, does not appear to be his own work, but rather that of an angel whose appendage he is. In his boundless work, he invents—locates—the articulation of archetypes and mythemes, he mimes the role of spirits, men, and elements. In particular, he is immediately interested in Nature observed in its infinitesimal details in order to grasp the homologies among all levels of the visible and invisible world.

The constitution of a profane science, resolutely separated from other domains of knowledge, resulted in alienating ideologies. It was against that separation that many theosophers were to rebel by developing a *Naturphilosophie* to which they were predisposed by one of the profound callings of theosophy: their interest in Nature and all its manifestations. The Reformation brought no remedy to this segregation, no more than it did to the subordination—which turned out to be artificial—of being and value under the "principles" of History. This Reformation limited itself to an attack on the separation of the sacred into a privileged category among cultural values.[2] On the other hand, if scholastic thought gave credit to reason and human freedom, its problem remained essentially that of knowing God within the framework of a philosophy preoccupied by the Platonic Logos and, especially, by an Aristotelian rationalism. Luther tried to oppose the irrational principal of faith to the rational principal of understanding: one may believe without understanding; one obeys upon hearing the call of the Word. The abyss between reason and faith simply became larger, but since Luther had gotten rid of rational understanding, some Lutherans turned naturally toward theosophy, seeking understanding through the marriage of speculation with illumination. The "organic" quality of Luther's thought has been noted in attempts to show that the fact of alchemical and even astrological speculation among Lutherans was not at all surprising.[3] Nevertheless, Lutherans today still set the *Naturphilosophie* of a Paracelsus against the theology of the omnipresence of Christ in the natural world and, in a general way, against the theology of Revelation.[4] A book like *The Chemical Wedding of Christian Rosenkreuz* (1616), by J.V. Andreae, more easily finds favor in the eyes of a Lutheran like J.W. Montgomery, who sees in the alchemical aspect of the work a legitimate application of faith to science and the possibility for science to account for faith, but Montgomery favors the theological level over that of alchemy (and, naturally, over psychology).[5]

Faith illuminated by a knowledge of Nature is in fact more an idea dear to Paracelsus—that famed physician and contemporary of Luther, who was quite indifferent with respect to formal religion and who cannot be considered to be Lutheran. All later theosophy was to retain his theory of the two torches; that of Nature, recognizable by its "signatures" (*signatura*), and that of the Bible (or grace). God wants to be recognized by His works. In the same

---

2. Cf. Gilbert Durand, *Science de l'Homme et Tradition, Le Nouvel esprit anthropologique*, (Paris, Sirac-"Tête de feuille", 1975, and Berg International, 1980).

3. John Warwick Montgomery, *Cross and Crucible; J.V. Andreae, Phoenix of the Theologians*, (La Haye, Nijhoff, 1973) t. I, p. 21: "Luther's thought was profoundly 'organic' in character, as Joseph Sittler has shown in his *Structure of Christian Ethics* (Baton Rouge, La., Louisiana State Univ. Press, 1958, cited by Montgomery on p. 21).

4. This is the case of Montgomery, op. cit., t. I, p. 197 ff.

5. Ibid., t. II, p. 273 ff.

light, Figulus (*Pandora magnalium naturalium aurea*, 1607) says that there are three books: Nature (the macrocosm), Humanity (the microcosm), and the Bible. That is because the works of Nature present, even in an incomplete fashion, the visible reflection of the invisible work of God. Nature showers us with signs by means of which God gives us the privilege of a fleeting glimpse of His Wisdom and of His *magnalia*: "In eternal matters, it is faith that makes works visible; in invisible bodies, it is the light of Nature that reveals invisible things.⁶" According to Paracelsus, experience (*Erfahrung*), should demonstrate every day the inanity of any pseudo-understanding founded only on logical reasoning (*logika*): "*Je gelehrter je verkehrter!*" In order to know God and to know how to cure illnesses, the quest for *sigilla* and for the invisible forces of Nature is more valuable than purely abstract reflection. What God has created contains in fact more knowledge (*Wissen und Erkenntnis*) than we possess in our isolated reason. Therefore, we discover God in His creation, just as all the parts of the universe are represented in Man—while the unaided formal logic professed by Aristotle or Galen, remains inappropriate for the study of Nature and even contradicts it.

For Friedrich Christoph Oetinger, the greatest German theosopher of the eighteenth century, the essence of personal religion is the *cognitio centralis*, which helps the Christian to see beyond the inevitable polarities of existence and, thus to find peace and joy in the recognition of the divine intention of ultimate harmony.⁷ In his *Etymologisches und emblematisches Wörterbuch*, Oetinger reserved one entry for *Wissen* and another for *Glaube*. "To know," he says, "is to see (to understand, to penetrate) a thing according to all its parts."⁸ Thus, Novalis was to say, superstition consists in taking the part for the Whole—and even for God himself.⁹ In the article "*Glaube*," Oetinger explains that faith consists principally "not in suppressing the syllogistic order of thought but in enlivening it."¹⁰ Novalis occasionally used a key word, *Illudieren*. Faith is *Illudieren*, which means that one posits an idea by hypothesis and the imagination while waiting for its possible verification. All true

---

6. Cited by Walter Pagel, *Paracelsus, an Introduction to Philosophical Medicine in the era of the Renaissance*, (Basel/New York, S. Karger, 1958) p. 67. "In den Ewigen dingen macht der Glaube alle Werk sichtbar: in den leiblichen unsichtbarlichen dingen macht das liecht der Natur alle ding sichtbar" (cited in ibid. p. 126).

7. Cf. good summary by F. Ernest Stoeffler, *German Pietism During the Eighteenth Century*, (Leyden: E.J. Brill, 1973) p. 116.

8. *Etymologisches und emblematisches Wörterbuch*, 1776: (reed. Hildesheim, Olms) 1969.

9. Theodor Haering, *Novalis als Philosoph*, (Stuttgart, Kohlhammer, 1954) chap. x.

10. Oetinger, op. cit., article "Glaube": "Gott und die syllogistische Ordnung der Gedanken nicht aufheben, sondern beleben" (Gal. III, 21).

knowledge supposes this anticipation (a priori) of true knowledge: Faith (belief) is knowledge from a distance, but knowledge is knowledge (understanding) of the present. The success of knowledge rests then on the power of faith, which arms and reinforces our energy. Here Novalis surpasses the teaching of the Epistle to the Hebrews; for him, it is not so much a matter of hope as of certainty. He later writes: "Faith is the action of the will on the intelligence"; and this statement is surprising for any person with even a superficial grasp of German Romanticism: "I am persuaded that through an unadorned technical intelligence and a calm moral sense, one may better arrive at true revelations than through the imagination (i.e., fantasy), which seems to lead us simply to the kingdom of phantoms, that antipode of the true heaven."[11] Indeed, everything remains as a simple belief or illusion, error and falsity, in as much as one is unable to link that which is established to the ultimate whole—to the absolute. This is why knowledge (*Erkennen*) seems like a widening (*Erweiterung*), a *Hinausschiebung*, of the domain of faith, which supposes that new intermediaries be established (*Setzen neuer Vermittelungen*); these resulting intermediaries (*Mittelresultate des Prozesses*) constitute the essential part of the cognitive process, which thus becomes a continuing faith (*fortgesetzter Glaube*). If this infinite always imprecise process were to stop, knowledge itself would cease to exist.[12]

FRANZ VON BAADER

Among the thinkers of modern Christian gnosis, it is perhaps Franz von Baader who spoke most of the connections between faith and knowledge. Several of his tracts, in their very titles, testify to the importance he gave to this topic of reflection: *Everything which opposes the entry of religion into the region of knowledge, or which does not favor that entry, stems from evil* (1825); *On the need, introduced by our era, for a more intimate relationship between science and religion* (1825); *On the attitude of knowledge towards Faith* (1833); *On the division between belief and religious knowledge—spiritual root of the decadence of religious and political society in our era as in all times* (1833); *On the binding tie which unites*

---

11. Above all, cf. Th. Haering, op. cit., p. 332 s. "Glauben ist Wirken des Willens auf die Intelligenz. Ich bin überzeugt, daß man durch kalten technischen Verstand und durch ruhigen moralischen Sinn eher zu wahren Offenbarungen gelangt, als durch Phantasie, die uns bloß ins Gespensterreich, diesen antipoden des wahren Himmels, zu leiten scheint" (quoted in ibid., p. 334).

12. Ibid., p. 96.

religious science and the natural sciences (1834).[11] He takes up this topic in other works as well, of course, and it is fitting that Eugène Susini, in his thesis on Franz von Baader, devotes a chapter to the "problem of knowledge" in Baader.[14] We shall limit ourselves here to certain essential points, taken from various places in his work, that are significant in terms of Baader's gnostic thought, including several of which, to the best of my knowledge, have not been raised before.

Baader takes up the Baconian idea of *harmonia luminis naturae et gratiae* in order to give himself a solid foundation consistent with the organicist aspect of his own theosophy.[15] This project manifests itself as early as his youthful writings, and one can join Susini in saying that "*toute l'oeuvre de Baader à partir de 1822 notamment. lutte pour la réconciliation de ces deux aspects de la vie de l'esprit: spéculation et croyance.*"[16] ("Baader's entire work, especially from 1822 on, struggles to reconcile these two aspects of the life of the mind: speculation and belief.") To Pascal's phrase: "*Toute notre dignité consiste en la pensée,*" ("All our dignity rests in thought") Baader adds that to think is the very nature of humanity and that Mephisto hates speculation.[17] The attitude preached by Mephisto entails a divorce between faith and knowledge, the consequences of which make themselves felt in other domains; it is the beginning of decay, whether individual or collective.[18] For Baader, all research starts with faith—contrary, he notes, to Descartes and to "all our philosophers" who begin with doubt or disbelief; for faith awakens research, carries it, guides it, assists it. Rousseau's *bon mot* ("*On cesse de sentir quand on commence à penser*") is false.[19] It is also dangerous because it contributes, Baader says as early as 1794, to the edification of one moral and religious system for the

---

13. *Alles, was dem Eindringen der Religion in die Region des Wissens sich widersetzt oder selbes nicht fördert, ist vom Bösen* (1825); *Ueber das durch unsere Zeit herbeigeführte Bedürfnis einer innigern Vereinigung der Wissenschaft und der Religion* (1825); *Ueber das Verhalten des Wissens zum Glauben* (1833); *Ueber den Zwiespalt des religiösen Glaubens und Wissens als der geistigen Wurzel des Verfalls der religiösen und politischen Societät in unserer wie in jeder Zeit* (1833). *Ueber den solidären Verband der Religionswissenschaft mit der Naturwissenschaft* (1834).
14. Eugène Susini, *Franz von Baader et le romantisme mystique. III. La philosophie de Franz von Baader*, t. II, (Paris, J. Vrin, 1942) cf. especially pp. 71 to 133. Cf. as well Staudenmaier, "Ueber das Verhalten des Wissens sum Glauben bei Fr. von Baader", pp. 179–181, in *Jahrbücher für Theologie und christliche Philosophie*, 2, 1834.
15. Cf notably *Ueber den solidären Verband . . .* , op. cit., t. III.
16. E. Susini, op. cit., p. 84.
17. Cf. ibid., p. 102.
18. *Sämtliche Werke*, edited by Franz Hoffmann, 1851/1860, see *Index*, t. XVI: "Glaube." Mephisto is here the figure in Goethe's *Faust*.
19. Ibid., VI, 139 ff. Baader cites this phrase of Rousseau's several times in his work: "We cease to feel when we begin to think."

head, and another for the heart, so that the true, concentrated light itself burns more strongly than the *chaleur sombre* (dark heat).[20] He will add later that love and knowledge (*Erkenntnis*), which is light, become true only in their marriage or solidification. In the same way that glass allows rays of light to pass through it, but not rays of heat, and thus yields to us only an unreal light, so a fire bound in shadows is but a devouring incandescence. If the head is the organ of light, the heart is that of feeling—of heat.[21]

One must proceed boldly: rather than spending one's time wondering if and how one can and should swim, it is better to jump into the water, invoking the name of God instead of surrounding oneself with instruments for learning.[22] Feeling and philosophy are linked: "The more superficial the feeling, the more superficial the speculation.[23] Similarly, "feeling and knowledge, faith and contemplation (*Schauen*), do not exclude but complete and reveal each other in their solidification.[24] Baader has only disdain for purely sentimental mysticism, which he often calls "pietism" and which he comes to qualify (in French) as "*religion des femmelettes*" ("religion of the womanish"). He never ceases to repeat that "science" should invigorate religious feeling and that in the nineteenth century, it is a difficult task to keep oneself as far from the pious lambs as from the impious goats.[25] Belief is an homage, an expression of admiration (*obsequium*) that stems from the rational order. In his study devoted to Lamennais, he refers to a phrase from Scripture ("*rationabile sit obsequium vestrum*") and observes that "rational faith" (*Denkglaube*) (from Professor Paulus) does not appear to him to be a new concept. We are a long way from "Credo quia absurdum. " By invoking the authority of Theodoret, Baader is also saying that blind faith is the source of all errors, of all misfortunes in the church.[26] In still more interesting fashion, he explains in his *On the attitude of knowledge towards faith* that humankind knows only to the extent that it knows "the known." In effect, Plato says that the spiritual eye sees and discovers only through another spiritual eye. In the same way, our knowledge is not obtained, as the rationalists say, *per generationem aequivocam*, nor from ourselves, but *per traducem*, that is, through real participation and insertion

---

20. SW, XI, 434.
21. SW, IX, 11; XI, 284 ff.
22. SW, VIII, 205.
23. "Je flacher das Gefühl, desto flacher die Spekulation," ibid., VIII, 187, cited in E. Susini, op. cit., p. 93; see also SW, VIII, 207.
24. "Gefühl und Wissen Glauben und Schauen treiben sich nicht einander aus, sondern ergänzen und bewähren sich in ihrer Concretheit." (SW, IX, 305).
25. Cf. p. ex. SW, XV, 405, 419.
26. Ibid., SW, X, 190.

(*Theilhaftwerden, Eingerücktwerden*), in—and into—a vision and a knowledge that exist and concern us a priori. Their original, superior, or central nature manifests itself to the individual, interiorly and exteriorly, by its stability (its ubiquitousness, and its "sempiternity"). The center and the periphery, internal and external "testimony," secret and public events, neither can nor should ever be separated. Malebranche is right ; for him we see everything through God, through a divine eye lost with the Fall but opened again to us by the Revelation, and which we rarely make use of, preferring to use our animal eye. "I am seen, therefore I see," says Father Bautain. I am thought, therefore I think! I am wanted—desired, loved—therefore I want, I desire, I love. Just as my movements lean on something mobile—for that which is content itself to resist me merely holds me up without giving me any real support—so the motivation of my will must itself be a will; thus the free movements of my reason must be of a more reasonable nature, knowing better how to understand me, and how to be understood by me.[27] As early as 1822, Baader writes in *Fermenta cognitionis* that Man's faith in God rests on the knowledge that we are to be seen, known, and as if pierced (*durchgesehen*) by someone we do not see.

The homological rapprochements Baader uses so liberally illuminate his thought in a poetical way. Here I think of certain passages he devotes to light, most notably when he explains in 1834 that all light is itself a vision or an eye, just as the eye is a light—even though logicians and opticians persist in speaking of a light that would itself be blind. "He who planted the ear, does he not hear?" Franz Hoffman will say in his commentary on Baader. "He who formed the eye, does he not see?" (Ps. 94:9; Prov. 20:12.) And Baader notes that Christ did not believe, but beheld (*schaute*)—this is why we can believe only in him. He is the contemplator (*Schauender*), the light of the world![28] It is not then an obscure, subjective, or incommunicable feeling, but a communicable knowledge, which is the foundation of Faith, the condition, Baader says in 1828 in his *Course in speculative dogmatics*. Without this knowledge, one could not speak of the obligatory nature (*Verbindlichkeit*) of faith, nor of any faith as law, nor of any disbelief as sin. Faith and knowledge are like movement and rest. Humanity can only believe by knowing, can only know by believing. Only one must not seek to believe where it is necessary to know, nor want to know where one should believe. The object of faith being a doctrine (a knowledge) or a fact, faith is not opposed to disbelief any more than knowledge is opposed to ignorance; true faith opposes false faith, true knowl-

---

27. SW, I, 348; cf. also p. 369 ff. Father Bautain is the author of *Enseignement de la philosophie en France*, Strasbourg, 1833.

28. SW, VI, 106 ff.

edge, false knowledge.[29] It is an error of theologians and philosophers, he writes in 1832, to say that learned (*wissend*) disbelief opposes ignorant faith, for one can refuse to believe in one thing only if one believes in something else.[30] In his 1833 study devoted to the connections between belief and knowledge, Baader returns to the notion of movement: belief is to knowledge what movement is to its foundation (*Begründung*). To accept support in order to move, to find a motive for free will—this represents the role of faith in the practice of reason (*Grund* in the natural realm corresponds to *Beweggrund* in the realm of the will). Let us recall a passage already presented by Susini: "I affirm that, just as one cannot move freely without taking a foundation, and just as one cannot take a foundation without moving freely, so one cannot make use of one's reason unless one believes freely, and believes without making use of one's reason."[31] This is an affirmation that appears to be inseparable from his theory of foundation. In his *Addendum to My Writing on the Quaternary of Life*, a text which he sent to G.H. von Schubert in 1818, he declares his agreement with Schirmer stating that thought (*das Denken*) is nothing else but "the faculty reassembling itself in the One," "the entry into self."[32] The entry (*Einkehren*) into self assumes a previous scattering—an "abyssality," as Boehme says—that is an *Ungrund*. The latter is situated at a lower level than union (*Einigung*) or foundation (*Grund*), for the foundation is always higher than that which depends on it—that which is carried, founded (*begründet*) in it. This autofoundation, this foundation (*Selbstergründung Begründung*), must therefore be considered as an elevation (*Selbsterhöhung Selbstpotenzierung*), as is suggested by Oetinger, and Saint-Martin in *L'esprit des choses* (t. I).[33]

As early as his 1786 journal, written in strongly lyrical accents (he is twenty-one at the time) Baader exclaims, "O if only my soul were the perfect image of divinity, of light, of the sun, which illuminates and warms everything about itself!" The next day, he adds that the feelings he experiences are no

---

29. SW, VIII, 28 ff.
30. SW, VI, 66.
31. E. Susini, op. cit., p. 132. "Ich behaupte, daß, so wie man sich nicht frei bewegen kann ohne Grund zu fassen, und wie man nicht Grund fassen kann ohne freies Bewegen, man auch seine Vernunft nicht gebrauchen kann ohne frei zu glauben, und nicht glauben kann, ohne von seiner Vernunft Gebrauch zu machen." (SW, I, 344).
32. "Das Denken," writes Schirmer, "selbst aber ist nichts anderes als das in Eins sich sammelnde Vermögen, das Sichbesinnen und Einkehren in sich." (cited by Baader in SW, XV, 349). This sentence is taken from Schirmers 1818 book *Versuch einer Würdigung des Supranaturalismus und Naturalismus*.
33. SW, XV, 349

longer thoughts lingering painfully in his brain, whose fibers they would burn (*durchglühen*). On the contrary, the light, finally reassembled as in a central foyer (*Brennpunkt*) transforms itself into a heat that flows sweetly through his entire being.[34] Thus we find the notion of foundation already posited here, and its significance is made more explicit in an 1835 text. There, Baader writes that the Hebrew word *bara*, which means "to create," is present as *bar* in the German *offenbar* (manifest), *gebären* (to beget), *Gebärde* (movement, gesture), etc., the root indicating a "placing in light" (*Inslichtsetzen*) or a discovery, and at the same time an upheaval that connotes uprooting at an unfathomable depth; a "foundation" that makes it possible to distinguish between the corporealizing, substantiating force of fire filled with light, and the decorporealizing force of fire that is void of light.[35] Faithful to his habit, he turns to etymology to make himself understood (little matter that etymology is at times scientifically fanciful, for it has the merit of clarifying his thought and proposing to us themes that are rich in reflection). For example, he places such terms as *glauben* (to believe), *geloben* (to promise solemnly), and *verloben* (to betroth) side by side.[36] The comparison with *verloben* is from Windischmann; this word signifies "to join," "to marry" (*sich verbinden, vermählen, eingeben*). A "promise" that supposes a will. No faith without will. But he substitutes for Saint Augustine's "*Nemo credit nisi volens*," "*Nemo vult nisi videns*," and he renders the German dictum "*Trau schau wem*" with "*Vide cui fidas*."[37] Baader does not omit noting that in *Andacht* (pious introspection) there is *denken* (to think). St. Peter in effect asks his community to give a rational foundation to its faith, by being always ready to defend itself in the face of any claim made by reason against the hope that exists in each of the community members (1 Pet. 3:15).[38] Our theosopher also compares the word *Manu*, the Hindu father of humanity, with the Sanskrit root *man* (to know), and notes that in Sanskrit the words *Manischa* (knowledge) and Manuschla (man) reveal the same analogy—just as one finds in Latin and English with *mens* and *mind*, and in German with *Mensch* (Man). Thus the word "man" meant "he who knows."[39] *Anerkennung*, impossible to translate precisely, includes, as Susini notes, the word *erkennen* (to know, to recognize) "and expresses at once the idea of believing in something and the idea of approving." *Anerkennung* is a

---

34. SW, XI, 25.
35. SW, IV, 279. For other passages relative to the "*Begründung*," cf. E. Susini, op. cit., t. XVI, Index.
36. SW, I, 364.
37. SW, I, 342 ff., 304.
38. Cf. Susini, op. cit., p. 100; cf. also SW, X, 23, note.
39. Cf. Susini, op. cit., p. 103; SW, I, 237.

synthesis of belief and admiration. The devil and the angel knew of (*erkennen*) God's superiority over them, but the angel acknowledged (*anerkennen*) this superiority, whereas the devil refused its "adhesion" (*Anerkennung*).[40] *Si non credideritis non intelligetis,*" Baader says, writing also that faith is the affectivity of knowledge.[41]

He often blames the philosophers who do not wish to articulate the two notions of faith and knowledge. Such is the case with Kant, Jacobi, and Herbart.[42] Faith is not a Kantian postulate.[43] Jacobi and Rousseau are too anti-rationalist;[44] along with them, Kant contributed to the development, in many, of a timidness where speculation is concerned.[45] For Descartes, all philosophy is foreign to Revelation. Hegel declared that one acquires a concept under the condition that one excludes affectivity—whereas the rational and the affective are irreconcilable only with an affectivity that is the enemy of reason, the only affectivity imagined by Hegel. Let us know, on the contrary, that Man does not guarantee his liberty by isolating himself, *à la* Robinson; he would then resemble an industry that renounced all capital, all credit.[46] Moreover, the opposition of the supernatural (or suprarational) and the "counternatural," or the antirational, is the cause of the consistent error of artificially opposing rationalism to supernaturalism: that which surpasses my nature or my knowledge, is not necessarily above that nature or that knowledge.[47] Cartesian doubt is thus quite far from the attitude of Paracelsus, for whom belief is the act by which the subject who believes opens himself in order to receive,[48] and we have seen that the philosophers generally have the tendency (a naive attitude, *einfältig*) to posit only our need to know and to understand, and not our need to be known and understood.[49] But though Germany is gravely responsible for the divorce of knowledge and faith, their reconciliation will also start

---

40. E. Susini, op. cit., pp. 115 and 129.
41. Ibid., p. 124.
42. SW, I, 372. For Kant, cf. also Susini, op. cit., p. 100.
43. "Man glaubt [. . .], was man begehrt, weil das Begehren (als Affect) bereits ein objectives Zeugniss in sich hat (non existentis nulla cupido), folglich kein blosses Wünschen, das Glauben kein (kantisches) Postulieren ist." (SW, III, 335, note).
44. Cf. Susini, op. cit., p. 91.
45. Ibid., p. 92.
46. Ibid., pp. 93, 111.
47. Ibid., p. 98.
48. Ibid., p. 118
49. SW, XV, 614.

from Germany.[50] Among the French, Baader thinks first of Saint-Martin, when he was considering those who attempted to denounce such a divorce: "I never cease to examine," writes the Unknown Philosopher, "whether in the ordinary conduct of Man, his will always awaits a decisive reason to determine itself, or if it is directed solely by the inducement of sentiment; I believe it to be open to one and not wholly dependent on the other; and I would say that, for the sake of the steadiness of his course, Man should exclude neither one nor the other of these two modes, for as cold and immobile as reflection without sentiment would render him, sentiment without reflection would be just as likely to lead him astray."[51] Furthermore, Baader notes, Saint-Martin said that "in the true order of things, knowledge and the delight in its object should coincide."[52] Theologians and philosophers should convince themselves of something that a connoisseur of the works of Saint-Martin, Joseph de Maistre, calls "*graciabilité*"—it is a matter (for philosophy and theology) of the possibility of reciprocally returning in grace.[53] One imagines that Baader, along with many other romantics, dreams of a religion that would be a science, and of a science that would be a religion.[54] Ultimately, he does not expect much from the thinkers of modern Protestantism, since most fall either into destructive nihilism or into "separatist," unscientific "pietism" (a mysticism)—he refers to the latter group as people of "weak health."[55] And one of the consequences of the Reformation was that there was "established between Protestants and Catholics the error which identified Protestantism with scientific speculation; the Protestant believed it necessary to keep his distance from the Catholic in order not to lose his science, and the Catholic believed it necessary to keep his distance from this same science in order not to lose his Catholicism."[56]

In consequence it is understood that knowledge should be militant.[57] The knowledge that is given (*gegeben*) to us for action (*Thun*)—for example,

50. Cf. Susini, op. cit., p. 94.
51. Saint-Martin, *Des Erreurs de la Vérité*, 1775, t. I, p. 65. Cited by Susini, op. cit., p. 87.
52. Cited in ibid., p. 111.
53. Ibid., p. 134.
54. Ibid., p. 97 (See also p. 100).
55. Ibid., p. 86 ff.
56. "Wie sich denn bald unter Protestanten wie unter Katholiken die irrige Meinung der Identität des Protestantismus und der Wissenschaftlichkeit festsetzte, und der Protestant sich vom Katholiken fern halten zu müssen glaubte, um seine Wissenschaft nicht einzubüssen, so wie der Katholik von letzerer, um sich nicht vom Katholizismus zu entfernen." (SW, VIII, 11).
57. Cf. passages highlighted ed by Susini, op. cit., p. 104.

for a mathematical figure, or for an experiment in physics—differs from the understanding obtained thanks to that action: this second knowledge is "proposed" (*aufgegeben*—Jesus said: "Practice my teaching, and you will understand its truth."). Action (*Thun*), moreover, is not the immediate result of *given* knowledge, but proceeds from belief, from hope, from trust, in science, just as all Faith—like all disbelief—is situated between a given (*gegeben*) knowledge and a proposed (*aufgegeben*) knowledge—which confirms that one must know in order to believe, and believe in order to know.[58] "*Scimus quia facimus,*" said Vico; "*scimus quae facimus, nescimus quae non facimus,*" says Baader: all theory of knowledge must begin not with the false equation of knowledge and being, but with the equation of knowledge and action.[59] Just as faith is a function of the will, so too are belief and understanding, liberty and understanding, action and understanding, belief and action, just as inseparable as attention and perception, inspiration and expiration. Orthosophy—the truth of knowledge—and orthodoxy—the truth of belief—complete each other.[60] The kind of belief that is anticipation of the future goes hand in hand with divination, but if the former is more active and creative, the latter is more passive and receptive.[61] In 1822 Baader explains to Prince Galitzin, to whom he dedicates his study devoted to the force of belief and divination, that for Paracelsus, belief is the act by which the subject who believes opens himself in order to receive; belief, then, would be "the subjective, psycho-physical act of opening oneself, and consequently of receiving (of opening in relation to a strong being, and of receiving a gift made by him); belief is therefore the necessary condition, as much for the surgeon as for the patient, for participating in the perfect manifestation of this force."[62]

We are not far from the Jungian process of individuation, since this opening must contribute to a new ordering, and to a new harmony of disparate elements. In his 1830 writing *On the Biblical concept of spirit and water*, Baader uses beautiful images to explain that the light that is bound in the head to coldness must descend into the heart, to marry there the love, which is full of warmth and which languishes in the shadows. Thus, he says, will the shadowy prison be broken, just as an angel of light descended like a flash of light-

---

58. SW, X, 23 ff.
59. Cf. Susini, op. cit., p. 70 ff.
60. Cf. ibid., pp. 101 and 119.
61. Cf. ibid., p. 117.
62. "Der subjective psychisch-physische Act des Sichöffnens, somit Empfangens (gegen einen und von einem Kräftigen) . . . , folglich die nothwendige Bedingung für den Operator sowohl, als für den Kranken, um der vollendeten Manifestation jener Kraft teilhaft zu werden." (SW, IV, 78).

ning into Christ's tomb so as to burst open the entryway. The difficult task that must be accomplished consists in dissolving the cold and the shadows—transforming them into water. Indeed, one observes in nature that luminous coldness—science, intelligence—and dark warmth—feeling—strive to unite: in the region of light water manifests itself in the form of tears—clouds, rain—and, again, water—dew—rises to regenerate itself by participating in the luminous fire of the sun. This coincidence of the production of water and the birth of light and heat prevails, the philosopher says, for all domains of life. "Nothing," according to Saint-Martin, "illuminates the mind so much as the tears of the heart. It awaits only these to show itself." ("*Rien n'éclaire autant l'esprit que les larmes du coeur. Il n'attend que celles-ci pour se montrer.*") A quotation that relies upon the great, general foundation concerning the production of water and light: the latter cannot show itself as long as there is coagulation. "*Beati qui lugent. . . .*"[63]

In one of the reflections inspired by Saint-Martin's *Tableau naturel*, the theosopher makes a significant remark that appears to me to illuminate further the problem of faith and knowledge, although in an indirect manner. He writes that the division of light into different colors is light's way of rendering itself perceptible, just as no sound and no word is conceivable outside the context of the sonorous figuration in which it is registered.[64] Therefore, one would have to pass through the game of colors in order to find the light, and through the game of language in order to reach the Word. But if our rational knowledge is capable only of conceiving the manner of the colors' relations to each other, that is, if it can know only structures, then we run the risk of not perceiving the light itself except as a simple abstraction. Baader, though, would not know how to run this risk because, for him, behind the color there is the Fire, or the lightning, which is personified energy and irreducible substance. He would no doubt take exception to current formalist structuralism less for its methods than for certain of its metaphysical positions. According to the theosopher, forms and structures do nothing but express a meaning, or rather they constitute the detour that this meaning borrows in order to manifest itself to us. Beyond the structures, there is the life; and, in that, there is our perception, our life. If understanding the relations among the colors leads to discovering the paths of the Light, it follows that in order to understand the origin of the Light itself it is necessary to experience the Fire—a personal experience that passes through faith, an igneous belief of an alchemical type.

---

63. SW, X, 4–6 (*Ueber den biblischen Begriff von Geist und Wasser*). Baader took a part of these considerations from Johannes Menge's book *Beiträge zur Erkenntniss des göttlichen Wortes und göttlichen Ebenbildes*, Lübeck, 1832.

64. SW, XII, 189.

And we know that, in alchemy, faith and knowledge are inseparable one from the other, as well as from action: "*Ora et labora*. . . ." Finally, when Baader speaks of faith and knowledge, of science and belief, of reason and religion, the opposition of the two terms should be regarded from three different points of view, which have been clearly distinguished and articulated by Susini: a) Science and religion should represent two distinct institutions; despite the Romantic "fusionism" noted above, Baader is not a partisan of theocracy. b) Faith and speculation about dogma should be reconciled, according to the principles dear to Baader, who claims to follow Joseph de Maistre in the essentials. c) The links between rational activity and belief concern the philosophical problem of knowledge in its entirety, and here Baader keeps himself always equidistant between reason and sentiment.[65]

Let us add that the interest he takes in the problem of the links between faith and knowledge, as well as the responses he gives to this question throughout his work, stem from the specifically theosophic position underlying his thought. As a gnostic—in the general sense of the term—he does not hesitate to affirm—resting upon the authority of Gregory of Nazianzus—the existence of truths that Jesus did not reveal completely to his disciples in order to avoid blinding them all at once, notably those truths that touch on the Holy Spirit.[66] Besides, whereas Bonald (whose thinking Baader knew and commented upon) speaks to us of the "traditions" of the Hebrews, Baader speaks of their "Tradition," the "mother-Tradition," while the "philosophy" appears to him as a kind of degraded tradition.[67] Fortunately, "radical" belief and understanding exist, "given" to the creature before the Fall, and "remaining" despite the state of sin.[68] Furthermore it is necessary that this belief and this knowledge, presented to us as roots, be developed by our own initiative. "*Non progredi est regredi*," he writes in 1833, adding that the dogmas are the principles of knowledge (*Erkenntnis-Principien*) of which we should ceaselessly make new and enlarged use, as is done with geometry and its axioms or by the gardener and his seeds. This is the response to those who refuse to admit new discoveries in religious understanding on the pretext that they would be incompatible with the permanence of dogma.[69] The Baaderian rec-

---

65. Susini, op. cit., pp. 95–97.
66. Cf. ibid., p. 105 ff.
67. Ibid., p. 109.
68. Ibid., p. 131.
69. SW, I, 361 ff: "Denjenigen, welche in dem religiösen Wissen keine Möglichkeit neuer Entdeckungen zugeben, weil diese mit der Permanenz der Dogmen unvereinbar wären, muß man zu bedenken geben, daß diese Dogmen Erkenntnis-Principien sind, von welchen wir stets neuen und weitern Gebrauch machen sollen, wie der Geometer von seinen Axiomen, oder wie der Gärtner von dem ihm anvertrauten Samen." (note).

onciliation of faith with knowledge is then inscribed within the redemptive program proper to all Christian theosophy: it is a matter of reintegrating into the state that is natural to humanity, a state for which we still possess a nostalgia, despite our condition as flawed beings. The destruction of original androgyny at the moment of the anthropocosmic drama separated in one fell swoop our affective power from our cognitive power; mental alienation corresponds to their absolute separation, whereas their union is necessary for love. The sleep of hypnosis temporarily reconstitutes this original union, contrary to what Kieser thinks, which explains why the mentally ill show themselves insensible to hypnotic action.[70] Whatever one thinks about the soundness of Baader's ideas on hypnosis, in my opinion his judgment is based on a sound intuition: the double necessity, for the equilibrium of the psyche, of a distancing proper to all truly symbolic activity, and of a perpetual and creative tension between elements which are at once opposed and complementary. For this reason we can regret the fact that Baader refused to speak more to us of mythologies. Legitimately anxious to safeguard the specificity of his Christianity in the face of the upsurge in Oriental, and particularly Indian, fashion, he concentrated chiefly on drawing his arguments for reflection from the Bible. But he was better armed than anyone to found a mythocriticism: his Christianity would have lost nothing, and he would doubtless have known, at least as well as Schelling, how to reconcile that Christianity and the mythical Imaginary of the pagan pantheons.

FROM TRADITIONS SHATTERED TO THE RETURN TO MYTH

What we call in the West "theosophy" corresponds to a project that begins to take shape during the Renaissance[71] and above all—though not exclusively—in the Germanic countries. The hermeneutics, philosophy, and spiritual alchemy that it proposes do not constitute an original method or reflection—a "tradition"—for it is a fact that the same attitudes are found elsewhere: one would be hard pressed to refuse John Scottus Eriugena the title of theosopher, and in non-Christian territory the Shiism that Henry Corbin made accessible to us appears essentially like a theosophy. Rather, what characterizes theosophy in the Western world from the sixteenth to the nineteenth centuries is the will, present in each of the theosophers, to unite by his own account that method, that reflection, that tradition—a will that manifests itself starting from the Renaissance, i.e., from the moment when the divorce between faith and knowledge is accentuated to the point at which disbelief

---

70. Cf. Susini, op. cit., p. 112 ff.
71. Hence Bernard Gorceix could legitimately entitle his thesis: *Valentin Weigel et les origines de la théosophie allemande*, (Paris, Presses universitaires de Lille, 1970).

and secularization are dissipating faith, and questions of the links of faith with knowledge are no longer posed in the same manner, if at all. Some aspects of esotericism since the death of Baader have greatly served to discredit theosophy, all the more since constituted religions and fixed ideologies had already held it in suspicion.

From the middle of the nineteenth century the theosophic source deteriorates, in the sense that we no longer see any notable personalities, despite the fact that there has always been, up until our times, epigones who were more or less unconditional disciples of Boehme, Oetinger, Saint-Martin, and Baader. Ultimately, it is significant that the word "esotericism," as vague as one could wish it, makes its appearance shortly before this decadence and the advent of table-turning. For if we observe that for the theosopher or the theologian faith and knowledge render an action or a practice legitimate and possible, we find that Allan Kardec's "religion" is constructed entirely on the basis of a *savoir faire*, of material experience. Baader's theories on magnetism were still founded on a theosophic perspective, in the sense that faith and knowledge were posited before the experiment itself. This was also the case with Jean-Baptiste Willermoz who, during the eighties, had neglected slightly his Masonic work in order to listen to the *"crisiaques"* ("magnetized women"). But if the Freemason from Lyon and the theosopher from Munich lent their ears, it was to hear a discourse that was to be interpreted in a theosophic key, a discourse that was not to be deviated from, whereas the experimental Christianity of Spiritualism is constructed on the basis of messages from the beyond. Since the middle of the nineteenth century, consequently, there is a general hesitancy concerning the meaning of the word "esotericism": that of hidden wisdom and knowledge—or of magical practices, occultism.[72]

If gnosis presents itself as a knowledge unable to do without a belief that involves the entire being in its origin, its present, and its future forms, then what can this belief be outside of the revealed religions? We find that for many minds it is Tradition; the same Tradition of which Baader spoke, but divested of its flowering within Christianity. The notion of "Tradition" in our contemporary Western world has the characteristics of being extremely imprecise and of plunging its roots into an Orient, revised and corrected by the dreams of Europeans. René Guénon, an exacting thinker who is often rigorous but seldom up-to-date on Western and, in particular Germanic, gnoses, has affirmed the legitimacy of this Tradition, which according to him would convey a doctrine that should be transmitted only via some very

---

72. A work which to this day is not devoid of worthy qualities, Robert Amadou's *L'Occultisme, esquise d'un monde vivant*, (Paris, Julliard, 1950), contributes to this confusion because of its title, for it really deals with esotericism.

selected channels. The success of Guénonism rests in large part on the taste for the Orient, widespread in Europe, especially since Romanticism, and on the fact that for many persons, Tradition naturally comes to occupy the space left vacant by faith. Guénon thought that the Catholic Church and Freemasonry represent the only two institutions that could be authentic depositaries of this Tradition, at least in part, and he never ceased to incite his readers and disciples to turn toward either the one or the other. At the same time, he warned against the danger we court by wanting to plunge ourselves into a culture different from the one into which we are born. Roman Catholicism interests Guénon less for its Christianity than for the way in which it reflects the Tradition that might have preceded it, which for him is more authentic than the Church of Saint Peter, more important than Christianity itself.

As for Freemasonry, the entire drama of its history, since its creation in 1717—in its contemporary "speculative" form—seems to stem from the fact that, at least in France and Italy, for a century it too often separated its primarily initiatory and symbolic vocation from belief in God, a relationship that the first "Constitutions" regarded as inseparable. The ineluctable consequence was a loss of interest in the initiation and the symbolism. Strictly speaking, no particular credo is obligatory to Freemasonry; it rests entirely upon ritual, not on dogma. In reaction to this secularizing evolution, a rite, such as the Scottish Rectified Rite, which inherits a significant part of Western tradition, notably Martinist, tends to admit only Christians into its fold. Today it appears as a Masonic rite whose initiatory and ritualistic practices intimately link the understanding of symbols, and even what can be termed Western gnosis, to an authentic Christianity. But in a great number of related societies that are not Masonic in principle, as is the case with many seekers of the truth, the very notion of faith has a tendency to be problematized: whether Christ is "cosmicized" to the point of being conceived as an evanescent fluid (and the abuse of the adjective "Christic" seems to me in this respect a telling sign); or whether—and this amounts at times to the same thing—the phobia of the Incarnation engenders a form of Docetism, which empties Christianity of its specificity; or whether Christ is reduced to one portrait among many others that hang on the walls of the gallery of "Great Initiates."

The Christian himself can reproach these systems for having the audacity to claim that they are still Christian, when they are all primarily a search for knowledge without the faith, which forms the basis of that knowledge and thanks to which it is deepened. More interesting, and above all more authentic, is Raymond Abellio's thinking,[73] because he makes no pretense of faith in

---

73. See for example Raymond Abellio, *La Structure Absolue. Essai de Phénoménologie génétique*, (Paris, Gallimard, collec. "Bibliothèque des Idées", 1965).

Christ, nor does he favor any revealed Book. For him, the universe has a meaning that we can decode, the language of God being inscribed in us and in Nature according to structures that He charges us to decipher, and which are expressed in the Bible or the *Zohar*, for example, behind their literality. He affirms the possibility for the consciousness to reveal itself to itself and, at the same time, to pierce the opacity of the world thanks to a process of transfiguration founded on the "reduction" so important to Husserl. His work is among the most interesting in contemporary gnosis, by virtue of its rigorous, convincing, and "initiatory" quality. It is knowledge in search of a faith. Abellio is a polytechnic student by training, and one observes a similar quest in other thinkers who are well-versed in the scientific disciplines, with this difference: for most, the emergence of a gnosis results essentially from a realization of the insufficiencies of official science and rationalism—whereas Abellio had received not only scientific, but also initiatory, instruction. Likewise, W. Heisenberg, whose *The Part and the Whole* reveals a long, personal journey that starts from the simple recognition of the experimental method (which is only one stage) as a way of coming to find, in the structure of matter, the numbers and the symmetries of Plato. Here, scientific knowledge leads to a gnosis—a word that Raymond Ruyer uses in the very title of *La Gnose de Princeton*.[74] In essence, what Heisenberg and the researchers of Princeton discover, as if by chance, is that the universe has a meaning, and that man and the universe go hand in hand with each other.

Since these voices of authority pointed out that in the so-called exact sciences the word "reason" could no longer be a synonym for "classical physics," other authors—and some editors—have sought to arouse opinion in the disarray caused by the defeat of scientism. The opportunity was a good one because faith, being removed, leaves a space whose void aspires to be filled, while at the same time the possibility of a new or "recovered" knowledge begins to take shape. Further, if we take care to define nothing, to go in all possible directions, then this remains as vague as one could possibly want it to be, and allows us to maintain the fantastic shiver set up by the discourse (easily terrifying because so difficult too decode) of infinite spaces. This might account for the success of the journal *Planète*[75] for several years. Its fundamental subject, as has already been noted, comes down to two implicit postulates: 1) There are more things in heaven and earth than are dreamt of in our philosophies. 2) There are more mysterious things in science than were previously believed. Upon these two postulates a double method is articu-

---

74. Raymond Ruyer, *La Gnose de Princeton. Des savants à la recherche d'une religion*, (Paris, Fayard, Collect. "Evolutions," 1974).
75. *Planète*, published from 1961 through 1968.

lated: a) Scientific enigmas are presented as metaphysical or religious mysteries. b) Religious mysteries are presented as scientific enigmas.

It is not in this way that we can today reconcile belief and knowledge, but rather by a return to symbol and myth. A knowledge that is that of symbol, but permanently undefined, tends to elude degradation and the entropy that threatens all information and to orient and channel belief in a sense always open and always to be rediscovered. The symbol threatens to objectify itself (as N. Berdiaev would say) if it does not insert itself into a dynamic and coherent whole—if it is not the image of an archetype, which itself finds a place in a complete, founding myth of any gnosis, of any knowledge of what we have been, what we are, and what we will become. There would not be a positive fusion of faith and knowledge, then, without the full adherence to a myth—in the lofty sense of this word. The fact of living the myth—the three panels of its triptych, simultaneously—of "enacting" it, constitutes the originality of the theosopher as opposed to the theologian. The entire work of Mircea Eliade rightly or wrongly tends to show that adhesion to a myth reveals itself as organically inseparable from an understanding of the world and of self. Myth, then, in its entirety, passes between belief and knowledge in order to reconnect them to a unique axis that assures the insertion of Man in every direction of space. From this follows, on the psychological plane, the "individuating" character of myth, which Jung, and later James Hillman in a different way, placed in a clear light; and this seems so true that the mere fact of studying these directions frequently reveals itself as a factor that helps to equilibrate the psyche. Above all, wholeheartedly adopting one of the directions for oneself entails a better comprehension of all the others, and knowing those helps to deepen the understanding of the one chosen. These observations do not apply as evidently to "idealist" gnoses, like that of Guénon, for whom the tangible universe is as if evacuated. Let us add that contemporaneous sensitization to the mythic, and hence to a certain way of understanding (to knowledge), can lead men to faith, as was the case with Albert Béguin, who came to Christianity under the influence of the theosophers of German Romanticism—though it can be difficult to distinguish between this kind of influence and the conversion that sometimes follows the reading or hearing of a sacred teaching.

Finally, it seems that the Christian theosophers share a common feeling against anything that interferes with admitting into the soul its divine model. This is why the distinction between faith and knowledge has scarcely any meaning for them, and if they speak of it at all, it is to speak about those for whom it is a problem. At times it is the theosopher's knowledge that develops and is challenged, and at times it is his faith that is deepened; but this comes to the same thing, to the extent that, finally, believing is a concept of disposition—one does not believe ceaselessly—and to the extent that the knowledge in question, which wants to seize reality itself and not merely to describe certain of its aspects, has few connections with science. Einstein said that science was not made to give flavor to the soup. The knowledge of Boehme and his brothers in theosophy is not only destined to *give* the flavor to the soup, but to make us *taste* it, a project that seems by no means to correspond to "Christian truths gone mad," but rather to signify an always healthy and perpetual return to participation on all planes, including that of the tangible; the plane that abstraction quickly causes us to forget, or even deny—the only one, in any case, that permits us to rediscover the absolute identity between the Man of Knowledge and the Man of Desire.

THE INNER CHURCH AND
THE HEAVENLY JERUSALEM

(FOUNDATIONS OF A COSMIC ANTHROPOLOGY ACCORDING
TO FRANZ VON BAADER AND CHRISTIAN THEOSOPHY)

For the second time we are assembled under the emblem of the University of
Saint John of Jerusalem,* a symbol that evokes the traditional Temple to
which each of us devotes himself to become the co-architect and laborer. Last
year the "traditional sciences" were the subject of a rather long and specific
methodological introduction in order that the great axes of our research and
the angular stones of the building could be defined. We are now working on
the Temple itself, the symbol of a city to rediscover, recreate, and rebuild: the
one that the Revelation of John permits us to foresee in Chapter 21 with its
evocation of a new heaven and a new earth, of a city that has itself become the
Temple of Light.[1] With the disappearance of the physical Temple, or rather
its apotheosis, comes the image of what is called the Inner Church whose
advent will be consecrated by the Heavenly Jerusalem.

The two terms (the Inner Church and the Heavenly Jerusalem) are
linked. But it must be clarified that it is a matter of a level of consciousness to
be acquired and a work to be accomplished: I will speak about this double
process, limiting myself in particular to Christian authors and to the period of

---

* Paper presented at the Conference of the University of Saint John of Jerusalem in Cambrai
(France), June 21, 1975.
1. Revelation 21:22 "And I saw no Temple in the city, for its temple is the Lord God the
Almighty and the Lamb."

history that includes some thinkers from the end of the eighteenth and the beginning of the nineteenth century.

THE REGENERATION OF MAN AND NATURE

Initially the Inner Church emphasizes the living faith in the Revelation of the Son of God; it reminds one that before one considers oneself Protestant, Orthodox, or Roman Catholic, it is important to know oneself as a Christian (a fact often forgotten), a certainty without which affiliation hardly has any meaning. The Christians who invoke the Inner Church's authority willingly say that they place the church of John or even the church of James above Peter's, but that does not necessarily mean indifference with respect to these formal religions. It inevitably happens that people invoking its authority have a tendency to repudiate the body of the church in favor of its soul, and that a too-great indifference to form entails a comparable indifference to substance,[2] as one often sees in pietist and quietist circles. But these tendencies could not define the Inner Church in terms of its own principle, nor would it be defined by a militant oecumenism, because there would be oecumenism only at the level of a true spiritual hermeneutics, of a *ta'wîl*.

It is not vague pietism because it assumes a combined process of speculative reflection, of *imaginatio vera*, and of the heart, which renders it inseparable from theosophic meditation. It is a matter of building in oneself a Temple, of acting not only as the spokesperson, but also as the architect of the universal Church which aspires to find, thanks to us, its *Leiblichkeit* (embodiment), as the German theosopher Oetinger states so well. Such a desire does not go against any denomination. I recalled last year that after Weigel, Paracelsus, and Jacob Boehme, a theosophic critique had been practiced against a theological trend that seemed to reduce Man to the state of a being cut off from any cosmic involvement, and to the role of a plaything in the hands of the Creator. This critique contradicts the assertion of the dualist temptation that we are, on the contrary, with God who needs us, the coordinators and the co-creators of a universe, awaiting His return. It also seeks to remind us that the absolute is already in us, not in some transcendental beyond or organically cut off from humanity, but in the *Seelenfünklein*, that tiny sensitive spark in our souls, which according to Meister Eckhart represents a fragment of Divinity itself; which he says it is up to us, with the help of grace, to transform into a living fire that will set the entire cosmos ablaze and cause the Holy City to descend.

In the time period about which I have chosen to speak today, the philosopher Hemsterhuis foresees an ideal society in the guise of a restored

---

2. Remark by Gabriel de Bray in a letter addressed to Maximilian I, 13–25 September 1820, in Eugène Susini, *Lettres inédites de Franz von Baader*, (Paris, P.U.F., 1967), p. 408.

and transformed mythical Greece, while Christian illuminism tends towards a faith capable of lighting up the entire universe: it is the manifestation of an autonomy of esotericism considered as interiorization—to repeat the felicitous expression of Henry Corbin. Let us look into a little book that well represents this Christian illuminism. The author is I.V. Lopuchin and its title is *Some traits of the Inner Church, of the Unique Way to Truth, and the Various Roads that lead to Error and Perdition* ("Quelques traits de l'Eglise Interieure, de l'unique chemin qui mène à la vérité, et des diverses routes qui conduisent à l'erreur et à la perdition). Written in Russian in Moscow from 1789 to 1791, published in 1798 in St. Petersburg, it has been translated into several languages (into French by Charles Auriat de Vatay, into German by Ewald and
. Jung-Stilling, and into Latin by Jung-Stilling).

Here are the basic points of the book that are so characteristic of the Inner Church.[1] Adam, created androgynous, did not know how to remain "in the areas of light," therefore God "exiled him." The first sign of repentance from the first Man became "the first rock upon which is built the Inner Church of God on Earth." It is in this Church that God "carries out the great work of regeneration." Jesus came to fulfill it on the cross "while mysteriously sprinkling all virtuous souls with his blood; with this clean tincture to renew one's soul in God." Not only did he change water into wine, but he will also regenerate the "mass of immaterial elements, from which he will form a new earth and a new heaven, when that which makes up the material world will crumble." The esoteric Church of Jesus Christ is "a way to enter into the true Church of Jesus Christ, which is within." The divine force, which resides in the depth of our inner being, begins to carry out its regeneration there, and it opens the way through which the kingdom of God can be manifested. This "living light" must penetrate us like a "leaven," renewing the three principles that constitute us: spirit, soul, body. Lopuchin writes:

> It is certain that Wisdom, which created everything, has exposed to her elect who love her, the secret of her creation, by which to them is revealed her most intimate work and the diverse action of the spirit of nature, deeply hidden and moved by the spirit of God in the elemental material (materia prima) in this ethereal world, from which everything has been made (Gen. 2:7). Since the fall of man she has been dressed in a coarse rudimentary covering which will live on until the joyful end of time, when from her will rise a new heaven and a new earth. Thus 'the priests and the doctors of the

---

3. For more details, cf. Antoine Faivre, *Eckartshausen et la théosophie chrétienne*, (Paris, Klincksieck, 1969), pp. 151 ff. and 223.

inner Church' are those who are able to exclaim with Saint Paul: 'It is no longer we who live; but Jesus Christ who lives in us.'

The building of this Church will be finished when there will no longer be any will that is not submissive to the will of God. Then death will disappear, Man will take on an ethereal form, one will see shine "a new heaven and a new earth."

One finds similar tones in Eckartshausen. He explains in *Ueber die wichtigsten Hieroglyphen fürs Menschenherz* ("The most important hieroglyphs for the heart of Man" 1796) that if baptism by water, that of John the Baptist, allows access to the exterior church, it is only a foreshadowing of the second baptism by the Holy Spirit, which was that of Jesus and is that which gives us access to another Church.[4] But nowhere does Eckartshausen tell us that the second one renders the first one useless. In *Einige Worte aus dem Innersten für die, die noch im Tempel und in den Vorhöfen sind* ("A few words from the most interior, for those who are still in the Temple and on its parvis" 1797) and *Ueber die Perfektibilität des Menschengeschlechts* ("On the perfectibility of Humankind" 1797), he carefully notes that there is, as one would say nowadays, something esoteric about the exoteric, and vice versa. In his vocabulary he uses the terms "exterior, interior, most interior." Thus, the symbols and mysteries are the exoteric part of religion and of the priests, who are themselves the exoteric part of prophecy. Likewise, the original light is the esoterism of the instrument or of the effect which is the esoterism of the form or of the phenomenon, etc.[5]

You will have noted in passing, among these authors, the importance of the natural and material world while awaiting the return. One might well say that in this tradition as in *Naturphilosophie* we are dealing with an amplifying interpretation of the passages of the Epistle to the Romans, 8:19–22:

> For the creation waits with eager longing for the revealing of the sons of God; for the creation was subjected to futility, not of its own will but by the will of him who subjected it in hope because the creation itself will be set free from its bondage to decay and obtain the glorious liberty of the children of God. We know that the whole of creation has been groaning in travail together until now;

This freedom, this glory of the children of God, is the Holy City, the Heavenly Jerusalem of Chapter 21 of the *Revelation*. Practically all Christian theosophers have made this parallel. Let us cite in the French domain one of the most well-known: Jean-Philippe Dutoit-Membrini, a Protestant minister

---

4. Cf. A. Faivre, op. cit., p. 379.
5. Ibid., p. 380 ff.

in Lausanne. He was the spiritual leader of a group of believers who gathered together those who were called the "inner souls," a brotherhood of Christians united by affinities, by similar reactions, with a free and spontaneous manner, reminiscent of the *collegia pietatis* of Spener. Dutoit is the author in 1793 of *La Philosophie divine, appliquée aux lumières naturelles, magique, astrale, surnaturelle, céleste et divine.* Commenting on the passage in this book cited from the Epistle to the Romans, Dutoit writes that "everything is fire in the universe" and he offers us this beautiful evocation:

> Thus bodies and the crudest matter are in an undeveloped sigh, in a stupor and in a deaf desire. They are like an internal fever, which ferments and seeks to extricate itself from that which is foreign to it. The most inferior bodies in the order of bodies contain and hold the most noble elements . . . to which they act as jailers. . . . And there is the silent groaning of matter and bodies, and the undeveloped desire for a more noble existence that will be their end upon becoming glorious bodies suitable for the glorious heavenly bodies of glorified Spirits . . . So the more noble Principles that [crude matter] hides, locks up and limes, as it were, extricated from that matter which is only a *caput mortuum*, and assembled, will be, as I have said, our glorious earth and matter shining in splendor. One sees examples and reflections of everything in nature, and this is reflected in the precious stones one finds in the bosom of the earth. The Holy City, the New Jerusalem will be just as and even much more brilliant to envision simply according to its glorious appearance.[6]

THE HOLY CITY ACCORDING TO BAADER

The task of Man consists then of helping God to lead Nature back toward its former perfection. Dutoit writes: "My Father (The Word as God) works until now, and I also work (as a God-human or a human inseparably united to Deity)."[7] We see this tradition magnificently orchestrated by the most prestigious German theosopher of the nineteenth century, Franz von Baader. Through him we better understand what the knowledge to be acquired and the work to be completed consist of. In a letter in French sent to Louis de Divonne in 1811, Baader speaks of an "exterior" that he pejoratively calls "peripheral" and that must not be confused with the exterior Church. Baader writes:

---

6. *La Philosophie divine*, t. III, p. 70.
7. Ibid., p. 72.

Our philosophers have created a terrible disorder in confusing this double manner of being in God, central or organic (regenerated) and peripheral or mechanical (unregenerated), and the atheists, who deny the living God in us, and who say to us that God is only outside of us (Nature, Fate, etc.), are correct in that this God is not really found in the heart of unregenerated Man or of the Devil, and that they do not find Him and they only sense Him around themselves as a terrible barrier.[8]

This quotation usefully recalls that the outer darkness is not the formal churches, which go hand in hand with the Inner Church. Baader, who is always careful to take into account the historic incarnation of Christ and His simultaneous presence in the universe, explains to us in 1828 in his tract *Ueber die sichtbare und unsichtbare Kirche* ("On the visible and invisible Church") that Jesus, by His ascension, transformed His limited earthly presence into a cosmic, although veiled, presence. This gives a cosmic dimension to the Christian church, which itself is the amplification of the national Jewish church. The "ferment" rendered possible by the *Menschwerdung* (the Incarnation) carries on its work through time until the One has penetrated the center of every individual form, that they may be subjugated (*subjcirt*), that they may be organically assimilated—in other words, says Baader, from the outside to the inside—in a word, until God is in everything. That is the foundation of the Inner Church according to Baader, but even better than Eckartshausen, he associates with this idea a dialectic that gives it strength and solidity. Indeed, he urges us not to imitate certain Protestant mystics who give greater importance exclusively to the inner, because he tells us that the very concept of real or living coincides with the identity of the outer and the inner, and the disidentity of the two is only a foreshadowing of death. Any "community" of the inner is absolutely linked to a "conformation" or corresponding outer embodiment, and there is no spirit that is not an "esprit de corps." On this topic Baader quotes, as he often does, this verse from the *Emerald Tablet*: "*Vis eius integra si conversa fuerit in terram.*" The two Churches are inseparable in their essence, and in their actions, without it being necessary, even so, to merge them. It is the union of the One and the individual.[9] Because the cause must take nature in order to manifest itself or to be rendered effective, he writes in 1834,[10] and throughout his entire work he allows

---

8. Eugène Susini, *Lettres inédites de Franz von Baader*, (Paris, J. Vrin, 1942) t.I, p. 269.

9. Baader, *Ueber die sichtbare und unsichtbare Kirche, so wie über die sichtbaren und unsichtbaren Wirkungen der sichtbaren Kirche*, in Sämtliche Werke, op. cit., VII, 211 ff.

10. *SW*, XV, 517.

us to understand that this divine manifestation is incarnated at the same time in the Churches and within us.

But this interior does not remain passive. The Great Work consists of making God's work and ours coincide perfectly in a double movement from bottom to top and from top to bottom, a process evoked in the *Emerald Tablet* by its striking turns of phrase and its poetry. By the same token, in 1816, Baader writes to C.D. von Meyer that in every plant two things, the earth and the sun, become one thing without merging, the body of a plant forming only if the sun becomes the earth and the earth the sun. Likewise Man and God join together thanks to Christ.[11] Baader compares God to an alchemist who uses a receptacle (the creature) to prepare the Tincture that he needs (His Son). According to Baader, the alchemist does not dispose of the receptacle once the work is finished. In the magnanimity of his joy before the completed task, he confers upon this receptacle the Tincture of eternal life.[12]

There is no descent without elevation, he writes in 1832 to Emilie Linder; if something comes down from above, something else must rise to meet it. Heaven aspires to join earth, Spirit aspires to join Nature, as the earth must rise up to heaven and Nature to Spirit without any of these merging notwithstanding. If the male's function is to entice the Spirit to his heart, it is incumbent upon the female to entice Nature or earth to this heart which is the central place above all else where the upper and lower meet, where man and woman become truly human. To find this divine center, man helps woman to elevate the lower while she helps him to lower the upper. In order to succeed, man tries to conquer the pride, coldness, and impatience that hinder the descent, while woman attempts to resist the faintheartedness, heaviness, and laziness that obstruct upward movement. Baader thinks that this anthropological trait allows one to understand the nature of the catastrophe that introduced the difference between the sexes, in other words, to better grasp the essence of original sin. Indeed, if a human being can only truly live in his heart, the central area, inside, located between the head and the base of the body, the heart must simultaneously attract to itself heaven and earth, which is rarely the case since one generally sees the heart owned in turn by heaven and earth, Spirit and Nature, whereas it must own both of them. God is God because He is found between Spirit and Nature, because He is both and at the same time above them. In creation, Man is the image of God because he is or must be the heart of heaven and of earth as well—a purely Biblical doctrine, adds Baader, but one which has been ignored for a long

---

11. Ibid., XV, 305.
12. Ibid., XV, 312, et E. Susini, op. cit. (ed. J. Vrin), p. 296.

time by philosophers and theologians. During the blessed moments when we have the impression of regaining this place, we not only have the intimate and heavenly feeling of what the whole of being is, but we know that such an accomplishment would allow us to act, like Orpheus, upon other men and upon Nature. If the untameable unicorn consents to lie next to the young virgin or to play at her feet, then creation will be achieved. In the first chapter of Genesis it is said that God put the finishing touches on the creation of heaven and earth by the creation of Man, and that it is only by residing in (*inwohnend*) Man that he was able to live in this creation; in other words, to celebrate the Sabbath in it. In a compelling parallel, Baader compares this first page of the Bible to the last of the New Testament, where this chapter of the Book of Revelation reveals that with the descent of the City of God (or the Kingdom of the children of God) the new heaven and the new earth will find their culmination. Because heaven, earth, and Man, created for eternity, must remain eternally, divine manifestation needs all three of them in its harmony.[13]

Baader also writes that Genesis begins with a dualism, the creation of heaven and earth, but that it ends with a creation that does away with this dualism: that of the human being who joins heaven to earth and the created world to the Creator. The Book of Revelation assures us that this function of Man is eternal, since the new heaven and earth are joined together forever by the future City.[14] God finds in Man his Sabbath, therefore there is a free mutual effusiveness from one to the other because both are found mutually: such is the sacramental union of the Creator in the creature, the eternal Sabbath about which the apostle Paul speaks. The Creation was too limited for God. He needed Man in order to deploy Himself liberally.[15]

Baader puts us on guard against pantheistic disorder; each organ of the whole keeps its individuality while contributing to the harmony of the Whole. The Holy City, once restored, will not abolish heaven or earth. He also puts us on guard against angelism: if Scripture teaches that men and women will be like angels, that does not mean that they will be angels. It is a matter of not confusing angelic nature with human nature, nor earthly nature with heavenly nature. Scripture explains: "a new heaven and a new earth." The New Jerusalem will have its seat on earth, but without merging with earth or with heaven; it will be the intermediary between the two, the link assuring their profound unity. This function of intermediary belonged to Man before his Fall since he was superior to heavenly and earthly creatures. Here once again we see the fundamental antidualism of Baader. He adds that Man was not created from the earth, but was first put upon it, not to leave it

---

13. SW, XV, 486 ff.
14. Ibid., 609.
15. Ibid., 641 ff.

later, nor to fall again onto it, but to cultivate it; in other words, to aid in its return to the Sabbath of God, to make it lose this "deformity" caused by the Fall and of which heaven has also been the victim. If we don't understand that, says the theosopher, we are blind to the Evil to which the world is exposed due to the fault of Man, to these corrupt practices that can one day go so far that, as Scripture says (Gen. 4:11–19; Lev. 16:34) the earth will no longer support us. It will spit us out or it will swallow us up. Baader repeats insistently that in the first two verses of Genesis "*tohu va bohu*" alludes to an earthly and celestial catastrophe for which God was not responsible, with the result that atonement is the aim of all creation described in Genesis, a restoration whose culmination is called the Heavenly Jerusalem towards which Man must work.[16] Does the world around us never cease to remind us of the pain of the Universe? "Through all of the beauty in Nature," he writes in 1820, "Man perceives in a way now muted, now strong, the sorrowful cry of Nature who laments having to wear the widow's veil because of Man."[17] Our work progresses in the following manner:

> The creature must not only . . . thrust himself towards what is above him so that this higher plane may elevate him to it while descending to him, but he also must at the same time raise to himself the lower, so that heaven and earth meet anew in this creature, that it becomes the place where they will celebrate their wedding and that which is above becomes similar to that which is below.[18]

Baader writes to Justinus Kerner in 1832 that Man achieves his true cosmic potentiality during those favored moments when the Spirit and Nature unite in his heart, which means when the heart is none other than the New Jerusalem, the City of God to which aspire the new heaven and earth.[19] Then would there no longer be any question of materialism or of idealism.

---

16. Ibid., III, 313 ff. Baader cites according to Johannes Menge, *Beiträge zur Erkenntnis des göttlichen Wortes und göttlichen Ebenbildes*, (Lübeck, 1832).

17. <<Durch alle Schönheiten der Natur hindurch vernimmt der Mensch bald leiser bald lauter jene melancholische Wehklage derselben über den Witwenschleier, den sie aus Schuld des Menschen tragen muss>> (SW, II, 120).

18. <<Die Creatur muss sich nemlich nicht nur gegen das ihr Höhere vertiefen, damit dieses in ihr niedersteigend sie zu sich erhebe, sondern sie muss zugleich das ihr Tiefere zu sich erheben, damit Himmel und Erde sich in ihr wieder begegnen, und sie die Ehestätte der Vermählung beider werde, damit das, was oben ist, dem gleich werde, was unten ist u.u.>> (SW, IV, 2310).

19. <<Tritt uns denn aber der Mensch als solcher und in seiner wahrhaften, zum Theil selbst kosmischen Virtualität anders als in jenen Silberblicken auf, in welchen Geist und Natur in seinem Herzen geeint sich finden, oder in welchen dieses Herz das neue Jerusalem (civitas Dei) ist, auf welches der neue Himmel und die neue Erde harren?>>

We need to qualify his position as being steadfastly "nondualist": in that he fits well into a Western theosophic tradition from which he does not deviate. Baader's originality consists primarily in the processes of his speculative thought, in his prodigious spirit of synthesis and in the genius of exhaustive expression. As we have seen, to the extent that this nondualism brings about a rejection of "angelism," Baader leans towards mistrusting Swedenborg. In 1834 he writes that the followers of Swedenborg are mistaken in saying that men and women become angels after their death.[20] And the following year he notes pertinently that the Swedenborgian idea of the beyond is not Christian because the Swede only talks about the immortality of the soul, which adds Baader, "demonstrates less perspicacity than the pagans who had certainly seen that a disembodied (*leiblos*) soul, therefore a soul without action, could be imperfect and insufficient."[21] Baader is generally suspicious of Swedenborg's descriptions, since he merely parades images without knowing how to distinguish different categories of spirits according to their respective value. Swedenborg is concerned with beauty, with esthetics, but his theosophy is hazy. It is not "incarnate" enough.[22]

We can not stress enough the importance of the *Menschwerdung*, the Incarnation in Baaderian thought. Thanks to that, this theosopher lives on, following the example of his precursors, equidistant between idealizing angelism and historic materialism. In short, he reminds us that it is not enough to stand up for ideal values, and that the Holy City vanishes like a mirage when one forgets not only about the idea of the *Leib*, the spiritual body, but also about the belief in the Incarnation of Jesus Christ, the Son of the living God. Maintaining a steadfast faith in this historic Incarnation is not the same as succumbing to a reductive historicism if one also maintains that Christ is a Cosmic Christ as well; but to deny this historical Incarnation is to succumb to the temptation of a doctrine that drains Christianity of its specificity. In 1816 Baader writes to Conrad Schmid:

> The hope of every Christian is built simultaneously on the forthcoming Revelation, general and personal, of Christ (as judge of the world), and on the interior Revelation, secret and individual. . . . The one who does not believe in the historic coming or the mystical

---

20. Ibid., III, 313 ff.
21. Ibid., XV, 529, et IV, 272.
22. Ibid., XII, 358 and 383. One reads nevertheless under the pen of Swedenborg: "If the Spirits had no organs, and if the Angels were not made of bodily substances, they would not have been able to speak, see or think" (*Arcanes célestes*, Paris, 1845–1889, t. III, p. 5 ff. #1533. Yet let us take note that these *Arcanes*, although presented as a vast commentary from Genesis, have practically no cosmonogic or eschatological dimension.)

(secret) coming of Christ, or whom this coming does not rejoice, is not a Christian.[23]

In a still more precise manner he writes to Johann Friedrich von Meyer in 1817:

> The Faith and Hope of a Christian who is familiar with the world (in other words the Faith in His worldly passage at a moment in history and the Hope of His return) [is] *as necessary* as the Faith in a Christ who manifests himself secretly.[24]

We understand why, like all of his predecessors, he stresses this point so much. It is that the embodiment raises an expectant suffering Nature towards heaven, while heaven aspires to consummate an eternal marriage with the earth. The Holy City, a result of that union, has as its first stone the heart of the Man-mediator. To this heart is linked the architecture of the Heavenly Jerusalem, a city to rebuild, just as the Masons labor to square off an uncut substance to make a cubic stone, a cornerstone of the Temple to be rebuilt. And since the University of Saint John of Jerusalem wants to contribute to this reconstruction, according to the methods defined last year, I want here to suggest a specific place while delineating the areas around which to organize the anthropocosmic building. It seems that the knowledge of this place can help us to bring forth the work that is only waiting to spring forth from our earth. Around this space it is our responsibility to build lodges—like those of the workmen—without a roof, so as to not lose sight of heaven from where the towers will descend, and to construct not only walls, but also, below ground, foundations without which the workers would be working on sand. It is on this double plan, horizontal and vertical, that I locate the knowledge to be acquired, and where I envision the work to be accomplished. An overly ambitious image? Perhaps . . . but we have the right to let ourselves be guided by our images, if we firmly maintain the quadruple axis, which is the basis for them and justifies them: our spiritual East, from which comes knowledge and where the angels live; our historic and apollinian West, domain of space and time; this human condition by which we are children of the earth; finally, the

---

23. <<[Ich muss] noch bemerken, dass die Hoffnung jedes Christen zugleich auf die zukünftige allgemeine persönliche Offenbarung des Christs (als Weltrichters) und auf innre heimliche individuelle Offenbarung desselben beruht (nach dem Spruch: ich werde mich Ihm offenbaren, etc.) und dass der kein Christ ist, welcher entweder das historische oder das mystische (heimlich) Kommen des Christs nicht glaubt und nicht sich freuend darauf hofft.>> In Eugène Susini, op. cit., J. Vrin, p. 293.
24. <<Der Glaube und die Hoffnung eines weltkundigen Christs (nämlich der geschichtliche Glaube seines irrdisch dagewesenseyns und die Hoffnung Seiner Wiederkunft) sey dem Christen *eben so nöthig* als der eines heimlich sich kundgebenden Christs.>> In ibid., p. 302.

Kingdom where our heavenly Father awaits the restoration of the ties that join God, Man and the universe.

The center of the cross is the site of the Inner Church upon which the Holy City can be built. Because this central point joins together the rays from the four horizons, it assures, once it is dynamically fixed, cohesion in the regained city. But it is especially the cross on Golgotha, which seems to be the model of such an axis; it is a gnostic model—in the etymological sense— because of the presence of the beloved disciple; it is historic because the Incarnation can only take place in history; it is earthly and anthropological because Jesus actually lived among us, and the tree from which the cross was made was actually rooted in our soil; finally, it is celestial and cosmic because the cross led to the descent into the underworld, to the Resurrection and to the Ascension of the One who said: "I am the Way, the Truth and the Life."

THE TEMPLE OF SOLOMON IN EIGHTEENTH-CENTURY MASONIC THEOSOPHY

Since the destruction of the Order of Jacques de Molay, several Masonic obediences have claimed to be the heirs of the Templars. However, neither in the following discussion nor in Willermoz's thinking was it ever a question of proving such filiations, which were in any case always hypothetical. It is merely a matter of recalling what the Temple as a symbol could and must have represented for the Beneficent Knight of the Holy City, and also, of course, for all Masons of the Rectified Scottish Rite (RSR), starting with the Apprentice degree. For this, there is no better way than to show, if only in broad strokes, the fundamental analogous relationships among the various parts of this Temple, the Man-Knight and the universe, the thematic relationships among these elements, and the numerological associations of all material and spiritual creation.

REBUILDING THE TEMPLE

Among the various teachings of transcendental Christianity, those of the eighteenth century Neo-Templars seem to be some of the most precious. In Germany the Rite of the Strict Observance (RSO) of Baron von Hund made reference to the "Templar" doctrine to which it claimed, more wrongly than rightly, to be the successor. For us here, the important thing is not a question of historical fact but of the symbolism itself. The so-called Lyon Reformation grafted itself onto the RSO and the merger appeared complete by 1782. At that moment it seemed as if the message of the eternal Temple had been clearly revealed to some "Men of Desire." Probably more than ever before, the Temple was at that time considered in terms of its tripartite aspect, but with the added symbolic underpinnings of an architecture of the universe, subtended by a coherent theosophy that was cosmogonic, cosmological, and eschatological.

We may recall that Martines de Pasqually hardly mentioned Solomon's Temple at all in his *Traité de la Réintégration des Etres* written in 1771,[1] but this was only because the *Traité* remained unfinished. With respect to the Temple, its entire theosophico-alchemical symbolism had the same basic meaning as Willermoz's symbolism. What documents are there that could enlighten us more fully on this subject? I know of four. Chronologically, the first is the *Conférences de Lyon* (1774–1776), the original of which is found in the Municipal Library of Lyon. Second, there are the three highly elaborated degrees of the Rectified Scottish Rite, a fine copy of which belonged to the Lodge l'Humanité à l'Orient de Crest and is preserved at the departmental archives of Valence. Third, we must mention the fourth degree of this rite, the Ritual of the Scottish Master of Saint Andrew, of which a fine 1809 copy can be found in the Municipal Library of Lyon. Furthermore, these four degrees are still very much alive today. As for the fourth document, it is of course the *Instructions secrètes aux Grands Profès* which I discovered in the legacy Bernard de Turckheim and published in an appendix to a book by René Le Forestier.[2] To fully understand the symbolism of Willermoz's Temple, one could hardly choose one of these sources over another. Nevertheless, the most important ones on which the present discussion will rest are the *Conférences de Lyon*, the ritual of the first degree and the *Instructions secrètes*. Let us plunge into the luxurious simplicity of this living symbolism.

---

1. Cf. two references to Solomon, pp. 110 and 125, in *Traité*, ed., Chacornac, 1899.
2. René Le Forestier, *La Franc-Maçonnerie templière et occultiste aux XVIIIe et XIXe siècles*, edited by Antoine Faivre, Paris, Aubier-Nauwelaerts, 1969 New edition: Paris, La Table d'Emeraude, 1988. Désaguiliers, in an excellent article on Solomon's Temple in the Rectified Scottish Rite, has already drawn attention to sources (referred to above) on the first four degrees: cf. *Renaissance Traditionelle*, 1972, no. 9–10: "Le Symbolisme du Temple de Salomon dans les quatre premiers grades du Régime Ecossais Rectifié." The *Conférences de Lyon*, or *Instructions aux Elus-Cohens* (1774–1776), are a collection of minutes of meetings held in Lyon by Jean-Baptiste Willermoz; the Elect-Cohens of Lyon in fact felt the need, after the departure of Martines De Pasqually, to compare and collate their interpretations of Martinesist doctrine, and to note down carefully the aspects of his oral teaching that had escaped them. Louis-Claude De Saint-Martin and Duroy D'Hauterive took part in these meetings. I have published these *Conférences* under the title: *Les Conférences des Elus-Cohens de Lyon: aux sources du Rite Ecossais Rectifié*, Braine-le-Comte (Belgium, du Baucens, 1975) 155 p., ill. As for the rituals of the first three degrees, the departmental archives of Valence have only the first and third degrees (1785–1787), but the Willermoz archives in Lyon have given us information on the second degree.

A SYMBOLIC TYPOLOGY

In the *Instructions secrètes* Willermoz taught the Grand Profès that Masonic initiation goes back historically to the Temple of Jerusalem. The Temple, unlike the pyramids of Egypt, was not the result of "an arbitrary choice of purely human convention." Now this is something that might shock historians, but we should not expect Willermoz to be a historian. His teachings were of a different nature. The continuation of this text is very interesting: "Destined to form a universal Emblem," the Temple of Jerusalem "was built according to plans drawn up by a superior hand" and its symbols "were not the invention of any man." This is why, he adds, "it is recommended to Masons to study, with constancy and without becoming discouraged, everything that has to do with Solomon's Temple, its proportions and its different parts, and the numbers that are pertinent; the era and the duration of its construction; the ground on which it was built; the number and type of materials and workers that were employed; finally the various upheavals that it has undergone. None of these objects were fixed upon without purpose; they all tend essentially to recount the history of mankind, and to demonstrate certain relationships with the Temple and with the Universe." Moreover, this created universe was "philosophically called the Great Universal Temple, of which Solomon's was one manifestation" (*Instructions secrètes aux Grands Profès*, in Le Forestier, op. cit., p. 1026).

The Apprentice degree of the RSR seems then to be a veritable propaedeutic to this Templar symbolism. We read: "The scene before you represents the famous Temple that was built in Jerusalem by King Solomon to the Glory of the Grand Architect of the Universe. It is the fundamental symbol of Masonry." Masonry was its heir, as is seen in a later degree: the fourth degree in fact asserts that "the Temple of Jerusalem is the fundamental, basic symbol of Freemasonry which was revived under various names, under different guises at different eras. . . . This remarkable Temple was and always will be, as much because of the great and astonishing upheavals it has undergone, the fundamental symbol of man and the universe." Let us now return to the first degree, where he recalls that Masons are in the process of reconstructing the Temple. The prayer of this degree begins as follows:
• "Deign to grant our zeal a happy success, so that the Temple that we have undertaken to raise to your glory. . . ." This is why the Apprentice has as his first task to rough-hew the uncut stone. "Brother Apprentice," we read in this instruction, "the unhewn stone on which you have just struck is a true symbol of yourself. Work without rest to hew it so that you may then be able to polish it, since this is the only means remaining to you to discover the glorious form of which it is capable, and without which it will be rejected from the construction of that Temple which we raise to the Grand Architect of the Universe." Moreover, in the instruction of this first degree the officiating officer asks the new member: "Why does the Temple of Solomon serve as a symbol for the

Masons?" Response: "To remind them that they must raise a Temple to virtue in their hearts with the same degree of perfection as that of Solomon's Temple." Of course, virtue must be understood in the context of the particular meanings and connotations of the period.

As we were saying, this symbolism goes back to a theosophical view of the world. The teaching of the RSR was progressive. The *Instructions secrètes* thus appear to be much more explicit in this regard, as do the earliest of our documents, the *Conférences de Lyon*, which are not specifically Masonic but are rather essentially Martinesist (i.e., inspired by Martines de Pasqually). We must understand that this duty to rebuild the Temple is meant to suggest a new Temple that resembles as much as possible the first one, which was destroyed. Willermoz and his Brethren were nourished upon and thoroughly steeped in a biblically centered educational background. Let us briefly summarize the specific era in history on which the esoteric doctrine of the RSR was so completely and harmoniously grafted. In 960 B.C. Solomon constructed the Temple of Jerusalem and during this time the country became a hereditary monarchy. Solomon's Temple replaced the Temple of Shiloh (about 1040 B.C.) which had already been used to house the Ark of the Covenant. Solomon's Temple gave the Ark a dwelling place worthy of itself on Mount Zion in Jerusalem because of the work of Hiram, who was its architect and also the king of Tyre. One essential fact to note is that the Ark, which had accompanied the armies of Israel in battle, thereby ceased to be a nomadic object. Consequently, the new edifice became the center of the world. All the more so as, constructed in seven years, it symbolized the creation in seven days. Its destruction in 587 B.C. as a result of the victory of the king of Babylon Nebuchadnezzar, who deported the Jews of Israel, was followed fifty years later by its reconstruction under Zerubbabel made possible by the victory of the Persian king Cyrus over Nebuchadnezzar.[1]

Thus, the fundamentals of the esoteric teaching underpinning the "Templar" theosophy of the RSR was based upon the following idea: that Solomon's Temple stood for the state of the universe and of Man before the Fall; because of this Fall, the building of Zerubbabel's Temple did not benefit to the same degree from the guidance of the Great Architect, that is, of God. In other words, the Temple of Zerubbabel represented the state of Man in the present and the state of the world into which we have been thrust. This second Temple stood as a symbol of humanity and of the universe taken in their historical unfolding. Therefore, for the Mason it is a matter of bringing to completion the work of Zerubbabel, or even of rebuilding another Temple

---

3. It was rebuilt between 20 B.C.–64 A.D. (Herod's Temple) and was destroyed in 70 A.D. in accord with the predictions of Jesus. On the Temple in the Scriptures, cf. especially Kings 1–10; 1–2 Chronicles; Ezra.

even better than Zerubbabel's. The objective was to rediscover the synchronic verticality of Solomon's Temple, or if you will, to escape the infinite vicissitudes of diachronic history. Martines de Pasqually wrote:

> It is by reflecting upon [his] glorious [state] that Adam brought to mind and carried out his evil intentions whilst in the midst of his first glorious abode which is commonly called the earthly paradise, and which we, in mystery, call the land raised above all senses. This site is so called by the friends of Wisdom, because it was in this place known under the name of Moria that the Temple of Solomon was later constructed. The construction of this Temple represented in a real way the emanation of the first man. To be convinced of this, one has only to remark that the Temple of Solomon was built without the use of tools made of metal: which shows to all men that the Creator formed the first man without the aid of any material, physical operation (*Traité*, p. 25).

In the *Conférences de Lyon*, Willermoz also taught that Solomon's Temple was built on "the mountain of Mount Mor," that is "the land raised above all senses" (p. 24),[4] and that this Temple was at once spiritual, corporal and temporal. The poetry that emerges from Willermoz's reasoning deserves some appreciation (p. 67, parag. V). The *Instructions secrètes* take up this theme, this time orchestrated in grandiose eschatological prophetism:

> All these things have been represented to us by the history of the Temple and by that of the Chosen People, but it is this latter that ought yet to furnish the most consoling model for mankind. Because tradition tells us that when the Jewish Nation has recognized and made amends for its crimes by a long and severe expiation, she will recover her original rights and be gathered again into Jerusalem. The Holy Ark hidden by Jeremiah in a cave, to which he sealed the entrance, will reappear in all its splendor, and the faithful tribes will look again on the walls of the holy city; perfect symbol of the first resurrection of man in his first incorruptible form, for all those who have laid aside flesh and blood in the tomb, in imitation of and through the help of the divine God-Man (p. 1044).

According to the Bible, the Holy of Holies was withdrawn from the Temple because of the betrayals of the people. Following this, the Assyrians destroyed the building, and the people were carried off to Babylon. In the same way, says Willermoz, since Man has fallen, the Spirit has withdrawn

---

4. The arabic numerals in parentheses refer to my numbering of the "paragraphs" in the *Conférences des Élus-Cohens de Lyon*, op. cit, except numerals above 1000 (*Inst. sec.*).

from his mind and Man's inner fire has grown dim just like the fire that Jeremiah hid in a well. In another typological comparison, Cyrus permitted the people to return to Jerusalem under the leadership of Zerubbabel and to rebuild the Temple. Even so, God is merciful and he helps us along the road to Reintegration. Zerubbabel, and later Nehemiah, rebuilt the Temple, but it was not as beautiful as the previous one. Likewise, the body of present-day Man is much less beautiful than the glorious body of Adam: "The men of today, who no longer have any idea of what has gone before them, are truly far from perceiving this degradation in our nature; they think that mankind is fine, and that everything around him is fine. Given over to the pleasure of the senses they make this body their Idol, and get from it the delights of the flesh, and have no other regret than that of knowing ahead of time that there is a moment when their supposed happiness must end" (p. 1043). "By the greatest of crimes, adds the *Instructions secrètes,* the Chosen Nation then lost the sacred promise given to her in trust, and which was her entire strength, a promise that was only fully and perfectly known by the High Priest, and for which the Masons have searched ever since with such great diligence. It was at this time that the second Temple was destroyed down to its very foundations, by the fury of the soldiers, blind agents of divine vengeance, and that the Jewish people were scattered among the nations and for centuries were delivered over to opprobrium and ignominy." Even so, the body of Man, which is to say his material temple, will be destroyed; even so, the Universal Temple, which is to say Nature or creation, will be destroyed as soon as the "source of power" ("central fire axis increate" in Martines de Pasqually's terminology), which is its alchemical support, is withdrawn. Then the entire universe will fade away (p. 1044).

In the degree of Scottish Master of Saint Andrew, a picture was presented to the candidate. It represented the Temple of Jerusalem in ruins, with two broken and overturned columns, the mosaic pavement and stairway of seven steps destroyed, and the altar of incense cracked open in the middle of the Temple, at the entrance to which is seen the Bronze Sea and its supports broken and scattered. Around these scenes chains and other symbols of captivity were represented. A second picture, unveiled before the candidate after the first, represented the Temple of Zerubbabel with the seven-branched candelabra, the Ark of the Covenant and the two cherubim, the porch of the Temple and the Bronze Sea reinstalled on its supports.[5]

The typological harmony of this vision of the world is clearly recognizable. The Jewish Temple, the body of Man, the universe itself, are so many Temples, which "figure one another," to use an expression of Willermoz (*"figurer à"* is frequently used in his writings). The human body is of course

---

5. Cf. Paul Naudon, *La Franc-Maçonnerie chrétienne,* (Paris, Dervy, 1970) p. 153. ff.

the first Temple in the scheme of our perception. It "figures" or represents the Masonic lodge. It must be seen as "a lodge or a Temple which is the reproduction of the general, particular and universal Temple" (p. 17), which are the different levels of the universe according to Martines's cosmology. But "if man's body is a Temple, then there ought to be religious rites to honor it" (p. 88). This brings to mind of course the words of Christ: "Destroy this Temple, and I will rebuild it in three days" (p. 45; 47). It would be difficult to separate all the Temples, so overlapping do they become, which is clearly in the best tradition of analogical thinking. Here is the essential point as made in the *Conférences de Lyon*: "The body of man and the Temple of Solomon are the reproduction of creation and the image of the Great Universal Temple" (p. 87). Martines de Pasqually wrote: "Adam, by the three spiritual (alchemical) principles (i.e., Salt, Sulfur, Mercury), which compose his visible material form, and by the proportions which rule them, is the exact representation of the general earthly temple, which we know to be an equilateral triangle" (*Traité*, p. 82).

One can roughly say—but this is already being false to any dynamic understanding of the symbol in its physical multiplicity—that there are four Temples: that of the Universe, that of Man, that of Solomon, and a nonrepresentational mystic temple, basically eschatological—although each person is to be part of its construction—which is in the anagogic sense, that of Zerubbabel. This summation may seem incomplete because a Temple can be at the same time much more and much less—but how can the macrocosm be distinguished from the microcosm? In the *Conférences de Lyon*, Willermoz tried to make his listeners understand this from within. What is a Temple? It is first of all each and every thing that has its vital force imparted to it by a "*véhicule*," such that an atom, he explains, is a Temple in and of itself (17). He adds that on the level of superior beings not subject to time, just as on the level of those that are, the Temple is the envelope that both houses these beings and that serves as a material receptacle for their action (p. 87, parag. II and III).

COSMOSOPHIC ELEMENTS

These alchemical allusions are not at all far-fetched or obscure. They illuminate this symbolism of the Temple in an ever newer light without which our understanding of this theosophical system would remain incomplete. What was it all about? God resolved upon and conceived the Temple of Nature as the result of a particular event, the Fall of Lucifer (*Instr. sec.*, p. 1027). The universe was created to serve as a repository, a prison, for the fallen angels, and later for Man after his Fall. God carved out a spatial and temporal sphere within the nonspace and the atemporality, which were pre-existent to these two falls from grace. This was done, one might say, to limit the damage, for the fallen beings could not break out of this sphere. It was not God Himself who made this sphere, but it was He who had it made through His agents. In the same way, it was not Solomon himself who constructed the Temple of Jerusalem, and David only made the preparations for its construction (*Instr. sec.*, p. 1029). The Great Architect of the Universe limited his role to impressing onto this work regularity, life, and movement, just as Solomon, who did not perform the work himself, but only gave the directives to his workers, heard "no sound of tools" (*Instr. sec.*, p. 1039). All life, each and every atom, is animated by a "véhicule" which, by the intermediary of a chain of agents of various ranks, receives a portion of the original impulse whose source is situated in the "divine immensity" (cf. *infra*). Each being, we have seen, is enveloped in a "temple" which serves as a receptacle for its action. This is why the Temple of Jerusalem is truly the symbol of the Great Universal Temple. Just as Solomon's Temple was destroyed when the glory of the Lord withdrew from it, so "the Great Universal Temple will cease when the divine action has withdrawn its Powers and the prescribed term of its existence is accomplished" (*Instr. sec.*, p. 1029). The "central fire axis," or "source of power," which surrounds the Great Universal Temple, that is to say, the entire universe, is like the cornerstone of this Temple. When God has utterly destroyed this axis, everything will fall back into the void, just as a living being dies when the effect of this axis ceases to act upon him and to maintain in him the cohesion of the three alchemical principles that are the necessary condition of all life .

Before the Fall, Man was not dependent upon this "central fire axis." But if the "original form of man," as Willermoz says, changed nature after the Fall, on the contrary "the visible appearance of this form did not change at all," because he was to be "a living image of the Universal Temple." This form is the personal Temple of Man, which is called the Lodge by the Masons (*Instr. sec.*, p. 1032). St. Paul wrote: Do you not know that you are God's Temple?" (1 Cor. 3:16), and "For God's temple is holy, and that temple you are. . . . ?" (1 Cor. 6:17). In his second Sermon Saint Bernard, speaking of the dedication of a church, alludes to the temple of stone: God does not inhabit it because He lives in Man, His image. This is why "the body of Man is the true Lodge of the Mason, or his own particular Temple." In the same way, the Sanctuary of Solomon's Temple was the invisible Lodge of the divine Spirit who came to dwell in it. In Masonry, the Lodge also symbolizes the place where the Brethren assemble because this place, Willermoz adds, represents the Universal Temple, that is to say, the created universe.

The *Instructions secrètes* recall that in a Masonic Lodge the outline of the Temple is drawn with white chalk, "to signify that the Temple will disappear when Christ comes to make the entire world a Temple of the Lord. This is why a Masonic Lodge is not exactly the representation of the Temple. In fact, the Lodge as a whole, in its entirety, is specifically not supposed to represent Solomon's Temple (*Instr. sec.*, p. 1038). Conversely, of course, the Masonic Lodge does represent the Universal Temple, that is, the entire universe.⁶ This Universal Temple, however, only encircles the two others, which are the particular Temple of our own body and the Sanctuary of Solomon's Temple, into which the Masons strive to enter. Most Masonic Lodges have a starry ceiling. During the Christian Middle Ages, the Temple lived in the collective mentality as a symbol of both the universal macrocosm and the human microcosm. This brings to mind as well the symbol of the square rule and compass, which were used in the form of a circle and a square in romanesque artistry and in its vocabulary to signify, among other things, immortal Man enclosed in a mortal body. The body of Man is at once Lodge and Sanctuary; the Lodge is at once the body of Man and the Masonic place.

It is not irrelevant to ask in what way the basic idea of this symbolism conforms to Biblical tradition. If we compare Solomon's Temple or the Tabernacle carried in the desert with the Temples of the other Eastern religions, we will understand better why this sacred bond with the God of Israel assumed this cosmic character. God Himself offers the figurative example of the Dwelling called to serve as bridge between heaven and earth: "According to all that I show you concerning the pattern of the Tabernacle and all of its furniture, so you shall make it." (Ex. 25:9); and again: "You have bidden me build a temple on your holy mountain, and an altar in the city where you have pitched your tent, a copy of the holy Tent which you prepared at the beginning" (Wis. 9:8). God resides in His celestial Temple ("From His Temple He heard my voice and my cry to Him reached His ears" (Ps. 18:6); "He who conquers I will make him a pillar in the temple of my God" (Rv. 3:12), and the material temple is one of the "copy and shadow of the heavenly sanctuary" (Heb. 8:5). Nevertheless, this cosmic symbolism conceived as a representation of the universe only appears explicitly in Philo of Alexandria and in Flavius Josephus. The latter wrote that "the purpose of each of the objects of the Temple is to bring to mind and to symbolize the cosmos" (*Ant.* III, 7,7); similarly, Philo writes: "It was proper that in building a sanctuary made by the hand of man for the Father and head of the universe, components were used that were like to those with which he made all things."⁷ We find this concept again in the Midrashim. According to an ancient rabbinic tradition, the three parts of Solomon's Temple were the *debir* (the Holy of Holies where the Ark was placed), which corresponded to the highest heavens, the *hekal* (porch), which corresponded to the rest of the earth, and the *ulam* (courtyard) which

---

6. According to the old rituals—especially those of the eighteenth century—the Lodge is not supposed to be taking place in Solomon's Temple but under the Porch of the Temple. The Lodge only stands before the House of the Lord, it is the road that leads to it.

7. *Vit. Moys.*, III, 6. These two texts are cited by Jean Daniélou in "La Symbolique cosmique du Temple de Jérusalem", *Annuaire 1953 de l'École Pratique des Hautes Études, Ve Section* (cf. "Symbolisme et monuments religieux," p. 61 ff.), from which I have borrowed the basic idea of this part of my analysis.

corresponded to the sea.[8] Admittedly, this symbolism is almost totally absent from the Old Testament because the presence of God in the Temple constituted, in the mind of its compilers, a reality that they considered more important than His presence in the universe. God chose to make Jerusalem His residence within the Temple of His Chosen People. That is why there was only one Temple of Jerusalem, while there were many churches or synagogues. Moreover, the divine covenant with the Chosen People would necessarily limit any projection of this onto a universal plane, but this symbolism is not truly absent from the Old Testament, if we allow that it is found there potentially. In fact it is in the New Testament that it is fully realized. It is in Christianity that we see why the Temple represents at one and the same time both a building and the human body, or even a group of disciples, and also that the representations can be multiplied infinitely (synagogues or churches), while always representing a single figurative model. There is only one Mount Zion, and while there may be several earthly cities, there is only one Heavenly Jerusalem. In the same way, each man is both similar to every other man but also unique. A microcosm of the universe, he is made up of a body, a soul, and a spirit (1 Cor., 15:44–45). Christianity conceives of immortality only in terms of the full restoration of the body through the spirit. As we will see, this triptych corresponds to that of the Porch, of the Temple proper, and of the Sanctuary.[9]

Willermoz and his Brethren did not give any real preference to the archetype of the Temple in the synchronic sense, however. They were acutely interested in what could be called historical temples, figurative symbols of the history of the human race. It is primarily in the *Conférences de Lyon* that we find telling remarks on this subject. We are not surprised to read that the first Temple was that of Adam. The author then mentions seven principal ones. After Adam came those of Enoch, Melchizedek, Moses (that is, the Ark of the Covenant), Solomon, Zerubbabel, and Jesus Christ. This typology expresses the "deliverance" and the "reconciliation." But "the others, such as Noah, Abraham, etc., are of a different type" (p. 17) and we will deal with them later. The author does not develop the symbolism of the Temple of Adam, which is to be expected, if one recalls the basic concepts of the cosmogony of Martines.

---

8. André Caquot. "La Religion d'Israël, des origines à la captivité de Babylone," in *Histoire des Religions*, t. I, (Paris, Gallimard, "Bibl. de la Pléiade", 1971) p. 421.

9. Curiously, a Mason by the name of Alex Horne, *King Solomon's Temple in the Masonic Tradition*, London, Aquarian Press, 1972, *never* refers to the R.S.R. in his somewhat deceptively titled work. It is a good work of erudition but is almost totally lacking in any clear understanding of symbolism.

As for Enoch, the text is even more interesting in as much as it brings in some ideas appropriated from the *Traité de la Réintégration* and not found in the *Instructions secrètes*. The Temples of Enoch, Moses, and Solomon correspond not only to stages of humanity, but equally to the three classes of spiritual beings of the universal creation (p. 67, parag. II; cf. also *infra*, on the idea of the ternary in creation). The Temple of Enoch, which followed directly that of Adam, "is completely spiritual"; its purpose is solely to teach divine law to mankind (p. 67, parag. III; cf. also *Traité*, p. 105). The Ark of the Covenant, or the Temple of Moses, symbolized the spirits of the supracelestial (p. 67, parag. III). The next two Temples, those of Solomon and Zerubbabel, contained the essence of the Martinesist typology. This essence is Christ, who is as clearly a Temple as Adam was.

For the Mason as for the Elect-Cohen, the Temple has a certain synchronic aspect in the sense that it symbolizes diverse spheres of creation (p. 17; cf. also *infra*, regarding this alchemical tripartism), such as the human body. It also has a diachronic aspect in the sense that it symbolizes certain stages in the history of the human species. And it symbolizes the Lodge and even Masonry as a whole, conceptualized both diachronically and synchronically, that is to say proceeding as much from linear history as from the immutable archetype. But the Temple is not an empty symbol, an abstract being. It has a distinct, concrete existence like the universe it symbolizes. God—so the Bible says—made everything according to number, weight, and size. Thus it is to be expected that in studying the Temple we find ourselves dealing with numbers. Let us take a closer look at the primary elements of this science of numbers.

ARITHMOSOPHIC ELEMENTS

Martines de Pasqually taught that the Universal Temple, Nature, is divided into three parts: terrestrial, celestial, and supracelestial. Likewise, Solomon's Temple had three parts: the Porch, the Inner Temple and the Sanctuary. Similarly the human body has belly, chest, and head. In each case the three parts are inseparable (*Instr. Sec.*, p. 1040). The ritual of the first degree clearly calls this tripartism to mind: "*Question*: How many parts are there to the Temple? *Answer*: Three. The Porch, the Temple, and the Sanctuary."[10] The Sanctuary of Solomon's Temple enclosed the Holy of Holies. Likewise, the terrestrial and celestial universes are separated from the divine vastness by the

---

10. Cited by Désaguiliers, op. cit., no. 9, p. 8.

supracelestial (cf. the diagram). Furthermore, Man's intellect is seated in his head, "as in the Sanctuary of his personal Temple," which is why one must be purified in order to enter one's true sanctuary, where one is to offer homage to the Divine. Head, heart, stomach; Sanctuary, Inner Temple, Porch; supracelestial, celestial, terrestrial. Everything "corresponds" (21).

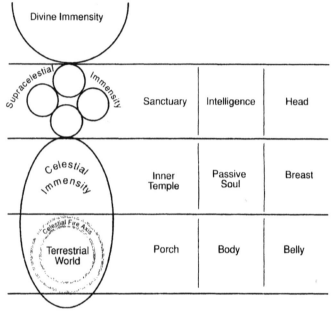

Sanctuary	Intelligence	Head
Inner Temple	Passive Soul	Breast
Porch	Body	Belly

There are agents who operate in each of these areas. The Porch corresponds to the earth and to the Bronze Sea, which was used for physical preparations of Temple offerings and stores, and also to the belly by reason of its material functions of growth and reproduction. The Inner Temple corresponds to the celestial. There we find the altar of incense, the twelve loaves of the shewbread, and the seven-branched candelabra. It is also the chest or the heart, the seat of animate life, the altar on which man must offer the daily incense to the Divine One. The Sanctuary therefore "figures or represents the supracelestial and man's head (*Instr. sec.*, p. 1041). Likewise, speaking typologically, when Moses went up on Sinai, he first made the people stay behind at the foot of the mountain, symbol of the earth, the unhappy abode of Man. Moses then went on further with Aaron and the seventy heads of the tribes, who were in turn left behind at a certain point, and continued on his way with Joshua for a while longer. This stage corresponds to the celestial. Finally, he completes his climb alone, and arrives at the sanctuary, the Holy of Holies, which corresponds to the supracelestial (*Instr. sec.*, p. 1041 ff.). Sinai also corresponds to the three circles of Martines's diagram: the base where the camp was, the sensual circle, the middle where Joshua stopped, the visual circle; and the top to which Moses climbed, the rational circle, dominated by the

Supracelestial (p. 82). The application of these concepts to matters of ritual are numerous. We will cite only one example. The apprentice candidate made three journeys, that is to say, three circles around the Temple that was traced out in the midst of the Lodge. This Temple itself had three enclosures, which represented not only the layout of Solomon's Temple but also the three universal divisions (terrestrial, celestial, and supracelestial) of this great edifice of Nature (*Instr. sec.*, p. 1045).

Just as it was comprised of three parts, so too did Solomon's Temple possess four lateral walls that enabled everyone to see it. Man has four limbs whose purpose is to carry out his actions upon his surroundings. The four walls, like these four limbs, can disappear without its tripartite essence perishing. This is because the functions of the Levites and those performing the sacrifices take place inside the Temple, just as "the seat of the sensual life resides essentially in the trunk" (*Instr. sec.*, p. 1040). This fourfold symbolism must be compared with that of the "tabernacle," that is to say, with the Ark of the Covenant built by Bethsaleel. This tabernacle "is the real symbol of the world, because it contains in its small expanse everything that the wide world contains in its immense space" (*Traité*, p. 359). It has four gates. The East gate, which Moses entered to invoke the inhabitants of the supracelestial, represents the heart of Man, because it is through the heart that the Creator directly reaches us with his favors through the agency of the inhabitants of the supracelestial. The West gate of the Ark of the Covenant corresponds to the eyes. The South gate corresponds to the ears (*Traité*, p. 356). As for Bethsaleel and his two associates, they "are a true reference to the three part number, which constitutes the vital force of the inferior spirits who produced the three spirituous essences from which proceeded all corporal forms" (*Traité*, p. 353). There are four divisions in the universe: the terrestrial, celestial, supracelestial, and the divine vastness (cf. diagram), the last three of which are the proper domain of Man. Likewise, Man has four principal organs "which are the heart on which the senses make their strongest impression, the eyes by which he obtains conviction, the ears by which he acquires the interpretation of that which he has seen and felt, and finally, speech, by which he makes use of and carries out results or product of the other three." The three spiritual forces in us depend on the primary force, which is divine and active, just as speech is the active organ that operates on the other three. In the same way, the East gate of the Ark built by Bethsaleel, which represents the power of the divine vastness, dominates the other three: the West gate, which refers to the terrestrial power, the South gate, which refers to the celestial power, and the North gate, which refers to the supracelestial power (p. 69). The Ark of the Covenant, as well as Solomon's Temple, "is a symbol of the Universal Temple or of Creation of which the temple or the body of man is also a representation." Moses here is like the Creator who ordered the spirits of the central axis to bring forth the three alchemical principles necessary for the construction of the universe. Bethsaleel meanwhile plays the role of the "spirits of the central axis who easily carry out their tasks using the vital force innate within them." Even the incorruptibility of the shittim wood signified the purity and the stability of the three alchemical principles "the action of which will stand firm for the duration of time prescribed by the Creator" (p. 70).

Let us continue this examination of the arithmological principles of the RSR, but limit ourselves to those numbers that have a direct relationship with Temple symbolism. When the Apprentice is asked where he has been accepted, he responds: "Into a just and perfect Lodge; 3 shapes it, it is composed of 5, 7 makes it just and perfect." In the *Instructions secrètes* Willermoz himself interprets this to mean the following. 1) The Lodge into which the Apprentice has been received is his own body, the Temple of his mind. This body carries the number 3 because it is made up of the three alchemical principles (Salt, Sulphur, Mercury). 2) Today, that is to say, since the Fall, this Lodge carries the inauspicious number 5 (cf. *infra*, regarding this number). 3) But then the number 7 makes the Lodge perfect, that is to say it then restores its former perfection. Seven is the number of completeness, the midpoint of the six-pointed star, the number of the Master, the sabbatical act of Man's creation. It is the day that completes the first six days (*Instr. sec.*, p. 1039). It is the number given to Man when God breathed life into Adam (*Instr. sec.*, p. 1040).

In fact, a Lodge or a Temple, necessarily presupposes a superior being to inhabit it. That is why the divine action rested on the seventh day in the created Universe, which was to constitute the Temple where its power would be made manifest to all temporal beings. Similarly Solomon's Temple was built "in six ages or years, and in the seventh it was solemnly dedicated to the Lord" (*Instr. sec.*, p. 1039). Let us take a look at the ritual for the Apprentice degree. A stairway of seven steps was drawn in the Porch section of the Temple. (Remember that the Temple was traced in the middle of the Lodge.) During his initiation the future Apprentice symbolically climbed up three steps and back down. It becomes even more interesting in the next two degrees. To become a Fellow-Craft, the candidate climbed up three steps, then two more, and then back down, thus the number 5. To become a Master Mason, he climbed up seven steps all at once (*Instr. sec.*, p. 1045 ff.), thus reaching the "interior". To fully understand the number 7, we must first speak of 6, which is not mentioned in the ritual phrase ("3 shapes it, it is composed of 5, 7 makes it just and perfect"), but which is nevertheless implicitly omnipresent. The number 6 represents the force that gave life to creation, but this was a passive life. Furthermore, the number 6 comes into play because the three alchemical principles added to the divine tripartism, which infused these three principles in order to "set them in motion and activity," ends up making 6. Also this remarkably even symbolizes the genesis of Solomon's star."[11]

---

11. Remember the traditional signs of the four elements: [∧] (fire), [∨] (water), [A] (air), [∀] (earth).

Animals are represented by the number 6, which is why they also are only represented, in a manner of speaking, by the number 2 (the two triangles). Although they have a body and a soul, they are without a mind. But man is a 3, because he is at once body, soul, and mind, which make up 7 (6 + 1). The number 6 is thus given to the journeyman "as representing the second degree of the temporal journey." It is the number 6, remember, which confers the "passive life" that existed when creation was completed on the sixth day when "animal life was given to the animals of the earth." But then came 7, which made both Man and the Lodge just and perfect (*Instr. sec.*, p. 1046). Furthermore, the Temple proper has four gates—and contains "four hieroglyphs" (67)—and the Porch has three gates (16), which also adds up to 7 and which also corresponds to the columns, to the seven gifts of the Spirit, to the candelabra, etc. (p. 21, cf. also pp. 27–28, about the Jachin and Boaz columns). Similarly, the dimensions of Noah's Ark all carried precise meanings.

Thus the Rectified Scottish Rite, as much in its "metahistorical" myth as in the actual facts of its history, reflects at one and the same time the two basic constituent vectors of humanity in its totality. The *Conférences de Lyon* express this in a simple and clear way. "The task of Masonry is the construction of edifices, firm foundations; we are thus spiritual Masons" (p. 17). Echoing this statement, the *Instructions secrètes* end with this sentence: "Do not lose sight, as Professed and as Mason, of the fact that the error of original Man hurled him from the Sanctuary to the Porch, and that the sole purpose of the Initiation is to enable him to climb back up from the Porch to the Sanctuary" (*Instr. sec.*, p. 1049).

Thus the reconstruction of the Temple must be the work of men, who are described as living stones in the beautiful parable (the 9th) of the *Pastor of Hermas* (first–second century): "And the stones, Lord, I said, which have come out of the depths and been set in order for this construction, who are they? — The first ten, he said, laid in the foundations, are the first generation of just men; the next thirty-five are the prophets of God and his servants and the forty are the apostles, the doctors who proclaimed the doctrine of the Son of God." Furthermore, let us add that this unhewn stone is Nature but also Man himself, and of course the expression "living stone" appears several times in the New Testament.

This is because the Rectified Scottish Rite is in the process of realizing anew the Temple. Without relying on any historical, diachronic affiliation with the long dead Order of Jacques de Molay, it attempted to build the Temple once more both in the vertical, archetypal sphere as well on the more concrete level, through its individual and collective activity. For the Mason this meant reconstructing the original Temple that existed before the Fall, so that God will come back to it and so that men themselves might return as prodigal children, bringing with them all Nature in this Assumption. Each and every act that works to achieve this goal is at once both material and spiritual. Such seems to be one of the meanings of esotericism, to the extent that *eisotheo* means: "I cause to enter." Such is also, perhaps, one of the meanings of the verse from the *Emerald Tablet*: "*Et vis ejus* [i.e., *Dei, unitatis*] *integra est, si conversa fuerit in terram*." "And his power [God's, the Unity's] will be whole and one, if it is converted into earth."[12]

---

12. Since the publication of this article in 1972, a fine book by Henry Corbin has come out, *Temple et contemplation*, (Paris, Flammarion, 1980) in which the author particularly discusses the configuration of the Ka'aba Temple as the secret of spiritual life, and the *Imago templi* vis-à-vis secular standards from Ezekiel to Philo, and in Meister Eckhart and Robert Fludd. Chapters VI–IX deal with Templar chivalry (without forgetting the drama *Die Söhne des Thals* by Zacharias Werner, nor Swedenborg).

THE CHEMICAL WEDDING OF
CHRISTIAN ROSENCREUTZ AS
PILGRIMAGE OF THE SOUL

"The Pilgrims of the Orient and the Wanderers of the Occident." This title struck me as provocative when Henry Corbin proposed it as the theme of our fourth Conference.* But he soon made plain that *Orient* and *Occident* would be understood here in a nongeographical sense: it is a question of a spiritual Orient in our Western world, and one can endeavor to define the specificity of this spirituality. We are indeed the heirs of a tradition that is specific, though smothered by the fashions, the sticky wickets, and the intellectual totalitarianisms that have scarcely ceased to prevail during the course of recent historical periods. It is a tradition whose knowledge can persuade us that the Western mentality is not necessarily condemned to the roving of a spirit lacking a Wisdom, which the Orient alone would possess; and that we do not have to go very far to look for the treasures to which our hearts and souls aspire, since they are right there, directly accessible, the fruits of a tree that stands in our own garden.

I have picked a fruit from this tree, the romance by Andreae. It grew beneath the rays of an Orient obscured by the wandering of a disoriented Occident (our travels to Katmandu are often nothing but rovings). Christian Rosencreutz, a mythic character who is said to have lived for 106 years, from 1378 to 1484, is the hero of this book in German entitled *Chymische Hochzeit Christiani Rosencreutz: Anno 1459* (The "Chemical Wedding" of Christian Rosenkreutz in the Year 1459), published in 1616 in Strasbourg. The author, Johann Valentin Andreae, was a young Lutheran from Tübingen. Christian, Andreae tells us, sought his way: "By chance, he heard about the wise men of

---

* Paper presented at the Conference of the University of Saint John of Jerusalem in Paris, June 18, 1977

Damcar in Arabia, the marvels of which they were capable, and the revelations that had been made to them about nature in all its entirety." Therefore he went to spend three years in Damcar—a mythic city—then crossed "the Arabian Gulf, made a short visit to Egypt, just to perfect his observation of the flora and fauna, then traveled back and forth across the Mediterranean, in order to get to Fez,'" traditionally a city of alchemists. Andreae thus develops his romance with the traditional tale of the voyage to the Orient from which Christian brings back to Germany the knowledge of the Arabs that has passed through Spain. But it concerns an acquired knowledge bearing on Islamic thought, and not an attempt to assimilate the religions of the Far East. The tradition that the hero is going to discover on the spot is the one embracing the three branches of the Abrahamic family. What he discovers over there by no means prompts him to change faith: he remains Christian. In fact, the semi-mythic Orient from which he relates his learning is "only a setting to facilitate the critique of a Europe free of cultural diaspora."[2]

SEVEN ALCHEMICAL DAYS

The mythic Orient, then, understood not only in the sense of a geographic locality adorned with the trappings of exoticism, but taken as a spiritual place is known, in the Christian tradition, as: *the Indies*. According to this tradition, a disciple asked Christ where the "way" is (Jn. 14:5). Christ replied that he would ordain him missionary to the land of the Indies.[1] Such is one of the paths of esotericism; it is a way to travel through, the way toward the interior (*eso-thodos*), *thodos* meaning "method." And Christian Rosy-Cross, at some length in this initiatory romance, undertakes his journey on the evening of Good Friday in order to conclude it on the Wednesday after Easter. The hero thus begins his narration, which is presented in the first person and which extends over seven days:

---

1. Bernard Gorceix, *La Bible des Rose-Croix*, (Paris, P.U.F., 1970), p. 5. This work comprises, in the French translation (the best in that language) by B. Gorceix, the *Confessio*, the *Fama*, and *The Chemical Wedding*, preceded by an excellent introduction by the translator. Roland Edighoffer's thesis, *Rose-Croix et Société idéale selon J.V. Andreae*, Paris, Arma Artis, Vol. I, 1982; Vol. II, 1987, the best work on the question to date (1994) appeared after publication of the present article in the *Cahiers de l'U.S.J.J*. See also Edgihoffer's synthetic approach: *Les Rose-Croix*, (Paris, P.U.F., collec. "Que Sais-Je?", 1982). And Joscelyn Godwin's translation and presentation of Andreae's *Chemical Wedding*, (Grand Rapids, MI, Phanes Press, 1993).

2. B. Gorceix, ibid, introduction, p. xxxiii.

3. Cited by Gerhard Wehr, *Esoterisches Christentum*, (Stuttgart, Klett Verlag, 1975), p. 273.

It was on the eve of Easter. I was sitting at my table, and as was my custom I had just come to the end of the conversation I was conducting with my creator in my humble prayer and meditated on the numerous great mysteries of which the Father of Light in his majesty, had given me ample revelation. I was also going to prepare a spotless unleavened wafer in my heart to sustain the gracious paschal lamb, when a wind began to blow gusts so cruel that I was sure the mountain in which my little house had been hollowed out was going to be split asunder by the violence of their assaults.[4]

Then he beholds a woman of marvelous beauty, who suddenly appears in an all-blue gown spangled with golden stars. She delivers an invitation to a mystic marriage, presented to him in verse form and signed: "the bride, the bridegroom." Next Christian has a prophetic dream; then he writes:

I equipped myself for the voyage, put on my white linen coat girded my loins with a blood red band that I crossed over my shoulders. I stuck four red roses in my hat as a sign of recognition. For traveling supplies I took bread salt and water on the advice of an initiate which when the time came, were of great help to me. Before leaving my hut, I knelt down, in my outfit and wedding clothes, beseeching God to bring everything to a successful end come what may.[5]

Then begins the second day. On leaving his cell, scarcely having entered the forest, it seems to him that the whole sky and all the elements have decked themselves for the wedding. He describes his voyage and the first evening at the castle, his hesitation among four ways of approach, passing through three enclosures, dinner, and a second dream. The third day, the day of the judgment of the unworthy and the giving out of the Golden Fleece, is also the one of carrying out the judgment in the garden, the castle visit, the hanging of the weights, and a third dream. Wedding preparations make up the subject of the fourth day: there are the scene in the garden and the presentation to the royal persons, as well as an astonishing theatrical presentation, then the death of the royal persons who are beheaded, and finally the shipping of the coffins in the night. The fifth day describes the trip on the water: the second garden scene and Christian's transgression during his visit to the underground dwelling of Venus, the fictitious burial of the royal persons, travel over water, the ceremony of the sea goddesses, the arrivals at the tower of Olympus, and a nocturnal scene. Then, on the sixth day, we are present at the resurrection of the king and queen who had been beheaded; the resurrection is carried out in

---

4. J.V. Andreae, *Les Noces Chymiques* . . . , in B. Gorceix, op. cit., p. 35 ff.
5. Ibid., pp. 36–44.

seven stages on the seven tiers of the tower of Olympus. The royal spouses sail away, and Christian converses with the old man, the guardian of the tower. Finally, the return to the events of the seventh day, with the giving out of the Order of the Golden Stone, the admission of the transgression and the punishment. An unexpected outcome ends the book, which remains incomplete and ends with these lines:

> In this place two quarto sheets are missing, and he [meaning the author of the book] has returned to his homeland whereas he had expected to be the gatekeeper in the morning.[6]

This mere summary of the "action" of the *Chemical Wedding* reminds us of the German romances of the Round Table, especially of Wolfram von Eschenbach's *Parzifal*, which dates from the beginning of the thirteenth century. On the other hand, this work was written at the time when baroque literature was springing to life in Germany and when the Mannerist current already sparkled with countless lights; it represents one of the most beautiful examples of this literature but at the same time is inscribed in a romantic chain whose most important preceding links, from the esoteric standpoint, are perhaps Francesco Colonna's *Dream of Poliphilo* (1499), the *Fifth Book* of François Rabelais (1564), and The *Voyage of the Fortunate Princes* by Beroalde de Verville (1610).[7] The beginning of the seventeenth century was also the golden age of literature and of alchemical or "hermeticist" iconography in Germany; between 1600 and 1618 in fact, Paracelsus, Jacob Boehme, Johannes Arndt, Valentin Weigel, and Heinrich Khunrath were published or reissued. The authors of the Rosicrucian manifestoes and the author of the *Chemical Wedding* also wrote as a function of the spiritual situation of their era: they attacked the dogmatism of the princes and the churches, the "Lutheran and Calvinist caesaro-papism"; they announced a general Reform, an upsetting and salutary restoration, and they prayed for its coming. Andreae conceived the Rosicrucian fable in order to effect a synthesis of pre-Baroque esotericism in a setting worthy of the cabinets of curiosities (*Kunstkammern*) of his contemporary Rodolph of Hapsburg.[8]

But this *Chemical Wedding* is above all an alchemical and mystical wedding; under the enlightening cloak of the symbol, it describes the process of the ascent of the soul toward God. On almost every page one finds references to the Great Spiritual Work. Thus, on the fifth day the six boats begin their sea pilgrimage, which recalls *The Odyssey*, or even Pantagruel on the way to

---

6. Ibid., p. 125. For the summary I have drawn from B. Gorceix, ibid., introduction.
7. Cf. ibid, p. ix ff.
8. Cf. ibid., pp. xx ff., xxxv ff.

the Enchanted Islands. Water, as we know, is often the symbol of Mercury, the figure of dissolution; in these themes and in the alchemical illustrations, there are numerous representations of boats sailing on a rough sea, or of islands surrounded by water-filled trenches that must be crossed, as the adepts of *The Wedding* try to do. This is a theme that at the time was also inserted into a genre, that of faraway travels—El Dorado!—and of mythology—*The Odyssey*, the expedition of the Argonauts. . . .⁹ But beyond the imagined representations there are the stages, the processes, of the pilgrimage of the soul. A pilgrimage, in reality, since the adept, who knows where he wants to go, seeks to rediscover the place where the soul is united with its God. Thus, during the sixth day the candidates are presented with ropes, ladders, and large wings. A circular trapdoor opens up in the ceiling, through which they see a lady who invites them to climb up. Christian, to whom a ladder chances to fall, thinks he is at a disadvantage; what follows shows the contrary, for those who use wings climb too quickly, and those who climb the rope blister their hands. The alchemist therefore chooses among three methods: either he toils without any outside help and dangerously exposes himself (the rope); or he progresses too hastily, which is harmful to the maturation of the work (the wings); or else he scales the intermediate steps rung by rung. This symbolism of the ladder, frequent in alchemical and spiritual iconography—a notable example being the bas-relief on the grand portal of Notre Dame de Paris—obviously recalls Jacob's ladder (Gen. 28:12) and appears to represent the stages of the so-called "humid" way as opposed to the "dry" way.¹⁰

The work is presented in the form of a septenary, which quite clearly represents the traditional operations of the Great Work. The action thus describes in seven acts—the "days"—the seven stages of alchemical transmutation. Before the final realization, a particularly trying ordeal awaits the adept, who must witness the beheading of the royal persons. But the phoenix, symbol of the resurrection, soon appears; its egg is cut up with a diamond; its blood brings back to life the royal couple whose nuptials will confer the title of "Knight of the Golden Stone" on Christian. That is the final purpose of the journey, the whole of the seven acts representing the pilgrimage itself. Of what does this peregrination consist?

In a work devoted to Andreae, J.W. Montgomery has attempted to extract the processional sense of the seven phases as it may appear to us in the

---

9. B. Gorceix, op. cit., p. 100, n.1. and R.J.W. Evans, *Rodolf II and his World. A Study in Intellectual History*, (Oxford, Clarendon Press, 1984).

10. Perhaps the ladder can be interpreted as representing the way termed "short," intermediate between the "dry" and "wet" ways. The rope then represents the wet way.

Chemical Wedding.[11] The first four stages correspond to what the alchemists call the *Nigredo* (black), the next two to the *Albedo* (white), the seventh to the *Rubedo*, in other words to the red work, the end of the Great Work. I draw upon the list proposed by Montgomery, interpreting it here in synthetic fashion.

Distillation opens the Work. It is the point of departure, getting under way. In his macrocosmic pilgrimage, Christian sees a raven, a dove, and a virgin in a sky-blue costume (first and third days). In his first dream he finds himself prisoner at the bottom of a pit, among other prisoners, all trying to climb on top of one another in order to get out. In like manner, Man knows the evils he suffers better through his relations with others. *Calcination* is next, since any alchemy traditionally begins with death: in the *Wedding* we are present first at the physical and spiritual ordeals, symbolized by dismemberings and tonsurings—the death of the self. Similarly, the white garments of the six sovereigns will become black. *Putrefaction*, the third stage, corresponds to the darkness in which Christian is chained up and which is a source of anguish for him (first and third days); it is also humanity hanging from the rope that is dropped down (first day). This is existential death, the loss of personal identity. In a like manner (days 4 and 7), the six sovereigns are beheaded. Finally, *solution–dissolution* occurs, the last stage of the *Nigredo*. Christian is wounded by a sharp stone, and he is weighed with other people on a scale that sorts out the good human wheat from the chaff. It is also the war between the forces of the good king and those of the Moor, or the transport of the corpses by boat, their purification and their dissolution (days 4 and 7), or even the calcination of the body of the bird whose ashes are then purified.

Then the ascent begins. Catabolism is dangerous because many are lost on the way; anabolism, the climb, is, in effect, the continuation. Alchemy puts the process called *coagulation* at the beginning of this "white work." Christian is pulled out of the pit, and he passes his trial successfully (days 1 and 3). The fiancée is saved by the good king; the liquified bodies are heavier than their living form; a dough is made from the ashes, from which will arise a *homunculus* and a *homuncula*. On the psychological level, that corresponds to the reordering of the heretofore fragmented elements of the personality. The following stage, the *vivification*, is symbolized here by the passage in which one sees Christian, freed from his chains, authorized to attend the "chemical marriage" (days 1 and 3), as well as by the sun that heats the solution in a large golden globe (we are present at the production of an egg as white as snow). The characters that may have been thought definitely to be dead come back

11. John Warwick Montgomery, *Cross and Crucible. Johann Valentin Andreae (1586–1654), Phoenix of the Theologians*, The Hague, Nijhoff, "Archives Internationales d'Histoire des Idées," no. 55, 2 vol. Cf. v. II, pp. 279–281.

to life again thanks to the flames from heaven (days 4 and 7). We can see self-realization there, the reintegration of the personality. Finally, the ultimate stage of the Great Work and true *Rubedo*: this is *multiplication*, or *projection*. Christian is entrusted with a message; he is given gold to spend and distribute on the way. He even sees himself awarded the privilege of freeing an emperor (days 1 and 3): the eggs, incubated for a long time, end by hatching. The fiancée takes the oath of allegiance, recovers possession of her kingdom, and gets crowned. The king and queen appear with great pomp (*"Vivat sponsus, vivit sponsa!"*), then embark on a ship of gold to participate in the great banquet (days 4 and 7). Thus the personality, reintegrated thanks to the passage to the sixth stage, is now found capable of radiating outwardly for the greatest good of others and of the world.[12]

GRACE AND GNOSIS OR THE CONJUNCTION OF OPPOSITES

This, in broad outline, presents Christian's pilgrimage, the interior voyage whose description borrows its structure and its symbolism from traditional alchemy. The book invites us to descend within ourselves, while being transformed. *Innenweg*, the inward or "intimate" way, the process of internal elaboration, of memorization: *er-innern* as the German nicely puts it, that is at once "to remember" and "to go deeply into one's self"; to have born or rather reborn what, in the germ at the bottom of the soul, aspires only to sprout in spite of our human condition as sinners. The pilgrimage toward the spirit, the *Wanderschaft zum Geist*, thus continues to be the main concern; the author, underneath the profusion of settings and symbols, proposes this pilgrimage to the Man of Desire anxious to go beyond the first level of reading. He is concerned less with a "mystical wedding," however, than with an alchemical wedding; the quest does not bear exclusively on interiority, since all Nature is assumed, included, in a process of transmutation by the spirit. Christian's pilgrimage, begun in the meditation cell, soon leads the hero into the "forest"; we see him lose his way, get his bearings, lose his way again in the meanders, the splendor, the misery of the world, and finally reappear quite different than at the beginning of the narration. He learns how to know the world because he is turned toward it; he possesses this *Weltzugewandtheit* at the same time that he descends within himself. It is a creative paradox, a constructive one—as characteristic of the great alchemical tradition, as it is of the teaching called "Rosicrucian" already given out by the two manifestoes of 1614 and 1615, the *Fama* having made Christian the student of Paracelsus and the reader, or the

---

12. Ibid., pp. 279–281.

coauthor of the mythic *Liber mundi*.[13] Knowledge and Faith, or light and grace, allow him to orientate himself during his journey.

But do grace and redemption occupy an essential place in alchemy? Doesn't the adept give instead the impression of a sort of demiurge seeking to scale the steps leading to the gates of heaven by his own means? That is the sentiment that a recent commentator on the *Chemical Wedding* expressed in regard to non-Lutheran Hermeticism, notably that of Paracelsus. Montgomery did recognize a Hermetist tradition in this romance teaching the need to join the macrocosm and the microcosm, or the universe and Man, by the affirmation of the central position of Christ at the intersection of these two vectors, which results in making the truth of the Gospel penetrate into all creation.[14] He notes, however, that the notion of the Redemption has little importance in Paracelsism, in which Man, the absolute center of the universe, must *rise* (a Neoplatonist idea), while the Christian revelation puts the accent on the *descent* of God come to save us, incapable as we would be of raising ourselves by ourselves to Him. In other words, this author seeks to oppose *Naturphilosophie* and the theology of the Revelation. To be sure, it seems that Andreae wanted to forget somewhat the Paracelsian *Naturphilosophie* explicit in the two manifestoes and oriented by Eros, on behalf of a theology of Revelation, putting the accent essentially on the Redemption.[15] *The Tower of Babel*, the title of a book by Andreae published in 1620 (*Turris Babel*), represents for the latter the overanthropocentric temptation to take the ramparts of heaven by assault, making use of an "occult wisdom," while according to the Gospel the descent of God into humanity, His death, and His Resurrection alone make salvation possible. No doubt Montgomery goes too far in considering the inverse, anabatic movement to be incompatible with Christianity, whereas it agrees very well with the faith provided that it is not favored exclusively. It does not appear to me that Andreae himself went that far in his own criticism. The problem is an important one, for by affirming that one has everything to expect from God and that unaided we are powerless, it comes to pass that God withdraws from our hearts and souls, and we no longer even take the initiative to start out on the pilgrimage toward the place where God and Man meet each other. On the contrary, the better way to meet is perhaps for each to go toward the other.

---

13. Cf. also Gerhard Wehr, op. cit, p. 231; and Antoine Faivre, "Voie interne et pensée ésotérique dans le Romantisme (France et Allemagne)," in A. Faivre, *Mystiques, théosophes et illuminés au siècle des Lumières,* (Hildesheim, Ed. Olms, 1976), pp. 191–200.

14. Cf. A. Faivre, "Roicruciana," in *Revue de L'Histoire des Religions,* (Paris, P.U.F., 1976), p. 158.

15. Andreae may have found the two manifestoes insufficiently Christian in the degree to which the latter, in preaching asceticism and celibacy, would suggest a radical opposition of matter and spirit.

This double movement accounts for what could well be the common denominator of Christian theosophy and alchemy, as it is expressed in the verses of the *Emerald Tablet*. The well-known text is given here not in the version that is usually quoted but in an English translation of the poetic, rarer version of Jacques de Nuisement published in 1621:[16]

> True it is; know with sure admiration
> That the high is the same thing as the low
> From all to one through one to all must go
> All wondrous effects of adaptation.
>
> One is turned to all through meditation,
> As nurse and womb and parents it shall know
> Earth the wind Diana and Apollo
> In this thing alone lies all perfection.
>
> Changed into earth its power is entire:
> Gently separate the earth from the fire.
> The subtle with great wisdom from the coarse.
>
> From the earth it climbs to Heaven then to aspire
> To earth once more where it will gain the force
> Of each the high and low that all require.

Andreae and his Tübingen friends specify and reaffirm, at the beginning of the seventeenth century, the need for a "pansophy" or "harmonic, ordered synthesis of all the sciences and all creeds . . . ; it is a question of realizing the

---

16.   C'est un point asseuré plein d'admiration
       Que le haut et le bas n'est qu'une mesme chose:
       Pour faire d'une seule en tout le monde enclose,
       Des effets merveilleux par adaptation.

       D'un seul en a tout fait la méditation,
       Et pour parents, matrice, et nourrice, on luy pose
       Phoebus, Diane, l'air, et la terre, ou repose
       Cette chose en qui gist toute perfection.

       Si, on la mue en terre elle a sa force entière:
       Separant par grand art, mais facile manière,
       Le subtil de l'espais, et la terre du feu.

       De la terre elle monte au Ciel; et puis en terre,
       Du Ciel elle descend. Recevant peu à peu,
       Les vertus de tous deux qu'en son ventre elle enserre.

       (p. 329 in: Jacques de Nuysement, *Traittez de l'Harmonie et Constitution Generalle du Vray Sel*, Paris, 1621.)

unity of knowledge, of reconciling the totality of knowing with the totality of faith."[17] It was at precisely at this time that alchemical thought and parallel traditions tended to fuse—as one sees with Jacob Boehme, a trend already perceptible in Paracelsus. One can show how this meeting of traditional mysticism and Paracelsian hylozoism, in Valentin Weigel (1533–1588), corresponds to the birth of what is called Germanic theosophy.[18] For the soul it means rising toward God through knowing and interpreting the scattered "signs" in the world, just as divine grace and the descent of God in Man allow us to understand this world and at the the same time hasten its reintegration. The pilgrimage, then, is ambiguous; it invites two simultaneous directions: starting from the divine grace in us, or from the knowledge of God, in order to understand Nature, to transform it; and starting from this Nature whose arcana lead us, stage by stage, to the knowledge of God. Therefore, we see why the *Chemical Wedding* is the first alchemical work cited by C.G. Jung in his work with the evocative title *Mysterium conjunctionis*.[19] And probably because it concerns a union, the pilgrimage is never truly finished but always to be resumed. Andreae's romance comes to an end *ex abrupto*. Goethe's long poem (*The Mysteries*), written in 1784–1785, before the voyage to Italy, also ends suddenly; one finds in it a remarkable allusion to the rose and the cross:

> The cross is tightly twined with roses
> Who has joined the roses to the cross?[20]

Who sees this image? The young Markus. After a long and arduous journey, he notices a cloister at nightfall, tries to make out the symbol, and hears:

> You come this way on wondrous paths,
> Says the kindly old man still approaching.
> Let these emblems convince you to stay
> Till you learn what many heros
> do with them .[21]

---

17. Cf. B. Gorceix, op. cit., p. xxiii.
18. Cf. ibid., p. lv; and by the same author: *Valentin Weigel 1533–1588 et les origines de la théosophie allemande*, (University of Lille III, thesis copy department, 1972), 500.
19. Cf. B. Gorceix, *La Bible des Rose-Croix*, op. cit, p. L.
20. P. 221: "*Es steht das Kreuz mit Rosen dicht umschlungen. / Wer hat dem Kreuze Rosen zugesellt?*"
21. Ibid., p. 235: "*Du kommst hierher auf wunderbaren Pfaden, / Spricht ihn der Alte wieder freundlich an; / Lass die Bilder dich zu bleiben laden, / Bis du erfährst, was mancher Held getan.*"

FROM VAGABONDAGE TO PILGRIMAGE

Markus and Christian are spiritual wanderers insofar as they lack a very clear understanding of the goal of their journey; they are pilgrims none the less, insofar as they know that a goal exists. Each of the two narrations puts both voyage and realization under the sign of the cross. Nevertheless, the Christian pilgrimage, viewed from a theosophical standpoint, is never intended to come to an end at a definitive resting place or a static satisfaction suppressing forward movement or annihilating the two movements directed toward each other. The theosophy based on a philosophy of Nature—in the Paracelsian sense and, later on, as in German Romanticism—introduces or reinstates into Christian thought a philosophy of life, a dialectical life exclusive of any static state. That is why one could, for example, compare Jacob Boehme to a spiritual wanderer who never agrees to a definitely concluded wedding but who remains prisoner of a dialectic. It is certain that Boehme sees dialectic everywhere, the tension of opposites, and places in the divine itself, hence at the ontological level, a never-resolved contradiction between a pole of light and a pole of darkness; for him all life, all creation, and all substantial reality rest on this polarity. Others, on the contrary, appear to have known about the marriage without the pilgrimage.[22] With regard to this Christian Hermeticism, one can speak of wanderers of the West provided that one does not mean by that the contemporary type of wandering, which is sterile, shorn of value and meaning.[23] For Boehme and his brothers in theosophy, death does not eliminate the eternal dialectical tension, the endless pilgrimage, since this *Lebensphilosophie* puts the dynamic and dialectical processes in the divine world as well. The very teaching of Christ seems to invite us to a never definitively interrupted trek. The wandering people of God traverse the history of peoples and cultures indefinitely, their God is a historic God who accompanies them, whereas the natural divinities of paganism were linked to places, to fixed localities. The experience of the pilgrim people is always to prolong, to resume: *er-fahren*, "to experience," means "to go," and at the same time suggest an elaboration, an internal process.

The alchemical allegory centered on Christian translates simultaneously the salvational work *in nobis* (Christian's pilgrimage) and *pro nobis* (the marriage of the King and Queen), but we are present less at the subjective marriage of the hero and Christ than at the description of the story of salvation and of Christ's union with the Church. Therefore the subject is not so much Christian's wedding itself, but rather a pilgrimage by which the hero recapit-

---

22. Cf. the work of J.W. Montgomery, op. cit., and A. Faivre, "Rosicruciana," cited article, p. 159.
23. Cf. Jean Bruns's book *Les Vagabonds de l'Occident*, Paris, 1974.

ulates what God has done for him through the entirety of the story of the salvation. The experience proper—this *Erfahrung*—would probably be incommunicable. The *Chemical Wedding* is presented therefore more as a spiritual
atlas than as the narration of an inner experience. This is the "*carte du tendre*"
in Christian Hermetist practice, not the romantic narration of an ineffable
true-to-life story.

It has been maintained that Andreae must have written the *Wedding* to
Christianize CRC (the Christian Rosencreutz of the *Fama*). The *Fama* relates
the hero's travels to the Orient, so far from Christian lands! It is about the
same character, always the lover of peregrination, like Pantagruel,[24] first the
pilgrim of the Orient and the Occident in the *Fama*, finally the pilgrim only
from the Christian Occident in the *Wedding*, that is, from the inner Orient, or
the mystic Indies. Christian probably did not spend much time visiting
Damcar and Fez, since these cities were supposed to be only places along the
way where one stops off only once, while the *Wedding* is placed entirely under
the sign of the Redeemer. Christian was never a true Western wanderer in the
negative sense, for his Orient was "oriented": the young adept was seeking to
educate himself through Islam and the Kabbalah. The disoriented taste for
the Orient among those who have lost their roots or who have cut them off:
that is true wandering, the roving that surrenders errant souls to the deadened
itineraries of a Jack Kerouac or to the mirages of Katmandu.

On the road to Emmaus the disciples were wandering about, despairing
of seeing the star reappear so that they might find their way again. They did
not know that very close to them, within speaking and seeing distance, was
the One whose coming they no longer dared to expect. Very close to us,
within the reach of our grasp and sight, riches wait to be taken back, consulted, meditated on, by each Man of Desire: these are the motifs of our
cathedrals, the liturgies of our churches, the symbols of our triple Abrahamic
tradition. It is incumbent on us to take back these messages, to reiterate them,
while "bringing back" their meaning. This is indeed a pilgrimage, that of setting out to study the texts of our predecessors. But this too can be a roving, a
wandering in a purely descriptive historical search that is taken as an end in
itself. Armed with historicism alone—in the sense that Henry Corbin gave
this word—we penetrate into infinite labyrinths, rove the microscopic instead
of taking ourselves as the microcosm and orienting ourselves in the macrocosm. It behooves us to know where we are not going—where we do not want
to go; but to advance toward *meaning* implies a compass.

Spiritual alchemy, in the sense in which we understand it here, is a magnetic needle. Its symbolism blossoms forth in polysemic fashion in bouquets
of meaning that mark the itinerary: we know then where we are going, even if

---

24. B. Gorceix, *La Bible des Rose-Croix*, op. cit., p. xi.

we sometimes find it difficult to understand how we are going there. Alchemy is a game—a serious game, *lusus serius,* to take up Michel Maier's title. Nevertheless, we are not going there as we would go toward an objective situated in the way a localized temple would be, for it is above all a question of finding, that is constructing, a *place*—but not a fixed point. Our voyage is infinite, because it is always pursued in a spiral. It is an eternal pilgrimage, which does not have at its end a paradise in which nothing would fade away any more; a permanent re-creation, as if it were less a question of succeeding than of always proceeding, and of knowing why. This form of pilgrimage is not based on an ideal of *perfection*—like holiness—but on an ideal of *wholeness.* We are not told that those who met Christ on the road to Emmaus would then be lost in the eternal immobility of some kind of unitive, if also cognitive, fusion. Let us imagine that, on the contrary, through this meeting with the Resurrected One they received the definite impulse toward a perpetual and at the same time eternally creative movement on the spiritual plane.

A spiral voyage then. And if the knot is never definitively tied, humano-cosmic harmony is revealed in that way as all the more creative, fecund, heavy with infinite begettings. Christian's chemical wedding does not end, the romance remains unfinished. I should like this paper to end as well, here, unfinished as it were, at the opening of these new crossroads.

MILES REDIVIVUS: ASPECTS OF THE CHIVALRIC IMAGINATION IN EIGHTEENTH-CENTURY ALCHEMY, FREEMASONRY AND LITERATURE

Right in the midst of the Enlightenment we come across the imagery of the knight. What is it doing there, and what need is it fulfilling? At the moment when the *Encyclopédie* was beginning to appear, when the *Aufklärung* was celebrating its first triumphs, this imagery stands in stark contrast to a dry rationalism, displaying a renewed creative presence, and exhibiting itself under new and diverse garb—thus the name of *miles redivivus*, which I suggest for following the knight, up to about 1815, in the three fields in which he manifested himself: the literature of alchemy, Freemasonry, and literature in the strict sense (novel, drama, epic).* Throughout Europe, but above all in Germany, which from the Renaissance until the present day has remained, more than any other country, the conservatory of most symbolic and initiatory traditions. Let us see what use was made of the orders of chivalry when taken over by myth, and let us try to extract some major themes.

Since the fifteenth century Europe has owed its popular vision of the chivalrous Middle Ages mainly to the *Chevalier au Lion* and *Amadis de Gaule*. This was so right through the eighteenth century, principally thanks to the books of the peddlar trade. To this must be added a periodically renewed interest in certain older works, such as Rixner's *Anfang . . . des Thurniers inn Teutscher Nation*, published in 1530. Understandably, the technical and pre-

---

* Paper presented at the Conference of the Committee of Studies on Symbology (in Tomar, Portugal) April 1983, and at the Conference of the University of Saint John of Jerusalem (Paris), June 1984.

cise details of this work and, above all, its numerous plates caused a ferment of imagination. The same thing happened in the eighteenth century with the *Mémoires sur l'Ancienne Chevalerie*, by J.-B. de La Curne de Sainte-Palaye (1753/1759), whose massive and erudite documentation, accompanied by a veritable apologia for knighthood, was to become a veritable mine for European storytellers.[1] These brief bibliographic citations give only a partial idea of the development of the chivalric element in the areas of Masonry and of literature, somewhat less so for alchemy. Writers on alchemy, whose discourse was as a rule less temporal, were chiefly interested in mythic paths already marked out in traditional mythological accounts. For instance, in 1758 Dom Pernety, while discussing "allegories which have a palpable . . . connection with the Hermetical Art," dealt successively with the winning of the Golden Fleece, the theft of the golden apples from the garden of the Hesperides, the story of Atalanta, the hind with the golden horns, Midas, the Golden Age of Man, and showers of gold.[2] The Golden Fleece was also a chivalric Order, not just a chapter out of Greek mythology. And in this regard the Order was of interest to Hermetic writers well into the eighteenth century.

HERMANN FICTULD AND THE
ORDER OF THE GOLDEN FLEECE

The expedition of Jason and the Argonauts lent itself marvelously to Hermetic and initiatory interpretations. In the richness of its *peripeteia* its imagery furnished an inexhaustible subject of meditation for symbolic alchemy. In 1731 there appeared in Germany, under the name of Ehrd de Naxagoras, a work of alchemy entitled *Aureum Vellus oder Güldenes Vliess*,[3] which related the story of Jason. Shortly afterwards in 1736, a 1607 book by

---

1. Translated into German under the title *Das Ritterwesen des Mittelalters nach seiner politischen und militärischen Verfassung* (Nuremberg, 1786–1790).

2. Joseph Antoine Dom Pernety, *Fables égyptiennes et grecques dévoilées*, Paris, 1758, pp. 433–580.

3. Hermann Fictuld speaks of a 1730 edition in his *Aureum Vellus*, p. 165 (actually 1731). I examined the 1733 edition (Munich Staatsbibliothek, call number: *Alch 245*, bound with other texts under the general title: *Opuscula Chymica II*). The title begins: Ehrd. De Naxagoras, *Aureum Vellus oder Güldenes Vliess: das ist ein Tractat. welcher darstellet den Grund und Ursprung des uralten Güldenen Vliesses . . .* Editio secunda, Frankfurt/Main, 1733, 2 vol., followed by a *Supplementum Aurei Velleris* by the same author, devoted to a sort of exegesis of the text of the *Emerald Tablet* (pp. 1-62). On Naxagoras, see Hermann Kopp, *Die Alchemie in älterer und neuerer Zeit*, Heidelberg, 1886, t. I and II, index. Since the French edition of this article, I wrote a book devoted to the theme of the Golden Fleece in Alchemy (*Toison d'Or et Alchimie*, Milan–Paris, Archè, 1991; English edition, revised and enlarged: *The Golden Fleece and Alchemy*, New York, S.U.N.Y. Press, 1993), in which I discuss the works of Naxagoras,

Johann Siebmacher carrying the same title[4] was republished in Leipzig. And in 1749 appeared Hermann Fictuld's book, perhaps the first to explain in a precise and systematic manner the alchemical content and meaning of the trappings of the Order of the Knights of the Golden Fleece.[5]

Who was Hermann Fictuld? We still don't know the identity of the person hidden behind this pseudonym. His works, however, all on alchemy or theosophy, have been preserved.[6] He maintained a correspondence with F.C.

---

4. Cf. H. Fictuld, *Prureum Vellus*, p. 164.
5. *Aureum Vellus oder Goldenes Vliess. Was dasselbe sey. Sowohl in seinem Ursprunge. als erhabenen Zustande. Denen Filiis Artis und Liebhabern der Hermetischen Philosophie dargelegt. auch dass darunter die Prima Materia Lapidis Philosophorum samt dessen Praxi verborqen, eröfnet von Hermann Fictuld*. Leipzig, bey Michael Blochberger, 1749, paginated 121 to 379. Pages 1 through 120 are entitled: *Azoth et Ignis das ist, das wahre und elementarische Wasser und Feuer— Oder Mercurius Philosophorum. . . .*
6. There is nothing in the biographies of Meusel, nor in any others that I was able to examine. The *Lexicon Pseudonymorum* of Emil Weller, Regensburg, 1886, does mention "Hermann Fictuld," but unfortunately does not tell us anything about his real name; the following works by this author are cited: *Contracta, das ist das edle Perlein [. . .] der himmlischen Weisheit*, 1734. *Chymisch Philosophischer Probierstein*, 1740, 1753, 1784. *Cabbala mystica naturae*, 1741. *Hermetischer Triumphbogen*, 1741. *Occulta Occultissima*, 1741. *Azoth et Ignis*, 1749. *Hermetica Victoria*, 1750. *Abhandlung von der Alchymie*, 1754. *Turba Philosophorum*, 1763. I examined at the Munich Staatsbibliothek: *Abhandlung von der Alchymie und derselben Gewissheit*, Erlangen, 1754 (call number: *Alch 247/5*, and another copy at the University Library, cote 8, Chem. 340). *Azoth et Ignis*, Leipzig, 1749 (call number: *Alch 247/1*, cf. also n. 2, p. 210, *supra*). *Der längst gewünschte und versprochene chymisch-philosophische Probierstein*, Frankfurt and Leipzig, 1740 (call number: *Alch 244/3*), along with a 3d ed., 1784 (*Alch 101*). *Chymische Schriften. Ans Licht gestellt durch Friedr. Roth-Scholtzen*, Frankfurt and Leipzig, 1734 (cote: *Alch 101 m*). *Hermetischer Triumphboqen auf zweyer Säulen der grossen und kleinen Welt bevestiget*, Petersburg, Copenhagen and Leipzig, 1741 (call number: *Alch 102*). *Turba Philosophorum*, n.p., 1763 (call number: *Alch 102 d*). Karl R. H. Frick, *Die Erleuchteten*, Graz, Akad. Druck und Verlagsanstalt, 1973, p. 313 ff., writes the following about this hermetic author: *"Nach einer Version soll sein Wahrer Name Johann Heinrich Schmidt von Sonnenberg gewesen sein. Geboren am 7. März 1700 soll er bereits mit 16 Jahren Gehilfe eines Regiments-Feldscherers zu Temesvar in Ungarn gewesen und von diesem in der Alchemie unterrichtet worden sein. Später wurde er angeblich mit einem Baron Prugg von Pruggenheim aus Innsbruck bekannt, der ihm weitere Unterweisungen ertheilte und sich mit ihm und einiqen anderen zu einem Rosenkreuzerzirkel verband. Nach einer anderen Version soll er Mummenthaler geheissen haben. in Langenthal geboren worden und 1777 im Alter von 78 Jahren verstorben sein. Im Hermetischen A.B.C. von 1779 soll schliesslich Fictulds wahrer Name Mummenthaler oder Weinstof gewesen sein"*. Joachim Telle (letter to the author, 14 April 1984) pointed out to me a translation, by Fictuld, entitled *Fürstliche und Monarchische Rosen von Jericho. Das ist: Moses Testament in Neue Sammlung von einigen alten und sehr rar gewordenen Philosophisch und Alchymistischen Schriften*, vol. III, Frankfurt and Leipzig, 1771. Foreword by Fictuld, 1760. There is likewise some biographical information about Fictuld in: *Sehr rare . . . Kunst-Stücke*, vol. III, Zittau and Leipzig, 1763, preface (new ed.). Finally, the Landesbibliothek of Darmstadt has a fairly large collection of this author's works.

Oetinger,[7] to whom moreover one of his books has been attributed. Further research may thus still hold some surprises about him. His reputation has not always been the best in our time, probably because he has not been read as he deserves to be read. One modern day critic, a highly respected scholar, has even called him "a charlatan!"[9] His books, however, interest me as much for their philosophical or theosophical content as for their historical value. In any event, Fictuld belonged to that theosophical trio of the first half of the century whose other two members were Sincerus Renatus and Georg von Welling.[10]

As is well known, the Order of the Golden Fleece was founded at Bruges in 1429 by Philip III the Good, Duke of Burgundy, father of Charles the Bold, who succeeded him and whose mother Isabella was the daughter of the king of Portugal. He instituted it on the day of his wedding, alleging that he would use it to undertake a crusade against the Saracens. In fact, the order was never put to this use, which only encouraged the purely Hermetic interpretations of Fictuld and other commentators before him. The chancellor of the order in the fifteenth century, Johannes Germanus, bishop of Chalon-in-Burgundy, was bothered by the too pagan—or too esoteric—reference to Jason and even requested, albeit without success, that the fleece of the Biblical Gideon be put forward in its place![11] And Charles the Bold, who spent enormous sums without anyone really knowing where his resources came from, was suspected of possessing the philosopher's stone. At his death, the order was already greatly reduced in membership, a situation that is still the case today.[12] This occultation itself was to give rise to alchemical allegorizing in somewhat the same way that the total disappearance of the Order of the

---

7. Cf. Oetinger to Castell, 13 May 1763, in *Oetingers Leben und Briefe* ed. by K. C. E. Ehmann, Stuttgart, 1859, pp. 655–670. Already called attention to by R. C. Zimmermann, *Das Weltbild des Jungen Goethe*, Munich, Fink, t. II, 1979, p. 370 ff.

8. According to R. C. Zimmermann, op. cit., t. 1, 1969, pp. 170 and 338, *Das Geheimnis von dem Salz*, Stuttgart, 1770, is by Fictuld.

9. R. C. Zimmerman, in ibid., p. 170 ("*Scharlatan und Pseudo-Rosenkreuzer*").

10. Principle work of Sincerus Renatus (*alias* Samuel Richter), *Theo-Philosophia Theoretico Practica*, Breslau, 1711. Cf. an interesting study of this work in R. C. Zimmerman, op. cit., t. I and II, name index. Georg von Welling, *Opus magocabbalisticum et theosophicum*, Frankfurt, 1719, several new editions. On Welling, see Petra Jungmayr's seminal work, *Georg von Welling (1655-1727). Sudien zu Leben und Werk*, Stuttgart, Franz Steiner, 1990.

11. Fictuld, *Aureum Vellus*, p. 223, based on Olivarius Marcanus.

12. The Order of the Golden Fleece is today made up of hardly more than a handful of members, primarily in Spain and Austria.

Temple after 1315 helped give credit to tales during the eighteenth century that the true Masons were the successors to the Templars.[11]

Fictuld did make some interesting historical suggestions in addition to the alchemical interpretation he gave to the regalia of these knights. He noted that the phrase "Golden Fleece" was not unknown in pagan and Christian Hermeticism or alchemy,[14] and that it was in that fortunate "*saeculum adepticum*," the fifteenth century, that the order had its foundation. Was this not the era of Pico della Mirandola, Cosimo de Medici, Theodorus Gaza, Thomas à Kempis, George Ripley, Isaac the Dutchman (Johann Isaak Levita), Salomon Trismosin, Basil Valentine, and Nicolas Flamel? Was it not the age of Bernard of Treviso, Thomas of Bologna, Raymond Lull, Edward IV of England, and Arnald of Villanova?[15] Well before Philip the Good's creation of the Order, The *Suidas* (the Sonda) had proposed an alchemical interpretation of Jason. Fictuld agreed with that, adding over and over again that this order founded in 1429, was conceived by the True Adepts to serve the Hermetic Art.[16] And our author also cited Aloisius Marlianus, Aurelius Johannes, the *Aureum Vellus* that appeared in Rorschach in 1598, *Das Güldene-Vliess* (by Johann Siebmacher) of 1607 republished at Leipzig in 1736, the *Aureum Vellus* of Johann Conrad Creiling, and those of Naxagoras, of E.H. ("*Jungfer*") of 1574, and of Johann de Monte Hermetis of 1680, without forgetting the treatise of Mennens that appeared in 1604 and was published again in the *Theatrum chemicum* of Strasbourg in 1623.[17] As for alchemical readings of the myth, Fictuld could have also mentioned John of Antioch, Eustathius, and the pseudo-Eudoxia Augusta, and could have cited Gianfrancesco Pico della Mirandola and Jacques Gohory as well![18] He reproduced a passage from a letter of Cornelius Agrippa who in 1509 wrote to Trithemius from Tollen telling him that he credited Philip III and Charles

---

13. Cf. *infra*, second part, dealing with Freemasonry.
14. *Aureum Vellus*, p. 257.
15. Ibid., p. 286. Fictuld was very curious about the history of Hermeticism; the *Probierstein*, cf. *supra*, p. 210, note 3, is basically meant as a history of alchemy.
16. *Aureum Vellus*, pp. 145, 150, 161 ff., 166, 218.
17. Ibid., pp. 164-167, 255. Cf., particularly regarding the 1598 *Aureum Vellus*: Salomon Trismosin, *La Toison d'Or ou la fleur des trésors* (text of the French edition of 1612, new translation of the German text of 1598), Paris, Retz, 1975, coll. Bibliotheca Hermetica, commentary and analysis by Bernard Husson and René Alleau.
18. Cf. the interesting study of these authors by Sylvain Matton in the preface to the facsimile edition of the *Fables égyptiennes et grecques dévoilées*, 1786 ed., Paris, La Table d'Émeraude, 1982. Let us also remember the presence of the Golden Fleece in the "third day" of the *Chemical Wedding of Christian Rosenkreutz*. See also my book *The Golden Fleece and Alchemy*, cited *supra*, note 3.

with the possession of supernatural secrets: "I was yet able to see for myself in Dijon the laboratory and the furnaces in the ducal castle and I was shown several writings and chymical characters on the walls, which are said to be in the handwriting of the dukes themselves."[19]

Philosophic gold was a substance that flowed from the outer planetary spheres, an astral, divine liquid, an igneous substance, the emanation of the goodness of God at the heart of all things, the soul, the seed, of life and of growth. Thus the word "*Vliess*" (fleece), related to "*fliessen*" (to flow), is well-chosen in German. The "*Goldene Vliess*" was made of this liquid gold, such that in choosing this beautiful symbol Philip III said more than he could have in many thick folio volumes.[20] This evocation, which did not leave out reference to the Soul of the World (*Anima Mundi*), clearly shows on what plane Fictuld meant to place his interpretation of the trappings of the knights of this order. These included the robe, the mottoes, the collar, the star, and lastly the double patronage of Mary and Andrew.

The annual *fête* was celebrated over a three-day period. On the first day, the knights wore purple robes; on the second, black, and on the third day, white. These colors were meant to suggest, according to Mennens, the astonishing mysteries of the Great Art.[21] The red robe was also meant to be worn on all other days of the year.[22] This could have been troubling for Fictuld, since the chronology of colors in the alchemical process was black-white-red (*Nigredo, Albedo, Rubedo*) instead! But this theosopher was able to get around the difficulty by proposing a fairly plausible hermetist interpretation. It was under the color purple, he noted, that the *materia prima* first appeared, which should not be confused with the final stage of *Rubedo*. The point was to find something that recalled coagulated blood, which was meant to be understood as the stain of original sin or at any rate some unstable state suggested by the *feces terrae* and the fig leaves of Adam and Eve. Thanks to the sacrifice of the Savior mortal Man could regain a stable state and thus rid himself of this red

---

19. *Aureum Vellus*, p. 255 ff.: Agrippa wrote that Philip the Good created the Order in honor of the holy mysteries (alchemical); moreover, Pico de la Mirandola, Cosimo de Medici, Theodorus Gaza, as well as others, shared the same interests as Philip regarding the hautes sciences. Agrippa added: "*Nach [Philippus] kam sein Sohn Carolus der gleichfalls theil an diesen göttlichen Geheimnissen gehabt und ein sehr kluger Mann soll gewesen seyn. Ich selbsten habe zu Diion noch das Laboratorium und die Oefen gesehen in der Hertzoglichen Burg, auch hat man mir daselbsten einige chymische Scripturen und Character an deren Wänden gewiesen die beyder Hertzogen eigene Handschrifften seyn sollen.*" Such is the testimony of Agrippa, cited by Fictuld.
20. Ibid., p. 217.
21. Ibid., p. 254: "*um mit diesen Farben die erstaunlichen Geheimnisse der grossen Kunst anzudeuten*".
22. Ibid., p. 260.

stain that nevertheless remains our sign on this earth and the color of the knights of the order throughout the rest of the year.

The red robe was put aside and replaced by the black one, for the "Philosophers" saw in this robe the beginning of the alchemical *Opus*, the doorway to the Palace of the King.[21] This is clearly the traditional *Nigredo*, and the reason why this second color is used is as follows. When the radiant light that is hidden "in the center of the robe"—that is, in our own hearts and in all physical matter—can no longer flow forth as it wishes to do because of the—red—impurities which act like a screen to it, the light withdraws into itself, into its center, leaving behind those impure parts which, because of this, and because they are from that moment on abandoned and left on their own, begin to rot, putrefy, and to turn black.[24] This putrescence must be melted away with the warmth of our tears "so that the soul, the pure seed, the divine tincture, the noble knight, can reappear in his pure vestments of innocence before the throne of divine grace."[25] On the third day, the knights put on a white damask robe because, according to the alchemists, this color represented the transition towards the red of perfection. White is light, seed, soul, life. It is Chaos that contains the *materia prima*. It is the original raiment of natural innocence. The secret fire of the Philosophers or aqueous fire—or rather igneous water—brought forth this white of perfection. But after the third day the knights put back on their red robes which, this time, symbolize the true *Rubedo!* Red thus does double duty, since on the first day of the following year's *fête* it again stood for the Fall of Man. Thus, Red = sin; black = despair and indecision; white = freedom; red = state of regeneration—then of sin again, etc.[26]

The robes were fitted with a wide hem on which Philip III had his symbol embroidered, a flint with a spark of fire (*Feuerstein und Feuerfunken*), and the motto: "Autre n'auray" [I will have no other] (*Non habeo aliud*). Fictuld interpreted this as: "I will have no higher knowledge than alchemy, I respect and venerate the single Chaos which has been revealed to me by God and my several friends." His son Charles the Bold changed this motto to: "Je l'ay empris" [I have undertaken it] (*Illud suscepi*), which our theosopher interpreted: "I am a prince and yet only a man, I will bear in mind my weaknesses,

---

23. Ibid., p. 261 ff.
24. Ibid., p. 263.
25. Ibid., p. 264.
26. Ibid., pp. 265–269. In the *Histoire des Ordres Militaires ou des Chevaliers*, "nouv. éd. tirée de l'abbé Giustiniani," etc., t. IV, Amsterdam, 1721, it says on p. 37 that the letters making up the name Jason correspond to the months when fruits are harvested (July, August, September, October, November). Moreover, on p. 43 this work confirms what Fictuld said about the robes. Also consult *La Toison d'Or*, by Kervyn de Letterhove, Brussels, 1907.

and what my father has bequeathed to me in matters of alchemy, I know for having seen myself.[27] Lastly, encircling the fleece itself, whose emblem hung like a jewel from a chain around the neck of the knight, was the motto: "*Pretium non vile laboris*"; that is, "Keep silent, contemplate my outer and inner truth because I am made of divine and not base gold, stone and steel spew forth sparks which, gathered in bundles, are the metallic gold of the chain that is before your eyes!"[28]

The most remarkable badge was without doubt the magnificent gold collar that has raised as much curiosity as it has admiration. This was a chain made of eight component sections in solid gold, each one adorned with two flints made of steel. As such, the collar was supposed to produce sparks, at least symbolically. To these eight parts were joined two others which hung from the collar and on which were found the symbol of the order, a medal adorned with the Golden Fleece made of golden wool with the motto noted above (*Pretium non vile laboris*). Fictuld remarked that the law tables of Zoroaster were worn in a similar manner. The fleece hanging from the chain symbolized the book made from rams' skins, or the scroll, according to the imagery of the ancients, on which the art of transmuting gold, among other occult arts, was written in gold letters.[29] Fictuld did not mention that the golden chain was basically a well-known symbol of Hermetism. German Romanticism would take this up toward the end of the century; the imagery recurs many times in Novalis's *Heinrich von Ofterdingen*, the finest initiatory novel of this school. Then there was the final badge, a star that was worn on the shoulder. With its six branches, it represented an "elementary" symbol of alchemy—in both senses of the word!—since all four elements were included in it and could be found in the marriage of water (the lower triangle point) and of fire (the upper triangle point), the other two elements being represented at one stroke in the closing of the triangles. Fictuld did not stress this imagery, which was very well known to his readers and which was not unique to the Golden Fleece. He limited himself to noting that it represented Azoth + Ignis, or the true Golden Fleece, the true *Signatstern* or blazing star.[30]

Why did Philip the Good choose the double patronage of Mary and Andrew? The thoughts of the Protestant Fictuld on the subject of the Virgin are not without esoteric or picturesque interest. Mary, who by her genealogy was a princess of the royal house, was born the poor daughter of Joachim. Likewise, the *materia prima* of the *Opus Magnum* was hidden from the eyes of

---

27. *Aureum Vellus*, p. 259 ff.
28. Ibid. p. 278.
29. Ibid., p. 276 ff.
30. Ibid., p. 282.

the uninitiated. Mary's was a sublunar quality, a cold and humid, terrestrial and elementary temperament. But along with this there was also in her an "innate Central-Fire."[31] Mary was endowed with a "lunar attraction," which drew toward her the emanations and exhalations of the stars and the upper regions. This, if we understand Fictuld correctly, allowed her to receive the infant Jesus. She was, at the same time, the image of the womb that was filled by the celestial emanations of the stars. The symbol of Eve, she represented the water flowing like a spring in *Mara*, and she was the image of the *materia prima*, of the lunar sulfur or seed, of the fountain where the King bathed, of water mixed with fire, of the fertile earth. She was also the fountain of fire and salt from which came the lunar temperament of her qualities, which were able to dissolve, ennoble and bring to perfection the solar virtues.[32] As for Andrew, etymologically he signified the "emerald stone" and was prefigured in the Old Testament by Zebulon, son of the patriarch Jacob. He possessed ascending qualities of the Sun and of Mars, received descending emanations of Venus, and symbolized primitive matter uniting with obscure matter, as shown by his missionary activity in the West (the "black" countries, since they are located towards the setting Sun). Moreover, he preached the Gospel where Jason had gone to search for the Golden Fleece with the Argonauts (Colchis, Scythia, Georgia). A confirmation that he represented the color black is the fact that the knights of the order honored him on the second feastday, precisely that day when they wore their black robes (Mary was celebrated on the third day). Black is filled with theological meaning, as Fictuld noted in other of his works.[33]

Other pages deal more specifically with the myth of the Argonauts. I will not linger over them here, because he makes no further mention of this

---

31. Ibid., p. 349: *"nach göttlichen Eigenschafften eine starcke Natur, sie war sublunarischer Complexion. irdischer und elementarischer Humeur, jedoch aber auch mit einem angebornen Central-Feuer verknupfft. das da in denen innersten Theilen ihres Leibes verborgen lag."*
32. Ibid. pp. 345, 350, 352.
33. Ibid., pp. 353, 356 ff. Paul-Georges Sansonetti pointed out to me that Charles the Bold added the X, but with two cut *"écotés"* (sprigs of laurel) to indicate that their rubbing together produced fire (the fire of the Holy Spirit, and the double flame of Dioscures come to mind!). Laurel is a symbol of Apollo. It increases the vitality (the idea of a universal vital force). Sansonetti also remarked that the collar of the Order sums up and brings together the fundamental images of several traditions: the striking of the stone evokes war of fire of time immemorial, and of humanity's first tool, but also the *Agni* of the Vedic tradition, the primordial "sparks" (escaped from the "vases") of the Jewish Kabbalah, and the fire rite of Mazdaism in Iran. A light which also makes me think of the light of *Xvarnah*, or light of glory (cf. Henry Corbin, *En Islam iranien*, [Paris, Gallimard, 1971], t. II, p. 156), the concept of which is itself organically linked to that of a knighthood based on a lineage of custodianship—and thus a fairly clear relationship between the "Xvarnah" and the "Grail."

order of chivalry but turns to hermetizing interpretations of mythology. For instance, Phrixus represents the solar sulfur and Helle the lunar mercury. These two children were born at Thebes, which symbolized the higher elements. Their mother Nephele (lunar) being unable to keep what Athamas (solar) entrusted to her, the children departed from the upper regions and, mounted on a ram, fell to earth in the land of Colchis like a shower of gold. Thessaly, from which Jason departed, symbolized the "one, great substance" of which the *Emerald Tablet* spoke ("*The S-Salia,*" Fictuld says, solar dust or Sulfur, life of fire and of love), while Colchis represented the fixed, incombustible elements that must be "separated out" in order to free the rarefied matter (the Fleece).[34] A long passage interpolated into this section is devoted to the text of the *Emerald Tablet.*[35] Other pages are purely theosophical, such as those where he mentions Lucifer, son of the Dawn and former high prince of the celestial choirs, who was made of an igneous substance that passes through everything and which, being somewhat the same as the substance of which the original Adam was made, was capable of contaminating him.[36] One point to note in passing, and also interesting because we are in the year 1749, is that Fictuld alluded to the Golden Rosy-Cross in relation to Hermes and the Argonauts.[37] Nine years later there appeared both the *Fables égyptiennes et grecques dévoilées* and the *Dictionnaire Mytho-Hermétique* by the Benedictine monk Dom Antoine-Joseph Pernety, who did not mention chivalry but who presented in the three volumes of these two works a veritable compendium of hermetist thinking applied to "ancient fables."[38]

CHIVALRIC HIGH DEGREES IN FREEMASONRY

At the time of the appearance of Fictuld's book, speculative Freemasonry had already been in existence for thirty-two years, and was in the process of adding its "High (or Side) Degrees." A good many of these were "chivalric," because at that time a speculative Freemasonry on the continent tended to consider itself a successor to the medieval orders of chivalry. Freemasonry

---

34. *Aureum Vellus,* pp. 309-319, 325.
35. Ibid., pp. 320-343.
36. Ibid., p. 318 ff.
37. Ibid., p. 341, an allusion to "*die goldenen Rosen-Creutzer.*"
38. The *Dictionnaire Mytho-Hermétique* was republished several times (cf. the reprinting of the original edition, Milan, Archè, 1969. A republication, also in facsimile, of the *Fables* using the edition of 1786, Paris, La Table d'Émeraude, 1982, with an introduction by Sylvain Matton, cf. supra, n. 6, p. 212). On Dom Pernety, see especially Micheline Meillassoux-Le Cerf, *Dom Antoine Pernety (1716–1796) et les Illuminés d'Avignon,* Mailand, Archè, 1992.

was based on three degrees (Apprentice, Fellowcraft, Master Mason), constituting what is known as "blue" Masonry, while the higher degrees,[19] belonging to a number of rites, constitute what is normally called "Scottish" Masonry. Clearly, it was these high degrees, the number of which varied according to different rites, that in the eighteenth century permitted the introduction of chivalric titles, which were linked to the esoteric symbolism of theosophical illuminism. The rapid evolution of Scottish Masonry toward this chivalric imagination is not at all surprising, seeing that there was a long defunct order, charged with history and mystery, that had already caused a great deal of ink to be spilt during the previous century.

This was the Order of the Temple. Why were the Masons so quickly intrigued by and drawn to this order in particular? Probably because it was more possible to make use of a long dead order or to claim to be its successor, since proof to the contrary will almost always be lacking. Pierre Dupuy's *Traités concernant l'histoire de France*, published in 1654 and a standard work on the Order of the Temple, was republished several times, notably in 1751, a sign of its success even before Rosa and Hund had introduced the Templar legend into German Masonry.[40] According to the legend, a certain masonic obedience (the Rite of Strict Observance, or RSO, founded by Baron Karl von Hund in 1764, but actually a little older under the name of the Chapter of Clermont) claimed to be the heir of the Knights of the Order of the Temple and its sole true descendant. Rituals and Instructions of the RSO developed this theme over and over again, circulating its claims also outside the lodges. The oldest version of the Templar legend that we know of is a Masonic

---

39. Cf. the still classic work of Gustav Adolph Schiffmann, *Die Entstehung der Rittergrade in Frankreich in der ersten Hälfte des 18. Jahrhunderts*, Leipzig, 1882. And more recently: James Fairbain Smith, "The Rise of the écossais degrees," in: *Proceedings of the Chapter of Research of the Grand Chapter of Royal Arch Masons of the State of Ohio*, vol. IX, Ohio, Otterbein, 1965. Adolf Hamberger, *Organisationsformen, Rituale. Lehren und magische Thematik der Frei-Maurerei und freimaurerartigen Bünde im deutschen Sprachraum Mitteleuropas*, 3 vols., + 1 vol. of bibliography, Eigenverlag, 1971–1973–1974, hektographiert (Hamberger is a professor at the University of Giessen). Works already cited in the excellent work of Karl R. H. Frick (cf. *supra*, n. 6).

40. On this we must also mention: Gurtler, *Historia Templariorum observationibus ecclesiasticis aucta* (1691). Schoonebeck, *Histoire de tous les ordres militaires ou de Chevalerie et des Ordres religieux* (1699–1700). For other titles—and they have been numerous on the subject of the Templars—cf. René Le Forestier, *La Franc-Maçonnerie templière et occultiste aux XVIIIe et XIXe siècles*, (Paris, Aubier-Nauwelaerts, 1969), p. 75 ff. and especially Georg Kloss, *Bibliographie der Freimaurerei*, (Frankfurt, 1844), pp. 155–163; republished in facsimile, (Graz, Akademischer Druck- und Verlagsanstalt), 1970. See also the fine chapters: a) in Jean Tourniac's book, *Vie et Perspectives de la Franc-Maçonnerie traditionnelle*, (Paris, Dervy, 1978 [nouv. éd], "La Chevalerie d'Occident") pp. 255–285; b) in Henry Corbin's book, *Temple et contemplation*, (Paris, Flammarion, 1980), chap. vi–ix .

Instruction dating back to 1760. Entitled *De la Maçonnerie parmi les chrétiens*, it taught that the first Christian "Masons" were Boethius, Symmachus, and Ausonius, succeeded by the canons of the Holy Sepulchre and, of course, the Templars![41] Moreover, even without any reference to the Order of the Temple, the question of the relationship of chivalry to Masonry was raised very early on. Already in 1675, and thus forty-two years before the birth of Speculative Masonry, Father Louis Maimbourg spoke of the Society of Free Masons "that is believed to have been formed at the time of the conquest of the Holy Land" in his *Histoire des Croisades*, which was published and translated several times. Elsewhere, a recently discovered document demonstrates the existence of a Chapter of Knights in an English Masonic lodge in 1710, seven years before the birth of Speculative Masonry! This order was founded by Frenchmen and was more free-thinking than religious, but it nevertheless used the vocabulary of Knighthood and had a Grand Master as its head. Finally, Ramsay, renowned for his famous Masonic oration of 1738 devoted to the origins of Masonry, evoked the orders of chivalry and spoke of "our ancestors the Crusaders" whose figurative secrets and signs "bring to mind either some part of our Science, some moral virtue, or some mystery of the Faith."[42]

The introduction of the Templar legend into Masonry was associated with a second, so-called Jacobite, legend that Hund early on linked to the former legend. The basis of the Jacobite fiction was to make the dethroned Stuart sovereign the contemporary representative of the Order of the Temple, equating him with the "Unknown Superior" of the RSO.[43] Hund

---

41. Cf. a good summary in Le Forestier, op. cit., p. 68 ff., and Schiffmann, op. cit., who reproduced the text of it on pp. 178–190 .

42. On Ramsay's oration, cf. G. A. Schiffmann, *Andreas Michael Ramsay, eine Studie zur Geschichte der Freimaurerei*, Leipzig, 1878, which reproduces the oration with an accompanying German translation. This text of Schiffmann was reproduced in facsimile and bound in a single volume with the same author's work cited *supra* n. 39, as well as with the study of Heinrich Lachmann, *Geschichte und Gebräuche der maurerischen Hochgrade und Hochgrad-Systeme*, Brunswick, 1866; the volume containing these 3 three facsimile reprints is entitled *Hochgrade der Freimaurerei*, (Graz, Akademische Druck- und Verlagsanstalt, 1974). In reference to the 1710 document: M. C. Jacob, "An unpublished record of a Masonic Lodge in England," in *Zeitschrift für Religion und Geistesgeschichte*, ed. by Ernst Benz and H. G. Schoeps, t. XXII, 1970. Jacob found among the papers of the "pantheist" John Toland a manuscript entitled *Extrait des Registres du Chapitre Général des Chevaliers de la Jubilation* (1710)—cited by Frick, p. 232.

43. The Catholic Charles I Stuart was executed in 1649 on the order of Cromwell. In 1660 the House of Stuart returned to the throne in the person of Charles II, succeeded by James II in 1685. The francophile policies of this Catholic king led the Emperor to support in opposition to him William of Orange's pretentions to the English throne. In 1688 William drove James II from the throne and the latter took up residence in the château of Saint-Germain-

found fertile ground for the adoption of this double fiction in the fact that before he had created the RSO, a Rite called the Chapter of Clermont had existed from 1758 to 1764 (including the well-known names of Lernay, Prinzen, and Rosa), whose fourth and fifth degrees were Knight of Saint-Andrew of the Thistle and Knight of God and His Temple, both of which exhibited a symbolism with dual orientation: Solomon's Temple and traditional alchemy.[44] The Instructions of this Rite taught that the principles of the Royal (alchemical) Art were recovered in the Temple of Jerusalem! Scottish hermetizing Masonry seems to have been born with this Chapter of Clermont, which was perhaps the first to fuse the three themes of chivalry, Solomon's Temple, and alchemy. It was also the womb in which, and from which, Hund was able to develop and enforce acceptance of his own rite, the RSO.

The sixth degree of the RSO was divided into three distinct categories of knights.[45] These knights adopted in addition a *nom de guerre*, which always began with "Eques a . . ." (e.g., Eques a Victoria, Eques a Pelicano, Eques ab Eremo). Jean-Baptiste Willermoz (Eques ab Eremo), before creating the Rite Écossais Rectifié (Rectified Scottish Rite) in the wake of and in competition with the RSO, had known of a degree called the Knight of the East in the third class of the Order of the Elect Cohens under his Master Martines de Pasqually. Through his Lyons lodge, La Parfaite Amitié, he was also familiar with a chapter of higher degrees which included, among others, the degrees of Knight Templar Grand Elect and Knight Rosy-Cross. These in no way laid claim to any affiliation with the Templar Order but were only an expression of the most current Masonic legend relating to Solomon's Temple. Lastly, Willermoz was part of the Grande Loge des Maîtres Réguliers de Lyon, founded in 1760, a rite made up of eight degrees the three highest of which were Grand Architect, Knight of the East, and Grand Master Scottish Knight of the Sword and the Rosy-Cross. Then in 1763 he founded with his brother the Chapter of the Knights of the Black Eagle, an extremely closed

---

43. *(Continued)*.
    James II from the throne and the latter took up residence in the château of Saint-Germain-en-Laye. With the backing of Louis XIV, James II was able to undertake a landing on the coast of Ireland, but eventually failed in this enterprise. His son James III mounted an invasion himself on the Scottish coast in 1715 but likewise failed. The latter's son, Charles Edward (1720–1788) attempted another restoration in Scotland in 1745, failed in his turn, and afterwards lived in France.

44. Cf. René Le Forestier, op. cit., p. 85 ff.

45. As did the CBCS (cf. *infra*, in reference to n. 49). The RSO degrees were: 1st degree: Apprentice-Fellowcraft-Master. 2nd degree: *Green Scottish*-Knight of the Eagle Rosy-Cross. 3rd degree: *Red Scottish-Ecuyer* Novice-Knight (several classes).

society, whose symbolism was strongly tinged with alchemy[46] and influenced by the Brethren of Metz. The Willermoz brothers, in fact, were well acquainted with a system in the Metz area—the Chapter of Saint Theodore—which was functioning in the beginning of the 1760s. The highest degree in this system was the Rectified Rite of Saint-Martin (named after the Roman knight who shared his cloak with a beggar) or the *Chevalier Bienfaisant de la Cité Sainte*, (CBCS), Knight Beneficent of the Holy City i.e., Rome).[47] This chapter also included a degree called the Knight Grand Inspector Grand Elect which tied in as well with the symbolism of alchemy—"Knight" in this context signifying "alchemist" for all intents and purposes![48] Picking up this term later on when creating his own Rite (the famous Rectified Scottish Rite) in the 1770s, Willermoz thereafter understood the "Cité Sainte" to be Jerusalem, or Palestine. This great reformer of Lyon, more than the System of Metz, would be behind the continuing renown of the degree of CBCS (an initialism synonymous with the RSR).

It has perhaps not been sufficiently noted that use of "CBCS" enabled Willermoz to allude to the Templars without expressly citing them at a time when, before the Convention of Wilhelmsbad (1782), it was still a question as to what interest any reference to the Order of Jacques de Molay could have for the new rite he was in the process of creating. In any event, he abandoned this reference at the Convention, and at the same time had it abandoned by the RSO as a whole. The RSO never recovered from this amputation, and expired from it soon afterward. The *Système de Lyon*, on the other hand, came out of it strengthened and is still very much alive even to the present day. Its ideals and its symbolism responded better to the underlying demands of the chivalric imagination, which was such a part of the collective mentality that it very soon tended to become timeless. The Holy City of the *Système de Lyon* was not Rome, but Jerusalem; its Temple was not that of Jacques de Molay, but of Solomon.

Moreover, we should recall that the tripartite division of knights, common to both the RSO and the RSR, owed nothing to the Order of the Templars; it merely distinguished the *milites* (noblemen of birth or ennobled by the Order of Saint-Louis), the *clerici* (Catholic priests or Protestant ministers), and the *equites cives* (magistrates, négociants, bourgeois).[49] Remember, too, that beyond the CBCS there was another, highly secret degree that was divided into two classes, that of Professed Knights (Chevaliers Profès) and of

---

46. Ibid., p. 279.
47. Ibid., p. 433.
48. Ibid., p. 325 ff.
49. Ibid., p. 423, and Frick, op. cit., p. 563.

Grand Professed Knights (Chevaliers Grands Profès).[50] *L'Ordre Intérieur*, that is to say, the degrees of Knight-Novice and of CBCS, claimed to continue the tradition of the *"Frères d'Orient"* (Constantinople, 1090!).[51]

The RSO, RSR, and other Rites mentioned above were not the only ones to include chivalric degrees. We will limit ourselves to a few examples. The fine and Christian Swedish Rite had a Scottish Master called the Knight of the East and of the Temple. One Scottish Philosophical Rite, founded in 1776 by Boileau and inspired by Rosicrucianism, included a degree of Knight of the Black Eagle.[52] It would have been surprising if the Philalethes, led by the indefatigable Savalette de Langes, had abstained from a similar reference: their *Chapitre des Chevaliers des Amis Réunis* was made up of a sixth class of Knights of the East, a seventh of Knights of the Rosy-Cross, and an eighth of Knights of the Temple.[53] But the Rosy-Cross themselves, that is to say the Golden Rosy-Cross, an obedience found widely throughout the German-speaking world in the 1770s and 1780s, had no chivalric degrees.[54] Perhaps this was because alchemy and hermeticism were already such an unmistakable and essential part of it that there was no need to pass through the intermediary of reference to an ideal. In any case, the magical and the practical seemed to win out over the ideal among the Golden Rosy-Cross. In compensation, perhaps, the hermetic order that succeeded the Golden Rosy-Cross in 1786 when the latter formally disappeared from the scene did include chivalric degrees. This was the *Système des Chevaliers de la Croix de la Trinité* (*Equites a Cruce Trinitatis*), founded by Assum, whose Grand Master was Karl von Hessen-Darmstadt (1749–1823). It transformed itself very quickly into the *Ordre des Chevaliers et Frères de la Lumière*—better known under the name of the Initiated Asiatic Brethern —the creation or rather the recreation of Ecker- und- Eckhoffen.[55]

In 1805 another lodge of high degrees called the Knights of the Cross, formed mostly of nobles, received its charter. It included an Inner Order called the Order of the Temple and, according to the official history of this lodge, during the French Revolution a certain Mathieu Radix de Chevillon is supposed to have recruited into its higher Masonic degrees several Brethren destined to become members in the Order of the Temple—that of Jacques de

---

50. In German: *"Schule der Ritter des Grossen Gelübdes."*
51. Ibid., p. 561.
52. Ibid., p. 505.
53. Ibid., p. 575.
54. This order disappeared when Frederick-William II succeeded Frederick II because the leaders had then attained their goal. With Illuminism on the throne and in the government, they no longer had any need for an order whose purpose was to serve their ambitious plans.

Molay! Another example, long after the Templar Strict Observance, of a certain collusion between the history of Masonry and that of the Order of the Temple.

The Templar legend of the eighteenth century proved abortive because the absence of well-founded historical references to it—the existence of a "filiation"—was well-compensated for in the mythologico-hermetical arsenal, which the epoch did not lack. From this time on, Masonic chivalry instead stressed either the symbolism of a symbolic Temple that was to be rebuilt, or a mythologico-hermetical imagery, or both at once. Now, we have seen that this imagery readily found the scenario it needed in the form of a famous legend of longstanding inspiration: that of Jason and the Argonauts. During the Enlightenment, the myth that proved to be a useful substitute for the Templar or Jacobite fictions was sometimes that of the Golden Fleece, done up for the occasion in chivalric guise, to which it lent itself so readily. If this myth rarely showed up explicitly in Masonic Rites in the strict sense, it was present in that para-Masonry of the Golden Rosy-Cross and other similar orders. In this regard, one of the first texts, and one of the most significant, is a manuscript dating from 1761 that is conserved in the archives of Dégh in Hungary. It deals with the ancient history of Freemasonry, of which it gives a Rosicrucian version. The Masons were supposedly the descendants of the Templars, who traced themselves back to the Company of the Argonauts, who went to Colchis and won the Golden Fleece![56] Moreover, the Rite of the "Academy of the True Masons" in 1766 had for its fourth degree a Knight of the Iris, for its fifth degree a Knight of the Argonauts, and for its sixth degree a Knight of the Golden Fleece. From this point on, the *Aureum Vellus* has been one of the symbols of the Rosy-Cross in the eighteenth century and of other lodges drawn to the tradition or modes of hermetic thinking.[57]

One could ask why the myth of the Golden Fleece rather than that of the Grail nearly won out as a paradigm of the initiatory quest during the eighteenth century. Was it because the Middle Ages tended to be forgotten during this period, in spite of the chivalric resurgence? Moreover, the Bible being *the* Book of the Western world, it was natural that the Temple of Solomon, which occupied such an important position in the Old Testament, a Temple always to be reconstructed, would become the fundamental symbol of Masonry, in as much as Masonry was rooted in the history of the construction guilds. The prestigious order of which Jacques de Molay was the last Grand Master and which was named after Solomon's edifice itself (the Temple),

---

55. Ibid., p. 78, following Wolfstieg, *Bibliographie der Frei-Maurerei* (no. 47, 598).

57. For the Swedish Rite, cf., Le Forestier, op. cit., p. 293. G. Kloss, op. cit., (cf. *supra* n. 40), notes p. 157, no. 2195, on the existence of a *Historia de la insigne Orden del Teyson de Oro*, by Julian de Piredo y Salazar, Madrid, 1788, 3 vol.

could hardly be expected to have faded from Christian memory. And if the medieval Grail was forgotten during the Enlightenment, this was because interest was more generally directed toward mythology, such as that of Greece, which lent itself readily to hermetic and alchemical readings.

The literature of the time (novel, drama, epic) naturally profited from this craze for the "chivalric," whether of an historical (Order of the Temple) or initiatory (Golden Fleece) nature. But in contrast to what was happening in the literature of hermeticism and in Masonry, literature proper did so by following sometimes contradictory and widely divergent paths.

CHIVALRIC LITERATURE IN GERMANY

Literature exploited the image of the knight and his accoutrements in ways obviously more precise and more varied than chivalric degrees, which were necessarily limited to certain schematic features, could do. Authors readily turned to specialized works on chivalry, such as those of Rixner or the contemporary La Curne de Sainte-Palaye.[58] When the need was felt, during the last third of the century, to find some sources of inspiration in the German national past that would allow an escape from foreign literary influence, chivalry began to blaze forth from a thousand literary hearths. Herder urged writers to return to the time of Charlemagne for inspiration and called for an exploration of the literature of the minstrels and knights (*Von Aehnlichkeit der mittleren englischen und deutschen Dichtkunst*, 1777).[59] This call went along with a dual renaissance of popular ballads led by Gottfried August Bürger (*Lenore*, 1774) and of the chivalric ideal led by R.E. Raspe, who beginning in 1765 called on Germans to revive their "chivalric romances" because they carried within them an authentic reflection of the past. Raspe's call, joined to those of Percy and Ossian, gave birth to the great and sudden medieval renaissance whose literary waves carried high both the knight and the, now gothic, ghost. With new life breathed into them, these two literary figures settled into a romantic landscape with which the popular or artistic tale would adorn itself as well. We have seen how Masonry profited from these encounters. All this assumed many different forms, because the imaginary realm of the knight developed along three fairly divergent directions in literature: a) the exaltation of the brave and valiant warrior knight; b) the popularization of the fig-

---

58. Although his influence must not be exaggerated. On this point and that which follows, see the excellent study by Gonthier-Louis Fink, *Naissance et apogée du conte merveilleux en Allemagne (1740–1800)* Paris, Les Belles-Lettres, 1966. The argument that follows is partly borrowed from this work.

59. *Werke*, II, p. 103 (Suphan ed.).

ure of the knight who took on a certain (rococo) spiritlessness; c) the initiatory message or journey.

Goethe's *Goetz von Berlichingen* (1774), written just before *Werther* on a
subject borrowed from the memoirs of a sixteenth-century Franconian
knight, belongs to this first aspect, that of the *Sturm und Drang*. Goethe made
his central character into a German Bayard, just, loyal, courageous, who
immediately appealed to the rebellious and patriotic youth who were his contemporaries. Similarly, the chivalric dramas of Joseph August von Törring
(*Kaspar der Thorringer*, 1770, and especially *Agnes Bernauer*, 1780) exalted
national sentiment by singing the praises of knightly gallantry and integrity.[60]
To the rococo aspect, so different from the preceding one, belong above all
several works of Wieland, not so much *Geron der Adlige* (1776), which glorified the moral and ethical ideal of the knight, as *Oberon* (1780), a verse narrative derived from both the adventure story and the Shakespearean fairytale.
Oberon is the tutelary genius and upholder of justice in the book of the same
name, but he is not the knight after whom the book is entitled. This knight
from the time of Charlemagne was the young Huon, Duke of Bordeaux, who
manages to rescue young maidens held prisoner by the giant Argoulaffre, flies
to the aid of a Saracen being attacked by a lion, and owes his victories neither
to enchantment nor to trickery. But overall *Oberon* remains close to baroque
opera, its lyricism is of an entirely musical nature. In fact Wieland did not set
out to rehabilitate the chivalry of the Middle Ages. Nor did he share the
admiration that Goethe, Herder, or Raspe expressed for the courage and
prowess attributed to that period in our history. Not only in *Oberon*, but also
in *Der Neue Amadis*, an historically evocative title, Wieland parodied the battles, carnage, and prowess of Amadis the Gaul.[61]

The moralism of numerous works, at least certain dramatic and epic
ones, went along with this rococo spiritlessness. In the novel proper one
meets less frequently the ideal of the valiant knight without fear or reproach,
and so the knight generally had no need for his armor or his shield. To the
desire of the reader to find himself plunged into a romantic world of moral
triumphs and trials is added a corresponding interiorization of the knightly
character, who thereby became more easy to identify with. But at the same
time a gap opened up between the period setting or dress of these works and
the action, because the realism of the medieval and chivalric settings no
longer existed except as a form of *trompe-l'oeil* or camouflage, simply a backdrop used to enhance the plot and give credulity to the moral lessons that

---

60. Cf. Otto Brahm, "Das deutsche Ritterdrama des 18. Jahrhunderts," in *Quellen und
    Forschungen zur Sprach- und Kultur-geschichte der germanischen Völker*, t. XL, Strasbourg,
    1880.
61. Fink, op. cit. p. 527 ff.

were the main concern of the reader. Even the legends of L.L. Wächter, who signed himself Veit Weber, seem sober next to the original *Amadis*. The tournament, which was less cruel and more sporting than the slaughter of battle, occupies a more important place in these works than it formerly did. And feats of arms often ceased to be the essential attribute of chivalry in authors as different as Christian Heinrich Spiess, C.A. Seidel, or J.A. Gleich. The main focus turned to knights errant, the upholders of justice and the redressers of wrongs. Ch.H. Spiess and Ch.A. Vulpius even condemned their knights to wander after death for having made too frequent use of their weapons! There is less of a longing for battles than for justice or for peace, and virtue has dethroned martial valor.[62]

We can see that the knights in the novels of many successful writers took on a certain bourgeois character, but this also happened to the knight in the work of the historian J. Möser (*Osnabrückische Geschichte*, 1768; *Patriotische Phantasien*, 1774–1778) who evoked local German provincial life with a triptych of a valorous knight, laboring peasants, and an honest burgher. Half of the novels by the famous Christiane Benedicte Eugénie Naubert (such as *Amalgunde*, 1787, and *Hatto*, 1789) were about chivalry, and it was from Möser that she drew her inspiration.[63] L.L. Wächter, alias Veit Weber, was the one who especially set the tone in this regard, for he sketched the pattern of the perfect knight on the model of Goetz von Berlichingen, a fearless warrior, a protector of widows and orphans but also a good father, a good husband, the incarnation of the ideal of the *pater familias* who was triumphant at the same time on the stage of the bourgeois drama. Wächters *Sagen der Vorzeit* (1787/1798), (Legends of Past Times), are not without interest in this regard. There is a bit of Rousseauism in him and in Mme. Naubert, both of whom were fond of setting the castle or solitary cottage of the virtuous knight against the princely palace that harbored a doubtful morality. Whereas La Curne de Sainte-Palaye had reproached the knights of earlier times for their disdain of culture, these novelists instead praised their simplicity and spoke of them as the guardian of tradition in opposition to those living at court. From then on this cliché was triumphant, and whatever the epoch being described, the same stereotype was always repeated.[64] The religious dimension was lacking from this knightly personnage, for he was a reflection more of the present

---

62. 62. Ibid., p. 527 ff.
63. Cf. ibid., name index. Mme. Naubert was famous enough to have some of her novels translated into French, for example the one she wrote under the pseudonym J. N. E. de Brock, *Les Chevaliers des Sept Montagnes, ou aventures arrivées dans le XIIIe siècle*, Metz, 1800. Of Spiess' work, cited above, there appeared one French edition, *Les Chevaliers du Lion*, 1800.
64. Fink, op. cit., pp. 507 ff., 517.

than the past, and very often "patriotism, xenophobia, anticlericalism, and naive Rousseauism"[65] were his defining characteristics.

More interesting still are the chivalric novels of an initiatory character. It was inevitable that they should have been written because Illuminism left its mark in many places in the enormous literary production of this era. Here, the knight has left the eagle's nest and shows up more often in the depths of the thick forests. This lent itself admirably to plot development and was highly suitable to the *roman noir* or gothic novel and also to the initiatory journey. One significant fact to note is that, with weapons being of much less importance, the pilgrim ended up taking the place of the knight. The knight himself became a pilgrim in Mme. Naubert (*Wallfahrten,* 1793; *Genoveva*), where, at various points on his way to the Holy Sepulchre or to Santiago de Compostella, we see him sold into slavery and subjected to trials that are so initiatory in nature that we lose any expectation of seeing him shine in combat any more. For Ch.H. Spiess and J.A. Gleich, the chivalric Middle Ages was first and foremost a land of testing and trials. But it is probably in the works of the Austrian J.B. von Alxinger and the Lithuanian F. Andreae, authors of chivalric adventures in the form of ballads and verse stories, that one finds the most interesting elements in this area.

In Andreae's *Rino und Jeannette* (1793–1794) the knight Rino takes us on a journey among the elementary spirits and leads us through labyrinths teeming with impenetrable forces. The adventures of Doolin, Alxinger's knightly creation in *Doolin von Maynz. Ein Rittergedicht* (1787), and *Bliomberie. Ein Rittergedicht* (1802)—where we come across invocations to Hermes Trismegistus and are treated to a lengthy description of some alchemical doings— are in a vein as rich and exciting as those of Rino. While enchantment masked the chivalric ideal in Wieland, it served to put the knight on a pedestal in the work of his two successors. At the same time, these narratives stood as role models for their readers. Andreae called on the warrior virtues of Germans as they faced the French Revolution and held up the Middle Ages in contrast to the decadence of the present and the knight in contrast to the burgher. In Alxinger, cosmopolitanism prevailed over patriotism, and his hero was shaped in the school of Masonic humanism. The trials he undergoes are intended to make a man of him—a "Brother." Similarly, Bliomberie belonged to a brotherhood whose members all pursue the same goal. Wieland's Huon, a dreamlike character, hardly gives any indication of his station, but Doolin and Bliomberie were truly and fully knights.[66]

---

65. Ibid., p. 527.
66. Ibid., pp. 243–250.

The famous drama of the Romantic Zacharias Werner, *Die Söhne des Thales* (*The Sons of the Valley*, 1804), is perhaps the most interesting historical fiction written during this period about the Order of the Temple. It was probably not as initiatory as some of its readers liked to believe, but it does contain some fairly specific allusions to certain high Masonic degrees of the eighteenth century, notably those of the Swedish Rite. The Masonic career of Werner himself has been the subject of several studies. And finally, let us recall that several editions of François-Just-Marie Raynouard's tragedy, *Les Templiers* (1805) were published in France.[67]

Parody did not lag behind. Theodor Gottlieb von Hippel was known primarily for his curious book of fiction entitled *Kreuz-und Querzüge des Ritters von A bis Z* (1795), which was published in two volumes and inspired both by *Don Quixote* and by *Tristam Shandy*. This was not an initiatory novel, but a *Bildungsroman* and above all a work of parody that contained many intriguing allusions to the Illuminism of the period. The very first page sets the tone: "The name of my hero is simply A.B.C. to X.Y.Z., of the Holy Roman Empire, Baron of, in, on, after, by and at, Rosenthal, Knight of numerous Orders of a sad and happy countenance."[68] We are treated to a detailed description of initiations within a certain Order of chivalry.[69] We are also presented with a certain Sir Rosenthal who rekindles the splendor of the Middle Ages not only by donning the vestments of a chivalric order but also by constructing on his property a small Jerusalem to which he has pilgrims come and in which he celebrates the feasts of his order! As a model for this

---

67. Cf. particularly, about Z. Werner, the thesis of Louis Guinet, *Zacharias Werner et l'ésotérisme maçonnique*, (The Hague, Mouton et Cie, 1962). On the numerous publications about the Templars at the turn of the century: Kloss, (op. cit., *supra*, n. 40), pp. 161–163 (regarding plays, cf. especially, pp. 300–302). Exactly contemporary with Werner's and Raynouard's plays were two 1805 publications which prolonged the satirical vein discussed *infra*, regarding Hippel; I think it is interesting to note them here because both titles contain the term "Knight of the Holy City" or "Jerusalem." First, there was the anonymous novel: *Emmanuel oder der schwarze Bund der Kreuzfrommen*, which also appeared under the title *Zenamide oder die Ritter der heiligen Stadt*, Altenburg, 1805, 2 vol. (cf. Kloss, p. 298, no. 3986 b). Secondly, the anonymous parody, which despite its title has nothing to do with the real Louis-Claude De Saint-Martin, *Leiden und Schicksale des unbekannten Philosophen Saint—Martin Ritter des Ordens der wohlthätigen Ritter vom neuen Jerusalem*, Erfurt, 1805.

68. Hippel, I: "*Der Nahme meines Helden ist kurz und gut: A.B.C. bis X.Y.Z. des heiligen Römischen Reiches Freiherr von in auf, nach durch und zu Rosenthal, Ritter vieler Orden trauriger und fröhlicher Gestalt.*" The chivalric or Masonic "Don Quixote" came out even before Hippel's novel: cf. E. A. A. von Göchhausen's novel of parody, *Freimaurerische Wanderungen des weisen Junkers Don Quixotte von Mancha und des grossen Schildknappen Herrn Sancho Pansa eine Jahrmarktsposse*, Leipzig, 1787, "*ohne Erlaubnis der Obern*" (cited in Kloss, op. cit., p 296, no. 3959).

69. Hippel, op. cit., II, 150 ff.

character the novelist might have had in mind a certain Weiher, of Neustadt near Danzig, who, having returned from the Holy Land, constructed an artificial Jerusalem for himself.[70] Rosenthal goes on a journey with his squire Michael who is clearly modeled after Sancho Panza, and they both perform their roles to the fullest, the knight aspiring to the highest ideals and the most profound mysteries of his order and his squire showing himself more interested in the practical success of their endeavors.

A need to create or to rediscover a sense of sodality[71] is evident in the century's chivalric resurgence. Disappointed in what philosophy and the church had to offer, some sought the means to realize this sodality in orders of a Masonic nature. They believed they could achieve it through men like Charles Stuart, in whom the champions of the Jacobite legend had placed their hope. But a person in his station neither could nor wished to play the role that was expected of him. In any case, the "Unknown Superiors" revealed themselves as nonexistent or ineffectual, when they did not turn out to be simply charlatans. These new deceptions led to a further interiorization of the idea of chivalry. It became more symbolic and spiritual by focusing on the Biblical image of the Temple to be reconstructed, and on the mytho-hermetical images of Jason and the Argonauts. In the fourteenth century, Rulman Merswin, spiritual leader of a chivalric community, had already spoken of "knights on a quest for chivalry," an expression which could apply even better to men of a similar mind in this century of the Enlightenment.

And so it was after the decline of the orders of chivalry that their myths and images developed and diversified along hermetical (alchemy) or associative (Freemasonry) lines, or in various literary forms. This evolution crystallized around two modes of expression. There was, on the one hand, a constant hermeneutic that rested on a symbolism already founded in a certain tradition. In this vein, Fictuld took on the role of interpreter of the trappings of the order founded by Philip the Good and, as we know, this sort of exegesis was fairly widespread at the time. The same is true of the mytho-hermetical commentaries of Dom Pernety on the tale of the Golden Fleece, which proceeded from a similar inspiration and indirectly gave new impetus to the chivalric myth itself. There was, moreover, a revival of the myth through ritual, through gesture and the spoken word; such was the history of the high Masonic degrees throughout the entire century and even beyond. Literature, when it did not merely expand upon moral and sentimental themes or create a fashion for certain medieval settings, was only a sounding board for this initiatory dimension.

---

70. According to Theodor Hönes, *Hippel, die Persönlichkeit und die Werke*, 1910, p. 72.

71. From the latin "*sodalitas*," or "*sodalicium*," that is, association, confraternity, guild; "*sodalis*" means *compagnon*, or member of a guild.

Chivalry was perhaps never as influential as when it became marginalized; that is to say, when the orders themselves had ceased to have any importance as official institutions. Once chivalry's political, economic, and military role had been relegated to the past, it discovered or rediscovered a certain spirituality, while becoming a storehouse of symbols and a repertory of generative images. Thereafter, in the midst of the spiritual desert of Enlightenment Europe chivalry became an empty vessel, which the *Imago templi* and the revived Quest filled by infusing meaning into the historic tradition and by remythologizing the relics of by-gone eras. And it really is the mythical we are speaking of, since chivalry was never truly an ideology, and even less so at the period we are considering than in the Middle Ages. But, as Gilbert Durand has recently reminded us, "myth unifies where ideology separates."

This was an evolutionary process and an active interiorization, typified by the transformation of the fully armed knight, with his lance and steed, into the trappings of chivalric orders (cloaks, collars) and the symbolic degrees of Scottish Masonry, which over time dissociated themselves from their more or less precise historical reference points. At the same time, they remained true to that which medieval chivalry had in common with Jason, which was the Quest, either terrestrial or maritime. Jason was the prototype of the knight, just as the ram was that of the Grail. Jason was thrust into a search for the Fleece, another empty vessel, just as the knights of the Grail went out in search of an empty tomb. In both cases, it was the creation, or the recreation, of a sacred space where the unfolding of the imagination was possible.

When in the midst of our quest for meaning we find ourselves plunged into a forest of symbols, Hermes is our guide. It was he who turned the fleece of the wonderful talking ram, the son of Poseidon, into gold. It was also he who was sometimes represented as *"krioforos"*—"ram carrier," bearing the ram on his shoulders. Ridden by Phrixos and Helle, who would fall to earth in the land of Colchis in a shower of gold, this animal was itself held aloft by Hermes. The image of Phrixos, an aerial and fugitive knight, complements that of Jason, mariner and conquering knight. It is up to each of us to discover his own land of Colchis and to meet up with a Pelias who will send him off, as well as to decide with whom to go, to choose his own ship Argo, his horse, or his ram, and to know who it is who carries his mount.

LOVE AND ANDROGYNY IN
FRANZ VON BAADER

It can hardly be denied that Baader is the greatest German, perhaps even European, theosopher of the nineteenth century, despite several attempts in recent years to present him in a way that corresponds very little to the actual thought and tradition he represents.[1] This "new Boehme"—*Boehmius redivivus*, as some and by no means the least, philosophers have called him—has fortunately never lacked in able and concerned exegetes who do him justice in a field that is rightly his.[2] Several attempts have been made to study his thought.[3] I have limited my approach to the main themes which seem to be the keys to his entire structure: faith and knowledge, light and fire, and

1. I find the work of Heinz-Jürgen Görtz, *Franz von Baaders anthropologischer Standpunkt*, (Fribourg–Munich, K. Alber, Coll. "Symposion," no. 56, 1977), to be typical in this regard. It is an excellent work, but one that casts a veil of modesty over the essentially theosophical aspect of Baaderian thought. This applies even to the book by Klaus Hemmerle, despite its good qualities, *Fr. von Baaders philosophischer Gedanke der Schöpfung*, which appeared in the same collection no. 13, 1963.
2. We mention here only: David Baumgardt, *Fr. von Baader und die philosophische Romantik*, (Halle–Saale, Niemeyer, 1927). Eugène Susini, *Franz von Baader et le romantisme mystique* (Paris, J. Vrin, 1942), 2 vol. Also the excellent study by Lidia Processi Xella, *La Dogmatica speculativa de Fr. von Baader*, (Turin, "Filosofia", series "Domenica Borello" (2), 1975), and *Filosofia erotica*, introduction, translation and notes by L.P. Xella, (Milan, Rusconi, 1982).
3. Aside from the references in the preceding footnote, consult the complete and fundamental bibliography by L.P. Xella, including all information available on him until 1977: *Baader. Rassegna storica degli studi*, 1786–1977, (Bologne, Il Mulino, 1977).

Sophiology.[4] Baader has been linked, and rightly so, to German Romanticism, which made "love" one of its preferred themes. Therefore, I feel it interesting to approach Baader's works under this new light, or with this new key. Above all, while doing so, to speak of androgyny in Baader's works obliges us to expound his conceptions of love. The work of rereading Baader yields very gratifying results to one who devotes himself to the matter.

In 1919, Giese had already dealt with the place of androgyny in "early Romanticism," and had devoted a synthetic and substantial section to Baader, based on some significant examples.[5] In 1955, Grassl published an annotated selection of the theosopher's texts, under the title *On Love, Marriage and Art.*[6] Two years later, a noteworthy anthology by Benz appeared, including introductory explanatory notes, in *Adam. the Myth of the Original Man.*[7] This quickly became the classic text par excellence on the theme of androgyny in Western theosophical tradition.[8] Here Baader is presented along with León Hebreo, J. Boehme, the English Boehmians, J.G. Gichtel, G. Arnold, the Bible of Berlebourg, Swedenborg, F.C. Oetinger, M. Hahn, J.J. Wirz, C.G. Carus, V. Soloviev and N. Berdiaev. Lidia Processi Xella recently completed a good Italian translation of Baader's main texts on androgyny,[9] prefaced by a long, scholarly study done by her, and this is certainly by far the best study to

4. "Faith and knowledge in Fr. von Baader and in modern gnosis," cf. in the present work, pp. 113–133; ("Ténèbre, éclair et lumière chez Fr. von Baader"), pp. 226–306,: in *Lumière et Cosmos*. (Paris, Albin Michel, coll. "Cahiers de l'Hermétisme", 1981); "Ame du Monde et Sophia chez Fr. von Baader", pp. 243–288, in *Sophia et l'Ame du Monde*, in the same collection, 1983; cf. in addition "L'imagination créatrice," pp. 355–390, in *Revue d'Allemagne*, Strasbourg, April 1981 (Italian translation in, *Conoscenza religiosa*, Florence, La Nuova Italia, April, 1981); and "Points de vue théosophiques sur la peine de mort", pp.17–24, in *Actes du colloque sur la peine de mort*, Paris, Association des amis d'Ivan Tourgeniev, 1980.

5. F. Giese, *Der romantische Charakter*, Bd. I, *Die Entwicklung des Androgynenproblems in der Frübromantik*, Langensalza, Wendt und, Klauwell, 1919. Cf. especially pp. 281–393. On Baader pp. 359–393.

6. Hans Grassl, *F. von Baader: Ueber Liebe, Ehe und Kunst. Aus den Schriften, Briefen, und Tagebüchern*, Munich, Kösel, 1953.

7. Ernst Benz, *Adam, der Mythus vom Urmenschen* (Munich, O.W. Barth, 1955).

8. Meanwhile, although unfortunately in the form of a summary, the thesis of W. Schulze had come out; it was especially dedicated to this theme in Oetinger: *Das androgyne Ideal und der christliche Glaube* (Diss. Heidelberg), (Lahr-Dinglingen, St. Johannis Druckerei, 1940).

9. Cf. *supra*, note 2: *Filosofia erotica*.

have appeared on this matter.[10] Throughout the course of this work, I have noted what is attributable to her.

The framework is organized around five main axes: ontological androgyny (in other words, based on divine, natural, and human principles); the myth of primitive Adam and his state of missing androgyny; the consequences of Adam's Fall, on human love, with dialectics and oppositions on one hand and the life of the couple and philosophies on the other. Finally, soteriology and eschatology are studied, based on the Baaderian ideas of knowledge and reintegration.

ONTOLOGICAL ANDROGYNY

General Principles

The Baaderian theory of Eros rests on the same principles on all three levels of the divine, natural and human; these principles are energized by their insertion into the scenario of the mythic drama. Before considering the three levels in their dramatic context, let us try to abstract the principles underlying them.

The idea of love is inseparable from that of the triad, through which we must understand the difference that unifies, and the unification that differentiates. The ternary also appears with hate since it is hate that brings together what is unequal, and reunites what is equal. Without original inequality there is no love; without original equality, there is no hate.[11] But, this is not what is essential, because Baader does not stop at the ternary. His theosophy, based

---

10. The study by L. P. Xella, pp. 7–79. Her translation of texts by Baader which pertain to androgyny, pp. 80–669; pp. 671–682, and an index. We should also mention two interesting works which have bearing on our topic: A. Rieber, "Sexualität und Liebe in ihrem Zusammenhang mit Schöpfung, Sündenfall und Erlösung bei Franz von Baader," in: *Salzburger Jahrbuch für Philosophie*, XIV, 1970, pp. 67–84. And P. Kluckhohn, *Die Auffassung der Liebe in der Literatur des 18. Jahrhunderts und in der deutschen Romantik*, Tübingen, Niemeyer, 1963. Finally, there are several interesting passages in: Willi Lambert, *Franz von Baaders Philosophie des Gebets (ein Grundriss seines Denkens)*, (Innsbruck-Vienna-Munich, Tyrolia Verlag, 1978), (cf. especially pp. 190–203. *Additional note:* Just after the publication of the present study (in French, 1986) another one appeared, by Bernhard Sill, *Androgynie und Geschlechtsdifferenz nach Franz von Baader. Eine anthropologisch-ethische Studie* (Regensburg, Friedrich Pustet, 1986, 498 p. After dealing with the history of the androgyne myth (pp. 36–136) and situating Baader in his philosophical context (pp. 137–172), the author gives a fine presentation of this theosopher's views on androgyny (pp. 173–248) and finally expounds his own reflections on them (pp . 249–334) . The notes (pp. 335–465) are followed by an excellent bibliography on this myth (pp. 467–498).

11. *Fermenta Cognitionis V* (1822–1824), II, 360 ff. In this note and the following, I refer to the edition of Baader's *Sämtliche Werke* edited by Franz Hoffmann (volumes and numbers in roman numerals, pages and number in arabic numerals).

on an essentially quaternary model, finds this structure in its eroticism on all three levels, and this is the key to what is going to follow. It is necessary to be aware that there are two forces existing on all levels: an active, masculine one, and a passive, feminine one; each force nonetheless possesses an aspect of the other one, resulting in quadrapolarity. Androgyny is thus ontologically set. When harmony reigns, the passive, gentle and moist feminine tincture[12] (this adjective should of course be understood metaphorically) spontaneously opens itself to the action of the expansive force, in order to constrict it and be constricted by it, whereas the active masculine tincture appears as a departure from itself, seeking to find a place in interiority. Their relationship is found reciprocally within the ascent and descent, which Baader calls *ascensus–descensus* and which is understood by him to be movement-in-rest and rest-in-movement. The feminine tincture tempers the masculine and receives warmth from it; the masculine is sustained by the feminine. There are four generative forces in this erotic-androgynous system, since each of the two tinctures potentially contains something of the nature of the other. The gentle feminine tincture looks for its corresponding gentleness in the harsh masculine tincture, to excite and provoke it out of its latency, so that by uniting with what is feminine within the masculine, it is able to soften the harshness and keep it from turning itself into a destructive fire.

Likewise and inversely, the harsh masculine tincture looks for its corresponding harshness in the feminine gentleness, to compel it to leave its passiveness, give form to what is still formless, and prevent this "water" from remaining stagnant and putrid. Thus, the feminine unites with the feminine within the masculine, and the masculine unites with the masculine within the feminine.[13]

The imaginary world of Baader is very spatial—its geometry is only understood organically—and it is full of forms which complete the quater-

---

12. "Tingieren" (to dye) does not have the same meaning for J. Boehme (cf. Baader, XII, 82) that it has in English (tint), i.e. to add a superficial color or an appearance. For him this word means a spiritual potentizing (potenzieren), a sowing, and it is located between the spirit and the body (Leib). "Tingieren" (ibid., 82, n), is the introduction of a vital form (Lebensgestalt) of one Being within another manner of existing, in opening the *Tinctur* which is hidden in this Being. The "Tinctur" is thus the living spiritual image between solely ideal Being and real Being; it could be heavenly, worldly or infernal. In the context of the present article we will see that it corresponds to the masculine and feminine aspects present in each human ("tincture" avoids saying "sex" which is solely the physiological transposition of "tincture" after the Fall).

13. L.P. Xella, *Filosofia erotica*, op. cit., p. 21 ff. One might compare this view with those of C.G. Jung (the theory of *anima* and *animus*, for example); L.P. Xella, (ibid., p. 22, n.19 a.b.c.) compares this with the views of R. Laing (*Intervista sul folle e il saggio*, a cura di V. Caretti, Laterza, Bari, 1979, especially pp. 144–154).

nary structure and lead back and reduce to some key notions, such as subordination, center and periphery. Love only exists in freedom; freedom needs
subordination and coordination in order to work, though some people think
that serving is not at all liberating.[14] Every union becomes one through
bondage; it is important for both parts to be different, much as in the case of a
musical chord. There is therefore a difference between maintaining one in
front of the other, or one below the other.[15] If I am below and want to raise
myself up, I must first pass through the mediation of my free self-abasement
and recognize the other as my superior.[16] Baader often uses the word "center"
to qualify the superior element, especially when it concerns the creature's
relationship with God—in other words, the periphery with the center. When
the periphery is filled with the center, it does not mean that the center is
"emptied"; creation, which should not be confused with God's self-evolution,
is not a process that consumes the Creator. On a human or animal level, the
body (periphery) is the pleroma of the head (center). In 1837, Baader cites
Nieuwentijdt, for whom the body can be considered as a development of the
head; for all that, the head is not the creator of the body, since both develop at
the same time in the embryo. Likewise, it would be erroneous to imagine an
active, masculine, motionless element situated exclusively in the center, and a
reactive, feminine, mobile element exclusively in the periphery. Indeed—and
this point is fundamental for understanding the theosopher's thought—the
expansion of the periphery occurs at the same time that the center opens, so
that in a normal state, i.e., in creative harmony, there is androgyny.[17]

We see the relationship of the two forces mentioned above from the
moment when "centering," the concentration, is inseparable from "departure," or from the fact that a periphery is created ("centering," says Baader, is
accompanied by "out of [ex-]centering"). On the divine world level, the identity of the *logos endetos* and *logos ekdetos*, or if you prefer—of the Son and
Sophia, (Virgin, mirror, eye) is a good example of the identity of the active
and reactive within all life-processes. The "ancient theologians and mystics,"
he writes in 1831 in a text dedicated to the notion of time, correctly liken the
reactive to the feminine (the prophet says that woman will encompass man),
since the feminine represents that which does not of itself have any value, that

---

14. L.P. Xella, op. cit., p.21.
15. *Ueber erotische Philosophie* 1828, IV, 165 ff. (roman numbers refer to *Sämtliche Werke*, 1851/1860).
16. *Ueber den biblischen Begriff von Geist und Wasser*, 1829, X, 3.
17. *Ueber den Paulinischen Begriff des Versehenseins des Menschen im Namen Jesu*, 1837, IV, 353. Bernhard Nieuwentijdt (1654-1718), mathematician, Cartesian adversary of Leibniz in the subject of infinitesimal calculus, and author of: *Het Regt Gebruik der Wereld Beschouwingen*, Amsterdam, 1717; *L'Existence de Dieu démontrée Par les merveilles de la Nature*. Paris, 1725.

which is nothing until it is itself freed, but like a mirror, carries the image in itself. The formation of an idea in ourselves can convince us of the soundness of this law of identity, or simultaneity of entry and departure: thought begins with an observation (*Anschauen*), and ends with contemplation (*Anschaulichkeit*) or "*Idea*," reminding us of the woman or Virgin who encompasses Man, of which she is the image or glory.[18]

Several texts, among them a course on speculative dogmatics (1838), insist on a third term that is inseparable from this coupling. Between the internal concentration and external excentration (out of centering), for example, which are "hidden" between the microphysic and the astrophysical "depths," there is an existing "true height" or "middle" (intermediary) whose role is to open both of them and bring them to light. Thus, says Baader, we can speak of androgyny as the union of two demicausalities on a backdrop or positive "middle" which unites, opens, and reveals them. The theosopher here reminds us of the importance of the "first two natural forms" (*Naturgestalten*) in Jacob Boehme's work. We have here both the concentrating, embracing sour (*herb*) form and the opening, bitter (*bitter*) form; the first descends and the other rises. Initially they lack the medium or positive foundation (*Grund*), because in Boehmian cosmogony they both arose from a negative medium, the "center of distress."[19] Instead of affirming each other and reaching harmony, they reciprocally deny each other, losing themselves in a perpetual ascent-descent deprived of internal law or measurement, much as one still finds today among intelligent or nonintelligent creatures. Similar to the manner in which a stone laying on the ground only appears to be resting, for the weight does not create union, so is our heart heavy, mean, and born to despair when it does not find anything that elevates it, and haughty (*hochfahrend*) when in its exaltation, it finds no limit to center it.

In connection with this, Baader brings up fire and water. If fire represents that which is elevated, it does not subsist without sustenance, in other words, without the "aqueous, descending spirit" which binds to it in order to allow both to find their support, bodies, and place (he uses the words "*Bestand*" "*Leib*" "*beleiben*," and "*bleiben*" here in a suggestive manner). Nourishment has no less need of hunger in order to materialize than hunger has need of nourishment. Woman needs man in the same way. Nevertheless, the first meeting of the two principles, which is negative, must be followed by a second or true foundation (*Gründung*), which is positive. According to Baader, theologians would do well to differentiate more clearly on this point,

---

18. *Elementarbegriffe über die Zeit*, 1831–1832, XIV, 141 ff.
19. Cf. my artcle "Feu, éclair et lumière chez Franz von Baader," in *Lumière et cosmos*, coll. "Cahiers de l'Hermétisme," (Paris, Albin Michel, 1981).

between what is the simple, immediate, created nature of the creature (for example, the nature this creature has when it comes into the world), and what is the divine relationship it acquires when by a second birth it is allowed to become a child of God. The creature is not immediately good and perfect; these two qualities wait to be "fixed" and consolidated.[20] The symbol that best designates the positive fixation or consolidation is shown in *Fermenta Cognitionis* as Mercury, because it accounts for the "androgynous nature of the spirit"; it expresses the identity of "content" and "form," or rather the identity of the principle revealed in them. Here we understand "content" to be the feminine factor that supplies the envelope; it is an intensive element, and has a tendency to be filled; "form" is to be the masculine factor that furnishes the soul, is an extensive element, and has a tendency to fill. The first factor is traditionally represented by " ☽ " and the second one by "O"; their union (the concept of union is represented by a cross) gives us the key Alchemist sign of Mercury: " ☿ ". The spirit, as Hegel saw it, is certainly life, center, middle.[21]

On the Divine Level

But, these diagrams and structures are inseparable from history—and above all, from metahistory. Everything obviously begins with the *Ungrund*, of which Jacob Boehme has revealed the mystery. In the beginning there was the passive desire of Divinity, comprised of the androgynous potentiality to be filled and made fertile. What characterizes a divine causality such as the Father is not so much the fact that it is without a cause, as that it is without foundation, i.e., deprived of a foundation on which to carry out its own activity in order to later rejoice on the Sabbath day of rest, as mentioned in the first book of Genesis. Thus there is originally an *Ungrund*; as in any beginning situation, it represents the potentiality and instability of the very figure, that it is a matter of moving within definite boundaries, from potency to act.[22] Jacob Boehme never speaks of the androgyny of the *Ungrund*; Baader, however, does bring up the two complementary aspects of mirror and volition, both without a beginning in the bosom of this *Ungrund*, just as Thomas Aquinas differentiates between the *Sapienta ingenita* (as *genitrix*) and the *Sapienta genita* (the virgin son, *Jungfrauensohn*) within the Father. The eternal Father,

---

20. *Vorlesungen über spekulative Dogmatik* 1838, IX, 213–219.
21. *Fermenta Cognitionis II*, 1822–1824, II, 325 ff. Thus one could say that the act of feeling, of sensing (*empfinden*), which is governed by the intention, by the content, is polarly opposed to contemplation (*Schauen*), which is governed by extension, by form.
22. Cf. L.P. Xella, op. cit., p. 34.

in the union of his fiery, eternal and harsh potency (*Potenz*) with the gentle luminous potency (Sophia), begets his Son.[23] Father, Mother and Son are the potencies within the *Verselbständigung*, the true individuation or conquest of authentic *Selbstheit*—the identity of Self on all levels.

He who is called Father–Being, the First Person, is already the result of a distinction, or the will to reproduce in the Son. The Son was potentiality, and begetting means to set into motion the potentiality of the feminine tincture and the potency of the masculine nature; it is the giving of nourishment to the appetite, of substance to nourishment, of meaning and consistency to desire; it is obliging the unstable duality to take root and form within a ternary.[24] On this divine level, we recognize the *descensus*, or first dialectic moment of entrance, during which the matrix is filled, and the *ascensus*, the moment the Son emerges. We know that this process repeats itself constantly. What Boehme and the theosophers who followed him see in the *Ungrund* is, above all, the source of a passive, feminine divineness and an active, masculine appetite, which arouse each other just as we have seen when nourishment (woman) arouses hunger (man) and hunger seeks nourishment. This dialectic of desire puts the *Ungrund* in a state of continuous inflammability, brought out in the Bible in the form of *ignis divinus*. Still it is necessary to differentiate between active inflammation, exemplified in anger, the fire of the Father, and passive inflammation, which means that the matrix, as the root of being, consumes itself and longs to be filled. Today we can still see how Nature, in spite of her profound degradation, had her origin in fire, as is demonstrated by electric and magnetic phenomena.[25]

Divine self-generation, which tends toward the *Verselbständigung*, is also called the "center of nature" by Baader; it is a passive moment represented as a triangle—figure of the root feminine principle—and inscribed within a circumference.[26] Every birth brings with it the danger of not being able to cross the fire of the Center of Nature unharmed (danger is often qualified by Baader as *Periculum Vitae*). The birth of a son brings with it the potentialization of the inflammability of feminine nature. Its appeasement does not indicate the extinction of initial desire–appetite, but rather its transformation into fulfillment and joy. The matrix finds its completeness whereas the Father, seeing a form given to his expansion, rejoices in the peace of the Sabbath. The

---

23. *Vorlesungen über spekulative Dogmatik*, 1838, IX, 213–219.
24. L.P. Xella, op. cit., p. 33 ff. We recall meanwhile that for Boehme the Being–Father is not the *Ungrund* but Nothingness.
25. Ibid., p. 35 ff.
26. Ibid., p. 34 ff. and especially *Vorlesungen über spekulative Dogmatik* cited above.

Son, or the reality of foundation, represents the correct relationship between the productive forces of the Father and Mother.[27]

Here one can insert an image that is frequently represented in Baader's texts: the one of three concentric circles generally brought out by the words: *pater in filio, filius in matre.* There is no being, he says in the manner of Saint-Martin, which does not have as its task to beget its own father. Lidia P. Xella clarifies this proposition, seemingly by drawing inspiration from C.G. Jung's quaternary. She implicitly shows one noteworthy difference between Baader and Boehme, since we know that Sophia is not considered as a fourth term for Boehme. It has to do with the androgynous and ontological quaternary structure brought up above: indeed, through the emergence of the Son, the latent masculine tincture becomes a reality in the feminine passiveness (one could also say that the Son is formed in and by a matrix excited to a state of activity). He does indeed produce the Father, but it is His passive aspect which becomes reality here. The Son is passive feminine tincture with regard to the Father, but is also active masculine tincture with respect to the Mother. Therefore, his double aspect is mediation, the possibility of becoming a quaternary of the Self, the *Verselbständigung*. The Son prevents the Mother from being a passive matrix with regard to the Father, and prevents the Father from condemning himself, by refusing to be abased to the eternal flame, in an act of self-consumption. As such, the matrix is indistinctness, without its own being or personality, and only able to make an offering of itself, while the Father is active–passive and the Son is passive–active, determined above the *Ungrund*, and constantly penetrating and emerging from one another in dynamic movement. This determination is the Spirit. Its movement is contained by the Mother who, from her maternal potentiality, was made the place of the reproductive process, the fourth term (neither creator nor created), in other words, Sophia.[28] Baader reminds us that St. Bernard denominates the Spirit as "the kiss of Father and Son," because those who kiss breathe together, and the union of both breaths creates something that then acts on them.[29] St. Bernard calls "breath" the kiss of he who breathes. The kiss is a kind of sanctifying Spirit that reconstitutes the primitive triad.[30] Father and Son are active while breathing the Spirit, and passive while undergoing its action. Just as the fire embraces the water, so the water embraces the fire. Their union is Mercury, i.e., the androgyny that arouses both again.[31] Let us note, however, that in

---

27. L.P. Xella, op.cit., p. 36.
28. Ibid. p. 37.
29. *Ueber das zweite Capitel der Genesis.* 1829, VII, 237, n. Cf. also Saint-Martin, *Esprit des Choses*, t. I, p. 205.
30. *Spekulative Dogmatik*, zweites Heft, 1830, VIII, 293, no. 7 and 237. Cf. also E. Susini, t. III, p. 572 ff.
31. *Ueber das zweite Capital der Genesis*, 1829, VII, 237.

Boehme's works, the coming together of masculine with feminine values is only conceived on a level of divine manifestation, and not on that of the *Ungrund*. There is not the least duality in the Absolute which is Boehme's *Ungrund*. But this, to my knowledge, was never stressed by Baader.

Pater in filio, filius in matre thus adds a supplementary element of androgyny to the already androgynous aspect suggested by the double movement. This key expression means that the producer is as much in his product as the product is in the producer. It centralizes itself while producing, and expands while constricting itself, and this by virtue of the principle expounded on above ("Centering is accompanied by out of [ex-] centering").[12] Creative and begetting love is always both paternal and maternal. Through its paternal aspect it fills, confers or seeks interiority, animates and makes corporal (beleiben). Through its maternal aspect, it gives form or cover, reveals, and pours out.

To say "*pater in filio*" means to recognize that God reveals himself through his genitus, as parents do through their child. As Father, God wants to possess his genitus; as Mother, He wants to be possessed by it. This explains the double activity: giving completeness (*Fülle*) and giving form or cover (*Hülle*). The image of fire, for example, that of a lamp light, helps to specifically understand this: fire, an animating activity, offers its base or dark element to a constructing and organizing activity, light, which will conceal the fire. This fire (heat or the Father) must be out of sight in order for the manifestation (light, the Son) to take place. But, this process is made possible by the presence of a mediator. In our elementary nature, it is the sun that centralizes the light and heat, the same as Christ does on another level. This third term hinders abnormal separation (for example, in our own lives the act of separating our brain—the light which gives form—from our heart—the warmth that fills).[13] The Father therefore unites his fiery and harsh potency with his gentle luminescent potency (Sophia, Idea) in order to beget his Son, to "fix him" (*fassen*), and endow him with the harsh potency of the Father while encompassing him with the gentle potency, which St. Paul calls the "eternal Mother on high" (for Boehme, however, it is not the Father who "sets" the Son, rather it is the Father who "sets" himself within the Son. . . .). This production of the *genitus* is not emanant, nor creating, nor bound to time; rather, it is immanent. If the idea of androgyny is comprehended, says Baader, then the Father will not be seen just as a fructiferous and begetting

---

32. *Vorrede zum zweiten Band der philosophischen Schriften und Aufsätze*, 1832, I, 410, ff.
33. *Religionsphilosophische Aphorismen*, X, 328–332. We note that for Boehme it is the feminine which provides the body or creates the body. Thus the masculine communicates the spirit, i.e., the fire of the soul, a hidden fire that becomes light. The body is formed by separating from water, by concretion.

potency (*Potenz*), which would indeed be detached from any kind of receptive potency that begets; he will not be seen as a male, comparable to what resulted from the separation of the sexes. In fact, one would not hesitate to speak of *genitrix* when speaking of God, and nor would this be contradictory to dogma.[14]

Pater in filio, filius in matre also expresses the "general law of every manifestation of a superior being within and by an inferior being," because manifestation is only possible "thanks to a free or constrained *occultation* of the inferior in relation to the superior."[15] Moreover, "all coordination is a reciprocal subjection," "all subjection is an occultation," or yet still: "all manifestation is conditioned by an occultation and all exteriorization by an interiorization."[36] just as light is conditioned by shadow, a revelation by a secret, and free activity by constraint and subordination of activity."[37] This also means that a being can only achieve its existence when another being is annihilated, as Meister Eckhart said when speaking of the Father who is consumed in the Son, or a producer in his product. Every producer becomes inflamed and, by consuming the darkness, begets the light. Creating is first the act of making an effort, with the intent of provoking a resistance of self, then reducing it until it is laid to rest. Fire rises up from the darkness and subsides into the light. While consuming the darkness, it acts as "father"; while subsiding in the form of light, it acts as "mother." The son is revealed in the mother, and the father in the son. In the same way, there is no domination without constraint or obedience, no language without hearing, and no science without faith.[18] Finally, "*pater in filio, filius in matre*" also reminds us that the producer is found within the product. Therefore, in seeing this product, one sees the producer as well (he who sees the Son sees the Father). The product is also in the producer, since whoever sees the Son sees him in the Mother.[19]

Sophia is a constraining force which confers an element of joy, sabbatical rest, and conquest of the self (*Verselbständigung*) on the unity of divine Persons in their distinction, mainly by the androgynous and dynamic eroticisms between Father and Son. The passage of *Ungrund* to *Begründung*, to the foundation, or to the Son as *Grund*—if you prefer—occurs with the formation of the image of the *Maya*, the feminine tincture, an original mirror in which

---

34. *Ueber den biblischen Begriff von Geist und Wasser*, 1830, X, 7.
35. *Sozialphilosophische Aphorismen*, V, 271 (cf. also E. Susini, t. III, p. 537).
36. VIII, 76 ff. (cf. E. Susini, t. III, p. 538).
37. V, 286 ff. (cf. E. Susini, t. III, p. 538).
38. IV, 227 seq.; V, 271 (cf. E. Susini, t. III, p. 538).
39. *Ueber den biblischen Begriff von Geist und Wasser*, 1830, X, 10 ff.

the images are still only potential. In this mirror as matrix, the Father seeks his own image, and his desire (*a visu cupido* . . .) returns to him reflected as admiration by the matrix itself, which through divine feminine tincture admires the superior imaginative potency of the divine masculine tincture. The *Maya* was the passive mirror as potential repose in the holy Ternary; Sophia is a passive mirror as real and active repose of the holy Ternary. *Spiegel, speculum*, mirror, *mirare, admiratio, miraculum—Wunder* (miracle), *bewundern* (to admire). . . . Wherever there is admiration there is always a hierarchical relation between "superior" and "inferior," which assures unity and a distinction between those so associated. In admiring the superior, the inferior leaves its own inferiority and "rises up" in some way. The superior that looks at and contemplates itself in the inferior, raises it to itself, without lowering itself down to the inferior level. "The superior," L.P. Xella so correctly writes, "is a miracle for the inferior and the inferior is a mirror for the superior: they thus meet without merging."[40]

But we know that this relationship is quaternary in the sense that the masculine unites with what is masculine in the feminine and the feminine with what is feminine in the masculine. "The expansive masculine potency finds its own repose, its own outline in moving and opening the feminine tincture and by limiting itself. This is why the deepest meaning of the relationship between movement and repose can only be obtained in the divine quaternary"—the fourth, passive term adds nothing to the Trinity because it neither creates nor begets; it reflects only the begetting and returns the image of the generative forces back to them; through this image, they can be perceived in their unity as well as in their differences.[41] The androgynous divinity is not, therefore, simply Father and Mother, but rather Father–Son–Spirit, and the process of foundation can only be quaternary, since it is the quaternary alone which can express *Verselbständigung*, i.e., access to the Self and to the personality of God in three equal and distinct Persons.

The essential of the above (especially where androgyny is concerned) can be regarded as a principle and as an act of language, in which existing languages are only bearers of witness for those who know how to see and hear. Baader freely speaks of the relationships existing between vowels and consonants. L.P. Xella has suggested an interpretation of the theosopher's ideas that seems to be heavily influenced by C.G. Jung. In summarizing her synthesis, we must begin by interpreting the repose within the matrix as a silence which longs to resound, as a hollow which waits to be inhabited (*Inwohnung*). The satisfaction of this desire is carried out through the mediation of lan-

---

40. L.P. Xella, op. cit., p. 38 ff.
41. Ibid., p. 40.

guage. When speaking of the word, one can also speak of androgynous quaternity because it can resound only to the extent it is listened to, and listened to only to the extent it resounds. It assumes a sound that is both active and passive: it expands in it, and is constrained and defined by it (the echo is a typical phenomenon whereby the original blueprint of Nature is manifested). At the origins of language there is a superabundance of desire and at the same time an ambiguity: silence is a feminine tincture (it would thus be feminine!) which, like the omnipotentiality of all sounds, longs to be filled and defined; it thus excites sound, the masculine tincture, which represents the appetite seeking a medium in which to express itself. Each needs the other so as to avoid both absolute mutism and inarticulate sounds.

The androgynous relationship of the two tinctures is reproduced in the word, which is thus *genitus*, through the cooperation of the vowel and consonant. The vowel, masculine tincture, needs the consonant in order to be able to express itself, and be fully articulate. The consonant, feminine tincture, needs the vowel in order to be expressed. It is obvious that from the outset, God would be the vowel par excellence which, in the superabundance of His sound, established within the intimate exchange among the Three Persons, allows its eternal natural matrix to give form and expression to the consonant of creation. Sophia, who is neither created nor creator, represents this balance and unison between the divine vowel and creating consonant. The Word inserts into Sophia the masculine-androgynous aspect, formative seminal word, and the feminine-androgynous aspect, thus exciting it to reproduce in Nature a seminal word united to sound, the giver of form. The signifying sonority of the divine Word thus both slips into the matrix to become a distinct signified and gives to it its essence, taking it from silence to life, according to the principle of the *Emerald Tablet*, so often cited by Baader: "*Vis ejus integra est, si conversa fuerit in terram.*"[42] One can therefore consider the divine eternity as androgynous, free *descensus–ascensus*, excitation and appeasement, the penetration and emergence of both tinctures in each other, through a third mediating term and quaternary totality.

On the Natural Level

Original Nature had to reproduce this ontological and divine plan. It was also androgynous and made up of a spiritual corporeality (*Geistleiblichkeit*), defined by two forces, an expansive one and another one containing it. The passive, gentle, moist feminine tincture (an "in-itself" and "interior of itself") opened spontaneously to the action of the expansive force to both constrict and be constricted by it. In this state of paradise, the active masculine tincture

---

42. L.P. Xella, op. cit., pp. 42–45.

revealed itself as fire aspiring to emerge out of itself, in search of the interiority of the other tincture; an elevation, since emerging and rising both precede
and condition the entry. Here, as on the divine level, we must try and grasp
the process in terms of magical imagination. Baader reminds us that we can
only comprehend the idea of androgyny if we know the meaning given by
Paracelsus and Boehme to "imagination" and "magic": for them, "imagination" is the root of all production; and love, appetite, etc., demonstrate aptly
that it is the *primus motor creans*.[43] The undifferentiated matrix, or principle of
nature, is passive receptivity, "magical inessentiality" but at the same time
potential mother of all the differentiations. Baader compares "magic," the
potentiality of all images, to the idea of natural magnetism, since he sees the
matrix as being capable of infinite splits, differentiations, and divisions, in the
desire it experiences to receive into its interior both the principle of the form
and the reality of all possible forms. The active excitation of the begetter's
(*genitor*) imagination—the principle of the form—makes the matrix pregnant
in order to contain it within its productive expansion, i.e., so as not to spread
out too far, and yet to define itself and return back within the limits of perfection. By returning to itself, it has become *genitus, imago* and at the same time
magia, the inessential *Maya*, has taken shape and become Sophia or the completeness of images in their essentiality. Sophia is thus ideal Nature, the place
where the *genitor* and *genitus* reflect one another and indissolubly blend, while
maintaining their differences.[44]

In order to understand Nature in its present state, it is not only necessary to know what the Judeo-Christian myth teaches about the Fall, especially
the creation of the universe based on the fall of Lucifer (cf. *infra*), but also to
know the mechanism of the relationships that unite all of Nature to God. So,
when the philosophers study the word "substance" (*Substanz*), they have a
tendency to forget that it is necessary to take this in its etymological sense of
"*Unter-halt*" (under-hold), meaning "to found" or " foundation."

The idea is that the producer is in balance with his product and united
(without blending) with it only upon entering profoundly in his product as
Mother and remaining poised above it as Father.[45] This holds true for Nature
as well as for the creature. In an 1834 essay dedicated to the ties of solidarity
between religious sciences and natural sciences, Baader notes that people

---

43. With regard to "magical imagination," cf. my article "L'imagination créatrice, fonction mag-
    ique et fondement mythique de l'image," pp. 355–390 in *Revue d'Allemagne*, Strasbourg,
    Société d'Etudes allemandes, April–June 1981, t. XIII, no. 2: *Hommages à Eugène Susini*. A
    second, more complete, edition, pp. 230–261 in *Conoscenza religiosa*, Florence, La Nuova
    Italia, April–June 1981.
44. L. P . Xella, op. cit., p. 19 ff.
45. *Vierzig Sätze aus einer religiösen Erotik* 1831, IV, 183.

have put a high value on Spinoza, but by following his idea of substance they have lost the essential understanding of the function of substantiation. It is necessary to know that the agent maintaining and keeping me is sacrificed in its movement toward me. While emerging (*Entäusserung*) it puts itself *below* me through love—a materializing descent that gives me support and allows me to rise and to exist. One must differentiate "*amor cadit*" from "*amor descendit*" and to avoid this error, complete the correct Hegelian idea of "*Aufhebung der Natur durch die Uebernatur*" with the idea of the *Erhebung* of this Nature, just as an artist "breaks in" his raw material in order to transform it.[46]

A little later, in a course on speculative dogmatics, Baader gave precise insight into how he conceives the relationship between Nature and the Spirit. Their "integration," or "disintegration"—their "separation" as far as we are concerned—are successive and reciprocal. Every descent, be it free or not, is disintegration and every ascent is integration, as one sees in the permanent descent of one, invisible and uncreated element in Nature; by this descent it decomposes into four elements and by ascending again it is reintegrated. For this one element, the earth is both the final step of the disintegrating descent and the first step of the ascent.

The descent is truly an off (ex-) centering while the ascent is concentration. There is a union between them when they manage to "settle" (*sich ponieren*) through means of a positive medium and mediator. This is why a being that has fallen into "disintegration" can only achieve its restoration with the help of an "integral" being that suspends the form of its own integrity and sacrifices itself to it in order to descend toward and bind itself to it [the being in disintegration].[47] We must therefore place the Nature–Spirit duality under the sign of androgyny. In a course on speculative dogmatics in 1838, Baader expressed a formula in a style probably consciously inspired by Schelling, but as if to correct the philosophy of identity:

> Since the concept of Spirit expresses that of the freedom of Nature and by the same token means the contrary of the absence of Nature (*Naturlosigkeit*), the absolute Spirit must simultaneously be absolute Nature. This idea of absolute identity of Spirit and Nature in God coincides with that of the identity of freedom and necessity.[48]

---

46. *Ueber den solidären Verband der Religionswissenschaft mit der Naturwissenschaft*, 1834, III, 345.
47. *Vorlesungen über speculative Dogmatik*, 1838, IX, 208.
48. Ibid., p. 218: "*Da der Begriff des Geistes jenen der Naturfreiheit somit das Gegenteil der Naturlosigkeit aussagt, so muß der absolute Geist zugleich die absolute Natur sein. Dieser Begriff der absoluten Identität des Geistes und der Natur in Gott fällt mit jenem der Identität der Freiheit und Nothwendigkeit zusammen.*" In the following, Baader made allusion to Edmund Burke, the author of *Reflexions on the Revolution in France*. On the nature of androgyny of the spirit, cf. also *Vierzig Sätze* (IV), 194 ff.

But, Baader does not state that for Boehme the absolute Spirit (*Ungrund*) is not Nature, not even absolute; this concept of identity is alien to Boehme.

PRIMITIVE ADAM AND FAILED ANDROGYNY

Before the Fall

The image of a primitive androgyne should be indulged in by our meditations because "without a clearing of this dark area of our nature, the mysteries of religion would remain impenetrable."[49] The present condition of Man itself is sufficient to cast a ray of light on the subject since both sexual potencies (fiery and aqueous) are found in each one of us, male or female. One of the two always overshadows the other in a given individual, a fact confirmed by phenomena of animal and plant nature.[50] On the other hand it is difficult to understand how theologians have remained so alien to the idea of primitive androgyny, since Mary conceived without the help of a man and Adam procreated without a woman.[51] If woman was created in the image of man, then man was conceived to be androgynous, which wasn't the case with respect to animals. But the first Man was not really created androgynous; rather, he received the mission of becoming it, by harmonizing both the masculine and feminine tinctures.[52] We must understand the concept of human androgyny as a function of the principles listed above, i.e., the complete union of cause and foundation (*Ursache* and *Grund*), "*genitor*" and "*genitus*," with their separation on the human level as that of man and woman, or as an actualization of time (Meister Eckhart said that all temporality is born of and subsists through separation of the Father and the Son).[53] Before the "sleep" in Genesis, 2:21, thus before the separation of the sexes, Adamic androgyny consisted in the identity of the principle or procreating organ and of that which gives form.[54] The question of the androgyny or nonandrogyny of Adam is in knowing if the distribution of double sexual potency (not only on a tincturial level—in two individuals and two different bodies) is primitive or if the differentiation presented in Genesis is already secondary at that point and preceded by a previous union into a single body. Baader's response appears to indicate no doubt on his part: the book of Moses speaks in favor of the second solution.

---

49. *Fermenta Cognitionis IV*, 1822–1824, II, 382.
50. *Vorlesungen über speculative Dogmatik*. 1838, IX, 211.
51. Ibid. 212.
52. X, 247, n. (cf. E. Susini, t. III, p. 366).
53. *Vorlesungen über speculative Dogmatik*, 1838, IX, 213.
54. XII, 409 (here Baader comments Saint-Martin's *Ministère de l'Homme-Esprit*).

When St. Paul says that in Christ we are no longer "man" and "woman" and that in Him we rediscover our lost divine image, this means that Adam was not initially conceived as "separated," As St. Augustine said, it is only later that the first Man was created with the *posse mori*; Baader preferred to call this *"posse mas et foemina fieri,"* which became later the "false desire" of Adam and the nocturnal aspect he took on.[55] Nevertheless, Adam had within him the differentiation of the two tinctures—certainly not a sexual separation in male and female—which would not have become externalized if Adam's Fall had not come about.[56] This failure to recognize the originally androgynous nature of Man is so great that one generally confuses the creation of Eve from Adam with the sexual division following his first Fall. This is why the androgyne has been described as incapable of reproducing itself.[57]

Contrary to other theosophers such as Johann Georg Gichtel or Antoinette Bourignon, who never spared any details in their concrete descriptions of the androgyne (external form, crystalline nature, impenetrability, etc.), Baader here shows evidence of prudence. To my knowledge, only one passage, in the *Aphorisms on Religious Philosophy*, which happens to have as its title *On the Androgyne*, contains a specific allusion. In this text, he first of all reminds us that Eve took on a different body, following a radical separation (*Scheidung*) into two parts of the essence or Adamic nature, and that this was not a consequence of an act of reproduction, which Adam would have been capable of, due to his androgynous nature. Otherwise, Eve herself would also have been androgynous. Here Baader specifically mentions the mode of reproduction in the primitive androgyne. It obviously took place without the help of sexual organs. It can be compared to the way he attained nourishment, i.e., without digestive organs, of which plant and sometimes animal nature offer us a glimpse. When Genesis says that man saw he was naked, it means he was ashamed to see himself endowed with separate reproductive and feeding organs. Saint Paul says that God will judge the belly with earthly food; he differentiates, in the noble sense, between belly (*Bauch*) and body (*Leib*). The androgyne would digest in the mouth, and procreate in the heart. At the time of the Fall, the stomach fell toward the bottom and the reproductive organs moved from the heart to the belly. "The woman—the earth—descended," says Saint-Martin, and Boehme teaches that the earth fell from the *puncto*

---

55. *Ueber den morgendländischen und den abendländischen Katholicismus*, 1840, X, 247.
56. *Vorlesungen über speculative Dogmatik*, 1838, IX, 221.
57. *Vierzig Sätze aus einer religiösen Erotik*, 1831, IV, 194 ff.
58. *Ueber die Androgyne*, X, 295. Concerning Adam's primitive sexuality according to Antoinette Bourignon, cf. Serge Hutin, *Les Disciples anglais de Jacob Boehme*, (Paris, Denoël, 1960), p. 27 ff.

solis.[58] Remember that as far as Boehme is concerned, the primitive body of Adam did not include sexual organs; he discovers sex by way of another body. The vision of sexual organs united in a single body, as brought out by Antoinette Bourignon, pertains to a "Boehmenism" that is far removed from Boehme. He would have trembled in horror at this!

It is therefore as "image of God" that Adam should have procreated. Baader obviously then quotes the passage which has caused so much ink to flow—Genesis 1:26-27: "*Then God said: Let us make man in our image, after our likeness: and let them have dominion over [. . .] So God created Man in his own image in the image of God he created him: male and female he created them. And God blessed them.*" One finds the same change in Genesis, 5:1-2: "*In the day that God created Man, in the likeness of God made he him: male and female created he them.*" The fact that in the second chapter it becomes a question of separation because it "was not good" that it did not take place, shows that Adam could not have been a male in the very beginning. Otherwise, how could he, without femininity, have been the image of God or even subsist? "Needless to say the text is interpolated." As far as the word "Elohim" being used to designate the creator in the plural is concerned, Baader explicitly states that this does not refer to any sexual duality in God.[59]

Unlike the animals, Adam was created by God—and not on his order; animals were created directly from the earth and other elements, immediately appearing as males and females, each sex materialized in a different body. Scripture shows us Man rising from the earth toward God and not formed, as Luther would have it, by a potter from a clump of earth.[60] Adam had not been created to be an earthly creature, but rather fell into this state. The author reminds us that the Kabbalists go so far as admitting two Adams, a first and a second. The first is described by the *Divine Philosophy* as "a divine being and Elohim," a spirit without an earthly body.[61] This one was lost. The second was an earthly body animated by a divine soul breathed into him, but not from the elements; it was to serve the Man–Spirit (*"L'Homme Esprit"*) as an instrument for carrying out the work of creation on earth which Lucifer's fall had corrupted (*verdorben*), and for transforming the earth into paradise. This is why the heavenly Adam was transported from the heavenly earth to the dark one, and united to earthly Adam in order to make one single person of him.

---

59. *Bemerkungen über das zweite Capitel der Genesis*, 1829, VII, 225.

60. *Vorlesungen über speculative Dogmatik.* 1838, IX, 210.

61. *Bemerkungen über das zweite Buch der Genesis*, 1829, VII, 226. Baader cites only the title of the work by Dutoit-Membrini. It is obviously *La Philosophie divine appliquée aux lumières naturelle, magique, astrale, surnaturelle, céleste et divine, ou aux immuables vérités* by Keleph Ben Nathan (pseudonym for Dutoit—Membrini), s.l., 1793, 3 vol. (title of t. III is slightly different).

From that time on, Adam was spirit-body-soul.[62] Jacob Boehme himself also noted that in order to be able to dominate and restore the already "corrupted" earthly nature, Adam would have had to possess this earth within himself— this *limus terrae*—as a constitutive element of his being. His duty would have been to uproot (*tilgen*) from himself the infection of this *limus*, which had resulted from lust (*Lust*) or Adam's element of temptation.[63] Boehme had also said that the soul of the earthly body has the image of this body, in the image of the *spiritus mundi*. But, the spiritual body identifies with Wisdom: when Adam lost this body, Wisdom disappeared. This differentiation of levels is very clear for Boehme.

Adam thus procreated, while remaining a virgin. Any true autonomization or autofoundation is only carried out by a fusion of opposites. This is the reason why Adamic tinctures did not have as their goal the actualization of their opposites. In other words, neither of them should have become autonomous but should have remained "*selbstlos*" in order for fusion (*Zusammenschliessen*) of both to be confirmed. The nonautonomization (*Selbstlosigkeit*) of one tincture coincides with asexualization. This is an idea that both Boehme and Plato have in common. Indeed, Baader does wonder, in "*Fermenta Cognitionis*" why the child attracts us so. Why does he/she awak- the memory or desire of a paradisical state of external nature in us? Because, that is what is still found vis-à-vis the spiritual or divine superior nature; it is what it should be—a tool without a will to reveal or a will that has not yet become its own autonomized spirit. We perceive the *Selbstlosigkeit* as asexual- ization in the innocence of a child. Might not the nostalgia for true love between man and woman and in the most noble of natures simply be a "com- plaint" expressing the sorrow of a lost paradise, or the pain of this rupture, or the inflammation that took hold of the external nature? The fiancée in the Song of Songs expresses the idea so well: "Oh! If only you were my brother!" The feeling of shame that takes hold of Adam after his sleep is first of all explained by the awareness of the autonomization of external nature: Animal and Spirit are only ashamed of their impotency, not of their potency; because animal potency will emerge detrimental to the potency of the Spirit, Man–Spirit ("l'Homme–Esprit") will be ashamed. The development of sexual

62. *Bemerkungen über das zweite Capitel der Genesis*, 1838, IV, 216. About this, Baader cites *Einleitung in die Bibel*, Strasbourg, 1820, p. 82, and Klein's *Schöpfung der Welten*, 1823.

63. *Bemerkungen über das zweite Capitel der Genesis*, 1838, IV, 226 ff.61. *Bemerkungen über das zweite Buch der Genesis*, 1829, VII, 226.

difference, and of the external inflammation of Nature will coincide with that of poison and death.[64]

Adam's mission was to maintain this state of androgyny within himself in order to "fix" himself in an image of God, which is itself neither male nor female. He necessarily had to undergo the temptation to not carry out this "fixation," since God wanted to put him to the test (*bewähren*—he had to "withstand the test"). This meant radically reducing to nothing (*tilgen*) the *posse mas et foemina fieri* (or "*posse animal fieri*") in himself so as to overcome the Spirit of the World (*Weltgeist*) both within and outside himself. This was the only way to make him submit, even though the true destination of Adam was to become lord and all-powerful king of the external world at the end of the tests, since the crown is only given to the winner. In order for the *posse*— his potentiality—to be reduced to nothing, it had to be excited as such; we have here the key to understanding a necessary temptation sent by God to the creature and putting that creature to the test. Adam was submitted to this temptation by Evil. Lucifer and his cohorts, however, were not previously submitted to anything originating in Evil, since it was still inexistent, and would only be a result of Lucifer's later lack of success in the test. We thus see, affirms Baader, that without the idea of androgyny, the central concept of religion, i.e., the image of God would remain incomprehensible.[65]

When God created Adam, he did not create him alone but also gave him the heavenly help of the Idea (Sophia)—androgynous itself, but not so for Boehme who believes that it perfectly transcends the sexes—with which he had to behave, above all *internally*, as an organ or image of God. If he had carried out this program properly, the two tincturial potencies (masculine and feminine) would have been *externally* bonded to each other to constitute androgyne, and the "*posse mas et foemina fieri*" would have been reduced to nothing in Adam.[66] Mediator between God and Nature, Man had to project his imagination in Sophia, in the divine Matrix so as to submit Nature to himself and be submitted to God. The active–masculine vis-à-vis Nature is passive–feminine vis-à-vis God. The "principle" is indeed masculine, and the "organ" is feminine, to the point where if Nature is "organ" with respect to Man, Man is "organ" with respect to God. Thus, the mystery of the relationship between the "principle" and the "organ" in God is that of the true constitution of the "divine Self," as L.P. Xella notes. It is thus also through the feminine tincture that Man should "imagine" passively "in" the Sophia, exciting the enclosed masculine activity within; this would have helped Adam to be

64. *Fermenta Cognitionis III–IV*, 1822–1824, II, 271 ff., 314 ff.
65. *Bemerkungen . . .* , 303 ff.
66. *Vorlesungen über speculative Dogmatik*, 1838, IX, 211 ff., n.

filled with the divine seed. This would have then allowed Man to project his active imagination on Nature, but we are going to see that instead of carrying out this program, he distorted these relationships.[67] According to the interpretation given by L.P. Xella, he should have stayed as the docile consonant, the instrument, allowing the divine vowel to express itself in creation vis-à-vis Nature. His role was to serve as a vowel which, pronounced by the intermediary of the natural consonant, would have restored Nature to its normal structure and complicity with God, which had been broken by Lucifer's sin.[68]

For Baader the vowel and consonant serve as a paradigmatic image: a creature can only be born in nature, he says, and light only reveals itself from fire; light takes the fire in it, like the creature assumes Nature, or as the vowel takes the consonants and reveals it. From that, explains Baader in a passage of *Fermenta Cognitionis*, we understand the tantalic anguish of that which cannot reveal itself, due to its inability to escape the fire.[69] Meanwhile for Boehme, and reiterated by Pierre Deghaye, we can add that within the relationship between man and Sophia, it is he who is the fire of the soul, while she is the spouse.

The Falls of Man

The relationship between vowel and consonant at the same time furnishes the key that opens the mystery of Adam's Fall. L.P. Xella has tried to show this, despite the relatively few passages dedicated to this image. One can say that Adam's sin—the first division of the two tinctures—was first of all consumed in the word. The Bible recounts how Nature was presented to Adam so that he might give a name to the animals. Now, animality represented, as did bisexuality—and animals were already bisexual for the most part—the division of the vowel and consonant that Adam had precisely to reunite and recombine in a Name. What he wanted, on the contrary, was to be given the Name by Nature, or to express himself and reproduce within bisexuality. Upon *"seeing"* (*mirare*) the bisexuality in Nature, Adam should have felt the desire to reunite the androgyny of this divided nature caused by Lucifer's sin. He should have—could have—rechanneled the factors of production, thanks to the Word (i.e., by the good giving of the Name), from the region of the belly to that of the chest. But, since he wished to have them remain in the lower region of the belly of bisexuality, he condemned himself to muteness. The human tongue lost its reproductive power, and it was necessary to wait

---

67. Cf. L.P. Xella, op. cit., p. 27.
68. Ibid., p. 45.
69. *Fermenta Cognitionis III*, 1822–1824, II, 254 ff.

for God to pronounce an even more resounding word—Jesus Christ—so that life could be given back to all of creation.[70]

To speak of name-giving (Gen. 2:19)[71] takes us directly to the Mosaic text, which Baader does several times during the first two chapters. We have even seen that one of the essays is entitled *Comments on the Second Chapter of Genesis, specifically concerning the relationship of the sexes instated by the Fall of Man* (1829).[72]

In light of these pages mainly, but also in other passages of his work,[73] it would be useful to now study Baader's interpretation of the Mosaic account of the Fall.[74] Let us recall, along with the theosopher, both Adam's Fall and the creation of Lucifer.[75] The sin of the prince of angels helps us to understand the sin of our first ancestor. Lucifer made the mistake of opposing the free "evolution" of the light. He wanted to capture it somehow, but at the same time he transformed it into a lightning bolt.[76] This event can be understood if one remembers the following principles, considered basic by Baader: a) a superior element places an auxiliary before (and out of) it so it may engender a product in conjunction—in "fixation" (*Fassung*)—with it; b) an inferior element possesses a superior element with the same goal of engenderment (begetting). Now, Lucifer and Adam made a mistake in the choice of the production auxiliary. Saint-Martin says that Man "transposed his love," and that he wanted a "low" base. . . .[77] Lucifer's imagination distanced itself from the middle (*Mitte*), or from the image of light. Adam's did the same, but in the case of the angel, the image directly fixed itself in the dark matter, in the "*centrum naturae*" (the "*Selbheit*" of Adam fixed in what is earthly, astral or external). Lucifer revolted whereas Adam only turned away from God because of "lowliness." The angel and his army, created suddenly, had no need to repro-

70. Cf. L.P. Xella, op. cit., p. 45 ff.
71. "[Because] out of the ground the Lord God formed every beast of the field, and every bird of the air, and brought them to the man to see what he would call them ."
72. The complete title is: *Bemerkungen über das zweite Capitel der Genesis besonders in bezug auf das durch den Fall des Menschen eingetretene Geschlechts-Verhältniss, aus einem Sendschreiben an die Frau Gräfin von Wielhorski geborene Fürstin Birron von Curland*, Theissing, Münster, 1833, IV, 209–220.
73. These passages are scarce. We remind ourselves that Baader only wrote articles, essays or course material.
74. As with the other themes and mythemes, I have assembled here all the relevant passages and writings of his works.
75. According to the classic outline, which is that of practically all Western theosophers.
76. *Vorlesungen über speculative Dogmatik*, 1838, IX, 223.
77. *Bemerkungen über das zweite Capitel der Genesis*, 1838, VII, 235.

duce. Their sin was not to make bad use of the will to reproduce—contrary to Adam's fault. God created the "earth" to stop or encompass the inflammation incited by the angelic revolt. Here Baader makes a link, in a suggestive manner, between the term *arrez* ("earth" in Hebrew) and *"arrêt"* (*"stop"*). . . . This earth began by water, i.e., with a first flood destined to extinguish the fire corresponding to or incited by the pride (*Hoffart*) of he who had just become a demon.[78] Having lost the most beautiful of his forms, he clothed himself in the ugliest fashion, and became mute;[79] he was "locked in" by God on this "earth" and then Adam was created to be the jailer.

The *Comments on the Second Chapter of Genesis* poses the same problem that seems to have been brought up in verses 2:18–19. In verse 2:18, God says: "It is not good for man to be alone. . . .," and interestingly enough, verse 2:19 in Luther's version of the Bible starts with the word "because": "because God, having formed different animals . . . made them come toward man . . .". In other words, it is because Man was put face to face with animal nature that it became necessary to give him a companion. According to Baader, the text here obviously has a lacuna, because this cause-and-effect relationship is hardly evident. The text is thus suggesting something else, namely that Adam went astray in this animal nature by penetrating it with the imagination, by placing his own image (*sich verbilden*) there, and covering himself within a double form. A Baaderian reading of the text would teach us the following: God says that it was not good for man to remain alone, and wanted to give him a companion similar to him, *because* after forming different animals and making them go toward man, man let himself be seduced by the animal nature, consequently he became imbalanced—hence the necessity that he be divided into two parts, or—that woman be created.[80]

In order to be able to accomplish his destination (Gen. 1:28) and exercise his mastery over Nature and the animals, Adam should not have let himself be tempted (by the *limus terrae*); but the possibility of temptation did exist in him. We have seen that what was created to be superior must first of all be "fixed" in a position of a hierarchical relationship, which itself implies a temptation to depart from that law. Every temptation that is overcome strengthens and fortifies; the presentation of animals was a temptation since Man had to name them, i.e., he had to assert his domination over them and take possession of them. Instead, he imagined "in" their nature and felt the need to mul-

78. *Fermenta Cognitionis IV*, 1822–1824, II, 315 ff.
79. *Bemerkungen über das zweite Capitel der Genesis*. 1838, VII, 238 ff.
80. Ibid., 226 ff. and E. Susini, t. III, p. 361 ff. The Vulgate also uses the adverb *"igitur"* in this place.

tiply thanks to the help of an external aid, thus losing the taste of his internal aid ("the woman of his youth," as Salomon says), or Sophia.

Adam's first sin was thus to make unlawful use of his ability to reproduce, which was paradisical and not animal-like. The "woman of his youth," as far as the eternal idea of God is concerned, could not have remained in Adam nor be "fixed" by him nor become substantially creaturelike in him unless he first placed in it—indeed, making only one single, indissoluble body (*Einleibigkeit*) with it—both the masculine and feminine qualities constituting his Adamic body. After his creation, both were well-balanced (*Temperatur*) and did not even have within themselves the possibility (*posse*) of being disconnected (even though Adam carried within himself the potentiality of an earthly corporalization). But, the sidereal or elementary Spirit of the World (*Weltgeist, Sternen- oder Elementargeist*) lustfully stared (*lüsterte*) at the heavenly virginal side of Adam, who made the mistake of letting himself be infiltrated and contaminated (*inqualieren*). The androgyne should have reproduced according to the laws of Paradise, through the union of both tinctures, but Adam was overcome by longing for paradisical begetting in an external body (in the external soul or *sidereal* spirit). Adam thus made illegitimate use of his masculine tincture, which became a main producer instead of staying confined to its role as an organ. Instead of passively conceiving in Sophia in order to actively conceive in Nature, he disrupted this relationship. Sophia withdrew, abandoning the masculine tincture, which was excited and condemned to consume itself in permanent inflammation. This means that the masculine tincture degenerated in fiery wrath and that both tinctures were disconnected from each other. That is why Adam fell into the temporal region, linked to the separation of the sexes.

The fiery eruption would have taken on even higher, more catastrophic proportions for Adam if God had not slowed up and stopped this devouring fire by detaching one of the two tinctures from Adam—the feminine one, or Eve. This division marks the flinging of Man into a temporal region, which was his safety at the same time. Baader characterizes this as the transformation into water of the contaminated Adamic feminine tincture, which in addition had been separated by God from the fiery masculine tincture. The two tinctures now found themselves placed in opposition. The water served as a stop (cf. *supra. "arrez"*), just as it did after Lucifer's sin. By relegating Man to "earth," God took a measure similar to the preceding one in order once again to limit the damage.[81] This separation was done by God through what Genesis calls Adam's "sleep"; when Adam is plunged into a consecutive ecstasy (*Ekstase*), unsettled in his natural abilities [faculties], he "goes out

---

81. *Bemerkungen über das zweite Capitel der Genesis*, 1838, VII, 238 ff. and *Fermenta Cognitionis IV*, 1822–1824, II, 315 ff.

from" himself and this emergence, along with the autonomization of the feminine tincture (or the creation of woman, if you prefer) at the same time fulfills the functions of the saving countermeasures destined to prevent an even deeper fall into the depths of animal nature. If, on the other hand, Adam had overcome the temptation before the animals, he would have confirmed his androgynous nature and in addition, all of external nature would have participated in his glory, as a blessing,[82] because thanks to him, it would have left the separatist state of generating potencies. One could state, along with L.P. Xella and a corresponding Jungian reading, that the orginal sin for Adam, a sin of the erotic imagination par excellence, consisted in his succumbing to the temptation of reducing the quaternary that was his mission to reestablish everywhere[83] to a relationship of dual opposition. Lead astray by his fault in animal nature and having lost his interior companion (Sophia), he became internally solitary and thus needed another companion "around him"—as the text goes. "It is not good for man to be alone" also pertains to God—hence the existence of Sophia. . . . But Adam is alone with himself in the end, since man and woman are two parts of the same divided entity, or two demi-persons. When the text says that God gave Adam a "companion," one must understand by this word that God gave him the possibility to reproduce physically. This companion is reproduction. . . .[84]

Whereas he could have believed it was possible to reproduce alone and affirm his own masculine tincture as unique, Adam (or rather the masculine tincture) was thus condemned to duality, to cast his semen, and to depend on the externality of the feminine tincture in order to obtain his own image. Nevertheless, sexuality at this stage did not yet have its present rigidity. The separation of the sexes did not only mean the absolute loss of innocence, it was above all the possibility of succumbing to the process of animal engenderment and alimentation.[85] Now, Adam and Eve succumbed and fell into bestiality. Much as water had diluted Lucifer's spirit of pride, the woman also—here playing the role of water—cut back the Adamic Fall in the sense that the tempter no longer had direct access to the Adamic interior, i.e., the fiery soul. It had indirect access, through the intermediary of Eve, resulting in the ambiguous role of EVA, who would have to become AVE[86] after having

82. Ibid., (*Bemerkungen* . . . and *Fermenta* . . . ,); cf. also *Ueber den verderblichen Einfluss* 1834, III, 301–308 and *Vorlesungen über speculative Dogmatik*, 1838, IX, 209 ff.
83. L.P. Xella, op. cit., p. 27.
84. *Religionsphilosophische Aphorismen*, X, 294 ff; XII, 229 about a text by Saint-Martin; *Fermenta Cognitionis IV*, 1822–1824, II, 315 ff.
85. XII, 409, about the *Ministère de l'Homme-Esprit* by Saint-Martin.
86. *Fermenta Cognitionis IV*, 1822–1824, II, 315 ff.

lost man. With the help of Eve, man should have—and could have—freed himself from the incestuous attraction of the world (*Weltsucht, Weltlust*). Anyhow, woman, compared to man, played only a secondary function in evil as well as in good: it still depends on man whether she begets God—or the Devil. Every woman conserves a vestige of Sophia (as helper, interior auxiliary of man) within herself, and Baader calls this the "feminine semen." An allusion to the "*semen mulieris*," as Boehme understands it, can be seen here. It is also the seed deposited in Eve's bosom, which then gives fruit to Mary's bosom. In the second stage of temptation, the tempter first took Eve as a carrier of the feminine semen.[87] Baader wished to explain the EVA–AVE parallelism in Latin verse:

> EVA et AVE produnt inverso Nomine quam sit
> Femina grande malum, Femina grande bonum,
> EVA parens mortem portendit AVE que salutem;
> Perdidit EVA homines quos reparavit AVE.[88]

At the time of the separation, there was also the possibility of reunification, simply by the ambiguity of the woman herself who, as exteriority, reminds Adam of the sin and of the loss of interiority. But, Eve tempted him toward exteriority, whereas the return to androgyny was still possible since there was no definitive split of the two tinctures. At the second level, man sinned by lusts of the flesh, by the voluptuous desire to undergo the power of a force that was inferior to him. According to the interpretation given by L.P. Xella, Adam's masculine tincture was not looking for the masculine in Eve at all i.e., for the divine memory of Sophia. In attempting to join directly with the feminine exterior—separated nature—he denied the feminine in himself, forever enclosing himself in his own triangle, the center of Nature where he would have to penetrate and "imagine" the divine. Her masculine aspect denied and thus condemned to passivity, Eve became inertia—which closed the matrix and made it sterile, condemning the masculine to impotency and condemning herself to undergo violence.[89] This second stage of temptation was that of the tree; to eat the apple meant to enter in animal nature in the most complete way, since apart from the first temptation, this entrance had somehow only been ideal or magical. "*Vis ejus integra, si conversa in terram. . . .*" One sees that the verse of the *Emerald Tablet* is applied to evil as well as to good! Reconstitution of the androgyne would have been possible if the Adamic couple had obeyed the divine commandment of "*Eritis Dei imago*"

---

87. *Bemerkungen über das zweite Capitel der Genesis*, 1829, VII, 226 ff.
88. Ibid., 231.
89. Here I am very close to L.P. Xella's exposition, op. cit., p. 28 ff.

and had submitted to the unifying superior principle of Sophia, surrendering itself to the process of conception—pregnancy in the image of God within both tinctures. The hardening of both was, on the contrary, the consequence of paying heed to the demoniacal invitation *"Eritis sicut Dei,"* since by each one imagining [conceiving] itself in its own abstraction, both tinctures reciprocally denied themselves. According to the Jungian perspective that L.P. Xella appears to hold, they situate themselves in a polarity that denies the quaternary circle by disrupting it in order to transform it into a true Ixion's Wheel.[90] This wheel holds a masculine tincture that knows no rest, as well as a feminine tincture that is petrified; it also holds the consequent wheel of days and years, which turns in an indefinite succession without allowing for any Sabbatical rest[91] in the present. The third, ultimate stage is that of the shame felt by Adam and Eve when they realized they were naked and corresponds to the complete development of the life of the belly, the shameful part of our present nature.[92] If the Spirit is ashamed it is not due to the sexual potency of its body, but to the fact that the animal potency seems detrimental to the potency of the Spirit.[93]

Temporal and animal masculinity and femininity are therefore not only the result of the androgyne's dissolution as a divine primitive image, but also—says Baader in an essay dedicated to the notion of time—products of extinction of this divine image. Dualism is only the *caput mortuum* of a ternary; at the same time the abnormality of the form or its division allows it to conclude in an internal rupture in the center of the invisible (or former) center of formation. Just as the parts in which the "all" or an organic continuum dissolve, were not "preformed" in the latter as parts, but are born when this "all" or this continuum disappears, likewise the present masculinity and femininity are something quite different from the tinctures that constituted the androgyne.[94]

The image of God in the cosmos (universe) should have been born as the *genitus* of an androgynous union between primordial Man and the divine Sophia. There had been "location," an active position (*Gesetztsein*); in the end there was just law (*Gesetz*). The creature underwent divine presence as air

---

90. Ibid. p. 48. With regard to the development of the theme of Ixion's Wheel in German Romanticism, L.P. Xella cites W. Hof, *Pessimistisch-nihilistische Strömungen in der deutschen Literatur vom Sturm und Drang zum Jungen Deutschland*, Niemeyer, 1970. Cf. also, in regard to Baader my article "Feu, éclair et lumière chez Franz von Baader" (cited supra).

91. L.P. Xella, op. cit., p. 48.

92. *Bemerkungen über das zweite Capitel der Genesis*, 1829, VII, 231.

93. *Fermenta Cognitionis III*, 1822–1824, II, 271 ff.

94. *Elementarbegriffe über die Zeit* 1831–1832, XIV, 142 ff.

weighs down upon the empty bodies void of that presence. In the same way
Nature can only withstand Man's violence because it is a closed matrix. The
Kantian imperative is only the fruit of original adultery; he blesses the
absolute passivity to which Man is condemned in relation to God, Man having denied the feminine tincture within himself and rendered the active masculine tincture impotent. Since the original sin, the divine generative force is
with Man in a relationship of *Durchwohnung* (God *traverses* Man) whereby
instead of the organ which he could and should be, he behaves as a simple
instrument of divine imagination, which he is capable only of undergoing.[95]

Several times Baader cites the patristic sources he is familiar with in the
field of androgyny. Gregory of Nyssa is the one who distinguishes a double
creation of Man: first of all he was created to be in the image of God, secondly, to be in the image of man and woman, so that even before Adam's
sleep, the first abuse of trust occurred through coveting.[96] Baader quotes
Maximos the Confessor[97] as well, and St. Augustine who confuses the present
face of Man—endowed with a belly and genital organs—with that of primitive Adam, and who does not differentiate enough between original Nature
and fallen Nature.[98] But, Baader's preferred source is John Scottus Eriugena.
He quotes him specifically at least four times when speaking about androgyny—in 1822, 1829, 1831, and 1841, but several times in other contexts.[99]
The text used is *De Divisione Naturae*, by the famous Irish philosopher who

---

95. L.P. Xella, op. cit., p. 30 ff.
96. *Der morgenländische und abendländische Katholizismus*, 1841, X, 128. Baader probably is allud-
    ing to the text by Gregory of Nyssa *De hom. opif.*, XVI ff., in Migne, t. ILVI, col. 178 ff.
97. Ibid., X, 128, but this name is only cited in passing. In Migne, the most significant passage is
    possibly t. XCI, col. 1308 ff.
98. Ibid., X, 128. Baader opposes to St. Augustine the Paulinian passages: 1 Cor. 15:21, 45 and
    Rom. 5:12. If before his Fall Adam had lived in the source of the four elements he would
    already have been created for death.
99. Cf. XVI, 441, under "Scotus Erigena" (index), and a note below. In 1822 it was in *Fermenta
    Cognitionis*, in 1829 *Bemerkungen über das zweite Capitel der Genesis*, in 1841 a text on
    Catholicism (cf. *supra*, n.3, p. 267). In *Fermenta Cognitionis*, Franz Hoffman, Baader's pupil,
    has added a note of reference to the most important passages of John Scottus Eriugena on
    androgyny (they almost correspond) in Migne, t. XXII (this is obviously about the famous
    work *De divisione naturae*) in col. 522–542, 582 ff., 775–782, 799, 807–816, 833–838,
    846–848. Hoffmann also cites Adolf Helfferich, *Die christliche Mystik*. (I, 215, 218, 229, 241;
    II, 73, 102, 108, ff.) and F. Staudenmaier, *Philosophie des Christentums*, I, 606, Oetinger,
    Biblisch-Emblematisches Wörterbuch, ed. Hamberger, 1849, 16, 70, 334, 498, and Friedrich
    Rückert, author of the poem *Tibetanischer Mythus*, in *Gesammelte Gedichte*, 1836, I, 57–59. It
    is interesting to note that F. Staudenmaier who is interested in John Scotus Erigena has also
    dedicated at least two writings to Baader (cited in Willi Lambert, op. cit., p. 322, and L.P.
    Xella, *Baader*, op. cit., index).

lived in Charles the Bold's court during the ninth century, and not his translation of texts by Dionysius the Areopagyte. Baader uses the edition presented
by Thomas Gale in 1681. Jacob Brucker had clearly understood in his *Historia
Critica Philosophiae*—a summary of the history of ideas published in the early
eighteenth century, and a longtime work of reference par excellence—that
the *De Divisione Naturae* exposes the "Alexandrian system of the
Neoplatonists [. . .], i.e., the emanationism received by the Orientals, the
Origenists, Synesius, Pseudo-Dionys and their like."[100] Baader may have been
familiar with the edition of this remarkable work that C.B. Schlüter, professor
at Münster, edited in 1838. The preface of the work contains a clearly formu-
lated wish: "May the image of this great genius take its place alongside Dante,
Bonaventure, and Jacob Boehme!"[101] On four occasions Baader cites the following passage:

> Homo reatu suae praevaricationis obrutus, naturae suae Divisionem
> in masculum et foeminam est passus, et quoniam ille divinum
> (angelicum) modum multiplicationis suae observare noluit, in
> pecorinam corruptibilemque ex masculo et foemina numerositatem
> Justo Judicio redactus est. Quae diviso in Christo adunationis sump-
> sit exordium, qui in se ipso humanae naturae restaurationis exem-
> plum (et initium) veraciter ostendit et futurae resurrectionis
> similitudinem praestitit.[102]

---

100. T.III, pp. 619–622, 1766 edition.
101. J. Görres also gave his opinion in *Die christliche Mystik*, I, p. 243 ff., Regensburg, 1836. Cf.
     several references in Dom Maïeul Cappuyns' *Jean Scot Erigène. Sa vie, son oeuvre, sa pensée*,
     (Louvain-Paris, Desclée De Brouwer, 1933), p. 260 ff., principally about how John Scottus
     Eriugena became fashionable in German idealism.
102. VII, 235; II, 318; XIV, 143; X, 128. This passage of *De divisione naturae* corresponds to col.
     532 of the *Patrologie Latine* of Migne, t. CXXII . Translation: "Oppressed by the error of his
     disobedience man suffered the division of his nature into male and female and as he did not
     want to preserve the divine mode of automultiplication which had been his, he was reduced
     by a just decree to proliferate in an animal and corruptible manner to start from the male
     and the female. This division began to be transformed in union in Jesus Christ, who in truth
     has shown in Himself an example and a beginning of the restauration of the human nature
     and furnished us with an analogy of the resurrection to come." Consult the work of Francis
     Bertin, in *L'Androgyne*, (coll. *"Cahiers de l'Hermétisme"*, Paris, Albin Michel, 1986). The
     double creation of Man (1) image of God, 2) image of man and woman) according to
     Gregory of Nyssa and Maximos agrees perfectly with Boehme. We will find useful hints on
     the theme in John Scottus Eriugena in *Jean Scot Erigène et l'histoire de la philosophie* (a collec-
     tive work), n. 561 of the "Collogues Internationaux du C.N.R.S."; cf . in particular pp.
     307–314, "Les origines de l'homme chez Jean Scot," by Francis Bertin. Cf. also the works
     of René Roques, of which one will find an annual synthesis in *L'Annuaire de l'Ecole Pratique
     des Hautes Etudes* (V Section, Sorbonne), since 1975, v. LXXXIII.

Consequences of the Adamic Falls

The Fall of Man had some repercussions in Nature, which transformed, would from now on find itself subject to exile and vanity (cf. Rom. 8:19–22). We have seen that the material finds its roots and its origin in the rupture resulting from Lucifer's fall. Any empowerment by the material can only be explained similarly in a separatist manner. Now, the perverted imagination of Adam—his sin—only served to accelerate this separating process, of which bisexuality is the image but which can be detected everywhere.[103] A great error made by many philosophers is to confuse the autonomization of external Nature with the nature of Man–Spirit.[104] If Man's misdeeds and crimes today hardly seem to affect the human form and that of Nature, it does not follow that that was the case originally, when he was "above" these forms which were more "open" to him.[105] L.P. Xella interprets Baader by noticing that even the physics of the entire universe is a spectacle of this original degradation. Attraction and repulsion are ontologically understood if one comprehends that the passive–feminine principle of the desire to be pregnant and fulfilled is, in an ambiguous way, accompanied in actual nature by the opposing negative desire to want to fulfill oneself. The forces of attraction and repulsion, like Newtonian gravity, do not have production as their end, but rather reciprocal neutralization leading to inertia. They are the effect and testimony of an ancient cosmic drama through which the universe lost the perfect copenetration, the intimate, fruitful union of its generative potencies. There is hardly any room left for the former erotic relationship between masculine and feminine forces, in which both of them were at once active and passive, full of desire for each other, and generating an incessant burst of life.[106]

Baader does not specify to what extent Man was actually at the origin of the present disorder on the cosmic level, but it seems largely due to the fall of Lucifer, with Man only accelerating the process of death. Whereas the feminine should unite with the feminine within the masculine, and the masculine with the masculine within the feminine, one finds that especially today there is a spectacle of juxtaposed parts, not integrated into any complete organism. However, electricity, just like animal magnetism and in Man "somambulism"—in the sense that this word had in the Romantic era—or states of trance, show that this forced condition is not the only natural mode possible. Meanwhile, Nature is presently the product of a materialization whose func-

---

103. *Fermenta Cognitionis V*, 1822–1824, II, 360 ff.
104. Ibid., (III), II, 271 ff.
105. *Bemerkungen über das zweite Capitel der Genesis*, 1829, VII, 238 ff.
106. L.P. Xella, op. cit., p.20 ff.

tion was to stop the fall of the cosmos (*arrez*-earth), since without this materialization the entire universe would probably have immediately been the prey and victim of centripetal and centrifugal forces a long time ago. The present cosmic order can thus be compared to a scaffold that one would not think of dismantling until the house was constructed. It serves as temporary support and as a foundation, while awaiting something better. . . . Inertia and gravity are only manifestations of the Fall, thus of sin, which caused Nature to lose its androgyny.[107]

According to the outline proposed by L.P. Xella, the active-masculine principle is indeed centrifugal when it takes itself as an end to itself, by being excited and rising in an absolutely autonomous manner, when it refuses to enter into feminine receptivity, so as to therein awaken its analogous masculine principle. It is therefore pure force which means to give itself only the outline of its form and to extend itself anarchically without being retained by anything. It loses itself in calcination; the unlimited expansion is only dispersion; and it is impossible for the fire to make a *genitus*, a Son who defines it. In the anarchical centripetality, on the contrary, the receptive-feminine principle becomes an autonomous generating power and refuses to open itself to any stimulating action by the active potency, therefore preventing the principle from swelling in this feminine principle. The matrix desires to be filled, and restricts itself, thus becoming increasingly concentrated, condemning itself to being available to any kind of degrading union. The centripetal and centrifugal forces are witness to this. The sin that contaminated the cosmos was one of disconnection and displacement of the generating potencies; it was a degradation of the original organism. Modern mechanical science only denies what now exists.[108] Magnetic poles thus attract each other, but remain separated in isolated masculine and feminine tinctures, in negative and positive poles—whereas in God they are active-passivity and passive-activity, not in polarity but in quaternary,[109] which is the case of any androgynous structure. Again, L.P. Xella's proposed reading evokes the thought of Jung.

The concept of eternity as finite time, the "bad eternity" of Spinozian origin, is never anything but the "degradation" of androgynous eternity, its deformation in a centrifugal sense, the absolutization of the temporal masculine tincture. Spinoza's error lies in having conceived eternal time as eternal movement, eternal and desperate flight, whereas divine eternity is actually unceasing production, a free game of *descensus–ascensus*, the reciprocal penetrating and emerging of both tinctures within each other, thanks to a third

---

107. Ibid., p. 23.
108. Ibid., p. 24.
109. Ibid., p. 36.

mediating term that is necessary in order for the dynamic quaternary to play fully and forever. There is no irremedial past because there is no stasis. There is also no inaccessible future because movement is not going to lose itself in an impotent flight from the center. Thus, what Spinoza said about eternity is only valid for "time," to whose laws the universe is subject for the moment. It is not valid for anything else. It is true that at this level, time is scission duality in which production is limited to itself; thus it is as sterile and impotent as the two separate absolutist tinctures must necessarily be. L. P. Xella effectively showed how in Baader this process of false autonomization is constitutive of all disorder and time: if the masculine is linked to continual movement, and if the feminine is linked to unmoving stillness, then the past and death appear. Nevertheless, in this ensemble of present–past–future that it constitutes, time is a feminine tincture for Man because it continually reminds him of his sin, making him feel nostalgic for his original androgyny, offering itself to him as an instrument for him to recompose it. L. P. Xella observed that for Baader it is a screen, a sign, an appearance. Just like any "external feminine tincture" it is neither truth nor nontruth by itself, since "true" and "false" only belong to eternity, to God, and to the devil. Time is directly linked to space since both are the fruit and testimony of the dislocation of productive cosmic potencies.[110] External space for us is the result of our magical adulterous union with bisexuality. The space of the primordial couple is the fetus given birth to by their imagination. Time occurs when that fetus places roots—fetus of the bastard formation that would have disappeared had Adam recovered in time and tried to restore the state of androgyny by giving in to divine Sophia. To be born and die, i.e., to live, is accompanied by the temptation to absolutize both tinctures in their separation or, on the contrary, to try to recompose them. Perseverance in the first is naturally the work of the masculine tincture to which, as we have seen, the active function alone belongs.[111] So, between birth and death, what is this situation of Man and love, confined to temporary time, which is the sign of our extralineality?

SITUATIONS OF HUMAN LOVE: DIALECTICS AND OPPOSITIONS

Center and Periphery, Androgyny and Hermaphrodism

The notion of center and periphery, applied both to space and time, can also be used to differentiate a "central sense" (*Centralsinn*). This means that in our

---

110. Ibid., 48 ff. (L.P. Xella reminds us here of the work by J. Sauter, *Baader und Kant*, [Jena, Fischer, 1929]). In connection with "finite time" and the "bad eternity of Spinozan origin" we note that the problem is not so simple because the nature which Baader calls eternal is no more than the absolute eternity, that of the Ungrund which has neither beginning nor end.

111. L.P. Xella, op. cit., p. 50 ff.

material life we only touch the peripheries of things with the peripheries of our senses, whereas with the *centrum* of each, we touch the very *centra* of things in the immaterial life.[112] Here we are reminded of the "moral sense" according to Shaftesbury, the "inner sense" of Hutcheson, and the "sympathy" of Burke. But in Baader the idea of "center" is truly theosophic in the sense that it is applied to all levels of relationships uniting God, humanity and the universe. Man is linked to God, as a point of a periphery is to its center, and he must remain there or risk losing himself in dissolution. The relationship between the center and periphery is loving and dynamic:

> Amor descendit ut elevet
> Abscondit ut se manifestat

This is indeed the mystery of the Creator's divine love: by concealing itself it freely descends into its sustenance in order to enter within. If it hides, it does so that the peripheral creature does not suffer the fate of Cybele who burned when she came into contact with Jupiter.[113] There is a simultaneity in the descent and the ascent, profiting that for which the descent took place. Thanks to this, the Spirit subsists and is affirmed vis-à-vis itself; it confirms the underlying image (*Bild*, or *Leib*) in its existence or reality. This image, face—or body—cannot be conceived by itself in an absolutely autonomous manner. In fact, it only finds its own reality when it is knowing and conceiving itself, a reality founded on an element above it that descends toward it. If it autonomizes (*Verselbstigung*) then it ceases to be *Bild*, i.e., image or body. Each link of a chain abandons its "atomistic egoism" a, b, c, d, etc., in order to allow each of the others to take their own place in relation to extremity "A" of the chain (one can imagine it suspended by "A"). If "A" were situated underneath the links, there would no longer be any solidarity and everything would fall into chaos. This is what happens with passion, as opposed to love.[114] True freedom needs both subordination and coordination, and without this freedom, there is no love—even though modern prejudices tend to deny the idea, fruitful as it is, of "liberating service."[115] The relationship of beings with God is the foundation of their being. Between them beings have relationships that have a relationship with the primitive and original Being. In a similar fashion, the interrelationship of the points of the periphery are normally mediated

---

112. *Vorlesungen über speculative Dogmatik*, 1838, IX, 220.
113. Baader writing to Stransky on Dec. 2, 1838, in *Nouvelles Lettres inédites de F. von Baader*, ed. by E. Susini (Paris, P.U.F., 1967), p. 335 ff.
114. *Elementarbegriffe über die Zeit*,1831–1832, XIV, 141 ff.
115. *Vorlesungen über speculative Dogmatik*, 1838, IX, 222.

(*vermittelt*) by the relationship that each one of them has with their common center. That is why fraternal love or love of one's neighbor is, as the Scriptures say, based on the love of God, just as hate for one's neighbor is based on the hate of God. I cannot be united with another person unless I am first directly united to God.[116] That is also why the unatonable crime is the one committed "against the center," in direct or total opposition; the "oblique" crime, peripheral and nontotal, falls or is depleted soon in the temporal movement—which is the centrifugal force turning around; this helps us to understand the identity of the notions of time and restoration.[117]

It is a law of physics, says Baader in his preface to Saint-Martin's work *The Spirit of Things*, that love makes the creature participate in divine nature. Any unifying act can only be carried out by an act of submission to a superior element or unifying principle that itself acts from top to bottom, i.e., from the inside toward the periphery and makes beings from the dispersing periphery unite by making them pass toward the internal center and gathering them together. This center is the "middle" (*Mitte*) of the absolute expansion and intension, or of the "indifference." Just as the sun draws the plant toward it, beckoning it to come out from the dark, earthly region or the root into the free region of air and light, so too is everything that is born, lives, and grows pulled from its own foundation (*Grund*) or abyss (*Abgrund*), from its own dark *Naturcentrum*. But, the creature has a tendency to fall into itself, unable to overcome the root-tendency of its being on its own; it is not a matter of destroying this root, but with overcoming it since it is a centripetal function, condition and carrier of life itself—as Jacob Boehme observed so well. Fire needs both air and nourishment; without one it is deprived of soul, without the other it is deprived of body. Likewise our soul needs to "take spirit and body" (*Begeistung, Beleibung*), i.e., it needs two midwives: one who will supply it with sidereal nourishment, and the other who will give it basic nourishment. The ternary which runs through the whole of life is that of the soul–spirit–body.[118]

Baader speaks again of the third term as a "heart center," which (so the *Forty Propositions for a Religious Eroticism* teaches) allows men and women to sustain and restore themselves communally. Likewise, one is "sustained" when one eats by an invisible, secret force that resides in the food and that puts us in communion with the other forces that produced it. It does not alter its very nature in the process, like the sun, which does not break up into numerous hosts but stays the same in the sky. In a similar force of a spiritual

---

116. This is about Lamennais' text *Essai sur l'indifférence*, V, 230.
117. *Vierzig Sätze aus einer reliaiösen Erotik*, 1831, IV, 199.
118. Baader's Preface to the German edition of *L'Esprit des Choses*, 1811, I, 60 ff.

nature, human beings join together; I cannot know another person as such unless he/she descends toward me, seeking the good or impersonal cause. *Materia* comes from *mater.* . . . Hence the originally androgynous nature of spirit, in which every spirit has its nature (earth) within and not outside of itself. Such is the great principle of substantiation: only a heart can nourish a heart, and man lives only by man, is nourished only by man, because we all participate in the "heart-center." We are so very scrupulous in the choice of our food, but so negligent or indifferent in choosing food for our heart![119]

Baader adds that this is why Saint-Martin can make us understand that lovers are the servants, priests, and visible agents of a superior Eros. One could even say that when they love each other, a superior being loves himself in them and through them! Any creature who loves only itself or who wants only to be an equal of God withers, preventing the divine process from working within, and awakening the "old serpent" within himself. The serpent is indeed *within* the creature and must not be confused with Lucifer or with any other external and previously evil creature. The love between two beings is not simply an exchange of identity (*Selbstheit*), since there is a superior third term that the meeting of lovers seeks to attract, just as the magical power of figures and talismans has as its function to descend and "fix" itself within the material boundaries of the spirit matching them "*Magia, imago, Magnet.* . . ."[120] But, as far as the spirit is concerned, here it is a question of it descending in order to then rise again, drawing upward to itself, raising what through love had been attracted downward. This third element—superior agent or superior principle—into which lovers enter, is indeed the Greek god Eros, on condition that we retain the true meaning of this name, without forgetting that all real love is of a religious nature.[121] The ascetics are often mistaken in their representation of the love of God, of the Creator, in contrast with the love between creatures, as if one should consider God *alongside* them. On the other hand, true religion expressly orders us to love creatures *in* the Creator, wherein, according to Meister Eckhart, they find their unity and completion.[122]

But for humanity in its present state there is no true unity or true completion, since the absolute reconstitution of androgyny is inconceivable. As

---

119. *Vierzig Sätze aus einer religiösen Erotik,* 1831, IV, 194. With regard to the "ursprünglich androgyne Natur des Geistes," we note that it is not at all clear what Baader intended with this. What is clear is that similar things nourish themselves by their like .

120. Preface to the German edition of *L'Esprit des Choses,* 1811, I, 60 ff. "To fix" is here "*bannen*" (today one says: "*auf die Platte bannen*", i.e., record (music, for example) on the wax surface of a disk—and it is surely in this sense that the idea expressed here is to be understood).

121. *Socialphilosophische Aphorismen,* 1828–1840, V, 264.

122. Ibid. V, 263. We recall here that Baader is the true rediscoverer of Meister Eckhart.

we have seen, the original quaternary was separated into a duality in which the active denies the passive, the masculine denies the feminine, and vice versa. The human being is condemned to procreate within a lower region where a perpetual battle reigns and where the two lovers are impotent to leave their state of duality completely. Amor is not Cupid; Hermaphrodite is a caricature of both Eros and the androgyne.

Amor, Cupid, and Hermaphrodite

The difference between our present temporal state and eternal life is comparable to that which differentiates a mechanism from an organism. This prompts Baader to say, in one of his "aphorisms on religious philosophy," that the Kingdom of God is a place that is organically complete, and that love witnesses the passage of the natural organism—i.e., rather mechanical—to a divine organism. But here it deals with love unencumbered with desire! True *Amor*, the theosopher continues, holds his torch toward heaven, and blind Cupid lowers his toward the receptacle of material senses. When Christ says that man and woman must make a single body, he means the suppression of separatist corporality, and that is also how one must understand the notion of androgyny, and not, as some do, as the absolute union of two bodies in one. Separation, but only to find themselves in the third term, since lovers can only love if Jesus lives within them, and they cannot love God if they don't love each other or if they deceive each other.[123] Baader has nothing against the fact that poetry or art in general embellishes sexual love and the instinct of reproduction, but he deplores the fact of artists showing so little of what has the most value in love. It has to do, of course, with what the Song of Songs expresses in the sentence: "Ah! if you were my brother, my sister!" We don't have to do as the *Naturphilosophen* who take marriage of the sexes for that of the hearts, or who take the *Spiritus Mundi Immundi* for that of the Holy Spirit.[124]

Contrary to those Spiritualists for whom the reconstruction of androgyny necessarily passes through a refusal of couple and marriage—as in the cases of Gichtel, Wirz, and several others—Baader is really a "professor of love" in the full meaning of the term, except that he would certainly not have appreciated the teachings, so prolific today, of the techniques on maximum sexual pleasure. For him it is not good for a human being to remain alone since the bond of love obliges lovers to renounce solitary self-completion; man and woman reunited must enter into completion (*Vollendung*) by means

---

123. *Religionsphilosophische Aphorismen*, X, 286 ff.
124. Baader in a letter, 1838 ?, in XV, 601.

of a solidarity, to the extent that faithful love will follow the loved one even to the doors of hell. That sexual love is initially a blessing is proven by the fact that it can often be a curse, especially since falling in love is part of human nature. The amorous state, that *"phantasmagoria* natural to the love of the sexes," which incites us to find the other more handsome or beautiful, more friendly, better, more perfect than he/she is in reality, "has deep meaning." As we will see, it is a gift or grace (*Gabe*) which should be interpreted as a duty to be fulfilled (*Aufgabe*), or a call (*Ruf*) before which a vocation emerges (*Beruf*).[125] But the carnal act remains ambiguous because we are tied—explains Baader in a letter to Johann Friedrich von Meyer—to a woman who is not "the woman of our youth" (Sophia), and who initially presents herself as an alleviation for the anger of our masculinity, without being able to radically extinguish it. This remark can obviously apply to both sexes. Baader means that the orgasm of animal reproduction is always a rebellion, even if necessary; it is the mark of original sin.[126]

"The destructive intoxication of sensuality" is even responsible for our difficulty in imagining heavenly begetting or our angelic state in heaven after death. One should meditate on Faust's verses where he says that in desire there is thirst for pleasure, and in pleasure one feels the bitter nostalgia of desire.[127] Then too, sexual instinct is often accompanied by an "internal hate." As proof, we see it dwindle or even completely vanish when true love appears! This is what liberates persons from each other but without detaching them. It "binds them positively." Bind, rebind, *religare*: true love, and not instinct or passion, is always of a *religious* nature.[128] The idea of binding and relation is also reconciliation, in the sense of "balancing" (*Ausgleichung*), since "*amor descendendo elevat.*" Indeed, reflects the theosopher on the second chapter of Genesis, an animal cannot embrace in the sense of holding in its arms, but Man can, thus carrying out this *Ausgleichung*, which allows the union of a higher element with an element lower than it (without our forgetting that for Baader woman needs man more than man needs woman, and that at any rate, he is the most direct way for her to reach God; that is similar to Boehme's thought). If it were true, as the osteologists would claim, that the arms are an extension of the sides, then while embracing a woman, a man would be

---

125. *Sätze über erotische Philosophie*, 1828, IV, 168 ff.
126. Baader writing to Johann Friedrich von Meyer (March 31, 1817), in *Lettres inédites*, ed. by E. Susini, (Paris: J. Vrin, 1941) p. 298. As an example, Baader uses the words of Eve who has just given birth to Cain: Gen. 4:1 ("I have gotten a man. . . .").
127. *Religionsphilosophische Aphorismen*, X, 343–346. Faust indeed says: "*In der Begierde lechz'ich nach Genuss./Und im Genuss verschmacht'ich vor Begierde.*"
128. *Uber das . . . Bedürfnis einer . . . Verbindung der Religion mit der Politik*, 1815, VI, 15.

attempting to reincorporate her into his thorax (chest or heart), from where she had emerged. Thus, *Ausgleichung*, the start of a return toward androgyny, is a gesture different from coupling *per se*, since the area of the belly is different from that of the heart. Coupling is not an act of union or love, rather it could be considered the contrary since it is the highest manifestation of egoism. Does it not end by a reciprocal collapse (*ein Ineinander-zu-Grunde-gehen*), and in sleep, the brother of death? The animal act is only really exorcised by embracing, i.e., by love. Baader here reminds us that the desire to devour and kill is linked in certain animals, just as in human beings, to the orgasm in coupling, on the principle that in temporal life extremes touch each other—like pleasure and pain, genius and folly, heroic action and crime, heaven and hell.[129]

As an extension to the preceding remarks, a passage from *Fermenta Cognitionis* places us on guard against the teachings of Kant, who speaks of love as a blind man speaks of colors. According to Spinoza's definition ("*ideo bonum est, quia appetimus*"), the philosopher does indeed define love as an inclination toward that which is advantageous for us. When encountering this thesis we must always remember that love is only love if it is without need or desire, and free vis-à-vis nature (*naturfrei*), which does not mean it to be deprived of nature (*naturlos*). Sexual desire must also be consecrated (*geweiht*) in the sense of "offering," in order to be transformed into true conjugal love. Sexual desire, representing the highest degree of "inflamed egoism" and thus "a total lack of love," tends ideally toward the dissolution of the "eternal sex," through the engulfment (*Untergang*) of the individual. Ideal human love, on the other hand, is the assumption of the "eternal sex" through the eternal unicity of the person, to the extent that the beloved becomes the part which represents the whole in the eyes of the lover, since God, or the Whole, pierces through the transfigured unicity of the person. As far as self-love is concerned, it is obviously legitimate, even obligatory, provided that I love myself only in God—but all the same, it is in God that I legitimately love my neighbor. Righteous self-love passes through my being, which is in God; false self-love through a nongenuine, illegitimate "self."[130]

That the "exorcism" of love (religious) is the single principle of any free association, that it elevates passions, i.e., subjugation (*Gebundenheit*), from the rank of bondage (*Bund*) to freedom, should not come as a surprise to us, if we have already accepted that sexual relations are in no way a return to the androgyny making up the integrity of human nature in man and woman.

---

129. *Bemerkungen über das zweite Capitel der Genesis*. 1829, VII, 236.
130. *Fermenta Cognitionis*, 1822–1824, II, 178 ff. Baader also writes: "*Die Geschlechtsneigung wird nur durch freie Resignation des Geschlechtstriebes zur Geschlechtsliebe*" in *Vorlesungen über Böhmes Theologumene und Philosopheme*, III, 403.

What carries out or expresses sexuality limited to itself is the physical and psychic effort that is consumed in a "double hermaphroditic frying pan" in which both partners tend to extract what they need from each other, for their own self-consumption. Mutual scorn and hate appear all too frequently,[131] in spite of the opposite appearance that hermaphroditic illusions tend to create. Baader returns to this illusion or confusion in several places of his work dealing with the difference between the androgyne and the hermaphrodite. If androgyny is the reunion of the active principle with the passive principle, or of the ternary center with the periphery in a single individual nature, then hermaphrodism would be the "difference" or disunity of the sexual attributes shown in its extreme "inflammation," thus in deformity.[132] To misunderstand that both sexes can neutralize each other positively (*sich aufheben*) in their difference leads to the confusion of heavenly androgynous nature with the bisexuality that is manifest in certain animals and which is only the caricature of the androgyne. At the same time, the hermaphrodites of pagan art have nothing to do with the Madonna of Christian art,[133] in which earthly femininity is not revealed as such, whereas the representation of the hermaphrodite sexually excites man and woman.[134]

In an essay published in 1834, Baader furnishes a long explanation of this. The title of the essay is: "*On the Pernicious Influence that Rationalist and Materialist Representations still exert on higher physics, higher poetry and the plastic arts.*" He observes above all that Christian iconography understood the need to make the Madonna a central figure or focus (*Focus*) above all religious forms in art and deplores the fact that the theologians have not followed the same way and seem to be unfaithful to the idea, which corresponds nonetheless to what they believe. The Madonna is pure; purity is above all unity, and only unity is productive. Therefore it is necessary for the heavenly, virginal, angelic-androgynous nature of the Madonna to be expressed likewise through the representations of Christ and the angels, such that in our contemplation, any and all masculine and feminine sexual desire in us is silenced, extinguished, and without constraint, and so that the spectacle captivates us, even if only momentarily, by its angelic nature.[135]

Pagan art will thus be a model that is useful to avoid, since hermaphroditus—i.e., the "focus of pagan forms"—is contrary to that which reunites the elements of the androgyne and the Madonna, gathering together two sexual

---

131. *Ueber den verderblichen Einfluss . . .*, 1834, III, 303 ff.

132. *Elementarbegriffe über die Zeit*, 1831–1832, XIV, 141 ff.

133. *Bemerkungen über das zweite Capitel der Genesis*, 1829, VII, 238.

134. *Vorlesungen über Jacob Böhme*, 1829, XIII, 132.

135. *Ueber den verderblichen Einfluss . . .*, 1834, III, 301–308.

potencies in their "polar inflammation." What these pagan works end up demonstrating, either openly or dissimulated, is always hermaphrodism. It should not come as a surprise that the oldest representation of Venus shows her as being bearded.[136] Even more so is the confusion, under this influence, of androgyne—which is the *union* of sexual potencies in a single body—with impotency—the absence of sex—and especially with hermaphrodism—which is the *coexistence* of two sexual potencies in a single body. It is not only the Greeks who create confusion with their bearded (*barbata*) Venus, for the Indians do as well with their *lingam*. It is just as erroneous to speak of hermaphrodism about two individual twins.[137] This is why the notion of the androgyne is actually Christian. All the materialistic doctrines of Man's primitive body contain the disbelief (or negation) of the Christian doctrine of the resurrection of the body.[138] As far as sexual love in art is concerned, this focus of poetry is generally treated frivolously or sentimentally. It is industrialized rationally, and "diabolized." But the true poet should never lose sight of the fact that love is the bond (*Bund*) or union, the "solidifying" element through which the two lovers present themselves before God in such a way as to mutually help each other to restore the virginal image that was extinguished or broken by the Fall, *also* the image and body of God.[139]

In assuming that a poetic talent were to undertake the dramatic representation of sexual love in its highest significance, different from Goethe's *Faust*, it would be necessary to take all this into account. Regarding the intentions of this hypothetical artist, Baader attempts to expound on what direction the author of such a drama should follow. It would be necessary to show the original androgyne gripped by the desire to taste what is earthly and animal, wandering within (*sich vergaffend*) both; an episode corresponding to the presentation of the animals in Genesis and the bestowal of their names by Adam. It would be necessary to show at the same time how he lost his divine, virginal image, how he became man and woman, how he found himself in another form upon waking, i.e., deformed (*verstaltet*). It would also be necessary to represent how the image fled at the moment of the Fall, how Sophia continued to appear to him and remind him of his heavenly humanity, and how this Wisdom, the light of life, shone like a star, an angel or a guide in the dark shadows of our earthly life, in order to show (*weisen: indicate; Weisheit: wisdom*) us the way to our "native land." In such a drama, the androgyne

136. Ibid., 305 ff. And *Vorlesungen über speculative Dogmatik*, 1836, IX, 136.
137. Ibid., 221. It is unfortunate that Baader did not develop this interesting idea about the twins.
138. Ibid., 221, 210.
139. *Ueber den verderblichen Einfluss . . .* 1834, III, 305 ff.

would not be the only one to have its place at the beginning of the story, since even today Wisdom appears in the souls of both man and woman and is reflected in each in order to play the role of the supreme "formational instinct" (*Bildungstrieb*) or *nisus formativus*.[140]

Humility and baseness, pride and nobility

This process of restoration, which the actions of Christ and Sophia are able to accelerate, or at least facilitate, is intended to reintegrate Man into his original quaternary state. Just as androgyny is quaternary, so too is it under the sign of a double polarity—but within which one polarity is essentially negative; thus, in several passages in his works, Baader states this law whose effects we feel in our human lives on a daily basis. The idea from which all the rest flows is that within a normal relationship between the sexes, man helps the woman to admire, and woman helps man to love. The woman acquires virility, and the man femininity. Whereas in a relationship without love, she helps him to become a serpent, and he helps her to become the spirit of Lucifer's pride. In both cases, the centrifugal and centripetal tendencies have escaped from the center (*dem Centrum entsinken*), an outline which symbolically accounts for the form of the serpent![141] This outline is ontologically founded; indeed, Man should have been the image of God. Now God is the middle (*Mitte*), par excellence, and thus Man must also be the middle. But we know that there is a centripetal tendency coexisting with a centrifugal tendency in each sphere, and that should not be imagined exactly like a circle with a center. The idea is rather in that the centripetal tendency corresponds to another tendency to incarnation (*Leibhaftigkeit*), and the centrifugal tendency to a need for active manifestation (*Lebhaftigkeit*). These two ideas call for analogies on different levels. Man is "noble" or "great" (*erhaben*) in love and in an elevated, majestic sense at the beginning, but the woman is "humble." The caricature of this outline is obviously despotism on one hand and baseness—the spirit of slavery and sensuality—on the other. Each of the partners undergoes both tendencies at the same time by virtue of the quaternary law; the despot is just as much a slave as the slave is a despot. It is important to be aware of this in all aspects of life, whether these be educational or pastoral, and not limit consciousness of it only to the relationship between lovers. Thus the *Aufklärung* made every effort to hide the "nobility" (*Erhabenheit*) of Christianity in order to show only the sweet and friendly side, while attribut-

---

140. Ibid. 307 ff. And *Religionsphilosophische Aphorismen*, X, 304–306. On Baader's idea of Sophia, cf. my article "Ame du Monde et Sophia chez Baader" in *Lumière et cosmos* coll. "Cahiers de l'Hermétisme", (Paris, Albin Michel, 1983).

141. *Vierzig Sätze aus einer religiösen Erotik*, 1831, IV, 194 ff. *Elementarbegriffe über die Zeit*, 1831–1832, XIV, 141 ff.

ing "nobility" to paganism! Baseness or sensuality, and pride tempt us all at once, even though one overtakes the other. They are the caricature or reversed, perverted effect of humility and nobility, the true constituents of the human being. Christianity delivered us from both of these perversions, in order to turn us into free beings,[142] at least theoretically.

These four qualities obviously manifest themselves in love, depending on which ones are allowed to prevail. The "profound sense" of ascetic and mystic doctrines regarding the reestablishment of the original androgynous nature of Man by religion—writes Baader in 1826 in a review on the *Essay on Indifference* by Lamennais—lies in the fact that pride (*Hoffart*) and baseness (*Niederträchtigkeit*) are considered by these doctrines to be enemies that are internally incompatible within us, while nobility and humility are actually a good, internal match.[143] In 1832 he evoked the anthropological tripartition of love in the head (brain), heart, and stomach, based on these ideas. Light is linked to the cold above, heat to the shadows below; both must unite at the risk of exposing us to the suffering and vanity of time. At any rate, the reunion of both results in a battle; it is our duty to assure this victory and not to succumb to divorce, which is always threatening to take root within us. Pride and baseness are light and heat that have become autonomous. To hold them together means we must maintain a correct "middle" (*Mitte*), the place of the "heart," and not fly unduly away to the heights or sink into the depths. What pushes us into succumbing to either temptation is not an energetic polarity, which would be ontologically founded, but rather an abnormal state of our nature.

The separation into sexes corresponds to that between heaven and earth, wherein the Book of Revelation by John says that thanks to mediation of the Kingdom or City of God, this separation will give way to an enduring and harmonious binding. This finally completed creation will thus have not two, but three "places"; there are only two at the present time because life of the heart "does not have" life of the head or stomach, but is "possessed" by each at their turn. Just as Man is ternary here, so original creation must not be conceived dually—like heaven and earth—because Man should be the third element, the mediator. This is why, in good magnetic ecstasy, or in any other less ambiguous state of human life known to religious or ecclesiastical tradition, when dominant manifestation of the life of feeling is discussed, it should not be said that the life of the head falls into that of the belly, nor than that of the belly—basic—rises abnormally. Rather, both combine harmoniously in their active "middle." To speak of it as "ecstasy" does not correspond to reality; rather, it is in fact a true "stasis" which is the anticipation of integration

---

142. *Vorlesungen über speculative Dogmatik*, 1838, VIII, 177 ff., 225.
143. *Recension der Schrift: Essai sur l'Indifférence*, t. V, p. 126.

and the "centering" of Man without which the integration of creation itself would not be possible.[144]

Above all, realizing this ternary junction within oneself is a measure of amorous realization. Man and woman complete each other by love, at least internally, and approach a state of androgyny. If, as we have seen, the woman helps the man to love, and the man helps the woman to admire, then neither remains entirely man or woman, to such an extent that he/she ceases to be a simple half. The human being lives on admiration as a spirit and on adoration as a heart. Just as man surpasses the woman in his ability to admire, so does she surpass the man in hers to adore. They need each other in order to be complete. The perversion of these two abilities chains lovers like a pair of galley slaves![145] In 1816 the theosopher writes to Christian Daniel von Meyer that if a plant, for its own existence, needs the sun to become earth and the earth to become sun, so too is the union of Man and God carried out through Christ. By 1832, as we see in a letter to his friend Emilie Linder, Baader's image had acquired strength and consistency, and the cosmic role of Man has been made clearly explicit. He explains therein that there is no descent without a corresponding elevation. The earth must rise toward the sky (heavens) and Nature toward the spirit, whereas the heaven (sky) descends toward the earth and the spirit toward Nature. At the same time, both terms must remain differentiated and not be mixed with each other. Likewise, if man's (male) function is to pull the high, the spirit, toward the heart, then it is woman's to raise the low, nature or earth, toward the heart, since it represents the "middle" where the two partners join and truthfully find their humanity. Man thus aids woman to raise the lower part (earthly) and the woman helps man to lower the higher part. Man must overcome his pride, his coldness or impatience, which resists this descent—this sacrifice—just as woman must resist any faint-heartedness, heaviness (weight), and laziness that oppose the elevation of the "low" part. Baader adds that consciousness of this mechanism allows him to better understand the nature of the original catastrophe that brought about the difference of the sexes.

He calls "feeling" (*Gefühl*) the "middle" or "heart" also, giving this word a precise connotation that it normally does not have. He also specifies in a letter to Emilie Linder that *Hoffart* (pride) should be understood as *Hochfahrt*, i.e., a voyage or departure on high, in the perjorative sense of abandonment of the "middle." If the "heart" is understood as such, then the couple becomes as Orpheus, who spreads the harmony obtained for himself over the whole of

---

144. *Vorrede zum zweiten Band der Schriften und Aufsätze*, 1832, I, 410 ff. Baader cites J. Menge here, *Beiträge zur Erkenntnis des göttlichen Werks*, Lübeck, 1822.
145. *Elementarbegriffe über die Zeit*, 1831–1832, XIV, 141 ff. *Socialphilosophische Aphorismen*, V, 349.

Nature. The possibility of the cosmic action of Man is understood even better if one considers God Himself—of whom we are the image—to be the middle or heart of the spirit and of Nature. Both are participating at the same time, maintaining themselves above one another. Unfortunately, theology is still on a level comparable to when our knowledge about electricity was limited to the observation that amber attracts lightweight bodies. We now know a good deal more about electricity, and likewise theology should take into account certain data! Is not Man's cosmic role mentioned in the first chapter of Genesis? One reads there that God completed the creation of heaven and earth with the creation of Man, in His image, wherein He could dwell, making His creation His resting place. The last chapter of Revelation also teaches us about the union of the new heaven and new earth. The heaven, earth and Man must remain eternally present, because the divine manifestation needs the harmony of all three.[146]

Hochfahrt, or the improperly undertaken voyage on high, the synonym of *Hoffart*—pride—is precisely the sin of Lucifer, Baader specifies on various occasions. It is the upright serpent of Isaiah. The twisted, lowly, and sneaky serpent of the woman, along with the preceding one, must be radically dissociated from each other in order to avoid their being joined together. The theosopher reminds us that sexual separation in the temporal region played the important role of "stopping" (*arrêt*) and limiting damage at the time of the Adamic Fall, since it actually *restrained* the "bad androgyny" from developing further, as would have happened if the separation had not taken place. But this also keeps the good androgyny from developing.[147] At any rate, if sexual love remains purely on an animal or natural level, it cannot become nobility and humility; at the same time, neither can it bind them together. This is detrimental to society because both potencies emerge first from the individual and then the couple, and extend into family and society. Meanwhile, if their reversed reflection does likewise, it will ultimately do so in order to cause misfortune and destruction.[148] In a short text entitled *On Unions*, Baader differentiates among the three cases that could arise. First of all, if masculine pride and the reptilian guile of the woman interpenetrate, they complete each other, thereby giving rise to a diabolical image. Indifference or "nothingness" as is often the case, could follow, which means that "man and woman manage their business externally, like Hans Stein & Co." Finally, there remains the possibility of reuniting both qualities through meditation of the "heart," their agent or higher principle—the re-linking—"religious"—principle without

---

146. Baader to Emilie Linder on May 7, 1832, XV, 486 ff.
147. *Vorlesungen über speculative Dogmatik*, 1838, IX, 211 ff.
148. *Sätze über erotische Philosophie*, 1828, IV, 175.

which the union would degenerate into banality or nothingness, or even into the diabolical figure purely and simply.[149]

SITUATIONS OF HUMAN LOVE: PHILOSOPHIES AND THE LIFE OF THE COUPLE

From the Gift of God to the Gift of Self, or the Birth of the Alchemical Child

The third means of union—the work to be accomplished—is not given directly, it must be created. During certain privileged moments a human being receives the revelation of this true vocation. In a passage in *Fermenta Cognitionis*, Baader cites Joseph de Maistre who speaks of "this degree of exaltation that raises Man above himself and places him in a state of producing great things," which also applies, adds the theosopher from Munich, to physical reproduction, since it only takes place by means of a "kind of ecstasy." Love liberates us from our impotence, makes us participate in our own productivity, since this alone is what is productive, whereas lovelessness is impotence, and hate is destructive.[150]

But, the exaltation or ecstasy into which we are sometimes plunged, without having sought them out, must be interpreted as a grace that has been granted us, a gift (*Gabe*) that must become a duty for us to carry out (*Aufgabe*). One must distinguish between love that is given, and love that is to be accomplished (*gegebene und aufgegebene Liebe*). This goes likewise for knowledge, he specifies in the text entitled *On Unions*. Being informed about the way a mechanism works or about the conditions of a scientific experiment to be carried out means that one has thereby acquired a form of knowledge. But this knowledge must be differentiated from that which one obtains by personal action, by reconstructing the mechanism oneself or by undertaking the experience personally. Likewise love, which is in a way "credited" to us, given by nature or favorable destiny, should not be received by us simply as a gift offered for our amusement or our enjoyment, but rather as a duty to be fulfilled, or a "problem" (*Problem*) to be solved. We are indebted from the very start and must acquit ourselves by putting ourselves into the "service of love" (*Minnedienst*) since this is the only service that will authorize us to appropriate this gift. We can imagine some orangutans who go to warm themselves one evening near a fire made by natives in a clearing, after the natives have retired into their huts for the night. The brazier will slowly go out, since it is not attended to and the monkeys will leave disconcerted; they will leave disappointed, without ever thinking of adding wood to the brazier. The same goes

---

149. *Socialphilosophische Aphorismen*, V, 339 ff.
150. *Fermenta Cognitionis II*, 1822/1824, II, 209.

for love that comes to us; we must attend to this gift from heaven—from heavenly beings—and we must know how, but, most human beings act like the monkeys in the parable .

Love is only understood by loving, and life by living. Just as one could say: "Have the experience, and then you'll know," one should say: "love, and you shall love," so that "the service of love" rendered to another person makes us receive both the love given to us and the love we bring, as is the case with maternal love.[151] Any love that comes without merit is comparable to a fragile newborn who has great need of all our care; again it is still only the fruit and image of its parents, but it is one who must become an active and autonomous image (*selbstisch*) of their spirit and their heart.[152] An alchemical child must be born, who by definition really only exists from the time of his/her second birth. The same goes for the love we bring to God; first we feel an impulse, which must be followed by an *amor generosus*, or *actuos*—very real and living. The deadened representations of love, in art that conceives love as leisurely enjoyment (*jouissance*), whether because of the edifying works of aesthetics or the *jouissance* of Romanticism, do not take these requirements and possibilities into account. On the contrary, it is here a question of putting into a new light the trials which lovers wait for while they are harmoniously and creatively building their work. "*Dii omnia laboribus (doloribus) vendunt.*"[153]

It is also completely natural for Baader to entitle one of his "aphorisms on religious philosophy" as: *Love is a child of those who are united in love.* Just as one speaks of "children of love"—and all children should be—so one must always be aware that in the beginning love itself is but a child. The theosopher continues: so, where does the prodigious and mysterious child called love come from? Just as parents keep their children with them for some time in order to raise them, so is God not content to just create beings; he later re-engenders them in himself. Whereas the child of flesh leaves his parents, or their life may be grief-stricken because of him, this mysterious child that is love never leaves his parents so long as they don't leave him; their life is not menaced by gloom, and it is a divine life they live. The marriage is often sterile, and sometimes parents bring fruits of a lesser quality, but the union of true and sincere hearts is always fertile and can rejoice unceasingly in the marvelous fruit it engenders. Such a union starts to form when the heavenly moments—those "eternal moments" that Shakespeare spoke of—meet our interior, and we fix (*fixieren*) them instead of sacrificing them to a temporal

---

151. *Socialphilosophische Aphorismen*, V, 347. *Vierzig Sätze aus einer religiösen Erotik*, 1831, IV, 196. *Sätze uber erotische Philosophie*, 1828, IV, p. 165 ff.

152. Ibid., 196.

153. *Sätze aus einer religiösen Erotik*, 1828, IV, p. 165 ff.

death, where they would disappear like abandoned or assassinated children. People who conclude that the amorous state is as fleeting as an illusion are mistaken. It is not illusory, as long as, instead of nourishing time with eternity, one manages to integrate and transfigure the temporal with the eternal.[154] Baader's beautiful idea suggests that on the one hand, eternity nourishes time, while on the other, Man gives the dimension of being (*l'étant*) to time, according to the grace received. Another aphorism of religious philosophy, entitled *Keys for understanding the mystery of love*, recalls how Sophia or "heavenly humanity" appears to the male-lover in the form of a female-lover while in an amorous state, and vice versa. Male and female thus have as their task to fix the sight of the heavenly virgin, which momentarily pierces through the clouds (to fix this *Durchblicken*). This appearance of Sophia explains the ecstasy of the amorous state and its "silver flash" (*Silberblick*)— and we know that we must see the superior "goal" of love by means of the incarnation of Sophia in us; because of us, this Sophia is deprived of her body, to which she has a right.[155]

Several passages in Baader's works insist on the necessity of trial in the elaborating process of the alchemical child. Even though the word "initiation" or "initiatic" doesn't seem to have been used here, it is nevertheless what this is about. A number of the *Forty Propositions concerning religious eroticism*, (a beautiful work dedicated to Emilie Linder), categorically insist on this point: friendship and love can only take root in adversity and unhappiness, without which there would only be camaraderie. If love can implant itself somehow without tears, it still does not take root without this dew. Love is only faithful and constant in those who have eradicated unfaithfulness and the possibility of denial from their being (as *posse mori*, according to the word of St. Augustine). God had created Man without sin, in a state of innocence, but he wanted the possibility of "fault" to be extirpated by action, by cooperation, and by the merit of Man himself. It is this way for any love, which begins in innocence but must undergo trials in order to be confirmed, to find its position and its stability (*bewährter Stand und Bestand*). It was not indispensable for Man to renounce or betray God, but temptation and resistance to temptation were necessary for Man's trial, so that his relation to God might be consolidated. It is this way for all love, including that of Man and Nature; likewise, it is the true principle of culture and fine arts. God's love for mankind, descends

---

154. *Religionsphilosophische Aphorismen*, X, p. 342 ff. "*Die Liebe selber ist ein Kind der in Liebe sich verbindenden.*"
155. Ibid, p. 304 ff.: "*Schlüssel zum Verständnisse des Mysteriums der Liebe.*" Cf . also my article "Sophia et l'Ame du Monde chez Franz von Baader" (cf. reference *supra*). The word "*Silberblick*" is a term borrowed from mining vocabulary. P. Kluckhohn (op. cit., p. 549, n. 1) comments that Baader is the first to use the word in this sense.

in order to elevate Nature, then extends horizontally in the form of human love, then descends even deeper as love of Nature in order to elevate Nature to mankind. But in order to establish the true dependent relationship of Nature on mankind, Adam had to be subject to a double temptation: to either make despotic use of Nature, or subject himself as a slave to her. In the first case, one forgets that it is God who is absolute Lord of Nature, and in the second that God is the only direct Lord of mankind. Lucifer succumbed to the first temptation, and humanity to the second.[156]

A long passage in *Propositions of Erotic Philosophy* is dedicated to these views. First of all Baader differentiates between two stages in the love of a created being toward its creator or towards another created being. The first corresponds to a state of unison (*unisono*) that has not undergone the trial (test) of confirmation; no "difference" (*Differenz*) has yet been manifested, but this state has within itself the possibility of differentiation, fragility, and mortality. The second stage corresponds to the extirpation of these three possibilities, from which true agreement or substantiation is born (*Substanzirung*).[157] We know that the relationship of a created being to another [of its kind] is determined by the relationship it enjoys with its creator; Man is with Nature and with fellowmen as he is with God. This means that in order to realize any love, divine mediation is needed, without which, free passage from the first to the second stage would be closed to us. We need this mediation even in our relationship with Nature. It is therefore useless to be afraid *of* Nature, which as Goethe so rightly said, is a fear "against" Nature. Experience shows that in the second stage love exerts a profound and beneficial liberating action, since it is then that it "is binding" (*reliirend*); this is a liberation that has consequences on Nature itself ("cult," "cultivate," "culture"—all mean the same thing).[158] Daily experience shows how reconciliation in love can operate; this contradicts the widespread prejudice according to which the best love never knows any misunderstanding, not even in the beginning. This would mean that the best love would never know forgiveness! Love does not consist in uniting already harmonious hearts, but rather in harmonizing. In friendship, in the love of parents for their children, in the love of a couple, it is often the deepest split that will allow the most solid unification. Blood poured from the heart is the callousness that will render the union durable.[159]

"In unison," writes Baader, "one does not hear dissonance, but it could appear. In a chord, dissonance is suppressed, overtaken, and no discord is

---

156. *Vierzig Sätze aus einer religiösen Erotik*, 1831, IV, 193, 198.
157. *Sätze über erotische Philosophie*, 1828, IV, p. 165 ff.
158. Ibid., p. 168 ff.
159. Ibid., p. 169.

feared."[160] Saint-Martin expressed the same idea in *On Errors and Truth* (*Des Erreurs et de la vérité*) in 1775: "Thus it is through the opposition of this disso-nant chord and all that derives from it, to the perfect chord that all musical productions are born. . . . If one allows the ear to hear only a continuity of per-fect chords, it will certainly not be shocked; but apart from the boring monot-ony that would result, we would find no expression or idea within. . . . As far as music is concerned, any result or product is founded on two dissonances resulting in a musical reaction. . . . If we bring this observation to sensitive things, we will see with the same evidence that they could/can only be born of two dissonances."[161]

The opposite would be remorse, indissociable from the Kantian type of moral imperative. The demons themselves believe not in God, but in trem-bling! What an error it is to replace religion by morality! To look for the Savior or safety in an imperative and not in a "dative"! Insolvency only appears when there is a claim made by the creditor. . . . Love is not only the child of abundance and poverty—what Plato saw—it is also the child of for-giveness and of repentance (which is not remorse), which means reconcilia-tion, because only the rich heart (*Gemüth*) forgives, and only the poor heart needs forgiveness. When there is true repentance or forgiveness between per-sons, these acts are not exerted by the persons themselves (*ex propriis*). It is a superior and mediating action that intervenes to give the richness of forgive-ness to one and the force of humbleness to the other. In any case, an act of reconciliation is religious to the degree it manifests this superior mediating action of the "highest" order; thus Baader says that there is something higher between the "governed" and those "who govern," which we tend to forget today. He means that especially since the French Revolution we consider the relationship between "governed" and those "who govern" in a "naturalist" way, that is, without any kind of mediating, binding, reconciliating, balanc-ing, binding (religious) power.[162]

Reconciliation does not place Man in his original state of innocence again but rather elevates him to the second stage of love. If an "organic reunion" is more solid than the preceding union, which has dissolved (*aufge-hoben*) in order to better reconstitute itself, it is because the unifying principle beckoned by this separation "possesses itself even more deeply, in view of the new emanation, which is going to be drawn out from the depths of itself." A scar in the organism prevents a new rupture in the future. God himself fol-

---

160. Cf . E. Susini, t. III, p. 550 (Baader, VIII, 187 paragr. 41) .

161. *Des erreurs et de la vérité*, pp. 51–516; already quoted by E. Susini, t. III, p. 551.

162. *Sätze über erotische Philosophie*, 1828, IV, p. 170 ff.

lowed this law in three great successive emanations. The sending of Man into
the world had been preceded by a break—that of Lucifer—resulting in the
mission of restoration that Man is responsible for. So God "fixed" Himself in
order to emanate Man ("*Gott fasste sich tiefer zur Emanation des Menschen*").
After the Adamic Fall, in view of a new emanation, God took hold even more
profoundly in His most intimate Self. This time only the indissoluble union
of the created being and the creator was initiated, along with God and the
world, and with that the highest elevation of the created being. Only blood
from the heart can furnish the cement for an eternal union; the blood of
Christ is obviously this blood par excellence through which the blood of the
"heart" (*Herzblut*) of Man or his "main soul" became fluid; from coagulate, it
was able to become eternal union by becoming accessible to the "passage to
the second stage of love"—love between humanity and Nature. One must
therefore be persuaded, first of all, that the ability of loving is even greater
since the coming of Christ, as our customs and social institutions evidence. As
far as love between man and woman is concerned, there is a clear difference
existing between Christian peoples and the others.[163]

An important nuance is strongly emphasized here by Baader. It is not
necessary to believe that the Fall of Man and his unfaithfulness to God were
necessary. Even without the Fall, Man would have had to go through the trial
of fortifying temptation, but this Fall was not at all inescapable. No more so
than doubt or error, which, as E. Susini noted, goes against Descartes. Baader
writes: "The maxim according to which all knowledge must begin with a
doubt must . . . also be rejected." Temptation is necessary, but not evil nor the
Fall. Admitting the ontological and necessary nature of evil contradicts the
fundamental tenets of the church. At any rate, only some of the angels followed Lucifer. Finally, "the fall of a girl is not the only condition necessary to
marry her"![164]

On Woman and the Couple

Baader assigns a fundamental role to woman in the human and spiritual realization of the couple and the whole of humanity. A letter written in 1839 to
his friend Stransky evokes the great mystery of love, thus of life, as "heavenly
music resounding even more perceptibly in the hearts of women than in
men—men should endeavor to give women only the text."[165] In a short essay

---

163. Ibid., 174.
164. Quoted by E.Susini, t. III, p. 554 (Baader, IV, 198, para. 37; VIII, 15, no. 1; VIII, p.139 ff.; I,
    p.328 ff.).
165. Baader to Stransky, October 3, 1839, XV, 626.

dedicated to "secret teachings" written by Martines de Pasqually, Baader reminds us that if evil action could only penetrate by way of the passive element (woman = water) in the active element (man = fire), then the good, reconciliating action should follow the same route. Indeed, woman (by this we mean: the feminine tincture in androgynous Adam, and now woman as distinct from man) serves as unconscious "conductor," of both good and evil action. She is the "base," just as the body is. He indulges here in one of those connections of which he is so fond: *Weib* and *Leib* ("women" and "body") must be respected, and not "spoiled" or dirtied because they have a blessing (*Segen*) within themselves. One must act prudently (*scheuen*) as far as they are concerned since they also hold a curse within![166]

A passage in *Fermenta Cognitionis* specifies that woman is above man to the extent that she is the unconscious carrier of the masculine desire to create, or the carrier of the image which is in man. However, she cannot reach consciousness of this image except through the help of the "awakening force" of man, which holds true for good as well as evil desire, for the seed of the woman and that of the serpent. Every woman is simultaneously EVA and AVE (Mary), and it depends on the work of man to determine which one of the two forms will reveal itself.[167] In the same collection, he makes a passing reference to Voltaire, an author he finds "sagacious": "Religion and love of women are founded on the same weakness"; indeed there may only be weakness in both cases. At any rate it is more often the fault of man than of woman if she brings demons into the world and not gods.[168]

Woman is the keeper of love, Baader says again in an 1828 text dedicated to erotic philosophy; only Christianity has known how to recognize this right fully, by procuring social freedom and honor for her, and it is normal for her to be attached to and to preserve this religion. Woman also preserves love, since as is well known, it is not love that takes the first step in man, but rather sensual desire (*Lust*). In a normal state, Baader says, sexual desire in woman follows love, and not the opposite. On the other hand, she is less able to separate or "abstract" desire and love. Thus man gives gives his worst part—sensual desire—consciously to the woman, while woman gives the best part directly and consciously to man. A virgin is an unconscious awakener (i.e., not

---

166. *Ueber des Spaniers D.M. de Pasquallys Lehre*, 1823, IV, p. 122: *"Verderbe es nicht. denn es ist ein Segen darin; scheue es aber auch denn es ist ein Fluch an ihm!"*
167. E . Susini, op. cit., t. II, p. 56 , no. 2. *Fermenta Cognitionis III*, 1822/1823, II, p. 255 ff.
168. Ibid. (IV), II , p. 316 ff. (Baader quotes John Scottus Eriugena at this point, *De divisione naturae*, according to the 1681 edition; see 1838 edition, II, p. 6–92 ff. to see how he thought like J. Boehme on this point).

guilty) of the desire of man and she consciously responds to this desire by giving love.[169]

In any case, Baader does not consecrate a cult of worship of woman
without some reserve, even independent of the fact that evil is introduced into
humanity through the channel of the feminine tincture. In a letter written in
1834 he explains that if the woman cannot dispense the Spirit or the sacra-
ments it is because she cannot, particularly in love, go beyond the "sidereal
constellation"—or superior instinct—whereas man does reach it. The danger
lies in making this "sidereal constellation" divine; it must always be placed
and considered in an area of its own.[170] If man can go directly to God, then
woman does even better by going through man (one wonders if for Baader
this is the preferable solution or the only possibility). Any true union implies a
subordination. We have seen that love is different depending on whether the
two members of the pair hold each other one below the other or one in front
of the other.[171] This applies to the relationship of the human being with God,
as well as to the one between man and woman. However, we know that in the
second case, a third term is necessary (God himself, or Christ), because the
idea of love is also that of a Triad. If St. Paul teaches (Eph. 5) that man must
love his wife—as the head does the body, or the Lord his community—and
that woman must venerate (*verehren*) man, this means that first of all man
must love woman by "descending" to her in such a way that by this "descent"
she is "elevated" (God first loved us in Christ, only the descent renders the
ascent, or love, possible). A man cannot love a woman who refuses this elevation. A woman cannot venerate a man who does not lean over her with love.
Paul presents both as being subject to the same unity, thereby presenting
them as a ternary. "Woman is only grasped in and by man, and man can only
develop himself in woman."[172] Then again, customs change, he confides in
1840 to his friend Stransky with some bitterness. We are witnessing a
"decline of the heart, in favor of a monstrous development of intelligence, in
such a way that women are losing their legitimate power over men more and
more—and through the fault of men. Women are only left with the bad arm
of sensuality without heart, and because they are women and not men, they
resemble phantoms of hybrid beings deprived of femininity. . . ."[173]

The attempt for a true union obviously rests on other bases. In *Forty
Propositions for a Religious Eroticism*, Baader is lavish with advice directed to the

---

169. *Sätze über erotische Philosophie*, 1828, IV, 175.
170. Baader to F. Hoffmann, Sept. 15, 1834, XV, 505.
171. *Sätze über erotische Philosophie*, 1828, IV, p. 165 ff.
172. *Fermenta Cognitionis V*, 1822/1824, II, p. 360 ff.
173. Baader to Stransky, Oct. 1 1840, XV, 37.

couple. He reminds us that if I love, it is myself I give in the gift I offer; if my wife loves me, it is myself she receives wth the gift. If I receive, it must be with the same amount of joy in letting myself join as in the joy felt by the other in wanting to join with me. He who knows how to give without pride can also take without being lowered—without "pressure"—he who takes while lowering himself can only give with pride.[174] This echoes a passage written about Jacob Boehme: when I love someone I deny myself and "rest" on the other; when someone loves me he denies himself and rests on me. . . . Love is thus a permanently alternating process of "giving" and "receiving." If I deny the other I find my own self denied—in any event, hate is unproductive; hence there is truth in the formula: "one for all and all for one." Such is the dialectics of difference and unity. The created being is a consonant separated from the divine vowel, but one which possesses the power to express itself when pronouncing this vowel. Meister Eckhart says that man is an adverb (*Beiwort*).[175] We have seen that this complementarity of vowel and consonant is obviously also applied to the love between man and woman.

Only love can make us really "liberal," because only he who knows how to love does not separate "right" from "duty," the act of ruling from the act of serving, the act of possessing from that of being possessed, etc.[176] Love makes us understand through the analogy of great mysteries. For example, if someone refuses our love and unhappiness comes of it, we can better imagine the suffering felt by God for the same reason.[177] But, how unhappy is he, this unfortunate being who cannot attach himself to a person he must hold in esteem, or even fear, and who feels inclination toward a person he must despise![178] Another one of the "forty propositions" puts us on guard against the "tantalism of the *philautia*." It is foolish to believe in any effective and successful *philautia* (self love), because it ruins the life of the couple. One can no more love oneself than one can hug oneself. He who seeks to love or admire himself only seeks, deep down, to refute, by means of the testimonies of others, his doubts about his own worthiness to be loved or admired. He never succeeds in refuting them and only empties himself more and more. *Philautia* denotes a deep emptiness; it is a tantalizing power that results from the refusal to admire and love those who deserve it.[179]

---

174. *Vierzig Sätze aus einer religiösen Erotik*, 1831, IV, p. 189 ff.
175. *Privatvorlesungen über Jacob Böhme*, 1829, XIII, 83.
176. *Vierzig Sätze aus einer religiösen Erotik*, 1831, IV, 186.
177. Baader in one of his correspondence, 1838?, XV, p. 602 ff.
178. *Vierzig Sätze aus einer religiösen Erotik*, 1831, IV, 189. *Socialphilosophische Aphorismen*, V, 349.
179. *Vierzig Sätze aus einer religiösen Erotik*, 1831, IV, 188.

One beautiful page of the *Forty Propositions* specifies the necessity of trial leading to reconciliation on the daily level of life as a couple, a law inscribed in divine creation and whose importance we have seen. He wonders what lovers have not felt that by forgiving and reconciling with each other they have entered more deeply into one another's hearts and more stably fixed the relationship with each other? Forgiving means making truly creative use of desire and imagination by somehow entering into the interior of the person who is regretful, thus renewing that person by our entry into him, and thus joining more deeply with him. What true love has not noticed that only the blood of the heart, which begins to drip like sacrificial blood when a fault is committed, is what is able to furnish the sealing cement to long-lasting friendship and love? Here one can speak of consanguinity in the deepest sense of the term . . . and he who has gone through this process of reconciliation is not far from the kingdom of God.[180] Baader then remarks that only love is really well-mannered (*artig*) and polite; there is always something distinguished about it, whereas lack of love is always coarse, even if one wants to give it the aura of politeness or gentleness.[181] Let us end with this *Reflection on a proposition recently rendered public against overpopulation* (1829). Dr. Weinhold has just proposed some contraceptive methods, but Baader responds that allowing the State to influence the population in such an area would bestow upon it powers that do not belong to it. Dr. Weinhold's proposition is close to that of Kantian morality, which sees marriage as a rental contract and not as a sacrament.[182]

Androgyny and Modern Philosophies

Baader's originality is also apparent in the way he associates two areas seemingly distant from one another, that of the androgynous quaternity of the human being and philosophy. L.P. Xella has attempted a connection between both ideas, which though not often explicit in the theosopher's writings, was nonetheless tempting. Philosophy, the highest point of elevation produced by humans, can testify to the fact that impotent isolation of one of the two tinctures corresponds to the sterile closing up of the other. Even the word—philosophia—should incite meditation on the divine quaternity in order to bring us closer. Philosophy for us should represent love of and for Sophia and should become a way for humanity back to God. It would also necessitate

---

180. Ibid., IV, 200.
181. Ibid., IV, 192.
182. *Socialphilosophische Aphorismen*, V, 281. Franz Hoffman mentions in a note that Schelling, Fichte, Hegel and Krause all spoke better about love than Weinhold and Kant.

going back once again through human history to its origins in order to understand how original sin has lead the flow of time astray.[183] This means that true philosophy is a theosophy that could help us to recompose the double tincture in the image of the Son, favoring the birth of the human person (*Verselbständigung*) as opposed to the affirmation of a false and egotistical self or unilateral abstraction of a single tincture. This is an apparently Jungian idea. In irreligious philosophies, the masculine tincture which by absolutizing itself denies the quaternary link between God and Man (*eritis sicut Dei*), also denies the feminine matrix or tincture, which seeks to be fertilized. By refusing this feminine tincture, the masculine tincture closes off divine action, stays empty, expropriates, and devastates the external being, or Nature. Corresponding to the industrial relationship we now have with Nature is the nihilism of philosophical speculations, which only seek to reflect and to locate themselves in the ego, as in the speculations of Descartes.[184]

Quoting Plato, but all the while taking his inspiration from Saint-Martin, Baader reminds us that knowledge originates from admiration. "The spirit of man, the Unknown Philosopher said, can only live by admiration, and his heart can only live by adoration and love." For Baader, loving means to recognize and admit an alterity, so that the correct relationship between subject and object is placed in admiration, one of unity in differentiation, one of a relationship between inferior and superior mediated by the "mirror" or the "miracle." True speculation, a word which comes from *speculum*, lies between "looking at oneself" and "admiring." It deals with an androgynous erotic link, since in its masculine tincture, the superior admires itself in the inferior, which holds its image, where it is grasped in femininity–passivity, bringing out the masculine aspect in the feminine tincture of the mirror. It brings out its own superior image, which is a miracle (*mirare!*). In admiration, the inferior is subject to the superior, which is inside of it and yet not annihilated by it. In turn, the superior raises the admiring inferior to its interior, thus becoming joined without being denied. We find once more our ontological androgynous quaternary, or the quaternary game of two tinctures, since here the superior unites to what is superior in the inferior, and the inferior unites to what is inferior in the superior. Thus the word voluntarily repeated by Baader is clarified: *Cogitor a Deo, ergo sum*. It means that I, the object of knowledge, recognize myself as the object of the knowledge of God.[185]

---

183. Cf. L.P. Xella, op. cit., p. 51.
184. Ibid. p. 52. E. Benz made a note that it was probably Baader who introduced the use of the term "nihilism" in German (cf. ibid., p. 52, note in which L.P. Xella gives an interesting bibliography on nihilism).
185. Ibid., p. 53. Cf. the good work of L.P. Xella, *La Dogmatica speculativa di Franz von Baader*, on Baaderian gnoseology. Turin, "Filosofia," Premi "Domenica Borello," 1977.

That is why post-Cartesian philosophy is a "bastard" product of time, a typical absolutization of the masculine tincture along with impotency and sterility, meaning nihilism. It lacks femininity, and refuses to admit its own inferiority and receptivity in relation to God.[186] This tendency was noticed by C.G. Jung and L.P. Xella. This philosophy is essentially erotic since for Baader it is from the desire that the two tinctures have that the whole process of production and creation emerges, and not from nothingness or matter. Any determination, figure, or true body (*Bild*) can only be understood as simultaneously filling and containing. Spinoza denied the passivity of philosophy—in any case, pantheism is a hermaphroditic caricature in this sense, and Spinoza's substance is neither God nor the cosmos since it wants to be both, just as the hermaphrodite does not overcome masculine and feminine, but instead provokes dualism. Here there is no fourth term.

L.P. Xella clarifies the hostility which Baader shows at several intervals towards Schelling's philosophy. This too could be qualified as "hermaphrodite," to the degree that the simple game of the double force of attraction–repulsion is divested of its erotic value and quaternary valency, thereby falling into static polarity once again. The systems of Spinoza and Schelling, which represent a guilty availability and inclination toward the binding with anything of an inferior nature and thereby descending below itself, correspond to the Adamic Fall into matter. It is thus to Lucifer—the superb "spiritualist"—that the other aspect of "despotic" will corresponds. One finds it in Fichtes system, and especially in Hegel's. For Fichte, the "I" rests on self-affirmation, denies God, which it identifies with the self, denies Nature, which it identifies with the "non-I," and thus denies the feminine tincture inside and outside the self. This "I" will no longer be able to generate on high by becoming fertilized by the divine Word, nor below by fertilizing Nature. In its unsatisfied need to be filled and to fill, it incessantly drives itself up against a sterile womb. This Fichtian "I" is unceasingly pursued by God who according to the teachings of Tauler, seeks the creature in order to generate His own son in him and to regenerate the creature by the intermediary of His own daughter. The Fichtian "I" pursues Nature unceasingly ; it remains the daughter of time, and is enchained to Ixion's wheel.[187] Self-love or egotism (*Selbstsucht*) appears along with the loss of true *Selbstheit*. It is when the truly constitutive principle of the State disappears that we then have a tendency to "constitute ourselves." According to Baader, the politicians of the times sacrificed to Fichteanism such that the way they constituted the State was actually a Fichtean way of founding oneself. After Fichte, the concept of

---

186. L.P. Xella, op. cit., p. 54.
187. Ibid., p. 56.

Studies in Esotericism 257

"taking" superseded that of "receiving" in philosophy, the same way "pride" had displaced humility.[188]

Fichtean philosophy stops at the *itio inter partes*, at the *bellum internecinum* between the two tinctures. Hegelian philosophy leads up to the triad and unfortunately, does not go beyond. That philosophy is characterized by a figure of the androgynous union, which would become rigid when the Word is produced. Hegelian dialectics also admits the necessity of a feminine tincture as an organ that affirms the masculine tincture—even though this terminology is not used—but which sees something alien in the second tincture, external to the masculine. It is thus reduced to a simple role of instrument. The Hegelian idea only seeks Nature in order to deny it, as if God had sought Man, or the finite the absolute, not to generate it and Himself, but to kill it. Determination (the Son) is too often interpreted by the philosophers as negation and limit as an evil within us. The Hegelian triad is a masked dualism in which father and son, masculine and feminine, continuously fight. The Father wants to be a Father, without passing through the narrow passages of the womb, as happens when pride absolutizes the masculine tincture. It alienates itself from Nature, throws the feminine organ out of itself, only to find it later before him as if it were an alien organ, as if it were nothingness.[189]

Is it not a paradox, but the effect of an inescapable process as well, that this Hegelian philosophy which proclaims the absoluteness of the Spirit and the triumph of Luciferian pride, can only be realized effectively in a form of low materialism? Does it not see the incarnation of an absolute in the physical person of the Head of State? Once the feminine matrix is denied, this philosophy is condemned to be a bastard product, in which humanity descends below its role as an organ of God, to be an instrument of the most infamous kind of union. The king usurped by Man in the invisible kingdom of the Spirit loses his mask and appears as a coarse body in the visible kingdom of politics.[190] We know that errors of this type, which are born of speculation, finish by truly invading Church and State. The two great Western churches do not escape severe diagnosis by Baader, since the Catholic church inclines to confuse the kingdom of God with simple material visibility, which is a form of petrification, while the Protestants confuse it with absolute invisibility, a dispersion of an internalness without foundation. Both participate in a mistaken absolutization of the two tinctures: one refuses to be put in motion and the other refuses to find a resting place; one defends the dogma as it is, thereby not seeing its dynamic seminal function, while the other rejects it without

---

188. *Vorlesungen über religiöse Philosophie*, 1826/1827, I, 161. *Sätze über erotische Philosophie*, 1828, IV, 171.

189. L.P. Xella, op. cit., p.57.

190. Ibid., p. 57.

understanding its formational function. Likewise, we have absolute monar-
chies, i.e., sterile closure, denied matrix, refusal of motion on one hand; on
the other, we have revolutions such as the French one, which deny the calen-
der, try to propose a new present, and reveal a purely destructive principle or
irrepressible motion which, by denying all formational principle, finishes by
denying itself.[191]

The link of solidarity between the head and the limbs, corresponding
respectively to monarchy and federalism or republicanism in the spiritual and
civil societies, is not always understood. These two principles are radically
separated. Each is made oppressed or annihilated by means of the other. The
deep nature of this kind of link is clarified if one understands the solidarity of
superstition and unbelief, of servitude and liberalism. We should not cast
away either one of these two poles by means of the other![192]

KNOWLEDGE AND REINTEGRATION

Love and Knowledge

If modern metaphysical errors and those of political philosophies are due to a
general ignorance of the great principles recalled by Baader, it follows that
the task of the contemplator of deep truths consists in bringing men back to
knowledge, or to a gnosis, a science that does not condemn one to erring. Has
Saint-Martin not reminded us that "science is not a leisurely occupation, but a
battle"? Since love is the great principle, it should be a science. Baader misses
no occasion to attack Rousseau and Jacobi, who claim that Man ceases to feel
when he starts to think or understand. It is an error liable to keep men in a
state of great uncertainty as far as religion and love are concerned, which are
confined to a vague area of clear-obscurity in our conscience or our reason.[193]
Believing does not suffice and only "maintains knowledge at its most inferior
level"—Baader writes to Jacobi in 1820[194]—and in addition declares he was
always against a "eunuch spiritualism,' which cannot help us understand the
mystery of love any more than bad naturalism can.[195] In order to be free in
relation to men and Nature, one must first help them to be free and that

---

191. Ibid., p. 58.
192. *Ueber den paulinischen Begriff. . .* , 1837, IV, 353.
193. Cf. for example *Sätze über erotische Philosophie* 1828, IV, 165 ff. and my article: "Faith and
    knowledge in Franz von Baader and modern gnosis," in the present work, as well as the
    work done by L.P. Xella quoted *supra*, n. 185.
194. *"Glauben ist Festhalten des Erkennens in seiner untersten Stufe,"* Baader to Jacobi, June 27,
    1806, XV, 204.
195. *Vorlesungen über J. Böhme's Theologumena et Philosopheme*, III, p. 402 ff.

obliges one to pass through knowledge. We have already seen that the ethical law can weigh down on us like an imperative, or air on a body when a vacuum has been created. But when it only traverses us, and does not dwell within us (*durchwohnen* is not *inwohnen*), it is because of this lack of knowledge that the law, living within us, becomes personal.[196] Knowledge is a duty; therefore Kant was mistaken in claiming that love cannot be commanded; this would go against the teaching of the Decalogue.[197]

Since knowledge, this form of gnosis, is such a marvelous and indispensable instrument, we are not surprised to see Baader attributing the faculty of androgyny to it. He explains this in a long essay published in 1807, dedicated to the use one can make of reason. He says that our faculty of knowledge (*Erkenntnisvermögen*) is bisexual, or rather androgynous. He compares it to the union of light and heat, since all light which is manifested is accompanied by a modification of temperature. When I am familiar with or recognize (*erkennen*) something above me, there is not only the manifestation of an internal light—since knowledge is not indifferent or deprived of effect—there is also internal heat. This is why admiration tends to become love or veneration, otherwise our heart (*Gemüt*) is bound, deprived of freedom.[198] Baader reminds us of one of his dearest ideas, namely that there is an analogy between the instinct of reproduction or engenderment and the instinct of knowledge.[199] A superior element inclines toward an inferior element, or "imagines" itself in it to be the foundation, just as the sun "carries" the earth or man carries the woman. The superior element fixes (*fassen*) and takes hold of (*erfassen*) it while becoming internal, it aspires to be glorified in it, to cover itself up by it, like an ornament. According to St. Paul, just as woman is the glory of man, so Adam is the image and glory of his God. The superior element actively imagines; one sees a passivity of the inferior element, which corresponds to active imagination, advance toward it to help and serve it. The spirit is the model of the inferior element, while the flesh is that of the superior one. The spirit searches to make itself flesh everywhere in order to find itself, feel, and spread out in joy, glorifying itself in the act of embodiment (*bildend*). The flesh is only nostalgia for a spirit that will come to animate and penetrate it, revealing itself in that flesh so as to raise it up to itself, in itself. In German, there is an etymological relationship between "meal" and "union" (*Mahl* and *Vermählung*), a relationship founded in real-

---

196. *Vorlesungen über speculative Dogmatik*, 1838, IX, 222.
197. *Ueber Religions- und religiöse Philosophie* 1831, I, 327.
198. *Ueber die Analogie des Erkenntnis- und des Zeugungstriebes*, 1808, I, 41.
199. Ibid., 44 (cf. also E. Susini, t. II, p.30 ff.).

ity, if one thinks of what the fact of eating and reproducing represent on different levels.[200]

The spirit of any created being is always pregnant (*schwanger*) with something, with a body in which it is represented and reflected. There is identity between its impetuousness (*Wallen*) and its will (*Wollen*), therefore the will acts in an organic manner—it is the "formational instinct." All that lives and comes to inhabit a body (*lieben, leben, leiben*) emanates from the androgynous desire (*Androgynenlust*), which is like a workshop or nuptial bed—the impenetrable and magical secret of all life. Keep this bed pure, and you will see the birth of a healthy life! Every created being, no matter on what level of life it is found, is both heavenly and earthly, or sidereal and elementary; the "sacrament of life" is given to him only in a double form. But it is not suitable for an inferior to take the superior for his wife, hence we can make sense of the following injunction: "Thou shalt not make any graven image or portrait of me," which leads back to: "You yourself must be my image and my symbol (*Gleichnis*)"! Of course, the superior is not suited to be subject to the inferior. We should neither serve what we have the duty to dominate, nor do the contrary—and so the distinction between baseness–pride and nobility–humility is clarified even more. This teaching also founds a knowledge of knowledge, since from that moment on, the fact of knowing—linked to the ideas of domination, formation, and engenderment—could not be separated from that of being known—linked to the idea of serving, being formed, receiving.[201] If knowledge succumbs to its object, i.e., to the matter to which it must give consistency (*Bestand*) and reasonable sense (*Verstand*), then it will return to darkness, as does man's heart when his love for someone succumbs to a poor, selfish sexual desire that renders the heart tight.[202]

Free inclination is that which comes from knowledge; the fact of having moved in a nonfree way, as in the case of passion, comes from a nonthought, thus ignorance. True life is freedom; the fact of having been tossed here and there, not knowing what one wants or do, corresponds to a "lack of life," necessarily accompanied by a movement that does not come from our innermost selves.

Baader notes that Lamennais in his *Essay on Indifference* was correct in recalling our love of Good as coming from the knowledge or recognition of that Good. In the case of blind instinct or nonfree passion, there is neither knowledge nor idea. If I know something, I am free with respect to it. Love is free. Knowledge liberates the knower from what is known. The animal level

---

200. Ibid., 44 ff. *Fermenta Cognitionis II*, 1822/1824, II, 178.
201. *Ueber die Analogie des Erkenntniss- und des Zeugungstriebes*, 1807, I, p. 44 ff.
202. *Ueber die Begründung der Ethik durch die Physik*, 1813, V, 17.

instructs us in this principle, since as instruments of objectiveness, the five senses slowly free the individual from the plant world. Jesus said: "You will know the truth and the truth will set you free"; He did not say: "You will only feel the truth, and you will figure it, etc." Certainly, it goes along well with feeling and representation, but only in the sense that clarification of the idea confirms the true feeling, fortifies it, and suppresses a nontrue feeling.[203] Knowledge and love are one and the same, finally, as already suggested by the biblical word "to know," which means "to be united to" (*cognovit eam*). By being filled with the idea that God loves him/her, Man receives the faculty of loving God in return (Anteros), of loving other human beings, and Nature. To this triple love corresponds a triple faculty of knowledge. The moral systems that deny this triplicity are atheist.[204]

The Self, the Couple, and Nature

To try to become familiar with the links uniting certain beings to others and to try to differentiate the diverse natures of these links are the responsibilities of anyone who contemplates the preceding ideas. There is too much of a tendency to confuse the coercive, external bonds (*Bande*) with those that are internal and free, and whose end is to protect (*Bünde*). Many people behave like the monkeys in the parable we cited earlier. Let us bear in mind that our nature continually needs us to deliver it from any antinatural—or non-natural—element that afflicts it. Let us proceed with ourselves the same way we would on the level of the State: those who govern should neither repress nor avoid revolutionary movements, but by means of a subtle chemistry, or the art of differentiation (*Scheidung*), should make use of the "evolutionary" elements accompanying them. The method for treating errors should be the same.[205]

Separating is therefore not suppressing, but putting something back in its correct place. This is the task we should be carrying out on ourselves, vis-à-vis our own kind and nature. Also, the word *Verselbständigung*, not very distant from the idea of Jungian individualization, corresponds to a process of identification, to a constant quest for Self, which L.P. Xella sees as being carried out through the quaternary dialectics we described above. It is about becoming conscious of the primitive androgynous scission, through a series of mandalas whose essential forms we have just highlighted, and of the dramatic disappearance of the feminine and despotic prevarication of the masculine, which had as a consequence the devastation of Nature, and nihilism in speculation.

---

203. V., 236. *Vorlesungen über Religionsphilosophie*, 1827, I, p. 237 ff.
204. *Vorlesungen über speculative Dogmatik*, 1830, VIII, p. 230 ff.
205. Ibid. IX, 223.

An initiatic, almost dramatic, aspect can be added to this, underlying the necessity of trial or "confirmation." Only love forgives, and it does so voluntarily because the humbleness and repentance that come to it help it to develop the richness and fullness of its tenderness.[206] Love that is given immediately is "natural" love, in the Pauline sense of the first Man created, out of whom the "Man–Spirit" has to come by suppressing this immediacy so as to transform it (*Aufhebung*). The result is love that is free in regard to Nature—but not deprived of nature (*naturfrei, naturlos*)—as is the sacred in relation to the sacrament, or a love "reborn" in which the relationship between lovers is different from that of the first stage. In divine love, for example, the Creator only reveals himself as the true father of His created being in the second stage.[207]

The dramatic aspect of all human love is heightened by the ontological significance of woman. It is known that in the first place, Eve is the external space given to man so that by finding a place in which to move, he would not hurl himself into the nothingness of the flight from the center. But once fixed in her externality, Eve represents the time given to him to regenerate himself in the image of the Son of God. She is, so to speak, the time of the formation of his seed from which he cannot escape without condemning himself to definitive deformation and making himself a prey of the demon. Being the feminine part of the separation, she represents the very place of space-time, the internal-external link, and thus partially shares the demoniacal condition. Man has within his possession the use of this externality for the sake of their mutual safety, by subjecting her, or damning himself to be subjected to her.[208] Love is only productive, in temporal reproduction or outside the realm of time, when it produces energies (*Kräfte*) and not created beings.[209] The second Adamic Fall took place through Eve, and by Eve reintegration was also initiated. Just as Adam's disfiguration into masculine and feminine images was first done internally and then was completed bodily, so too must the restoration of this divine image pass through the nothingness of this disfiguration, first internally and then externally. Love's goal is to help man and woman complete each other, so they may become a total human image. Man leaves with displeasure what he entered with pleasure. The internal and abstract masculinity and femininity, opposed egotistically to love, are the cross which lovers can help to carry and bear in their lives. This process of rebirth through love should be the object of dramatic themes, thinks Baader, and literature

---

206. *Vierzig Sätze aus einer religiösen Erotik*, 1831, IV, p. 192 ff.
207. *Sätze über erotische Philosophie*, 1828, IV, 167.
208. Cf. L.P. Xella, op. cit., p. 49 ff.
209. *Fermenta Cognitionis V*, II, 360 ff. (#29).

could play a larger role in describing the war against the devil who is the enemy of marriage, or of love because it concerns rebirth. This would be more profoundly true and poetic than what we are generally told by novels and dramas.[210]

The sacrament of marriage is a result of the eternal dimension of union, since what is purely temporal has no need of sacrament. In order to reconstruct the lost androgyny, thanks to this, man must help woman liberate herself from her femininity as incompleteness, and woman must help man in the same goal so that both will be reborn in the complete original image of humanity, at least internally, so they can cease to be semi-human beings, semi-wild beings (*Wildheit*, wild state, meaning distancing—*Entfremdung* from the divine life). In a word, they must become Christians, or be reborn, having found the wholeness of their human nature once again.[211]

It must therefore reach the point at which both beings constitute only a single being; each is half of the other, and for that to happen "each one of them is obliged to divide up, go out from the self, and penetrate the other with the half of his/her being, abandoning the other half." Baader represents this idea in the following way: A/B and a/b; the love realized will be A/b and a/B, which indicates exchange and copenetration. Since on the other hand we know that love does not become realized in two different units but in a superior third term, the outline of true love would look as such: AbaB.[212] Reciprocal elevation leads to what Baader would accept and probably call the alchemical egg, which "in such ecstasy, can only be understood thanks to the common elevation of both lovers in a third, superior principle . . . which the Greeks personified in Eros (the god that represented love)."[213]

If this restoration can be done through love between the two sexes, then the ascetic who has made vows of chastity must be careful not to reconstitute the divine image in a bad way. Thus, women especially have sought not the nothingness of their feminine desire, but a conjugal relationship with Christ, their fiancé and heavenly spouse. The third term, in such a case, disappears. This third term can only be possessed by the couple when both partners are linked within the same Christ in whom, as St. Paul said (Gal. 3:28), there is neither male nor female.[214] That is why one can conceive of a man abandoning his masculinity in order to become a father, or a wife abandoning her femi-

210. *Religionsphilosophische Aphorismen*, X, p. 1304 ff.
211. *Ueber den verderblichen Einfluss . . .* , 1834, III, 306.
212. Cf. E. Susini, t. II, p. 546; Baader, I, 231.
213. *Eos. München Blätter für Poesie, Literatur und Kunst*, 1829, p. 248 (quoted by Susini, t. III, p. 548 ff.).
214. *Der morgenländische und abendländische Katholizismus*, 1841, X, 247.

ninity so as to become a mother—*virgo parturiens*, Sarah; the solitary woman does indeed have the possibility of engendering more children than she who has "known" man.[215]

Life as a couple is thus only secondarily made up of reciprocal exchanges. It must first and principally realize the "integration" of androgyny. Each of both partners should be completed with the help of the other and the superior element, Sophia or Idea, who makes her home in both of them. There should therefore be mutual help to become links on the same chain. "Man as a soul searches for the image of the woman for his own image of man, and the woman as a soul searches for the image of man for her own image of woman."[216] When Paul says that "within the Lord woman is not independent of man, nor man of woman" (1 Cor. 11), he is showing us that the Lord is restorer and founder of our lost androgynous nature. At the time of resurrection there will not be a man and woman stuck together to make a complete human being, because Aristophanes, says Baader, did not correctly interpret Platonic androgyny. Those who would have been males will have Christ as their fiancée, not by uniting to their animal masculinity but in suspending it (*aufheben*), and those who would have been females will have Christ as their fiancé, by suspending (*aufheben*) their animal femininity.[217]

We know that it is not possible to isolate the human couple and their relationships with the divine world from the vast togetherness, of which Nature is an integral part. Knowledge and reintegration also go through Nature. Space and time, at least that which appears to us as such, were conceived in the mind of Man from the magic, adulterous union of Man with bisexuality. This is at least how it appears to be, and this is the way through which we must pass to come to some understanding of Nature, however little that may be. Adam was conscious of space from the of the first Fall. The Adamic couple was conscious of time from the moment of the second Fall since it was a heightening of the first. This consciousness we have of time and space is a result of a bastard formation linking both tinctures in a forced connection. Dissolution of it grants us freedom, androgyny and true fertility, but is accompanied by suffering in virtue of the alchemical principle of *dolor ex solutione continui*. All human production in time has the characteristics of birth and death. It is *Begründung* and *Entgründung* at the same time. Each birth presupposes and implies a death because the "negative foundation"—bisexual humanity—and death by destruction are born precisely in time. The pleasure

---

215. *Fermenta Cognitionis II*, 1822/1824, II, p. 225 ff.
216. *Vorlesungen über speculative Dogmatik*, 1838, IX, 221.
217. *Bemerkungen über das zweite Capitel der Genesis*, 1829, VII, 238. Cf. also E. Susini, t. III, p. 574.

of coupling, be it legitimate or adulterous, can only provoke a painful birth since the *genitus* must always kill its negative possibility: if it is the Son it must kill the bastard himself, who is a product of the demon; it will try to kill the Son or prevent his conception.[218]

Thus we are plunged into a universe that is fundamentally ambiguous. Besides, it is more "formless," even more "repulsive," than what actually meets our eye. The mercifulness of God dissimulates this aspect from our view by offering a covering, matter, so that the appearance becomes more tolerable. This appearance, or *"Maya,"* is in itself neither truth nor lie. Baader often plays with this idea: *schonen* ("to spare" in the sense of "to be sparing of") is related to *schön,* "beautiful." God thus wills beauty in Nature so as to spare our eyes, hiding the abyss of chaotic forces from us, or the "radical carbon" behind a face of light. Without this envelope we would be frightened and horrified, just as the epidermis englobing the most beautiful human form prevents that form from revealing its real anatomical truth: *"Non impune videbis!"* Just as love produces tricks so does it produce art: and Baader connects *Lust* to *List* ("desire" to "trick"), *Kunst* to *Gunst* ("art" to "favor").[219] Nature must serve as a spiritual stepping-stone for us. To this effect we serve it just as it can serve us. The union of man and woman thus builds a body, like a scaffold in which an androgynous divine personality can grow. Our body is a plan, a sketch, which is given to us in order to comprehend and interpret the Holy Scripture and the data offered by physiology under a double light. For example, from the fact that arms are only the prolongment of the ribs, one can infer that the androgynous union is situated in the region of the chest. The natural physique, which bears the imprint of creation, makes us pass—without any solution of continuity—to a divine physique, a *corpus spirituale* in the image of God. Nature must thus be known and loved. Whoever does not love his brother, says St. Paul, does not love God, and Baader adds that he who does not love Nature or does not lovingly care for her, loves neither his neighbor nor God. *Cultur* is likened here to *cultus.*[220] Cult, humanity, *culture* all have the same source, like three forms of love which simultaneously appear and disappear. Where one is missing, so are the others.[221] "Physics itself, similar to a mute and innocent animal, had to bear witness against the false prophets who have made bad use of it."[222]

218. L.P. Xella, op. cit., p. 50.
219. Baader, I, 127, VII, 299 (quoted by E. Susini, t. III, pp. 577 ff., 581).
220. *Bemerkungen über das zweite Capitel der Genesis,* 1829, VII, 239.
221. V, 275 (quoted by E. Susini, t. III, p. 561).
222. *"Die Physik selbst, jenem stummen schuldlosen Tiere gleich, musste gegen die schlimmen Propheten zeugen, die sie misbrauchten."* (V, 6. Cf. also X, 127).

There is nothing surprising in the dramatic relationship of Man to Nature, since it is so inscribed in the Judeo-Christian theosophical myth setting. In a letter to Constantin von Löwenstein-Wertheim in 1828, Baader lets us know that a certain von Schenk was so interested in his ideas on love that he wanted to take them to the stage, in a drama that would have dealt especially with "reconciliation." Baader adds that he himself sees the deep reason of human culture in the love of Nature—of "mother earth"—and he attributes the cause of earth's distancing from us (*Entfremdung*) to technical mobilization (*Entfremdung*). By losing our indissoluble union with the earth, we have abandoned our love for her, and we find ourselves in the same "rational" relationship with her as the man who would be content to have an exchange with his wife where everything would eventually lead to two columns of "debit" and "credit."[223] Our relationship with the earth is like our most intimate relationship with a human being. As Baader writes in 1838, if the power and victory of love over all obstacles are expressed not by breaking them with violence but by penetrating them with a subtle *spiritus* while waiting for better times, so is matter, which supposedly is incompressible, but not impenetrable by a superior substance's action. The effects are felt by Nature, who is waiting for her complete dissolution.[224]

We have seen why inertia and gravity are in fact nothing other than a precarious balance, a provisional organization of a devastated universe, aspiring to a regained transparency. There is no solution of continuity between the ethical and the physical. But, one must act on this devastation. The bastard *genitus* must be exterminated, and a new, organic, living space must be regenerated in the new Son. There is no reintegration of Man if Nature is not a participant. Nature is not just traversed, supported, or disintegrated by dissociated masculine and feminine forces. She is above all a principle that is feminine with respect to humanity, a consuming desire wanting to be filled by mankind so as to carry in her womb the "good son," or image to which she is assigned, but which has been lost in the centripetal implosion caused by the centrifugal explosion of Lucifer's sin. As L.P. Xella explained in her study on the erotic philosophy of Baader, Nature is thus an omnipotent matrix for Man where he can spread out, so he can return to himself, simultaneously giving himself a form and reconciling Nature with the divine principle of the form. She is profoundly and radically ambiguous for this reason.[225] By reminding us of the sin that devastated her, Nature awakes in us the nostalgia and need for a sacred androgynous union, while she continues to tempt us so that we hesitate

---

223. Baader to C. von Löwenstein-Wertheim, March 26, 1828, XV, p. 444 ff.
224. Baader in one of his correspondences (around 1838), XV, 601.
225. Cf. L.P. Xella, p. 25.

between this sacred union and an adulterous one. Like any feminine principle, Nature is neither negativity nor evil in herself. She is not, as Hegel suggested, the fall of the Idea. It is Man who can choose to generate evil and the
negative through her.

Modern industrialization uses Nature as a simple material tool, and
reduces it to pure passivity, obliging her to also deny her internal masculinity,
and to hostiley close herself to our actions. At the same time, Man is condemned to impotency, to the procreation of bastards in which he will not be
able to recognize himself, and who in turn will not recognize themselves in
him, revolting against him. Nature, who has been raped, is comparable to a
material that is refractory to artistic creation, and Man is comparable to an
artist deprived of malleable material. His reproductive ability no longer finds
a container to spread out in, and thus ends by accepting to subordinate himself to the inferior principle that should have raised him. The rapist is here
condemned to be raped. But his role was and still remains one of generating
himself to become the image of God in the cosmos, thus regenerating it and
stopping the dislocation wrought by Lucifer's sin.[226] We can add that Nature
is not only a feminine principle, for Boehme and Baader.

Art is part of Nature's regenerating enterprise. For Baader, this idea
goes without saying, and this is probably the reason why this theme is not as
developed as one might wish. He likes "the artistic representation of the
transfiguration of the earthly body," since it represents a "cessation of weight
and of being in darkness." This was Raphael's error when he placed shadow in
his painting on the transfiguration, rendering the character suspended in the
air somewhat disturbing. This also brings to light a connection between the
words *Licht* (light) and *leicht* (lightweight). Art, which is of heavenly origin,
must make eternal Nature appear in the framework of temporal Nature.[227]

God, Christ and Sophia. The "Saved Savior"

The fall of proud Lucifer had not touched God "in his heart," but that of
Adam, seduced by the senses, did, explains Baader poetically in *Forty
Propositions*. That is why love, which saves and helps, came from the heart of
God and by the means of the Incarnation—which began at the very moment
of the Fall—started the work of reconciliation or reunion of God, humanity,
and Nature. It is the work of the history of the world on a large scale, and of
each human life in particular. Love, says John, is and was a part of God when
he created the world and Man. But, when Man fell, love came from God and

---

226. Ibid., p. 26.
227. Quoted by E. Susini, t. III, p. 585 (VIII, p. 133 ff., X, 102).

went into the world as the saving Word. At the time of the Adamic Fall, the heart of God was directed toward Man in order to reform what was formless. The ray of divine love, or Jesus, went into Sophia, the matrix of all archetypes, and became Man–Spirit in the archetype of Man. And so, natural incarnation started in time.[228] Since then, divine grace has always been at work everywhere. The German word corresponds etymologically to a free "lowering" of divinity, since "*Gnade*" (grace) is related to "*gnieden*" or "*niedern*."[229] God is with lovers as the third term that lowers itself toward them; they must let themselves be absorbed by Him, lose themselves in Him (*an Ihn*), but to find themselves entirely united to Him, "because the perfect unity is found only in our individual joining with God, and only after this is done will we naturally find ourselves as brothers of one another." "Cohabitation" (*Beiwohnen*) between two individuals, or a single one with God, does not call for their fusing, but rather for their mutual differentiation. As far as this is concerned, Baader attacks the Guyonian mysticism of fusion in *Fermenta Cognitionis*. Differentiation is no more a separation than union is a fusing.[230]

To say that love is a duty and recall that it is a divine commandment, means that it is in the power of anyone to open or close oneself to what God expects when a commitment is made with someone. "*Pflicht*" (duty) comes from "*Verflochtensein*" (to be united, interlaced, together); likewise, "duty" and "love" both suggest the idea of a bond. The first indicates that a power moves through (*durchwohnen*) the parts, but the second, love, since it is free from the weight of the law, attracts, fills, occupies (*innewohnen*), much as air entering a body in vacuum liberates the body from air pressure. This is why the Scriptures are an accomplishment of the Law, and why the weight of the Law only expresses the lack of "inhabitation" (*Inwohnung*). That which does not possess a center which carries it, and harbors only a force that "goes through" (*durchwohnend*), is indeed heavy. God only aspires to live within us, and every successful couple is Sophia's resting ground.

---

228. *Vierzig Sätze aus einer religiösen Erotik*, 1831, IV, 199. In Boehme, God is already incarnated in the holy element, which is the flesh of the angels, and which would be the luminous flesh of Christ.

229. Ibid., 192. "*Die Sonne geht zu Gnaden*," the Ancient ones used to say, according to Baader, to indicate that the sun sets.

230. *Bemerkungen über einige antireligiöse Philosopheme unserer Zeit*, 1824, II, 459 (the quote in French in the text is perhaps from Saint-Martin). *Fermenta Cognitionis II*, II, 227, n.: Baader quotes a text from Madame Guyon: "Just as a river is water which has come from the sea and yet *very different* from the sea, since it is found outside of its origin, it tries by all means to come closer to the sea, until it does, and fuses and mixes with it, just as it was before leaving it. It can no longer be differentiated." Already quoted by E. Susini, t. III, p. 533.

The aphorism of religious philosophy dedicated to the androgyne specifies this idea of dwelling. Baader recalls that Voltaire wrote about the subject
of the divine ternary in *La Henriade* (Chapter X): "Power, love and intelli-
gence/United and divided, make up his Essence." Baader objects that the persons of the Trinity are not "united" because they are already "one," and this is
not the same thing. They are not so much divided as different. What we
sometimes call the composition (*Zusammengesetztsein*) of a substance or
nature is none other than a disturbance (*Versetztheit*) of the members or elements which make it up. We only find absolute differentiation and unity in
God. On the other hand, it is the triple relationship of God to Man that this
verse expresses the best: as far as love is concerned, God "*inwohnt*" the soul of
Man; as far as power, he "*durchwohnt*" it (Man as nature and created being); as
far as Wisdom (*adjutor*, which is also "woman" in Genesis), he "*beiwohnt*" him.
This "*Beiwohnung*," this "*verbum apud Deum*" (*logos exdetos*), or this "*verbum
apud hominem seu creaturam*" (since Wisdom, in the Book of Wisdom, is
named as God's and the creature's playmate, and we cannot understand "*apud
hominem*" or mediation if there is no "*apud Deum*") are no longer understood
by theologians who have become silent about this Sophia (i.e., about the unity
and differentiation of "*logos endetos*" and "*logos exdetos*") because they see a
fourth person in it—a hypostasis—in God, or as Schwenkfeld says, a wife of
God.[211]

In *Forty Propositions*, Baader proposes another etymological connection
destined to clarify the process of reciprocity, and this concerns the word
"*Glauben*" (Faith). If the beloved gives him/herself to me, I am indebted, and
vice versa. Likewise, God cannot give Himself to me if I do not give myself to
Him, and if I give myself up to Him, I am his creditor (*Gläubiger*).[212] Another
thought from the same collection sees the process of reciprocity in a different
way. If I give joy to the one I love, I free myself of a need or pain, and if I
remove a trouble, I receive joy from it. That means there is "acknowledge-
ment"[233] (almost in the exact commercial sense of the word!) between both. I
am grateful to someone for loving me but I cannot love anyone who returns
nothing to me. That is why God often complains in the Scriptures on how
few men let themselves be loved by Him. He suffers only by being able to love
so few of them effectively. Baader had already said in his 1828 *Propositions for
an erotic philosophy* that if all noncommunicated joy is sorrowful to the lover,

---

231. *Religionsphilosophische Aphorismen*, X, p. 294 seq.
232. *Vierzig Sätze aus einer religiösen Erotik*, 1831, IV, p. 184 ff.
233. Ibid., 185. Expression borrowed from accounting: "*Die Liebe schreibt alles mit doppelter Kreide
an.*"

then any communicated pain is changed into something that is almost joy. This also happens in Man's love for God and explains the origin of prayer.[234]

God unceasingly searches for the creature, in order to find in it the matrix or the vase, and a place to celebrate the peace of the Sabbath: rest in movement and movement in rest. After Adam's sin, He left his innermost self, his *aseitas*, so as to give us His Son. In 1840, in a letter to Stransky, Baader evokes this sacrifice of the Father through a beautiful alchemical image. From the fiery red lion (the red, masculine part of the tincture and the white lamb (the white, feminine part of the tincture) is born the pink lion (*rosin*) or knight—the young man with a virgin heart. Blood and nerves represent this double tincture in animal nature, which Baader sees as perfectly united in the figure of Christ. Baaderian christology of course develops the themes of reunification, of the joining of opposites, and of androgyny. This is not the place to expound on his christology in detail, so I will limit myself to a few remarks which best illustrate the point. In a letter to C.D. von Meyer, the theosopher reminds us that if the plant unites earth and sky without mingling them, in order for the body of the plant to exist, the sun needs to become earth and the earth to become sun. The same goes for Christ who, first-born of all created beings and first to be resurrected, is the union of God and Man.[235] Our Savior is androgynous to Baader—but let us note here that Christ was probably not androgynous for Boehme! In any case, He is married to heavenly humanity, and each human being should take part in this marriage (Eph. 5:32).[236] Just as Christ unites God and Man, He also brings divine Love and Wrath together, as we read in the *Fermenta Cognitionis*.[237]

This is also not the place to present the rich and complex Baaderian sophiology, which I tried to do in a preceding article.[238] (Besides, the preceding pages contain the essential points on the Love-Sophia relationship which are found throughout the work.) A few additional quotes will suffice to illustrate this. In a letter to Passavant the theosopher makes the "remarriage" with Sophia a sacrament par excellence; thus, the very accomplishment of love—as well as this remarriage—is the "original poem of Man!"[239] Several passages in the work insist on the fact that if Sophia is considered woman for man, or man for woman, she still is of higher birth than we ourselves. She is therefore

234. *Sätze über erotische Philosophie*, 1828, IV, 176.
235. Baader to C.D. von Meyer, March 2, 1816, XV, 305.
236. *Ueber den paulinischen Begriff*..., 1837, IV, 353.
237. *Fermenta Cognitionis III*, 1822/1824, II, 254 ff.
238. Cf. *supra*, n. 4.
239. August 12, 1816, XV, 313.

really neither woman nor man, so that when she lives within us, all sexual desire is extinguished. She lives in the androgynous image (*Bildniss*) or immortal created being in the depths of our very selves.[240] Since the androgyne conditions this dwelling of the heavenly Virgin and conditions the dwelling of God in us, we must distrust the error committed by certain mystics who perceive the relationship of the human being with God like that of man with woman, in the current sense.[241]

One of the *Courses on speculative dogmatics* contains a rather interesting sophiological development, which was perhaps not brought up in the works dedicated to Baader. After mentioning that according to Meister Eckhart temporality is born and subsists only by the separation of Father and Son. Baader mentions a "solar tincture" and an "eternal tincture," separated from each other by a border (the word "tincture" here means "tincturial nature," an idea that is current in Boehme and Paracelsus). While the external solar tincture, which he also refers to as an external Venus or external Sophia, is bisexual (man and woman, or fire and water, thus double tincture), the internal or eternal tincture is not. This is because it is a participant in the Father and the Son, which are One. However, both of them—the external and internal—are only two aspects of a same entity. The obviously double external tincture—masculine and feminine—becomes one, while penetrating the internal tincture. A fiery divine principle that "cuts out the man or woman from the human being" is balanced between the solar and eternal tinctures, so that the human being, while penetrating Sophia by fire, is drawn into it. The eternal tincture should not be exposed, desecrated, or divulged, because this fire will burn anyone who touches it improperly.[242]

Another passage of the work is found in one of the *Courses on religious philosophy* and concerns the theme of the saved Savior. It is such a romantic theme that the *Naturphilosophie* adopted it as a myth that is more implicit than explicit. This is the one about the captive light, captured, which was awakened by another light that had remained free; or of the opposition between the weight and the light, the first serving as a dead term in which the primitive energies were engulfed. Baader does not make this connection with light and weight in the way Schelling does, but rather presents the idea in the following way. He first notes that the teacher, through a motion of love, tries to withdraw the weight of ignorance and error from the student so that light enters into him. But the teacher himself will stay enclosed within a certain opaque-

---

240. *Vorlesungen über J. Böhme*, 1833, XIII, 185.
241. *Ueber den verderblichen Einfluss . . .*, 1834, III, 303. Baader notes that Thomas Aquinas maintained this true idea of virginity with Mary, against the opinion of the Scotists.
242. *Vorlesungen über speculative Dogmatik*, 1838, IX, p.213 ff.

ness (*in Trübung*) as long as the student will not give him back the light he obtained thanks to him. "Likewise, the Savior must save his Savior once again." Such is the great mystery of religion: God exposed Himself freely to the sufferings of the intelligent creature, by descending toward him through love ("*Amor descendit*"). Man, in turn, can liberate the heart of God from this freely adopted "*suspension*," in other words "save his Savior." "Happy is he who understands this mystery of Christianity!" This soteriology is also applied to Man in his relationships with Nature and other human beings. If Nature is before us in order to help us, she expects that we then help her, by assuming the pain of her "nonintegrity" so as to deliver her from it. It is only by the "integrity" of Man, which he cannot find without the help from Nature, that she will reach her full state of completion.[243]

BAADER AND HIS TIME

Jacob Boehme, theosopher par excellence, but not a *Naturphilosoph* in the romantic or Oetingerian sense of the word, hardly sought to support his speculations by science. Baader however, incorporates into his mystical *Naturphilosohie* the scientific support of a era fond of great syntheses. Infatuation with doctrines on polarity encourages or incites his meditations, since like Schelling, he believes in the need to become a speculative observer of Nature. We can add ethical sensitivity and an interest in aesthetics, which was generally stimulated in his contemporaries by the works of Winckelmann, and Humboldt, who had attracted attention to the hermaphrodites of Greek art.[244] Baader smelts this within the crucible of his theosophy—without really giving full justice to Plato nor a very clear concept of the hermaphrodite—and he feels very much at home with esotericism even before German Romanticism became preoccupied with Boehme. His interest in the idea of androgyny came about in 1796, in his correspondence with Jacobi about the Kabbalah.[245] He says that the eye is a feminine faculty, since it harbors nostalgia for the fertilizing ray; likewise, the ray seeks out this nostalgia as a fiancé does the open arms of his fiancée. Ontological complementarity and unity announce later developments .

The time when his thought was elaborated and its foundations being laid also corresponded to a favored facet of sensitivity at the beginning of the great Romantic era: Friedrich Schlegel and Schleiermacher expound on the

---

243. *Vorlesungen über religiöse Philosophie*, 1826/1827, I, p. 161 ff.

244. Cf. Giese (op. cit., *supra*, n. p. 236), pp. 370 ff., 381, 390 ff. on this point and others that follow. On Schelling, cf. p. 301 ff.

245. Baader to Jacobi, June 16, 1796, XV, 165 and November 19, 1796, XV, 168.

idea and present the image they have of woman. Woman, a superior type of humanity and gifted with the same rights as man, actually exercises them less by rash social reforms, than by embodying the philosophical viewpoints inspired by Schelling, Schleiermacher, or Novalis. These are real beings, after all, who always incite our interest, and who are linked to the first Romanticism, and who acted on the latter like leaven on dough; such are Caroline, Dorothea, Sophie, Therese, Henriette, Rachel. In this context, the originality of Baader is twofold. First, woman as a "lived" experience does not seem to constitute a true fermentum of personal inspiration for him. Although he has a strong taste for the "beautiful sex," we do not have the impression that a real female human being has influenced him in his theories. At least his work does not carry any trace of this, except perhaps toward the end of his life, when Romanticism first entered into history. An unhappy countess, present in his correspondence, somehow pulls out some strains, but not any real themes.[246] The second originality, which would be useful to insist on further, carries us to the very theory of the androgyne.

Man and woman, indeed for romantic Eros, are two single parts of a "Whole." Baader adds a third term to this duality: the Idea, which realizes a tripolarity. And, we have also seen the large place he grants to quadripolarity. That allows him to show how complementarity is at least as internal as it is external, whereas for the great authors of those times it was presented above all as something internal.[247] Baader at first believed that Schelling was on the path of meditation toward androgyny and its polar mysteries, due to the kind of research he conducted; however, he never really arrived where Baader expected him. If we put aside the intuition of some previous theosophers such as Eckartshausen,[248] or those of the later *Naturphilosophie*—such as Joseph Görres or J.F. von Meyer—inspired more or less by Baader himself, we will find that most points of comparison with him are found in painters, poets, or novelists.

In spite of his *"reale Psychologie,"* Novalis did not clearly address the issue, which Runge has clarified a little, which Ritter has announced somewhat more adequately, and which Baader has elaborated on by refusing to treat sexuality as a marginal problem. If the *Hymns to the Night* are a celebration of the ecstasy linked to each individual death, then the book *Heinrich von Ofterdingen* indicates initiatic progress in comparison, because of the fact that

---

246. XV, pp. 178, 181, 106, 203. . .
247. Cf. especially IX, 209; VII, 238. And Giese, p. 375.
248. Eckartshausen preceded Baader with this theory on love; cf. for example *Aufschlüsse zur Magie*, t. II, Munich, 1790, p. 14 ff., and my work about this author on a general scale, *Eckartshausen et la théosophie chrétienne*, (Paris, Klincksieck, 1969).

a victory has been gained over the Ego. The victory is in the superior idea of transformation in this world, even if through the intermediary of the dream. The magic idealism of Novalis points toward theosophy in the sense that he prepares the way, but Baader is perhaps the only one to bring a dynamic, "organicized" Platonism to the level of real life through his speculative discourse, of which Sophie's fiancé, the creator of Mathilde, had poetic intuition, without ever speaking openly about androgyny. The graphic writings of Philip Otto Runge, leading to a renunciation the Novalis type, open upon the idea of romantic Death and Night and point the way toward perfection or a form of completion. Runge had an experience of mystical pessimism concerning the life of the sexes. If his four *Hours of the Day (Tageszeiten)* go back to an androgynous quadripolarity in Nature, then the myosotis inscribed in the work (cf. painting *The Early Morning [Der Kleine Morgen]*, a pictoral completion of the first of four drawings) seem especially to evoke the Platonic nostalgia for the other "half."[249] At practically the same time, *Fragments*, by Johann Wilhelm Ritter,[250] ensures the transition between Novalis and Baader. Ritter was indeed the first to truly raise the problem, by isolating it from the question of the sexes; i.e., by carrying it into the whole of Nature. The context is thus woven, engaging Baader ever more resolutely in what he believes to be the true Western esoteric tradition, whereas his illustrious predecessor Saint-Martin had hardly attempted to speculate on androgyny.[251] Baader's work meanwhile continues to enrich literature and speculation,[252] the echo ceasing only when art and philosophy refuse to take root in theosophy.

---

249. Cf. Giese, p. 357 ff.

250. *Fragmente aus dem Nachlasse eines jungen Physikers*, Heidelberg, 1810; (facsimile, Heidelberg, L. Schneider, 1969). Cf. A. Faivre, "Physique et métaphysique du feu chez J.W. Ritter pp. 25–52, in *Les Etudes philosophiques*, (Paris, P.U.F., 1983, #1.)

251. For Saint-Martin, the difference of the sexes does not extend "beyond bodily form and faculties". Cf. *De l'esprit des choses*, t. I, Paris, 18, p. 211 ff.

252. Until our own days! This influence, found indirectly by W. Lambert in certain contemporaries, should be studied further. See op. cit., *supra* n.10, cf. p. 200, n. 239. And the collective work edited by Peter Koslowski, *Die Philosophie, Theologie und Gnosis Franz von Baader's*, Vienna, Passagen Verlag, 1993.

THE METAMORPHOSES OF HERMES:
NEOGNOSTIC COSMOLOGIES
AND TRADITIONAL GNOSIS

For Basarab Nicolescu

The theme chosen for our fifth annual session* invites us to question two means of contemplating, two qualities of vision. By "the eyes of the flesh" I refer to those of the man of science whose knowledge rests on experimentation, the postulate of possible objectivity, and the difference between the subject who observes and the object that is observed. For the scientist as such, it is not a matter of tasting the flavors of the world, but rather of describing its components. Einstein said one day that "science is not made to give the soup flavor"; in fact, it is possible to see the Universe as a blind mechanism governed only by chance and necessity. But Einstein also said that "God does not play at dice": meaning thereby that there must be an order that is not due to chance and that would thus justify the quest for meaning—for the "why" and not merely for the "how." The positivist scientist would answer that before finding meaning I should first exhaust all feasible possibilities allowed by the eyes of the flesh, by an external process, in a "disinterested" way. But since I myself am part of this world, its meaning, if there is any, does concern me, and I can certainly question this without waiting for several more centuries rich in discoveries to elapse; this is called pursuing metaphysics.

Science and metaphysics were paired for a long time. But, Kant gave some tough blows to both, as Bergson noted in *La Pensée et le mouvant*, and "they still have not recovered from their surprise. Our mind willingly resigns

---

* Paper presented at the Conference of the University of Saint John of Jerusalem in Cambrai, June 1978.

itself to seeing relative cognition in science and empty speculation in meta-physics."[1] In fact, the essential characteristic of critical philosophy had been to leave the monopoly on the study of Nature to the sciences, hence the Bergsonian reaction to this aspect of Kantism, which was absolutely nothing new, since after Kant the whole German *Naturphilosophie* movement became engaged in tearing away this monopoly from positive science:[2] Ritter, Baader, Schelling, and Saint-Martin all possessed the "eyes of fire." We understand by this term the vision of a revelation of prophetic character that illuminates the world and mankind. In Heraclitus—not only because of the fire which he speaks of—in Ezechiel's description of the four living beings, in Ibn' Arabi or Sohravardi, in Jacob Boehme, or even in the unknown authors of the Chinese *I Ching*, it seems that by means of dazzling revelations or progressive inspira-tion certain beings receive knowledge of the ultimate principles of reality of the world through immediate, nondiscursive means. We can call this "gno-sis," without intending to designate the particular movement that is currently termed "Gnosticism," and which developed in the early centuries of Christianity. Gnosis then is the term used here to designate a cognition that is necessarily of the religious type since it deals with the "why" of the Universe and its meaning; this cognition and knowledge are not necessarily strangers to organized religions: there is often just as much gnosis in certain of the Church Fathers as there is in nondenominational Christian theosophy.

It happens that scholars possessing knowledge through eyes of the flesh use the images perceived by the eyes of fire. This was frequently the case prior to Kant, thus Newton is not only the scholar that he is known for having been. Impassioned by symbolic alchemy,[3] he always considered the mind to have direct access to experience, he believed in the existence of a *sensorium Dei*, which means that God intervenes in Nature through the intermediary of that medium. Paradoxically, from Newton on, physics and metaphysics would increasingly diverge. Let us bring up some of our contemporaries, chosen exclusively from those we would designate as scientists and who, by a second criterion, would borrow from traditional gnosis some of the images that the eyes of fire had perceived. I am not suggesting that these enquiring minds are absolutely representative of all of modern science, even within their respec-

1. Quoted by Michel Ambacher, *Cosmologie et philosophie*. Preface of René Poirier, Paris, Aubier-Montaigne, coll. "Presence et Pensée," 1967, p. 216.
2. Cf. *Epochen der Naturmystik*. Edited by Antoine Faivre and Rolf Christian Zimnermann, West Berlin, Erich Schmidt, 1979.
3. Cf. Jen Zafiropulo and Catherine Monod, '*Sensorium Dei*' *dans l'hermétisme et la science*, (Paris, Les Belles Lettres, 1976). Betty J.T. Dobbs, *The Foundations of Newton's Alchemy or the Hunting of the Greene Lyon*, (Cambridge University Press, 1975), and *The Janus Faces of Genius (The Role of Alchemy in Newton's Thought)*, (Cambridge University Press, 1991).

tive fields, and I will not speak about the scientific value of their theories or their systems. Some call themselves the "new gnostics," and speak of "neo-gnosis"; this means they are looking within traditions for symbols that allow them to enlarge their conceptual universe or to render it accessible when the discourse of "positive" science does not suffice. This rather new phenomenon is hardly surprising if one thinks of how present physics tends more and more to offer models of the universe, and how life sciences find themselves constrained to suggesting hypotheses about meaning.

Three questions will serve as clues for us: 1) the problem of origins 2) the problem of the relationships between mind and Nature 3) the new logics of the concrete.

The Problem of Origins

The problem of origins—that is to say, when, how, and why did the world begin to exist?—is found within objective science and metaphysics, but also in religion, since every cosmogonic myth proposes an account of the origin of the universe. Human thought has always hesitated between a representation of an infinite and that of a finite universe; of infinite or finite space itself.[4] Since, thanks to Einstein, one believes one can deny the existence of space void of matter, ever-increasing numbers of scholars are depicting space–universe as a finite sphere outside of which there is nothing else, not even space; space would therefore be finite, but without limits (much the same as our globe has no limits of length, since it is spherical).

One can then understand how the theories of Georges Lemaître, an astrophysicist and priest, have continued to hold the attention of the scientific circle. Although presented a half century ago, it is appropriate to recall them here, because of the success they still enjoy. Lemaître stands in the wake of the finitism that the Christian Middle Ages had inherited from Aristotle.[5] "We can conceive," writes Lemaître, "of space beginning with a primitive atom and the beginning of space marking the beginning of time."[6] Closer to our own time is G. Gamov who identifies himself with the school of Lemaître. For him, cosmic history is preceded by an initial moment that is characterized by a singular state of matter–energy, and he holds that the evo-

---

4. Cf. Alexandre Koyré, *From the Closed World to the Infinite Universe*, (Baltimore, John Hopkins Press, 1957).

5. Finitism which is also summarized by Kant's *thesis* on the first antinomy.

6. Quoted by Jacques Merleau-Ponty, *Cosmologie du XXe siècle. Etude épistémologigue et historique des théories de la cosmologie contemporaine*, (Paris, Gallimard, 1965) p. 333.

lution of the universe was dominated by the expansion of space.[7] At its origin the universe would have been very dense, thus very hot, and because of its high temperature would have been composed entirely of radiation. It would appear that this hypothesis is accepted by most astrophysicists at the present time. One piece of fundamental data would be assured from that moment on: "something" would have had to have been generated approximately ten billion years ago, in a period before which neither the universe nor space existed. This event would have been the primitive atom of Lemaître, of a very small dimension (the latter is still a matter for debate). Its temperature was so high during the first fraction of a second of its existence that its radiational energy created a cosmic explosion, the "big bang" or *Urknall*, which was followed by a period of diminishing radiation and heat. This consequently increased the density of the first particles of matter, neutrons, which later became protons and electrons, these latter constituting the atoms of hydrogen. Since then, the universe itself has not ceased to expand.[8]

The relationship between the brief description above and "gnosis" in the sense given here, is shown when we realize how closely some physicists have tried to connect this with the account of the creation of the world in the first chapters of our Judaic cosmogony. For the French microphysicist and epistemologist, Jean Charon, this reconciliation takes the form of a veritable mythical evocation. He does not hesitate to bring even closer what contemporary cosmologists are currently saying in terms of Einstein's theory of relativity, and what Genesis teaches about the light created "in the beginning": In this beginning the Universe was filled with electromagnetic radiation at high temperatures, that is to say, filled with light. He notes that Genesis and the astrophysicists agree that matter was created only later, after light; he describes these origins just as well as the *Natur*-philosophers of the time of Romantic era, all the while trying to retrace the brief, early history of matter, which began to be formed from the radiation of photons after that first fraction of a second of expansion. First we see the neutrons being born; next, the neutrinos; then the positive and negative electrons. These functioned to provoke the universe out of its static state, the universe having existed in a period of "waiting" before their appearance, which was limited to a spherical space filled with "black" electromagnetic radiation at 60,000 degrees. There was thus no specific matter, no "mind." It was only the light that reigned before the appearance of the first pair of electrons (+ and –). Their appearance, in

---

7. G. Gamov, *La Création de l'univers*, (Paris, Dunod, 1956) (book in which he summarized the whole of his work). Cf. also Stephan Weinberg, *Les Trois Premières Minutes*, (Paris, Seuil Ed.,1978).

8. The "big bang" theory is not shared by all cosmophysicists; cf. namely the very different theses of Hanus Alfven and Oscar Klein.

fact, did bring a "mind" to the universe. One could consider this appearance as an act coming "from the exterior," and thus having divine origin; this of course could result in the idea of an *ex nihilo* creation.[9]

Who is this God who thereby creates the universe? The neo-gnostics have a tendency to consider this God both as a multiple being and as a dynamic energy, a concept linked to the German theosophy of the Baroque age, which was later defended by Romantic *Naturphilosophie*. Edgar Morin, one of the major French epistemologists of our day, would perhaps refuse the designation of neognostic, but he does not deprive himself of drawing on hermetist symbolism. In the first volume of *La Méthode*, entitled "La Nature de la Nature,"[10] he envisions *"Elohim"* as the God-Creator by distinguishing him from *"Adonai"*—Lord–God—and from *"JHVH"*—God–Legislator. "The singular plural of *Elohim*," he writes, "accounts for *unitas multiplex* of geniuses whose vortex constitutes a *generator*. One can envision these geniuses in materialistic terms, in the form of motivational energies—that is to say, as having a whirlwind form—or in terms that are simultaneously magical and spiritualist. . . . Thus the idea of *Elohim* unites and translates . . . the idea of a vortex of genesis, the idea of a creating power." In a way that resembles the way in which the protosolar vortex is transformed into order, *Elohim*—the thermodynamic Vortex—without ever ceasing to be supremely *Elohim*, makes room for *JHVH*, God–Organizer which is not solar but cybernetic. Morin adds that the *I Ching* "brings in the most exemplary image of the genesiac and generic identity."

Origin is not only that by which everything begins, it is also that by which everything, unceasingly, takes its existence and form. Morin sees an alchemical notion here and does not hesitate to call it by the traditional name of "Philosophical Mercury," thereby evoking the presently troublesome difficulty experienced by modern science in specifically stating what one should understand by *"elemental unity."* Perhaps, he observes, an ultimate or first individualizable and isolable reality does not exist, but rather a *continuum* (*bootstrap* theory), a kind of unitary root outside of time, outside of space. "If the atoms are not opened out into the environment, might they not be opened inwardly, into the unconceived and unknown of the physis?"

The Problem of the Relationship between Mind and Nature

Behind the nature grasped by our immediate perception and our methods of scientific investigation—behind the *"natura naturata"*—is there not an active

---

9. Jean E. Charon, *L'Homme et l'univers*, (Paris, Albin Michel, 1974), p. 188; *L'Esprit cet inconnu*, (Paris, Albin Michel, 1977), pp. 198 ff., 203.

10. Edgar Morin, *La Méthode I: La Nature de la Nature*, (Paris, Seuil Ed., 1977), p. 228 ff.

and living nature—a *"natura naturans"*—of which the first would be only the effect or the continuation? Is not "nature naturing" a life or a mind whereby the "nature natured" would be only the outward appearance? To Einstein, for whom "space empty of matter does not exist," Charon responds by completing the formula: "the space empty of living does not exist." The gnostics have tried to address and respond to what is perhaps the most fundamental philosophical question ever, that of the relationship between mind and Nature. When microphysicists and astrophysicists pose this same question, they seem to take up or rediscover, in a different language, the hypotheses or ideas that previously belonged to some religious traditions.

E.A. Milne, one of the greatest contemporary cosmologists, has done his best to assure a reconciliation between "natural philosophy" and Christian teaching by consistently refusing to separate theology from physics. He is the first philosopher of Nature since Leibniz who has tried to define the universe as an ideal community of conscious monads, to preface the objective description of the physical world by that of intersubjectivity, and thereby to go beyond the traditional opposition of subject and object. For Milne, the meaning of science is "the giving of insight into the mind of God." He proposed a new idea of the idealism of space, very different from what Kant had set forth, departing from the transcendental reduction of Euclidean space and Galilean time. Milne has links with Leibniz because of his metaphysics of the spatial relationship: space is the mode of coexistence of thinking monads; it should be considered thus, even before making it the immediately obvious predicate of material beings.[11]

In a work that caused some scandal, Raymond Ruyer spoke to us of the "gnostics of Princeton and Pasadena,"[12] using this term to refer to the scholarly university physicists at those universities. Gathered together in a sort of club, anxious to preserve their anonymity, they developed, Ruyer informs us, a philosophy inspired by the most advanced scientific research and molded after the ideas of ancient gnostics. These thinkers date back to approximately 1970; Ruyer had had the opportunity to enter this seraglio and obtain authorization to divulge that philosophy, on the condition that he not reveal the names. One wonders, about the reason for such a clause, given the fact that the ideas in mention were not of a type to worry the government or disturb public morale. Personally, in fact, I greatly doubt the existence of this association, which seems to me to be a sort of fictional vehicle designed to expose

---

11. E.A. Milne, *Modern Cosmology and the Christian Idea of God*, Oxford, 1952, quoted by Jacques Merleau-Ponty, op. cit. pp. 169,171, 442. Note incidentally that Milne said he was against the hypothesis of a finite Universe.

12. Raymond Ruyer, *La Gnose de Princeton. Des savants à la recherche d'une religion*, (Paris, Fayard, coll. "Evolutions," 1974).

certain ideas. But there is no doubt that these ideas are current in the scientific world, and not only in the United States. In this sense, Ruyer's book is a testimony.

According to the "gnostics of Princeton"—as we shall denominate them for reference in this paper—one should refuse to oppose mind to matter, subjective to objective, consciousness to the thing. They declare themselves essentially antimaterialists. For them, physical and material reality cannot precede consciousness. This "gnosis" proclaims itself deist as well. Essentially it connects with one of the permanent traits of gnosis, that which always considered the mind to be indissociable from physical or chemical phenomena. Ruyer seems visibly pleased to tell us that the gnostics of Princeton are all interested in a book by Samuel Butler, *God the Known and the Unknown* (1879), where they read that the unity of all living beings is one great living being of which organisms of all species constitute the cells. This is a current idea in the Philosophy of Nature. Traditional Gnosis also poses the existence of an omnipresent, living reality, capable of provoking the appearance of thought in space, thought that also resides in the mineral realm and is manifested in the behavior of even the most rudimentary living organisms. These scholars adopted the term *"holon,"*[11] previously used by Arthur Koestler, to designate the "sub-unities" of space, the same carriers of mind which were called *"aeons"* by the ancient gnostics. There would be aeons in us who know how to create life and whose knowledge would greatly surpass our own. Like the *aeon*, the *holon* would represent the spirit emanated from universal intelligence.

Towards 1930, well before Koestler, Eddington had suggested that elemental particles could be intelligent matter. In 1964, D.F. Lawden, a mathematics professor at the University of Canterbury in New Zealand, held that "the continuity of nature entails that consciousness or intelligence be a universal property of matter: even elemental particles would be endowed with this up to a certain point." At about the same time, in 1963, V.A. Firsoff, whose work has an important place in the neognostic bibliography of Ruyer's book, expressed the same idea: "Intelligence is an entity or universal interaction of the same nature as electricity or gravity and there must be some existing *formula of transformation*, analogous to the famous equation of Einstein $E=mc^2$, in which intelligence would be put into the equation with other entities of the physical world." A complex structure like a galaxy, which resembles an organism and possesses a kind of nuclear, not chemical metabolism, very likely possesses, adds V.A. Firsoff, an intelligence, perhaps even of a superior kind. "If intelligence is a universal property of matter, the universe then rep-

13. Ibid., p. 63.

resents a terrifying amount of mental potential, and *anima mundi* must exist."[14]

For the gnostics of Princeton, "the mind becomes a keyboard, before playing its tunes on itself having become keyboard."[15] Thus the mind uses the brain, which is matter; there is disjunction between one and the other; between the form as thematic idea and the form as structure in space. But the mind (or the form as thematic idea) should not be pictured as independent of a matter by which it risks being devoured. This would lead "to mythologies and digressions of ancient gnosticism about the *Pneuma* and the mind, conceived as completely independent of Matter."[16] We see that the gnostics of Princeton, and apparently Ruyer himself, limit "ancient gnosis" to only one of the gnostic schools from the early Christian era, the same one that had made Irenaeus anxious. It is sufficiently well-known that Western gnosis, in the broadest sense of Hermetism or Christian esotericism, has continuously—with the exception perhaps of Swedenborg—placed the idea of *Menschwerdung*, incarnation, at the very center of its speculations, and that it has always insisted on the existence of organic relationships between mind and matter, unlike "ancient gnosticism" according to Ruyer, i.e., that of certain gnostics of early Christian times and unlike the spirit of Catharism. The verse of the *Emerald Tablet*: "*Et vis ejus[=Dei, Unitatis] integra est, si conversa fuerit in terram,*" so often quoted in Western alchemy and Hermetism, has expressed this idea for centuries.

One of the noteworthy tendencies of the gnostics of Princeton is their disinterest in Eastern exoticism. They say that one should be nurtured by one's own tradition, or by an already well-assimilated one. Zen Buddhism is a curse in the West, since it means "techniques and consistent works beyond values and norms, beyond psychic montages"; hence it suggests absurd gestures professing to go beyond meaning and inspires artistic and pretentious hoax by those who have nothing to create or say.[17] This trait shows how much closer the relationship is of the alleged gnostics of Princeton to Christian Hermeticism, for whom incarnation is the cornerstone. The idea is secularized here, but it has nevertheless inherited some of the traditional gnostic concepts. These montages play the role of the mind "becoming incarnate, distributing itself into managing schemes, using the already incarnate, and continuing with incarnation, organizing and constructing. . . .; Phenomenon . . . which explains the creation of the form by the mind, of the *gross body*

---

14. Cf. V A. Firsoff, *Vie, intelligence et galaxies*, (Paris, Dunod, 1970), pp. 121, 127.
15. Raymond Ruyer, op. cit., p. 173.
16. Ibid., p. 166.
17. Ibid., p. 198.

by the *subtle body.*"[18] One can consider philosophies and religions not only as research and discoveries of truths, but as inventions of montages, with the "speculative and mythological 'gravy.'"[19] There is, then, in this prevailing thought described by Ruyer, a sense of the concrete, a taste for both material and intellectual fulfillment, a wisdom that aims to reconcile the body and the mind; but there is also a deepseated agnosticism, since only the montages are important, the rest is only the "gravy," and one can do without it.

The idea that matter is inhabited by the mind is found in the heart of Jean Charon's reflections, who professes to make known the "different aspects and consequences" of the physics which he believes in and which he himself qualifies as "neognostic."[20] In order to introduce this type of physics he doesn't hesitate to first take care to set the stage for us, revealing to our amazement an awe-inspiring panorama whose colors remind us of the evocations of Romantic gnosis. The Universe can be portrayed as a huge ocean. Water is the space–time of matter. The air above the ocean is the space–time of the mind. Soft waves render the surface iridescent; an image that symbolizes the undulating quality of gravitational space. Tiny bubbles of air enclosed in thin layers of water drift here and there; these are the electrons; some among them swim in the vortex; these are the atoms. The electrons are mind floating on matter. Little by little the water evaporates into the mist and one day, billions of years later, there will remain only a mass of small iridescent bubbles flying ever higher into the skies. . . .[21] In order to give scientific credence to these images, Charon proposes a theory that he believed demonstrable in 1975,[22] and from which the following would result.

The stable particles, those which are of almost infinite duration, contain a "space–time" that can never lose its informational content. They make up a large part of the particles of our body and subsist beyond our bodily death; they are the electrons of all the atoms of which our body is composed. Each one of these electrons possesses in itself the totality of information characterizing what we call our mind, our own person, our "I." By virtue of the negentropic play of their spins, our electrons receive information indefinitely without ever losing any.[23] Since they are carriers of the psyche, they commu-

---

18. Ibid., p. 216.
19. Ibid., p. 220.
20. Jean Charon, *L'esprit* . . . , op. cit., p. 16.
21. Ibid., p. 94.
22. Jean Charon, *Théorie de la relativité complexe*, (Paris, Albin Michel, 1977).
23. Complex theory which cannot be expounded on here in great detail. Consult ibid., and *L'Esprit* . . . , op. cit.

nicate with each other, a fact which would explain telepathy as well as the organization of elemental matter ("psychism of elemental matter"). The informational part they receive—the world "consciousness" they have accumulated—remains forever ingrained.[24] As the picturesque image of the ocean has already suggested, if the universe one day began again to contract, there would be a fundamental difference between the new order of things and the state that preceded the *big bang*: just as prior to that moment no particles were existing, after the contraction, the space of the universe would be filled with positron/electron pairs; that is to say positive and negative electrons—a final phase that would represent a differentiated state, the carrier of all worldly memory. The heavy particles, neutrons, would continue to disappear "until all our aeonic "I"s were reunited in a huge structure, even more negentropic than in the past, reaching the place where time seems to be stopped, where the mind has ultimately led this gigantic evolution, the green grazing grounds where the universe finally holds her breath."[25]

One could have said[26] that the story of the universe is that of genes making up chromosomes, with the individual representing the vehicle. We see that Charon situates the center of evolution even lower: no longer in the genes, but rather in the electrons; therefore the mind spreads to all matter.[27] Teilhard de Chardin also sought to give life to matter: "We are logically forced," he writes in *Le Phénomène humain*, "to assume the existence in rudimentary form (in a microscopic, i.e., infinitely diffused state) of some sort of psyche in every corpuscle." And Charon reminds us that Teilhard designated this psyche "the within of things"—a within, a nature naturing, which might have been able to build the first living structures. Teilhard and Charon draw on the traditional thought previously expressed in the *Nous* of Anaxagoras— the idea of mind associated with each seed of matter, participating in its behavior; they rediscover what Thales had affirmed ("all things are filled with gods") before Schelling viewed matter as "the mind lying dormant." But Charon resolutely digresses from Teilhard, the Jesuit who thought that that which is elemental is nothing in evolution; all spiritual affairs of the world are carried only by an infinitesimal number of organized structures: human beings. For Charon on the other hand, if Man is part of this affair, "he cannot constitute the axis."[28] In the same way, whereas Teilhard sees our mind spread

---

24. Ibid., pp. 42, 46 ff., 104 ff., 139, 141.
25. Ibid., pp. 241, 255.
26. For example, E.O. Wilson, *Sociobiology*, (Havard University Press, 1975), Jean Charon quotes this work in *L'Esprit . . .* , op. cit., p. 190 ff.
27. Ibid., p. 190 ff.
28. Ibid., p. 102 ff.

over the unity of elemental corpuscles forming us, Charon thinks that our mind, our "I," is completely contained within each of the electrons of our body and not in the other particles that make us up.

The reflections of Edgar Morin are quite different. He declared, as did many others, how important it is to see the notion of matter increasingly disappear: a particle for example doesn't exist by itself as an entity, and one sees "the all" being born of its parts, with the result that our world seems formed and created on the basis of abstractions. "We are actually condemned," he writes, "to know only a universe of messages, and nothing else beyond that. But at the same time we have the privilege of being able to read the universe in the form of messages. . . . We walk, wander, in a forest of symbols *that observe us with familiarity*."[29] Matter is not material on the microphysics level, but we have not yet expelled from science the idea of the mind. The departure of the mind—this "metaphysical wanderer"—has left an enormous gap that *information* has claimed, and still sovereignly claims today, to fill.[10] The relationship between information and form remains no less a mystery. The mystery whose essence Morin sought to grasp is perhaps nothing more than the relationship between what one calls Nature and the mind.

First one identifies a purely arbitrary sign, chemically located in the nucleic DNA where it is found like an engram or a file; a living, existential form departs from there. How does one go from one to the other? Nobody has yet been able to answer this question. In the same way, how is the passage of the arbitrary sign, located in a cerebral neuron, carried out to mental recall? Neither in the case of genetic reproduction nor in memory can we say that the new being is already preformed and that recollection was already filed and boxed away, like a photograph. We still do not know how forms revive and regenerate. In order to find out one would have to develop and encourage a "thermodynamics of forms," which is what René Thom also made a plea for, so as to establish a true theory of information.[11]

In an enticing and helpful work,[12] Fritjof Capra, professor at the University of California in Berkeley, proposes "to explore the relationships between the concepts of modern physics and the basic ideas of philosophical and religious traditions of the Far East." Such a program shows a taste that differs from that of the Princeton scholars, with respect to the East. Despite the misgivings that may be prompted by the book's title and statement of its subject, this book is one of the most serious of its kind; through his double

29. Edgar Morin, op. cit., p.356. The expression is an allusion to the famous sonnet by Baudelaire.
30. Ibid., p. 360.
31. Ibid., p. 363. Cf. René Thom, *Modèles mathématiques de la morphogenèse*, Paris, 1974, p. 179.
32. Fritjof Capra, *The Tao of Physics*, (Berkeley, Shambhala, 1975).

speciality, the author does indeed know what he is talking about. He strives to show that modern physics—essentially microphysics—obliges its seekers to undergo a genuine epistemological conversion in which the teachings of the Hindu *Vedas*, the Chinese *I Ching* and the Buddhist *sutras* can be of great help, because the thought of all these fields seems oriented in the same direction. Incidentally, he also notes that a true parallel exists between this direction of thought and the extracts of Heraclitus, the Sufism of Ibn'Arabi, and the teachings of the Yaqui medicine man Don Juan.[33] Let us hope that the author will one day substitute the Western for the Eastern tradition, in a comparably serious work, and call to mind its alchemical, theosophical, and hermetist aspects.

Capra shows that one should not look for the forces at the origin of movement outside the objects, as the Greeks wanted to do, since they are an intrinsic property of matter. In the same way, the eastern conception of the divine is not that of a God who directs the world from above but of a principle controlling everything from within.[34] To the physicist Capra, the universe appears as a "cosmic dance"—title of one of the chapters of his book—in the image of cosmological diagrams from India: nothing is closed; there is no dead matter; rhythm is everywhere in musical numbers and in cosmic choreography; it is found as much in the infinitely great as in the infinitely small. He insists on the idea of participation, which even in the laboratory tends to supplant that of observation—a familiar idea in Eastern religious teaching. Buddhists received the object as an event, not as a substance, as a something. Things are *samskara*—events, acts. Everything is time and movement and microphysicists are now obliged to picture the world as such. Buddhists and Taoists say that ultimate reality is a void—*sunyata*—a *living* void that gives birth to all the forms of the phenomenal world.[35]

Let us conclude this part of our discussion with another example. Capra summarizes the so-called *bootstrap* theory,[36] which seems to be somewhat influential in modern microphysics. Contrary to the Newtonian universe, which is constructed on basic entities (building blocks), this theory teaches that the cosmos is a dynamic network of interconnected elements. The properties of the parts in this network are not fundamental features because they all follow each other's properties; their mutual interrelations determine the entire network's structure. As in Eastern cosmology, the universe would thus

33. Ibid., pp. 8, 19.
34. Ibid., p. 24.
35. Ibid., pp. 204, 212.
36. This is the theory of Geoffrey Chew; cf. G. Gale, "Chew's Monadology," in *Journal of the History of Ideas* vol. XXXV, April-June 1974, pp. 339-348.

present itself as an interconnected "all," in which no single part would appear more fundamental than any other, with the result that the properties of any part would be determined by those properties of all the others. "All is in each thing and each thing is in all." It is as if each particle contained all the others while nonetheless remaining a part of the others! The monads of Leibniz did not have windows and only some were reflected in others, but in the *bootstrap* theory, an emphasis is put on the interrelation and interpenetration of all the particles of the universe. It is the return of the old doctrine of universal interdependence to a science that at the height of its triumph believed it had chased away that doctrine for good.[17]

If universal interdependence tends to supplant mechanical indifference, the laws of this interdependence bring honor back to the dynamic, polar, and dialectic schemata that were not entirely forgotten since Presocratic times and that are organized around arithmological laws in which one finds Pythagorean numbers, geometric models (*Yin-Yang*, spiral, etc.), and principles such as the one of complementarity. It is worth noting that one is now familiar with three or four "interactions" upon which the universe rests and which constitute what one calls "matter." They are respectively: the strong interactions that link protons and neutrons together, thus giving the nucleus a tremendous cohesion; the gravitational interactions that determine the formation of stars, the concentration of galaxies; and the electromagnetic interactions that link electrons to nuclei and atoms to molecules. One may also add the so-called "weak" interactions to that list.

Jean Charon sees in the electron a space with ever-increasing negentropy, where the mind develops little by little, making use of the "spiritual" properties that reside in four "psychic" interactions: Reflection, Cognition, Love, and Action.[18] They can be brought to eight, number indicating perfection of the fulfilled world according to traditional arithmosophy, if we include the four interactions of physics. For Charon, the mind presents itself stably in two complementary forms, the positive electron and negative electron, which comes close to the *Yin* and *Yang*.

New Logics of the Concrete

The *physis* of today, notes Edgar Morin, is rediscovering its generic fullness which the Presocratics had recognized, hence the possibility of a new metapysics where "*meta*" means both surpassing and integration, rather than "extraphysical." That *physis* makes us "rediscover Nature in order to redis-

---

37. Fritjof Capra, op. cit., p. 286.
38. Jean Charon, *L'Esprit . . .* , op. cit., p. 217.

cover our Nature, just as the Romantics had felt, who were the authentic keepers of complexity as against the century of great simplification."[40] Morin certainly saw that the universe, which had been deprived of its spirits, geniuses, and agent intellects by an unduly triumphant science erasing all that was generative and productive in her, is now reenergized and vitalized, once again "populated," since no one can any longer seriously conceive of energy in simple atomistic and isolating terms. Everywhere throughout the universe there exists what Morin calls a "Shakespearian dimension"; the world opening up "is more Shakespearian than Newtonian. Epics, tragedies, and buffooneries are played out."[41] Objects give way to systems, while essences and substances give way to organization; complex unities replace simple elemental ones.[42] Morin sees Heraclitus as one of the first to have uncovered the notion of antagonism behind the apparent harmony of spheres, and in an impressive list after Heraclitus: "Nicholas of Cusa, Hegel, Lupasco, Thom, each in his own way." Thus, even thanks to modern science, the notion of a circular or spiral movement made up of dialectic oppositions has been revealed to us: "The suns make the wheel—the planets, the cyclones, the spinning cycles of days, seasons, oxygen and carbon."[43] Hegel, adds Morin, did not see that the great time of "Becoming" (flux) is syncretic, something generally ignored by all the great philosophers of this genre.[44]

The universe now appears to be tripolar: it possesses disorder, organization, order. A fourth term resets in motion these three poles: the interactions (strong, gravitational, electromagnetic), and Morin presents this as the point in the middle of the tripolar triangle.[45] This is why the world is not built on the model of our cybernetic machines; in fact, even if their principle does provide a host of enriching concepts such as retroaction compared to interaction, loop compared to process, regulation compared to stabilization and especially finality compared to causality, it fundamentally lacks a principle of complexity that would allow one to include the idea of disorder and to conceive of the idea of antagonism and conflict as part of the natural order of mechanistic-beings. The vocation of scientific thought now is to bring two opposite ideas

---

39. Ibid., p. 219.
40. Edgar Morin, op. cit., pp. 368, 371, 373.
41. Ibid., pp. 82, 278 ff.
42. Ibid., p. 123.
43. Ibid., p. 225. By and about René Thom, consult *Morphogenèse et imaginaire*, (Paris, Les Lettres Modernes, coll. "Circe," #8–9, 1978).
44. Edgar Morin, op. cit., p. 87.
45. Ibid., pp. 51 and 59.

to think coherently together, to find the *"meta"* point of view relativizing contradiction, to associate antagonistic notions by rendering them complementary. The bond and complex unity have supplanted the alternative.[46]

To this ternary and quaternary unity one can also add a perhaps even more fundamental bipolarity. The *bootstrap* theory already drawn up suggests the existence of two complementary faces of reality, with only one remaining accessible to our investigations. Like Jean Charon, Edgar Morin sees in the image of *Yin* and *Yang* the simultaneous representation of harmonious order and vortex antagonism. However, he notes, the symbol degenerates when antagonism loses itself to the static perfect image of a pure closed circle. Frequent references to the Presocratics are found in the cosmogonies, writes Morin, because they had, through the themes of fire, water, and air, conceived of the vortex turbulence as genesis and *poiesis*. One must first understand that for the philosopher-magis of the Greek Islands, fire, air, and water were not simple elements nor primary principles, but rather the *"dynamic first modes of existence and organization of the Universe."* Modern chemistry would do well then to see not only their composition and state in the elements, but also their mode of organization.[47]

The observations of epistemologist Edgar Morin rely on discoveries made by physicists and biologists. One of them, the microphysicist Niels Bohr, explicitly embraced a Presocratic, traditional idea. In 1927 he expounded his theory of the principle of complementarity in which the corpuscular image and undulating image complement each other, in the same way that the Neoplatonist Iamblichus, sixteen hundred years before him, had postulated the coexistence of two realities—the discontinuous and the continuum. In 1947, while receiving the Danish Order, Bohr chose the *Yin* and the *Yang* for his coat of arms, along with the legend: "Contraria sunt complementa."[48] Symmetry and Dissymmetry were thought of as the result and principle of experimentation, yet also as reference to a tradition, in this case Platonism. The famous microphysicist, Werner Heisenberg, submits the following:[49] "Elemental particles can be compared to the regular bodies found in the *Timaeus* of Plato"; and: *"In the beginning there was symmetry,"* this pronouncement is certainly more accurate than Democritus' proposition: "In the

46. Ibid., p. 251 ff.
47. Ibid.
48. Cf. Gêrald Holton, "The Roots of Complementarity," in *Eranos Jahrbuch 1968*, t. XXXVII, (Zurich, Rhein Verlag, 1970), p. 51 ff.
49. Among other works by this author, cf. namely *Physics and Philosophy* New York, Harper, 1958.

beginning there was the particle."[50] The gnostics of Princeton themselves also attach importance to the fact that particles can only be created and annihilated by pairs, which implies that their 'heres' are paired; molecular biology constantly faces the surprising fact that one molecule 'recognizes' another at some distance away: an unsolvable mystery for those who would like to lean on a 'punctualist' explanation."[51]

There would be a great deal to say about the present status of names in both the biological and microphysical sciences, showing to what extent positivism has been surpassed and replaced by ideas reminiscent of arithmosophy. One could cite numerous authors on this subject but who do not refer directly to any form of gnosis in particular. There is the case of one epistemologist, a polytechnician named Raymond Abellio, who proposed a sixfold structure called the "absolute structure," which is capable of taking into account all phenomena. Retrospectively, we see that Abellio clearly deserves an important place among contemporary neognostics but since his reflection simultaneously departs from both "Tradition" itself and from science, he is not really considered part of those to whom I limit myself during this report; i.e., those who have recourse to gnostic ideas as though by a fluke or by sheer luck and thereby seem able to render their intuition more accessible or to break free from the rut of positivism. Nonetheless, Abellio represents a unique case in the sense that he does adhere to a kind of gnosis that is largely the result of his own meditation and reasoning. If he does lean on a fair number of the aspects of gnostic traditions—I am not saying "neognostic"—it is because he considers them to be much more an ensemble of coded messages whose study would increase our cognition of the universe, than a body of teachings carrying a definitive truth. His work *La Structure Absolue*[52] will probably remain one of the major works on the philosophical reflection of our times, but his other publications are of equally great interest. To recall here two examples dealing with this subject, Abellio noted that the genetic code, a true "dictionary" of sixty-four words or codons organized around the logic of complementarity, corresponds precisely to the sixty-four hexagrams of the *I Ching*, and the four "letters" constituting the basis of this code are combined into two pairs of binary oppositions, like both *Yin* and *Yang*. The *I Ching* thus appears as a "complete model."[53] It is also true that when nuclear physicists want to bring

---

50. Ibid., already quoted in my report "Philosophie de la Nature et Naturalisme scientiste" in *Cahiers de l'U.S.J.J.*; 1974 seminary, #1, (Paris, A. Bonne, 1975).

51. Raymond Ruyer, op. cit., p. 65.

52. Raymond Abellio, *La Structure absolue. Essai de phénoménologie génétique*, (Paris, Gallimard, coll. "Bibliothèque des Idées," 1965).

53. Raymond Abellio, *La Fin de l'ésotérisme*, (Paris, Flammarion, 1973), p. 127.

some order to the profusion of particles, they are led to visualize senary constructions or *quarks* for which the elements of symmetry and dissymmetry are combined in exactly the same way as in the absolute structure Abellio has discovered.[54]

While Abellio recognizes that "Tradition" can teach us a great deal, Stéphane Lupasco seems not to have consulted it at all. However, the Lupascian critique of formal Aristotelianism and Hegelianism recalled the steps of alchemical dialectics and Presocratic intuitions so much so that, throughout his later years, Lupasco became more and more interested in the ancient models of thought which, he discovered, so closely resembled his own. His open-mindedness and his flexibility of expression helped steer him away from any kind of dogmatism. Like Abellio, though in a somewhat different sense, Lupasco posed the idea of a double crossed contradiction: the addition of the antagonistic coupling of potentialization–actualization to the bipolar pair of homogenization–heterogenization. A good balance of the four terms engenders creative harmony. Lupasco's way of thinking challenges the totalitarianism of the logic of identity and tries to locate negentropic tendencies at play in Nature. It refuses even to consider that contradiction and conflict, mainly on a psychological level, could constitute the morbid.[55]

Gnosis, Neo-Gnoses and Science

Psychoanalysis, especially the Jungian type of analytical psychology or André Virel's genetic psychology,[56] could also be considered as a kind of neognosis, by reason of its frequent and explicit references to some gnostic traditions. But we have had to limit ourselves here to discussion of the already enormous field of physical sciences. Perhaps it has been enough to show how men of science are inclined to collect some fragments from unjustly hidden, traditional teachings. Modern science is not then entirely the pure quantitativism that René Guénon saw;[57] it sets the tone by seeking unprecedented paths and a

---

54. Ibid., p. 128.
55. Among the numerous other works by Lupasco, we quote *Du rêve, de la mathématique et de la mort*, (Paris, Christian Bourgois, 1971).
56. In his book *Histoire de notre image*, (Geneva, Mont-Blanc Ed., 1965, coll. "Action et Pensée"), one of the most interesting ever produced by contemporary psychology, Virel proposes a reading on mythology and alchemy which usefully completes that of Jung. The adjective "genetic" could have been listed somehow in the subtitle, as in the subtitle of Abellio's work (cf. note 52), since it also deals with genetics, even though in a different sense. The restrictive limits of the present report do not allow me to specify to what extent emphasis on morphogenesis, in its broad sense, means a positive return to unjustly forgotten traditions.
57. Cf. René Guénon, *La Régne de la quantité et les signes des temps*, (Paris, Gallimard, coll. "Idées," 1970. First edition, 1945).

new epistemology. The reaction against scientism, just as characteristic among many scholars who are not "neognostics," represents one of the significant trends of the twentieth century; Pascal's maxim seems more relevant than ever: "A little bit of science distances one from God, a lot brings one back." In the same way, Edgar Morin finishes his book by making a plea for "a science that takes in the possibilities of self-knowledge, is open to cosmic solidarity, does not disintegrate the face of beings and existing beings, and recognizes the mystery that is in everything."[58]

Nevertheless, epistemology is not in itself enough to create a philosophy, much less a gnosis. One must beware of three dangers. The first one is to read into these authors, with the exception of Abellio and Lupasco, something other than good reasons to be wary of totalitarian positivist science and the chance rediscovery of traditional images. The second one is to pass unjustly from a metaphysics born of a new epistemology to a "gnosis" born of the result of experiments carried out by the mere "eyes of the flesh." Gnosis resulting from the "eyes of fire" is neither metaphysics nor a diffusible science. Knowledge is not cognition. Science moves toward multiplicity; gnosis always leads to unity, even if this unity proves to be complex. One should avoid mixing chemistry and alchemy, astronomy and astrology, and talking about a hyperchemistry or even a scientific astrology.

The third pitfall is just as dangerous, since it is presented under a fascinating guise. While reading Ruyer's book, one is struck by the playful aspect of the "exercises" of the gnostics of Princeton. "There is an experimental side to New Gnosis. The neognostics have existence before them like the players of Eleusis, and the rule is to discover the rules of the game."[59] Hence their taste in science-fiction also: Fred Hoyle, recognized as a scholar and author of science-fiction, is given a prominent place in the bibliography of Ruyer's work. It seems to me that Hermann Hesse already described these games and players in his novel *Das Glasperlenspiel*,[60] where the game, which is itself free and sophisticated, is reduced to an ensemble of formal exercises while representing, in the eyes of the characters, the highest possible intellectual and spiritual activity. If gnosis does not ignore the aspect of play, its game is *lusus serius*, a serious game, like that of *Sophia* playing with divinity at the dawn of creation.

The sophianic game: this is what the insight of the flame (the "eyes of fire") allows one to shed light on. One finds such insight where cognition merges with knowledge, procuring a religious type of revelation, expressed

---

58. Edgar Morin, op. cit., p. 387.
59. Raymond Ruyer, op. cit., p. 223.
60. First Edition of *Das Glasperlenspiel*, (Zurich, Fretz and Wasmuth, 1943).

first in the form of the storyline of a "foundational Myth." There is no genuine gnosis without prior adherence to an "account of origins" unfolded through symbols, endlessly penetrated by a spiritual hermeneutics, which, thanks to the "eyes of fire," "searches everything, even the depths of God."[61] Now, these accounts, hierogonies, do not fall under the rubric of scientific process. The taste for dialogue today readily prompts us to abandon all specificity of that which actually constitutes the object of our specific traditions. It would be childish to forget that a good number of neognostics empty the myths of all their specificity: "What is fascinating [!] about this gnosis [of Princeton]," writes Ruyer, "is that it never loses itself freely in the myth."[62] Later he writes, in a passage significantly entitled *La Vision sans yeux et l'aveugle absolu*: "New Gnosis is not mythology. The gnostics simultaneously welcome the myth and vigorously reduce it."[63] Notwithstanding, the relationship of these seekers to symbolism and rites seems rather ambiguous: "A bond between gnostics and Freemasons certainly does exist, although it is difficult to define since diverse branches of Freemasonry in the United States are very multifaceted. There are reciprocal borrowings; but the gnostics are hostile to symbolism."[64]

As a matter of fact, every complete myth can only express itself through a symbolic scenario, that is to say it is polysemous and not simply allegorical. When Edgar Morin sees this world offering itself to us as: "more Shakespearian than Newtonian" and "playing tragedy and buffonery,"[65] he is not discovering its scenario, simply because only the "founding" myth can furnish the key; insight of the flame is not without this gnosis—nor this gnosis without insight of the flame. In the Old Testament one has the account of Genesis and of the vision of Ezekiel. In order to shed light on the world and on Man, the gnostic eye must first be illuminated by a revelation of this sort, which alone allows it to see; then the illusion of history will disappear and the visible and invisible universe be revealed in their light, the subtle bodies will reveal their transparency and insight of the flesh be seen in its own order. It can be understood, then, why the supporters of the "new gnosis," in a broad sense, necessarily separate themselves, *volens nolens*, from traditional gnosis. The neutralizing of the myth out of the range of their knowledge and discourse engenders three consequences which, although they are perhaps inescapable, render this knowledge incompatible with gnosis. It has to do

61. 1 Cor. 2:10.
62. Raymond Ruyer, op. cit., p. 60.
63. Ibid., p. 75.
64. Ibid., p. 215.

with pantheism, which they generally profess, with the absence of reference to the original Fall, and with the negation of any form of anthropocentrism.

Pantheism, or Spinozism to be more precise, asserts itself unambiguously in the Princeton Gnosis: "God or *Unitas* is not a Being or an Individual who contemplates the universe from the outside. It is a Unity of domain, a Unity of this total Surface-object." Indeed: "that the Universe be *gnostic* in an etymological sense, that is to say consciousness searching light, is really obvious. Gnostics do clarify just that."[66] Raymond Ruyer, after the new gnostics, takes to task precisely the prince of Christian theosophy, Jacob Boehme; Ruyer speaks to us of the "huge error of Jacob Boehme who . . . imagines the *unitas* like an eye which is watching, sees itself and creates vision. For [Boehme] the divine Absolute wants to know itself. . . . Since there is nothing beyond the Absolute, it must divide itself into eye and mirror, so as to be able to look at itself. . . . There are less naive philosophers who say just about the same thing. . . . Their 'Subject' . . . is always the eye of Jacob Boehme."[67]

The absence of reference to an original catastrophe by which the universe actually started or to a "Fall" responsible for the present state of Man was already notable in the work of Teilhard de Chardin,[68] a thinker whom nevertheless one still called a "Christian." Sign of the times. . . . Without exception, the same absence seems to characterize all the neognostics. One would find it very difficult to come up with any text of Christian gnosis in which this original element did not serve as a fundamental and permanent reference.

Finally one notes that they have a strong tendency[69] to reduce Man to the role of Man accessory element of the universe, indeed, an absolutely insignificant one. "*Alles bezieht sich auf den Menschen*," said Oetinger, strikingly summing up the thought of his predecessors, especially that of Jacob Boehme. At the same time, while the eighteenth century was announcing a new Philosophy of Nature, Saint-Martin was reminding us that it is necessary to explain things with reference to Man and not with reference to things. Certainly for Princeton gnosis the appearance of the mind in space and time does not prove that matter is primary and essential but that there is a "Beyond" beyond space and time;[70] an almost spiritualist thesis that nonethe-

---

65. Edgar Morin, op. cit., p. 82.
66. Raymond Ruyer, op. cit., p. 293.
67. Ibid., p. 71.
68. One is aware that original sin is skipped in the work of Teilhard. When I enquired about this during a seminar on the illustrious Jesuit, the commentator Claude Cuenot answered: "Teilhard was not very interested in that, but rather in other, more important questions."
69. Here, on the other hand, Teilhard does not share this tendency.
70. Ibid., p. 297.

less concludes: "New Gnosis, far from being a new type of humanism, is more of a new theocentrism."[71] And again: "Man must keep his humble, momentarily correct place of simian in the world."[72] In the same way for Jean Charon: "My thought is that of my thinking electrons. There is more than analogy here, there is identity. There are not two types of thinking beings in the universe; there are the aeons (i.e., electrons), and that's all."[73]

Neognosis only resembles traditional gnosis in that it borrows from it what is the most external. If one wants to compare them with each other one finds no common point at which their specificities merge, since neognosis can only describe actions, whereas gnosis accounts for the acts themselves. That is why I accept the somewhat severe judgment imposed by Etienne Perrot: "The new Gnosis of the end of the twentieth century can only rejoin the victorious scientism of the nineteenth century one day at the museum of thought, scientism that had prided itself on having extinguished certain stars, stars that would never light the sky again."[74] Such a judgment is aimed only at some of the authors quoted in this report, certainly not at others; it essentially concerns Jean Charon and the gnostics of Princeton.

Once we recognize the futility of trying to unite the irreconcilable at all costs by looking for an average, artificial term or common denominator that is purely formal and heavily laden with misunderstandings, it would seem permissible to look at the world that is described by experimental science today, by reading it in the light of a revealed tradition. This dangerous, but profitable process was attempted by most "philosophers of Nature," in the sense given to the word here. Although the distance separating the two banks seems long, one can at least visualize the construction of a bridge, allowing one to move from one side to another. The bridges separate as much as they link together. A new *Naturphilosophie* could constitute an intermediate link of this kind; it could maintain the role of ontological cosmology, long time awaited in vain. A true theology would complete this *Naturphilosophie*, by one subsisting partially on the other; but it would be a theology capable of assimilating all the riches of the world, of making itself metaphilosophical and metagnostic at the same time, and whose organization would be analogous to what medieval Christian theology conceived in the twelfth century. Such a *Natur-*

---

71. Ibid., p. 297.
72. Ibid., p. 14.
73. Jean Charon, *L'Esprit* . . . , op. cit., p. 195.
74. Etienne Perrot, preface to the work of Marie-Louise von Franz. *Nombre et Temps, Psychologie des profondeurs et physique moderne.* Preface and translation by Etienne Perrot, (Paris, La Fontaine de Pierre, 1978) (*Zahl und Zeit*, Stuttgart, E. Klett, 1970).

philosophie would make an effort to compose a new cosmology—a new way to consider the order of the world—placed under the double and complementary sign of anthropology and comprehension of reality.[75] This comprehension would be of a multiple reality, and far from limiting itself to a project of insipid and abridged rationality, would associate the flesh with the flame, as in the verse of Péguy:

> And the supernatural is itself of the flesh
> Both the tree of Grace and the tree of Nature
> are entwined like two heavy lianas
> Over the pillar and profane temples.
> They have articulated their double binding.[76]

Ixion, according to the Greek myth, chased Hera, queen of the heavens, thus of Nature, to violate and force her. But Hera escaped. Zeus, incensed by Ixion's attitude, trapped him by putting in Hera's place a hazy, illusory mist whom he called Nephele. Ixion chased her and raped her, mistaking her for Hera. He soon was bound to a rolling wheel of unquenchable fire which moved incessantly through space, infinitely devouring its victim. Alongside this image, in contrast to it, let us evoke the dynamic harmony, the "founding" act upon which the Genesis opens: Joseph Haydn understood the *Creation* of the world; his music did not fly forth from the fire of Ixion's wheel, but from the flash of primordial light which inflamed the world so as to embrace it with love.[77]

---

75. One can read an interesting article on this subject by Dominique Dubarle, "Epistémologie et Cosmologie," in *Idée de Monde et Philosophie de la Nature*, (Paris, Desclée, 1966), pp. 124, 126. Under a different perspective, cf. also Stanislas Breton, "Monde et Nature," in ibid., pp. 71-92. Among the most illuminating works published since the present article was written, see primarily the fine book by a microphysicist who is a reader of Jacob Boehme: Basarab Nicolescu, *Science. Meaning and Evolution (The Cosmology of Jacob Boehme)*, New York, Parabola Books, 1991. B. Nicolescu is also the author of *Nous, la particule et le Monde*, Paris, Le Mail, 1995.

76.   Et le surnaturel est lui-même charnel
        Et l'arbre de la Grâce et l'arbre de Nature
        Se sont étreints tous deux comme deux lourdes lianes
        Par-dessus les piliers et les temples profanes.
        Ils ont articulé leur double ligature.

77. The presentation of this paper was followed by the audition of *Und Gott schuf das Licht* (a passage of Josef Haynd's *Creation*).

A BIBLIOGRAPHICAL GUIDE
TO RESEARCH

INTRODUCTION

This bibliography presumes to serve only as a guide for research. It is limited chiefly to some of the most serious historical and critical works, the most up-to-date or representative of research on Western esotericism in general or on some of its currents and aspects in particular. In order not to overstep the limits of this volume, I have had to omit the works of the esotericists themselves, even of the most important, and I have limited myself to recent, solid studies devoted to certain authors and currents of thought. Among these I was able to include only books, leaving aside many interesting articles from journals and collective works. (Nevertheless a journals and serials section is included.) It seemed to me that some recent editions or reprints of works by great authors—when provided with scholarly notes and commentary and recent enlightening prefaces—must also figure here (hence Jacob Boehme's *Epîtres théosophiques*, Oetinger's *Lehrtafel*, Saint-Martin's *Oeuvres Majeures*, or Baader's *Sämtliche Werke*).

I also had to give up the idea of a list by theme: in such a limited panorama this would have been too arbitrary. There is therefore no rubric for astrology, otherwise it would have been necessary to make room for the many other mancies. However, astrology is obviously present here, as is, for example, the Tarot. I used thematic classification only within one historical rubric, the teeming seventeenth century. I retained three thematic rubrics, alchemy, esoteric freemasonry, and the Tradition, because of their historical connotations. Furthermore, I indicated publications among the journals and serials in which excellent thematic orientations are to be found. Finally, I included titles of library and exhibit catalogues, as such works are valuable research tools when they are accompanied by enlightening commentary and scholarly notes.

The distinction between "General works" and "Tradition" may appear artificial, but I am committed to a designated space to the treatment of the notion of "Tradition" in our period. Those who work on its history often have a "traditionalist" stance of their own, whether they deal with what I have called in Book I the first, the second, or the third way. But I have cited them above all as historians of esoteric ideas or of the Tradition, and less as traditionalists. It is often just such authors, after all, who help us to understand how the Orient is now part of esoteric imagination in the West. Furthermore, I have regrouped under a single rubric the period from the end of the nineteenth century to the present. This may also appear arbitrary, given the diversity of currents, but supplementary subdivisions would have weighed down the already ramified schema of this bibliography, and, in a bibliography as general as this, it seemed fastidious to make distinctions between new religious movements, new magical movements, initiatory societies, etc.

In the fourth section ("From the second to the fifteenth century"), the small number of references to Gnosticism and the absence of Catharism should not be surprising. This restrictive presentation is a result of the proposed definition of Western esotericism as a form of thought that is even more strongly nondualistic than nonmonistic, and for which the notion of "dualitude" is rather more constitutive (see the introductory chapter in this book). But comparative esotericism must obviously take into consideration these two currents, which are, on the one hand, dualistic Gnosticism, and on the other, Catharism. Nor can it ignore many works of philosophy, anthropology, and history, such as those of Mircea Eliade. It would also certainly have to reserve a specific place for the works of Carl Gustav Jung and his disciples, thanks to which an important strain of esotericism was restored in an interesting manner, with a view to a better understanding of the psyche. Having limited myself to a critical bibliography, I would gladly have cited solid overall studies on the relation between this branch of the humanities and esotericism. Now, I know of no such study; but readers may find the possibility of documenting this question from certain books, journals, or serials cited here. This question is, after all, closely tied to the question of the links that are being established today between esotericism and science, links which throw into relief a *Naturphilosophie*, in the sense that German Romanticism gave to this term. It seems that, as yet, no historical and critical work devoted to this aspect of twentieth century thought exists. Bearing in mind these lacunae, or these gaps, the panoramic table used for the bibliography follows:

General works
Alchemy
Esoteric Freemasonry
From the second (*Corpus Hermeticum*) to the fifteenth century
Renaissance and the seventeenth century:
    A) Varia
    B) The reception of Alexandrian Hermetism
    C) Christian Kabbalah
    D) Paraclesism and Philosophy of Nature
    E) Rosicrucianism
    F) Theosophy
Eighteenth century
Romanticism and *Naturphilosophie*
Late nineteenth century and the twentieth century
Concerning "Tradition"
Esotericism and Islam
Esotericism, Literature, and Art
Journals and serials
A word about libraries

GENERAL WORKS

Alchemy and the Occult. A Catalogue of Books and Manuscripts from the Collection of Paul and Mary Mellon given to Yale University Library. Vol. I–II: *Printed Books 1472–1623*, compiled by Ian MacPhail with Essays by R.P. Multhauf and Aniela Jaffé and additional Notes by William McGuire (vol. I, 276 pp; vol. II, 581 pp.). New Haven: Yale University Library, 1968. Vol. III–IV: *Manuscripts 1225–1671*, compiled by Laurence C. Witten and Richard Pachella with an Introduction by Pearl Kibre and additional Notes by William McGuire (vol. III, 402 pp.; vol. IV, 853 pp.). New Haven: Yale University Library, 1977. Illustrated. A most useful tool for research.

Alchemy: A Comprehensive Bibliography of the Manly P. Hall Collection of Books and Manuscripts, Including Related Material on Rosicrucianism and the Writings of Jacob Boehme. Ed Ron Charles Hogart. Los Angeles: The Philosophical Research Society, 1986, 314 pp., illustrated.

Amadou, Robert. *L'Occultisme: Esquisse d'un monde vivant*. Paris: Julliard, 1950, 254 pp. New expanded edition: Paris: Chanteloup, 1987. A Small work that has become a classic. The title leads to confusion since the author means by "occultism" what we understand as "esotericism."

Astrology, Science and Society: Historical Essays. Ed. Eddy Patrick Curry. Woodbridge: Suffolk (England): The Boydell Press, 1987, 302 pp. Proceedings of the Warburg Institute colloquium (March, 1984), of which twelve participants are represented here. An important text, not only in relation to astrology.

Benoist, Luc. *L'ésotérisme*. Que sais-je? series. Paris: Presses Universitaires de France, 1963, 126 pp.

Bibliotheca Magica dalle opere a stampa della Biblioteca Casanatense di Roma (secs. xv–xvii). Florence: Leo S. Olschki, 1985, introduced by Mino Gabriele, 225 pp., illustrated.

Biedermann, Hans. *Lexikon der magischen Künste (Die Welt der Magie seit der Spätantike)*. Graz (Austria): Akad. Druck- und Verlagsanstalt, 1986 (see new ed., Munich: W. Heyne, 1991. Very precise and useful.

Bonardel, Françoise. *L'Hermétisme*. Que sais-je? series. Paris: PUF, 1985, 127 p. A good, short introductory text to Western esotericism.

Chevalier, Jean. *Dictionnaire des symboles: Mythes, rêves, coutumes, gestes, formes, figures, couleurs, nombres.* 4 vols. Paris: Seghers, 1973. Vol. 1, 371 pp.; vol. 2, 397 pp.; vol. 3, 391 pp.; vol. 4, 424 pp. (first edition, 1969) Useful, with an excellent bibliography.

Corsetti, Jean-Paul. *Histoire de l'Ésotérisme et des Sciences Occultes.* Paris: Larousse, 1992, 343 pp., illustrated. An excellent synthesis, from the origins to the nineteenth century.

(Le) Défi magique. Edited by Massimo Introvigne and Jean-Baptiste Martin. Lyons: Presses Universitaires de Lyon, 1994. Vol. I: *Esotérisme, Occultisme, Spiritisme,* 337 pp. Vol. II: *Satanisme, Sorcellerie,* 364 pp. Proceedings of the colloquium held at the Bibliothèque Municipale of Lyons (6–8, April 1992). Many interesting contributions on the history of esotericism, mostly of the 19., and 20. centuries.

Dictionnaire des Sociétés Secrètes en Occident. Published under the direction of Pierre Mariel. Paris: Culture, Arts, Loisira, 1971, 479 pp., illustrated. Includes some of the worst, but also some of the best material. Clear and practical.

Dictionnaire Encyclopédique de l'ésotérisme. Paris: PUF. Forthcoming, 1996.

Eliade, Mircea. *Occultism, Witchcraft and Cultural Fashions.* The University of Chicago Press, 1976, 148 pp.

Epochen der Naturmystik: Hermetische Tradition im wissenschaftlichen Fortschritt (Mystical Approaches to Nature; Grands Moments de la Mystique de la Nature). Ed. Antoine Faivre and Rolf Christian Zimmermann. Berlin: Erich Schmidt, 1979, 459 pp. A collective work. From Ficino and Agrippa to Schelling, also looking at Paracelsus, J. B. Van Helmont, Swedenborg, Oetinger, Martines de Pasqually, Saint-Martin, Goethe, Blake, Newton, and Baader.

500 Years of Gnosis in Europe: Exhibit of Printed Books and Manuscripts from the Gnostic Tradition. Moscow and St. Petersburg. Organized by the Bibliotheca Philosophica Hermetica (Amsterdam) and the M. I. Rudomino Russian State Library for Foreign Literature. Amsterdam: In de Pelikaan (Bibliotheca Philosophica Hermetica), 1993, 312 pp. This catalogue, edited by Carlos Gilly and Franz A. Janssen and introduced by Joseph R. Ritman, is bilingual (English and Russian). Both illustrations and texts constitute an excellent mass of information.

Frick, Karl R. H. *Die Erleuchteten. Licht und Finsternis: Gnostisch-theosophische und freimaurerisch-okkulte Geheimgesellschaften bis an die Wende zum 20. Jahrhundert.* 2 vols. Graz (Austria): Akad. Druck- und Verlagsanstalt: Vol. 1, *Ursprünge und Anfänge.* 1975, 345 pp., illustrated; Vol. 2,

Geschichte ihrer Lehren, Rituale und Organisationen. 1978. 582 pp., illustrated. Also, from the same author at the same publisher: *Die Erleuchteten: Gnostisch-theosophische und alchemistisch-rosenkreuzerische Geheimgesellschaften bis zum Ende des 18. Jahrhunderts. Ein Beitrag zur Geistesgeschichte der Neuzeit.* 1973, 635 pp., illustrated. Historical syntheses concerning the initiatic orders, with an effort at philosophical clarification and a great selection of texts and documents. An invaluable research tool.

Gnosis und Mystik in der Geschichte der Philosophie. Ed. Peter Koslowski. Zurich/Munich: Artemis, 1988, 408 pp. This collective work contains articles on Paracelsus, J. Boehme, H. More, F. Baader, R. Steiner, etc.

Hermes Trismegistus, Pater Philosophorum. Tekstgeschiedenis van het "Corpus Hermeticum" (catalogue from the exhibit organized by the Bibliotheca Philosophica Hermetica in Amsterdam, in 1990). By F. van Lamoen. Amsterdam: B. P. H., 1990, 151 pp. An excellent bibliography on the reception of the *Corpus Hermeticum* in modern times.

(De) Hermetische Gnosis in de loop der eeuwen (Beschouwingen over de invloed van een Egyptische religie op de cultuur van het Westen). Ed. by Gilles Quispel. Baarn (Netherlands): Tirion, 1992, 672 pp. Illustrated. Collective work with articles by J.-P. Mahé, C. Gilly, J. Ritman, etc.

Hidden Truths. Magic, Alchemy and the Occult. Ed. Lawrence E. Sullivan. New York: MacMillan Publishing Company, 1989, 281 pp. A reprinting of articles by Ioan P. Culianu, Allison Coudert, Mircea Eliade, Antoine Faivre, Nathan Sivin, etc., from *The Encyclopedia of Religion*, ed. Mircea Eliade, MacMillan, 1987.

Lubac, Henri de. *La postérité spirituelle de Joachim de Flore.* 2 vols. Le Sycomore series. Paris: Lethielleux. Vol. 1, *De Joachim à Schelling*, 1979, 414 pp.; vol. 2, *De Saint-Simon à nos jours*, 1981, 508 pp. This book is not presented as a work on esotericism, but several chapters deal directly with the subject. A beautiful synthesis showing the relationships among different currents of thought.

Merkur, Dan. *Gnosis. An Esoteric Tradition of Mystical Visions and Unions.* Albany: SUNY Press, 1993, 387 pp. A brilliant exposé of Gnostic visionary techniques from Hellenistic and Jewish Mysticism, through the Islam to medieval neoplatonism and Renaissance alchemy.

Microcosme et Macrocosme. Université de Tours: Bulletin de la Société ligérienne de philosophie. Number 2 1975, 108 pp. By R. Thom, G. Durand, M. de Gandillac, J. L. Vieillard Baron, J. F. Marquet, P. Demange, H. Corbin.

Miers, Horst E. *Lexikon des Geheimwissens.* Freiburg i. Br.: Goldmann Verlag (6th ed., 1986). Can be used to complement Biedermann's *Lexicon* (cf. *supra*), but is not always reliable.

Modern Esoteric Spirituality. Eds. Antoine Faivre and Jacob Needleman. New York: The Crossroad Publishing Company, 1992; vol. 21 of World Spirituality: An Encyclopedic History of the Religious Quest. 413 pp., illustrated. A presentation by several authors of most of the Western esoteric strains of modern times.

Peuckert, Will-Erich. *Gabalia: Ein Versuch zur Geschichte der Magia naturalis im 16. bis 18. Jahrhundert.* Berlin: E. Schmidt, 1967, 578 pp. Somewhat disorganized, but a great wealth of information here.

Riffard, Pierre. *L'Occultisme: Textes et recherches.* Idéologies et Sociétés series. Paris: Librairie Larousse, 1981, 191 pp., illustrated. Interesting and unpretentious, tasetful populariazation.

———. *Dictionnaire de l'ésotérisme.* Paris: Payot, 1983, 387 pp., illustrated. An attempt at classification, with copious references.

———. *L'ésotérisme: Qu'est-ce que l'ésotérisme? Anthologie de l'ésotérisme occidental.* Bouquins series. Paris: R. Laffont, 1990, 106 pp. An interesting introduction to this discipline, with a judicious selection of texts.

Serant, Paul. *Au seuil de l'ésotérisme: Précédé de "L'esprit moderne de la tradition," par Raymond Abellio.* Correspondences series. Paris: Grasset, 1955, 255 pp. A stimulating account by an author, inspired by Guénon. The preface is one of R. Abellio's major texts.

Sladek, Mirko. *Fragmente der hermetischen Philosophie in der Naturphilosophie der Neuzeit.* Berne: P. Lang, European University Publications, 1984, 208 pp. Philosophy of the *Corpus Hermeticum* and the forms it has taken in Giordano Bruno, Henry Moore, Thomas Vaughan, and Goethe.

Thorndike, Lynn. *A History of Magic and the Experimental Science.* 8 vols. New York: Columbia University Press, 1984. (First edition, 1923–1958). Vol. 1, 835 pp.; vol. 2, 1036 pp.; vol. 3, 827 pp.; vol. 4, 767 pp.; vol. 5, 695 pp.; vol. 6, 766 pp.; vol. 7, 695 pp.; vol. 8, 808 pp. Covers the whole period from the first to the seventeenth centuries: magic, astrology, alchemy, philosophies of nature, etc. The stress is on the "occult sciences" rather than on theosophy or philosophy. Indispensable, considering the breadth and quality of information.

Tomberg, Valentin. *Meditations on the Tarot.* Warwick, New York: Amity House, 1987, 658 pp. (German edition, 1973; French edition, 1980. The book was written in French.) This is not a treatise on the Tarot. The Greater Arcanes serve as a pretext for meditations on Western theosophy and its traditions. A great book. Appeared without author's name; cf. my analysis in *La Tourbe de philosophes*. Paris: La Table d'Emeraude, 1981, numbers 14, 15–16, 17.

Tuveson, Ernest Lee. *The Avatars of Thrice Great Hermes: An Approach to Romanticism*. London and Toronto: Associated Univ. Press, 1982, 264 pp. Philosophy of the *Corpus Hermeticum* and the forms it took during the Romantic era in the Anglo-Saxon context.

Weeks, Andrew. *German Mysticism from Hildegard of Bingen to Ludwig Wittgenstein (A Literary and Intellectual History)*. Albany: SUNY Press, 1993, 283 pp. This book provides useful insights into mysticism and theosophy in Germany and shows how both interact.

Wehr, Gerhard. *Esoterisches Christentum (Aspekte, Impulse, Konsequenzen)*. Stuttgart: E. Klett, "Edition Alpha," 1975, 314 pp. As the title suggests, this is not a history. The emphasis is on spirituality. Some fine treatments on the Middle Ages. The modern period is scarcely touched upon (except for the twentieth century).

―――. "Fermenta Cognitionis." A series. Freiburg im Breisgau: Aurum. Eleven small volumes appearing from 1978–1980, of about 100 pp. each, all edited by G. Wehr. Invaluable short introductory texts to the works of the great authors. The series includes: *Saint-Martin; Valentin Weigel der Pansoph und esoterische Christ; Paracelsus; Meister Eckhart; Jacob Boehme der Geisteslehrer und Seelenführer; F. C. Oetinger; R. Steiner als christlicher Esoteriker; Der anthroposophische Erkenntnisweg; Novalis, das Mysterium "Christus und Sophie"; Christian Rosenkreutz Inspirator neuzeitlicher Esoterik; Franz von Baader*.

ALCHEMY

Alchemy and the Occult . . . Cf. *supra*, General Works.

Alchemy: A Comprehensive Bibliography . . . Cf. *supra*, General Works.

Die Alchemie in der europäischen Kultur und Wissenschaftsgeschichte. Ed. Christoph Meinel, Proceedings of the Colloquium at the Herzog August Bibliothek in Wolfenbüttel (2–5 April, 1984). Wiesbaden: Harrassowitz (Wolfenbütteler Forschungen, 32), 356 pp. illustrated. A grouping of seventeen contributions, all of the first rank. An indispensable work.

Alchemy Revisited. Ed. Z. R. W. M. von Martels. Proceedings of the Colloquium at the University of Groningen (17–19 April, 1989). Leiden/New York: E. J. Brill (Collection des travaux de l'Académie Internationale de l'Histoire des Sciences, 33), 1990, 284 pp., illustrated. Same remark as above, thirty-one contributions.

Alchimie. Cahiers de l'Hermétisme series. Paris: Albin Michel, 1978, 221 pp., illustrated. Texts by A. Savoret, B. Husson, K. von Eckartshausen, A. Faivre, et al. Contains a bibliography of French language alchemical literature since 1945, by J. J. Mathé and A. Faivre.

Alchimie et Philosophie à la Renaissance. Eds. Jean Margolin and Sylvain Matton. Proceedings of the Colloquium of Tours (4–7 December, 1991). Paris: Vrin, 1993, 478 pp. Thirty-five contributions.

Alleau, René. *Aspects de l'alchimie traditionnelle.* Paris: Editions de Minuit, 1970, 238 pp. (first edition, 1953). Principles and symbols, followed by texts and documents.

Birkham, Helmut. *Die alchemistische Lehrdichtung des Gratheus filius philosophi in Cod. Vind. 2372. Zugleich ein Beitrag zur okkulten Wissenschaft im Spätmittelalter.* Vienna: Oesterreichische Akademie der Wissenschaften, 1992. Vol. 1, text edition, translation, index, 347 pp., illustrated; vol. 2, introduction, commentaries, 494 pp. This is a presentation of the medieval text of Zadith ben Hamuel. The introduction and commentaries in Vol. 2 concerning the history of alchemy are particularly interesting.

Bonardel, Françoise. *Philosophie de l'Alchimie: Grand Oeuvre et Modernité.* Cf. *infra*, Concerning Tradition.

Buntz, Herwig. *Deutsche Alchemistische Traktate des XV. und XVI. Jahrhunderts.* Phil. Diss. München, 1969, 228 pp., illustrated. A good general introduction, practical bibliography, and two studies: on Arnauld de Villeneuve and on Lambspringk.

Burckhardt, Titus. *Alchemie: Sinn und Weltbild.* Olten and Freiburgti. Br: Walter Verlag, 1960, 228 pp., illustrated. French version: *Alchimie. Sa signification et son image du monde.* Basel: Thoth, Stiftung L. Keimer, 1974, 231 pp., illustrated. English version: *Alchemy, Science of the Cosmos, Science of the Soul.* London: Stuart and Watkins, 1967, 206 pp. Baltimore: Penguin Books, 1971. One of the most interesting philosophical approaches.

Coudert, Allison. *Alchemy: The Philosopher's Stone.* London: Wildwood House, 1980, 239 pp., illustrated.

Crisciani, Chiara. Cf. *infra*, Gagnon, Claude: *Alchimie et Philosophie au Moyen Age.*

Dobbs, Betty J.T. *The Foundations of Newton's Alchemy or, the Hunting of the Greene Lyon.* Cambridge: Cambridge University Press, 1975, 300 pp.

————. *The Janus Faces of Genius. The Role of Alchemy in Newton's Thought.* Cambridge: Cambridge University Press, 1991, 359 pp.

Duval, Paulette. Cf. *infra*, From the second to the fifteenth century.

Duveen, D. I. *Bibliotheca Alchemica et Chemica: An Annotated Catalogue of Printed Books on Alchemy, Chemistry and Cognate Subjects in the Library of Denis I. Duveen.* London: E. Weil, 1949, 699 pp., illustrated. New edition, Utrecht: H. E. S. Publishers, 1986.

Eliade, Mircea. *Forgerons et alchimistes.* Paris: Flammarion, 1977, 188 pp. (first edition, 1956). English version: *The Forge and the Crucible.* London: Rider, 1962, 208 pp. One of the first truly reflective philosophical works on alchemy by an academic.

Evola, Julius. *La Tradizione Ermetica.* 1931. French version: *La Tradition hermétique (Les Symboles et la doctrine—L'Art royal hermétique).* Paris: Éditions traditionnelles, 1968, 244 pp. A classic much read and consulted; but the author has a rather personal conception of alchemy.

Faivre, Antoine. *The Golden Fleece and Alchemy.* New York: SUNY Press, 1993, 140 pp. Original French edition: Mailan/Paris: Arché, 1990.

Ferguson, John. *Bibliotheca Chemica. A Bibliography of books on Alchemy, Chemistry, and Pharmaceutics.* 2 vols. London: Academic and Bibliographic Publications, 1954, 487 pp. and 798 pp. Facsimile, London: Starker Brothers, s. d. (first edition, 1906). An indispensable research tool.

Gagnon, Claude and Crisciana, Chiara. *Alchimie et philosophie au Moyen Age: Perspectives et problèmes.* Montreal: Éditions L'Aurore Univers, 1980, 83 pp. a remarkable work; indispensable.

Gagnon, Claude. *Analyse archéologique du "Livre des figures hiéroglyphiques" attribué à Nicolas Flamel (1330–1418),* S. l. Philosophy dissertation. Université de Montréal (typescript, 1975), 381 pp.

————. *Description du "Livre des Figures Hiéroglyphiques" attribué à Nicolas Flamel, suivie d'une réimpression de l'édition originale et d'une reproduction des sept talismans du "Livre d'Abraham," auxquels on a joint le "Testament" authentique dudit Flamel.* Montreal: L'Aurore, 1977, 193 pp., illustrated. Completes the research and the results of the preceding work. The best text on this complex historical question.

Ganzenmueller, Wilhelm *L'Alchimie au Moyen Age.* Verviers: Éditions Marabout, 1974, 187 pp. Revision and notes by R. Delhez. First edition: *Die Alchemie im Mittelalter.* Paderborn: Bonifacius, 1938; reprinted 1967 (Hildesheim: Olms, 240 pp.).

Haeffner, Mark. *The Dictionary of Alchemy (From Maria Prophetissa to Isaac Newton)*. London: Aquarian Press, 1991, 272 pp.

Halleux, Robert. *Les Textes alchimiques*. Typologie des sources du Moyen Âge occidental series, 32. Turnhout (Belgium): Brepols, 1979, 153 pp. One of the best historical introductions and bibliographic orientations.

Holymard, E. J. *Alchemy*. Harmondsworth: Penguin Books, 1957, 288 pp. New edition, 1968. A clear, richly illustrated exposé.

Hutin, Serge. *L'Alchimie*. Que sais-je? series. Paris: PUF, 1971 (fourth edition updated), 128 pp. English edition: *A History of Alchemy*. New York: Tower, 1971, 120 pp. The most concise of the introductions.

Jabir Ibn Hayyan. cf. Lory, Pierre.

Kahn, Didier. *Hermès Trismégiste. La "Table d'Emeraude" et sa Tradition alchimique*. Paris: Les Belles Lettres (series "Aux sources de la Tradition"), 1994, 137 pp., illustrated.

Kopp, Hermann. *Die Alchemie in älterer und neuerer Zeit. Ein Beitrag zur Kulturgeschichte* vol. 1, *Die Alchemie bis zum letzten Viertel des 18. Jahrhunderts*, 260 pp.; vol. 2, *Die Alchemie vom letzten Viertel des 18. Jahrhunderts an*, 425 pp. Heidelberg: Carl Winter, 1886; reprinted 1962 (Hildesheim: Olms). I make an exception in citing an older work; such is the great richness of this work. Obviously dated on some points, it is still one of the most complete historical exposés.

Kren, Claudia. *Alchemy in Europe. A Guide to Research*. New York/London: Garland Publishing, Inc., 1990, 130 pp. This almost complete bibliography will certainly long remain an indispensable tool for research. It presents articles as well as books and is intelligently divided into sections like "Research Aids," "Medieval Alchemy," "Alchemy and the Arts," "Alchemy and the Spiritual," etc.

Lindsay, Jack. *The Origins of Alchemy in Graeco-Roman Egypt*. London: F. Muller, 1970, 452 pp., illustrated. New edition New York: Barnes and Noble, 1976. Basic text. Wealth of documentation and extensive bibliography.

Lory, Pierre, Jâbir ibn Hayyan. *Dix Traités d'alchimie (Les dix premiers Traités du Livre des Soixante-dix)*. Translated and introduced by Pierre Lory. Paris: Islam Sindbad, 1983, 318 pp.

Monod-Herzen, George Edmont. *L'Alchimie méditerranéenne. Ses origines et son but. La Table d'Émeraude*. Paris: Adyar, 1962, 214 pp., illustrated.

Obrist, Barbara. *Les Débuts de l'imagerie alchimique (XIVè–XVè siècles)*. Paris: Le Sycomore 1982, 328 pp., illustrated.

Pelvet, Pierre *L'Alchimie en France dans la Première moitié du XXè siècle.* Université de Paris X: Nanterre. Dissertation, December, 1980, typescript, 380 pp. with analytic table. On Jollivet-Castelot, Fulcanelli, Eugène Canseliet, and their milieu. A very interesting text.

Pereira, Michela. *The Alchemical Corpus attributed to Raymond Lull.* London: The Warburg Institute, 1989, 118 pp.

Pritchard, Alan. *Alchemy. A Bibliography of English Language Writings.* London: Routledge and Kegan Paul, 1980, 439 pp. A nearly exhaustive bibliography of all the texts (articles included!) in the English language. Indispensable.

Rabinovitch, V. L. *Alchimia kak phienomen sriednieviekoï kulturi.* Moscow: Nauka, 1979, 269 pp., illustrated. Interesting and well documented. A Russian bibliography. This author has published various works on alchemy and symbolism since 1970.

Read, John. *Prelude to Chemistry. An outline of Alchemy, its Literature and Relationships.* London: G. Bell and Sons Ltd., 1936, reprinted 1966 (Cambridge, Mass.: MIT Pr.). 328 pp., illustrated. A solid study, at once synthetic and precise, and highly readable.

Ruska, Julius. *Tabula Smaragdina. Ein Beitrag zur Geschichte der hermetischen Literatur.* Heidelberg: C. Winter, 1926 (Heidelberger Akten der Von-Portheim-Stiftung, 16), 248 pp. A great classic on the history of the *Emerald Tablet.*

Telle, Joachim. *Sol und Luna. Literar- und alchemiegeschichtliche Studien zu einem altdeutschen Bildgedicht.* Hürtgenwald (Germany): J. Pressler, 1980 (Schriften zur Wissenschaftsgeschichte, 2), 273 pp., illustrated.

―――. *Rosarium Philosophorum. Ein alchemisches Florilegium des Spätmittelalters. Faksimile der illustrierten Erstausgabe Frankfurt 1550.* Edited and commented by J. Telle. Translated from Latin into German by Lutz Claren and Joachim Huber. Weinheim (Germany): VCH Verlag, 1992. Vol. 1, 192 pp. (facsimile); vol. 2, 270 pp. (Telle's presentations). Vol. 2 is an excellent survey of alchemical literature related to the famous *Rosarium Philosophorum.*

Thorndike, Lynn. Cf. General Works.

Van Lennep, Jacques. *Art et alchimie: Étude de l'iconographie hermétique et de ses influences.* Art et Savoir series. Brussels: Meddens, 1966. 292 pp., illustrated.

―――. *Alchimie. Contribution à l'histoire de l'art alchimique.* Crédit Commercial de Belgique; distribution: Dervy-Livre, 1985, 502 pp. This superb catalogue, the only one of its kind, was brought out for the alchemy exposition in Brussels (December 1984–March 1985).

Weisser, Ursula. *Das "Buch über das Geheimnis der Schöpfung" von Pseudo-Apollonius von Tyana.* Berlin/New York: de Gruyter, 1980 (Ars medica, III/2), 258 pp.

We also have available a very large part of the Latin texts of alchemy, thanks to the recent facsimile publication of collections made in the seventeenth and early eighteenth centuries. The most important are:

Bibliotheca Chemica Curiosa, seu rerum ad alchemiam pertinentium thesaurus instructissimus. 2 vols. Ed. by J. Jacob Manget in Geneva in 1702. Editor Arnaldo Forni, s.d., 1977, In-folio, vol. 1, 938 pp.; vol. 2, 903 pp.

Musaeum Hermeticum Reformatum et Amplificatum. Edition of Frankfurt, 1678. Reprint Graz: Ak. Druck- und Verlagsanstalt, 1970, Introduction by Karl R. H. Frick, 863 pp.

Theatrum Chemicum, praecipuos selectorum auctorum tractatus de Chemiae et Lapidis Philosophici. 6 vols. Argentorati: 1659/61. Turin: Bottega d'Erasmo, 1981: Vol. 1, 794 pp.; vol. 2, 449 pp.; vol. 3, 859 pp.; vol. 4, 1014 pp.; vol. 5, 912 pp.; vol. 6, 772 pp. Each volume contains an index. Installment added: Introduzione, by Maurizio Barracano, I-xxxviii pp.

Among collections of texts in other languages, we cite:

Theatrum Chemicum Britannicum. Containing severall Poeticall Pieces of our Famous English Philosophers, who have written the Hermetique Mysteries in their owne Ancient Language. Faithfully Collected into one Volume, with Annotations thereon, by Elias Ashmole, Esq. qui est Mercuriophilus Anglicus. London: 1652, 494 pp., illustrated. Newly published in facsimile at Hildesheim (Germany): Olms, 1968, with a preface by C. H. Josten.

Alchimie. Textes alchimiques allemands traduits et présentés par Bernard Gorceix. L'Espace intérieur series. Paris: Fayard, 1980, 238 pp. Pp. 11–64, presentation of the texts by B. Gorceix; most are situated in the Paracelsian tradition.

Scherer, Richard. *Alchymia. Die Jungfrau im blauen Gewande. Alchemistische Texte des 16. und 17. Jahrhunderts.* Presented and edited by R. Scherer. Mössingen (Germany): Talheimer (Texte aus der Geschichte (1)), 1988, 333 pp., illustrated. Following an introduction by the editor is a selection of texts (all of them in German version), each accompanied by an explanatory note (texts by G. Tancke, B. Valentine, R. Bacon, the Rosicrucians, etc.).

Also notable are the journals:

Ambix. The Journal of the Society for the Study of Alchemy and Early Chemistry (since 1937). Three issues a year, each about fifty pages, constituting a volume. 40 volumes have appeared. Cambridge: Hoffers Printers. This is a most documented journal.

Cauda Pavonis. (The Hermetic Text Society Newsletter). Ed. Stanton J. Linden. Washington State University, Dept. of English. Since 1982. Two issues per year, from twelve to twenty pages each. Contains essentially reports, recensions, and analyses. Very good quality; literary orientation.

Chrysopoeia. Revue publiée par la Société d'Études de l'Histoire de l'Alchimie. Directed by Sylvain Matton. Milan: Archè; and Paris: J. C. Bailly. Since 1987 (quarterly). The most copious serious periodical devoted to the domain of alchemy.

The Hermetic Journal. Ed. Adam McLean. Quarterly until 1988 (42 issues published, about forty pages each); annual since 1989 (around 160 pp.). Edinburgh, 31 Royal Terrace, EH 7-5 AH, England. Uneven quality, but many excellent articles and iconographies. McLean also publishes new editions of alchemical and theosophical texts.

La Tourbe des Philosophes. Revue d'Études alchimiques. Paris: La Table d'Émeraude. Since 1977, quarterly. About sixty pages per issue. Inspired by E. Canseliet and Fulcanelli. Many articles on practical alchemy.

ESOTERIC FREEMASONRY

Benimeli, José A. Ferrer. *Bibliografía de la Masoneria. Introducción historico-critica.* Universidad de Zaragoza, and Universidad Católica Andrés Bello de Caracas, 1974, 387 pp.

Benimeli, José A. Ferrer. *Masoneria, Iglesia e Illustración: Un conflicto ideológico-politico-religioso.* 3 vols. Madrid: Fundación Universitaria Española (Seminario Cisneros), 1976/1977, vol. 1, *Los bases de un conflicto (1700–1739),* 440 pp., illustrated; vol. 2, *Inquisición procesos históricos (1739–1750),* 546 pp., illustrated; vol. 3, *Institucionalización del conflicto (1751–1800),* 725 pp., illustrated. An indispensable research and reference tool. Many developments on the subjects of freemasonry and esotericism.

Fabry, Jacques. cf. *infra*, Romanticism and Naturphilosophie.

Le Forestier, René. *La Franc-Maçonnerie templière et occultiste aux XVIIIe et XIXe siècles.* Edited by A. Faivre with addenda and notes; preface by A.

Faivre, introduction by Alec Mellor. Paris: Aubier-Nauwelaerts, 1970, 1116 pp., illustrated. Reprinted by La Table d'Emeraude, Paris, 1989. An indispensable work, not only for freemasonry of the era, but also for Illuminism.

Freimaurer und Geheimbünde im 18. Jahrhundert in Mitteleuropa. Ed. by Helmut Reinalter. Frankfurt: Suhrkamp, 1986, 404 pp. On the Rosicrucians, the Asiatic Brethern, etc.

Frick, Karl R. H. Cf. *supra, Licht und Finsternis,* etc. (under General Works).

Galtier, Gerard. *Franc-Maçonnerie Egyptienne, Rose-Croix et Néo-Chevalerie. Les Fils de Cagliostro.* Paris: Rocher, 1989, 474 pp.

Geheime Gesellschaften. Ed. by Ludz (Peter Christian). Heidelberg: L. Schneider, 1979 (Wolfenbütteler Studien zur Aufklärung, 5, 1), 461 pp.

Guinet, Louis. *Zacharias Werner et l'ésotérisme maçonnique.* Paris: Mouton, 1962, 426 pp.

Illuminisme et Franc-Maçonnerie. Special issue of the *Revue des Etudes Maistriennes,* nr. 5–6, Paris: Les Belles Lettres, 1980, 345 pp. (Proceedings of the Conference in Chambéry, May 1979). English translation: *Maistre Studies,* translated and edited by Richard A. Lebrun. Lanham (MD): University Press of America, 1988, 297 pp.

Keller, Jules. Cf. *infra,* Eighteenth century.

McIntosh, Christopher, Cf. *infra,* Eighteenth century.

Möller, Helmut, and Howe, Ellic. *Merlin Peregrinus. Vom Untergrund des Abendlandes.* Würzburg: Königshausen und Neumann, 1986, 341 pp., illustrated. This study concentrates on the occultist Mason Theodor Reuss, and provides a rich documentation on the fringe Masonry at the turn of the century.

Naudon, Paul. *La Franc-Maçonnerie chrétienne (La Tradition opérative, l'Arche Royale de Jérusalem, le Rite Écossais Rectifié).* Histoire et Tradition series. Paris: Dervy, 1970, 236 pp.

———. *Les Origines religieuses et corporatives de la Franc-Maçonnerie.* Histoire et Tradition series. Paris: Dervy, 1979, 348 pp. (first edition, 1972).

———. *La Franc-Maçonnerie.* Que sais-je? series. Paris: PUF, 1963, 128 pp. The most practical and perhaps the best of the introductions.

Partner, Peter. *The Knights Templar and their Myth.* Rochester (Vermont): Destiny Books, 1990, 209 pp., illustrated.

Porset, Charles. *Les Philalèthes et les Convents de Paris. Contribution à l'histoire de l'ésotérisme maçonnique à la veille de la Révolution.* Paris/Geneva: Champion/Slatkine, Nouvelle Bibliothèque Initiatique series, forthcoming.

Presenza di Cagliostro. Cf. *infra*, Eighteenth century.

Tourniac, Jean. *Symbolisme maçonnique et tradition chrétienne.* Histoire et Tradition series. Paris: Devry, 1982, 276 pp. (first edition, 1965).

Among the most informed and worthwhile journals:

Ars Quatuor Coronatorum: Transactions of Quatuor Coronati Lodge No. 2076. An annual volume of 250–270 pp., 107 issues published up to 1994.

Les Cahiers Verts. Publication du Grand Prieuré des Gaules (Neuilly-sur-Seine, France). Since 1969; twelve issues published to 1993. A very knowledgable journal, concentrating on the Rectified Scottish Rite.

Renaissance Traditionnelle. Quarterly, since 1970; 93 issues published to 1993. 50 to 80 pages per issue. Founded by René Desaguliers. Extremely serious and documented. Unfortunately, difficult to obtain, even in libraries.

Travaux de la Loge nationale de Recherches Villard de Honnecourt. Neuilly, G. L. N. F., biannual, 26 issues published in the current format, to 1993, each between 200 and 300 pp. A good periodical in French. Easily obtained in bookstores.

Zeitschrift, and *Jahrbuch der Forschungsloge Quatuor Coronati.* Bayreuth. Appears irregularly in varied formats. A mine for the historian. Volumes of up to 400 pages. In one issue (1976, 383 pp., and Nachtrag, 1984) the catalogue of the Masonic Library of Bayreuth (the work of Herbert Schneider) was published—but this is only one example among other publications in this periodical.

Among the most important Masonic dictionaries, we point out:

Lennhoff, Eugen, and Posner, Oskar. *Internationales Freimaurer Lexikon.* Graz: Akad. Druck- und Verlagsanstalt, s.d., 1780 col. (reprint of the 1932 edition). The most practical of all the dictionaries.

Wolfstieg, August. *Bibliothek der Freimaurerischen Literatur.* 4 vols. Hildesheim: G. Olms, 1964 (reprint of the 1911 de Burg edition), vol. 1, 990 pp.; vol. 2, 1041 pp.; vol. 3, 536 pp.; vol. 4, 598 pp. A reference tool whose scale has never been surpassed.

Ligou, Daniel. *Dictionnaire universel de la Franc-Maçonnerie: Hommes illustres, pays, rites, symboles.* Under the direction of Daniel Ligou. Daniel

Beresniak and Marion Prachin, eds. Navarre-Prisme, 1974, 1398 pp., illustrated.

Finally a series of works was published during the 1980s by the Aquarian Press (Wellingborough, Northamptonshire, England), on the Golden Dawn and on Freemason authors of esoteric works such as A. E. Waite and W. E. Westcott. It is worthwhile to consult the books of Francis King, Ellic Howe, R. A. Gilbert, etc., published in this series.

FROM THE SECOND (*CORPUS HERMETICUM*) TO THE FIFTEENTH CENTURY

Alverny, Marie-Thérèse d'; Dannenfeldt, K. H.; Silverstein, Theodore. "Hermetica Philosophica," and "Oracula Chaldaica" in *Catalogus Translationum et Commentariorum: Medieval and Renaissance Latin Translations and Commentaries. Annotated lists and guides*, pp. 137–164. Ed. by Paul Oskar Kristeller Vol. 1 (I–II) Washington D.C.: The Catholic University of America Press (Union Acad. Int.), 1960.

Bejottes, L. Le *"Livre Sacré" d'Hermès Trismégiste et ses 36 herbes magigues*. Brussels: Impr. de Barthélemy, 1911 (reprint Paris: Trois Mondes, 1974), 201 pp.

Berthelot, Marcellin. Cf. above, under "Alchemy."

Blanco, A. G. "Hermetism. A Bibliographical Approach," in *Aufstieg und Niedergang der römischen Welt*, vol. 2 (4. Teilband: *Religion*). Ed. W. Haase. Berlin/New York: W. de Gruyter, 1984, pp. 2240–2281.

Bonardel, Françoise. *L'Hermétisme*. Cf. above, General Works.

Brehier, Emile. *La Philosophie au Moyen Age*. L'Evolution de l'humanité series. Paris: Albin Michel, 1949, 470 pp., illustrated.

Casaril, Guy. *Rabbi Siméon Bar Jochai et la Cabbale*. Maîtres Spirituels series. Paris: Éditions du Seuil, 1961, 187 pp., illustrated. A small, practical introductory work.

Christ, Plato, Hermes Trismegistus. The Dawn of Printing. Catalogue of the Incunabula in the Bibliotheca Philosophica Hermetica. Catalogued by Margaret Lane Ford. 2 vols. Amsterdam: In de Pelikaan (Bibliotheca Philosophica Hermetica), 1990, 207 pp. and 410 pp., illustrated.

Cousins, Ewert H. *Bonaventure and the Coincidence of Opposites*. Chicago: Franciscan Herald Press, 1978, 316 pp. A remarkable work of synthesis. New and fertile insights.

Dannenfeldt, K. H. Cf. *supra*, Alverny (*Catalogus Translationum*).

Davy, Marie-Magdeleine. *Initiation à la symbolique romane*. Paris: Flammarion, 1977, 312 pp. (First edition, *Essai sur la symbolique romane*, 1955.)

————. *Initiation médiévale: La Philosophie au XIIe siècle*. Bibliothèque de l'Hermétisme series. Paris: Albin Michel, 1980, 297 pp.

Delatte, Louis. *Textes latins et vieux français relatifs aux Kyranides*. Liège and Paris: Faculté de Philosophie de Liège, and Droz, 1942, 364 pp.

Duval, Paulette. *La Pensée alchimique et le Conte du Graal: recherches sur les structures ("Gestalten") de la Pensée alchimique, leurs correspondances dans le conte du Graal de Chrétien de Troyes et l'influence de l'Espagne mozarabe de l'Ebre sur la pensée symbolique de l'Oeuvre*. Paris: Champion, and Lille: "Reproduction des Thèses", 1975, 386 pp., illustrated.

Festugière, André-Jean. *Hermétisme et mystique païenne*. Paris: Aubier-Montaigne, 1967, 333 pp., illustrated.

————. *La Révélation d'Hermès Trismégiste*, 4 vols. Paris: "Les Belles-Lettres," Vol. I, 1981, 441 pp.; vol. II, 610 pp.; vol. III, 314 pp.; vol. I, 319 pp., illustrated. (First edition: 1949–1954). A basic work on the Hermetica.

Fowden, Garth. *The Egyptian Hermes. A Historical Approach to the Late Pagan Mind*. Cambridge Univ. Press, 1986, 244 pp. New edition: Princeton Univ. Press, 1993.

Gagnon, Claude. Cf. *Supra*, Alchemy.

Gallais, Pierre. *Perceval et L'Initiation: Essai sur le dernier roman de Chrétien de Troyes, ses correspondances orientales et sa signification anthropologique*. Paris: Sirac, 1972, 312 pp., illustrated.

Gandillac, Maurice de. Cf. *infra*: "Pensée encyclopédique au Moyen Age," and "Pseudo-Denys."

Garin, Eugenio. *Moyen Age et Renaissance*. Paris: Gallimard, series "Bibliothèque des Idées," 1969, 273 pp. (Original edition: *Medioèvo e Rinascimento*, 1954.) A collection of particularly well-documented and enlightening articles and essays.

Gilson, Étienne. *La Philosophie au Moyen Age, des origines patristiques à la fin du XIVe siècle*. Paris: Payot, 1962, 782 pp. (first edition: 1944.) For our purposes, É Bréhier's text is preferable, although the two complement each other.

Goetschel, Roland. *La Kabbale*. Que sais-je? series. Paris: PUF, 1985, 126 pp. The most reliable historical guide among the short works devoted to the Kabbalah. An indispensable handbook.

Gorceix, Bernard. *Le Livre des Oeuvres divines* of Hildegard of Bingen. Spiritualités Vivantes series. Paris: Albin Michel, 1982, 217 pp. An excellent introduction by the translator, B. Gorceix, pp. i-ci.

―――. *Les Amis de Dieu en Allemagne au siècle de Maître Eckhart.* Spiritualités Vivantes series. Paris: Albin Michel, 1984, 302 pp. The basic text on Rulman Merswin and the Green Island.

Halbronn, Jacques. *Le Monde juif et l'astrologie. Histoire d'un vieux couple.* Followed by an essay by Paul Fenton, preface by Juan Vernet. Milan: Arché, 1985, 433 pp., illustrated (first edition, 1979).

Halleux, Robert. Cf. above, Alchemy.

Hermes Latinus. Editio Critica. Corpus Christianorum series, starting in 1994. Series directed by Paolo Lucentini. Turnhout (Belgium): Brepols. The critical edition of the Latin Hermetica, from late antiquity to the middle ages.

Hermes Trismegistus. *Poïmandres. Traités II–XVII* (of the "Corpus Hermeticum"). *Asclepius. Fragments extraits de Stobée.* Texts established and translated by A. D. Nock and A. J. Festugière, 4 vols. Paris: "Les Belles-Lettres," 1954–1960. Vol. 1, 195 pp.; vol 2, 196–404 pp.; vol. 3, 93 pp.; vol 4, 150 pp. This ensemble obviously complements Festugière's work, *La Révélation d'Hermès Trismégiste* (cf. *supra*), the two works constituting an indispensable research tool.

Hermes Trismegistus, Pater Philosophorum. Cf. *supra*, General Works.

But let us not forget the following:

Hermetica: The Ancient Greek and Latin Writings which contain Religious or Philosophic Teachings Ascribed to Hermes Trismegistus; edited with English translation by Walter Scott. 4 vols. Oxford: Clarendon Press, 1924/36. (Facsimile: Boston: Shambhala, 1983/85): Vol. 1, *Introduction, texts and translation*, 1924, 549 pp.; vol. 2, *Notes on the Corpus Hermeticum*, 1925, 482 pp.; vol. 3, *Notes on the Latin Asclepius and the hermetic extracts of Stobaeus*, 1926, 626 pp.; vol. 4, *Testimonia, with introduction, addenda and indices by A. A. Ferguson*, 1936, 576 pp. New edition, in one volume, with an interesting preface by A. G. Gilbert. Solos Press, England, 1992, 255 pp. Scott's work is not outdated by A. J. Festugière's edition (cf. above). Vol. 4 in particular is an unequalled study with regard to the testimonia.

Hermetica. The Greek Corpus Hermeticum *and the Latin* Asclepius *in a new English translation with notes and introduction.* By Brian P. Copenhaver. Cambridge University Press, 1992, 320 pp. The most recent scholarly presentation and translation.

(De) Hermetische Gnosis in de loop der eeuwen . . . Cf. *supra*, General Works.

Hillgarth, J. N. *Ramon Lull and Lullism in 14th century France.* Oxford: Clarendon Press, 1971, 504 pp., illustrated.

Jamblicus. *Les Mystères d'Égypte.* Text established and translated by Édouard des Places. Paris: "Les Belles-Lettres," 1966, 224 pp.

Jonas, Hans. *The Gnostic Religion.* Boston: Beacon Press, 1958. French translation: *La Religion gnostique. Le message du Dieu Étranger et les débuts du christianisme.* Translated by Louis Évrard. Paris: Flammarion, 1978, 506 pp. Contains an appendix, "Le Syndrome gnostique," pp. 443–463 (first edition, 1974). A remarkable historical and philosophical study. An indispensable book for the study of gnosticism.

Kahane, Henry et Renée. *The Krater and the Grail. Hermetic Sources of the Parzival.* In collaboration with Angelina Pietrangeli. Urbana: Univ. of Illinois Press (Illinois Studies in Language and Literature, vol. 56), 1965, 218 pp., illustrated.

Kahn, Didier. *Hermès Trismégiste . . .* Cf. *supra,* Alchimie.

Kibre, Pearle. *Studies in Medieval Science, Alchemy, Astrology, Mathematics and Medicine.* Ronceverte, West Virginia and London: Hambledon Press, 1984, 376 pp., illustrated. (A collection of twenty articles.)

Lubac, Henri de. Cf. *supra,* General Works, for vol. 1.

Mahé, Jean-Pierre. *Hermès en Haute Égypte.* Vol. I: *Les textes hermétiques de Nag Hammadi et leurs parallèles grecs et latins.* Québec: Presses Universitaires de Laval, 1978, 171 p. Vol. II: *Le Fragment du "Discours Parfait" et les Définitions hermétiques arméniennes,* same publisher, 1982, 565 p.

Marx, Jean. *La Légende arthurienne et le Graal.* Geneva: Slatkine, 1974, 410 pp., facsimile of the PUF edition, 1952.

Matt, Daniel Chanan. *Zohar, The Book of Enlightenment.* Translation and Introduction by Daniel Chanan Matt, preface by Arthur Green. New York: Paulist Press, "The Classics of Western Spirituality," 1983, 320 pp. An interesting selection; instructive notes and introduction.

Mopsik, Charles. *Zohar.* Translation, annotation, and foreword by Charles Mopsik. Followed by the *Midrach Ha Néélam,* translated and annotated by Bernard Maruani. 2 vols. Éditions Verdier, vol. 1, 1981, 671 pp.; vol. 2, 1984, 555 pp. Finally, a complete French translation of the *Zohar,* which more than replaces the very outdated translation by Jean de Pauly. A good introduction and critical guides.

Naudon, Paul. Cf. above, Freemasonry.

(Le) Néo-platonisme. Paris: C.N.R.S., "Colloques internationaux du C.N.R.S." (Proceedings of the colloquium of Royaumont, 1969), 1971, 496 pp.

Oracles Chaldaïques. Avec un choix de commentaires anciens. Text established and translated by Édouard des Places. Paris: "Les Belles-Lettres," 1971, 252 pp.

La Pensée encyclopédique au Moyen Age. (A collective work) Neuchatel: La Baconnière, 1966, 125 pp. Instructive articles on the "Summae," notably: Isidore of Seville (J. Fontaine); Hugues of St. Victor (J. Châtillon); Vincent de Beauvais (M. Lemoine); Raoul Ardent (J. Gründel), Bartholomew of England and Alexander Neckham (P. Michaud-Quantin); and an excellent text by M. de Gandillac, "Encyclopédies prémédiévales."

Picatrix. The Latin Version of the Ghayat al-Hakin. Edited with introduction and notes by David Pingree. London: The Warburg Institute, 1986, 326 pp., illustrated.

(Des) Places. Cf. *supra*, Jamblicus and "Oracles Chaldaïques."

Poirion, Daniel. *Le Merveilleux dans la littérature française du Moyen Age.* Que sais-je? series. Paris: PUF. 1982, 127 pp.

Pseudo-Denys l'Aréopagite (Oeuvres du—). Translation, commentary and notes by Maurice de Gandillac. Bibliothèque Philosophique series. Paris: Aubier-Montaigne, 1980, 406 pp. (first edition, 1943).

Puech, Henri-Charles. *En Quête de la Gnose.* 2 vols. Bibliothèque des Sciences Humaines series. Paris: Gallimard. Vol. 1: *La Gnose et le Temps, et autres essais*, 1978, 300 pp.; vol. 2 *Sur l'Évangile selon Thomas. Esquisse d'une interprétation systématique*, 1978, 319 pp.

Ribard, Jacques. *Le Moyen Age: Littérature et symbolisme.* Essais series. Paris: Champion, 1984, 169 pp. An excellent short work devoted to the symbolism of numbers, colors, animals, plants, names, space, time, objects.

———. *Chrétien de Troyes: Le Chevalier de la Charrette. Essai d'interprétation symbolique.* Paris: Nizet, 1973, 185 pp. Chrétien de Troyes is read from the perspective of a Christian hermeneutic, Lancelot is an Arthurian Christ.

Ritter, Hellmut. "Picatrix, ein arabisches Handbuch hellenistischer Magie," in *Vorträge der Bibliothek Warburg.* Leipzig: Teubner, 1923, pp. 94–124.

Roques, René. *L'Univers dionysien: structure hiérarchique du monde selon le Pseudo-Denys.* Paris: Éditions du Cerf, 1983, 392 pp. (First edition, 1954).

Ruska, Julius. Cf. above, under Alchemy.

Sansonetti, Paul-Georges. *Graal et Alchimie.* L'Ile Verte series. Paris: Berg International, 1982, 214 pp., illustrated.

Saxl, Fritz. *Verzeichnis astrologischer und mythologischer illustrierter Handschriften des lateinischen Mittelalters.* Vols. I–III. Heidelberg: C. Winter, 1915/1927 (and Studien der Bibliothek Warburg). Leipzig: Teubner, 1923.

Schaya, Leo. *La Création en Dieu à la lumière du judaïsme, du christianisme et de l'islam.* Mystiques et religions series. Paris: Dervy, 1983, 564 pp.

Scholem, Gershom. *Major Trends in Jewish Mysticism.* Jerusalem: Schocken, 1941, 454 pp. Several new editions. Incontestably the best introductory text to the Kabbalah.

Other important works by the same author:

———. *Zur Kabbala und ihrer Symbolik.* Zurich: Rhein, 1960, 303 pp. English edition: *On the Kabbala and its Symbolism.* New York: Schocken, 1965, 216 pp.

———. *Ursprung und Anfänge der Kabbala.* Berlin: de Gruyter, 1962 (Studia Judaica, 3); 434 pp. English edition: *Origins of the Kabbalah*, ed. R.J.Z. Werblowsky. Princeton University Press, 1987, 487 pp.

———. *Kabbalah.* New York: Meridian Books, 1978, 494 pp. illustrated (first edition: Jerusalem, 1974).

———. *The Messianic Idea in Judaism and other essays on Jewish Spirituality.* New York: Schocken, 1971, 504 pp.

Scot Érigène (Jean) et l'histoire de la Philosophie, in *Colloques internationaux du C.N.R.S.*, number 561, 1977, 484 pp. (1975 colloquium, contributions from F. Bertin, J. Trouillard, P. Lucentini, J. Chatillon, et al.).

Scott, Walter. Cf. *supra, Hermes Trismegistus.*

Sfameni Gasparro, Giulia. *Gnostica et Hermetica: saggi sullo gnosticismo e sull'ermetismo.* Rome: Ed. dell'Ateneo, 1982, 386 pp. Deals especially with hermetism and Hermes Trismegistus in primitive Christian literature.

Silverstein, Théodore. "The fabulous cosmogony of Bernardus Silvestris." *Modern Philology* (A Journal devoted to research in Medieval and Modern Literature). Chicago: University of Chicago Press, 46 (August 1948): 92–116.

———. "Liber Hermetis Mercurii Triplicis de VI Rerum Principiis." *Archives d'Histoire doctrinale et littéraire du Moyen Age.* Paris: J. Vrin. 1955–56: 217–302.

———. Cf. also *supra*, Alverny (*Hermetica Philosophica*).

Thorndike, Lynn. Cf. *supra*, General Works. Vols. 1–4 of *History of Magic* are fundamental for the Middle Ages.

Wehr, Gerhard. Cf. *supra*, General Works.

RENAISSANCE AND SEVENTEENTH CENTURY

A) Varia

Agrippa Ab Nettesheim, (Henricus Cornelius.) *De Occulta philosophia.* Introduced by Karl Anton Nowotny. Graz: Akad. Druck- und Verlagsanstalt, 1967, in folio, 915 pp., illustrated. (First edition, 1533).

Cassirer, Ernst. *Individuum und Kosmos in der Philosophie der Renaissance.* Leipzig: Teubner, 1927, 458 pp., illustrated. (English edition: *The Individual and the Cosmos in Renaissance Philosophy.* Oxford: Blackwell, 1963, 199 pp., and Pennsylvania Univ. Press, 1972.)

La Città dei Segreti. Magia, astrologia et cultura esoterica a Roma (xv–xviii). Ed Fabio Troncarelli. Milan: Franco Angeli, 1985 (collected articles).

Culiano, Ioan P. *Eros et Magie à la Renaissance.* 1984. Paris: Flammarion, 1984, 418 pp. English edition: *Eros and Magic in the Renaissance.* Chicago Univ. Press, 1987, 264 pp.

Evans, R. J. W. *Rudolf II and his World (A Study in Intellectual History) (1576–1612).* Oxford: Clarendon Press, 1984, 323 pp., illustrated (first edition, 1973). Remarkably well documented, irreplaceable study of the milieu.

French, Peter. *John Dee. The World of an Elizabethan Magus.* London: Routledge and Kegan Paul, 1972, 243 pp., illustrated.

Garin, Eugenio. *Lo zodiaco vita.* Bari: Laterza, 1976. English translation: *Astrology in the Renaissance. The Zodiac of Life.* London: Routledge and Kegan Paul, 1983, 145 pp.

———. *Medioevo e Rinascimento: studi e ricerche.* Bari: Laterza, 1954 (new edition, 1966, 354 pp.).

Godet, Alain. *Nun was ist die Imagination anders als ein Sonn im Menschen (Studien zu einem Zentralbegriff des magischen Denkens).* Diss., University of Basel, Zurich: A.D.A.G. Administration & Druck, 1982, 282 pp. Many well-chosen references and citations. An original work that deserves to be better-known.

Huffman, William H. *Robert Fludd and the End of the Renaissance.* London: Routledge, 1988, 252 pp.

La Magia naturale del Rinascimento: testi di Agrippa, Cardano, Fludd. Introduction by Paolo Rossi. Torino: Utet, 1989, 134 pp., illustrated.

Il Mago, il cosmo, il teatro degli astri. Saggi sulla letteratura esoterica del Rinascimento. Collective work introduced by Gianfranco Formichetti. Rome: Bulzoni, 1985, 238 pp.

Navert, Charles G. *Agrippa and the Crisis of Renaissance Thought.* Illinois Univ. Press, 1965, 374 pp.

Die Okkulten Wissenschaften in der Renaissance. A collective work brought out by August Buck and the Herzog August Bibliothek of Wolfenbüttel. Wiesbaden (in Kommission bei O. Harrassowitz), 1992 (Wolfenbütteler Abhandlungen zur Renaissanceforschung, 2), 293 pp., illustrated.

Science, Pseudo-Science, and Utopianism in Early Modern Thought. A collective work introduced by Stephen A. McKnight. Columbia and London: Univ. of Missouri Press, 1992, 221 pp. On alchemy, Hermetism, Newton.

Peuckert, Will Erich. *Pansophie. Ein Versuch zur Geschichte der weissen und schwarzen Magie.* Stuttgart: Kohlhammer, 1936. New edition, Berlin: Erich Schmidt, 1966. Somewhat disorganized, but a great wealth of information.

Seznec, Jean. *La Survivance des dieux antiques.* Paris: Flammarion, 1980, 337 pp., illustrated. English edition: *The Survival of the Pagan Gods: the Mythological Tradition and its Place in Renaissance Humanism and Art.* New York: Pantheon, 1953, 376 pp. (new edition 1961).

Shumaker, Wayne. *The Occult Sciences in the Renaissance (a Study in Intellectual Patterns).* Berkeley and Los Angeles: Univ. of California Press, 1979, 282 pp., illustrated (first edition, 1972). Astrology, hermetism, magic, alchemy: One chapter is devoted to each of these branches.

Thomas, Keith. *Religion and the Decline of Magic. Studies in Popular Beliefs in 16th and 17th century England.* London: Weidenfeld, 1971. New edition: Penguin Books, 1980[4], 853 pp.

Thorndike, Lynn. Cf. *supra*, General Works. Volumes 5–8 contain a rich material for the period.

Turner, Robert. *Elisabethan Magic. The Art and the Magus.* Longmead (England): Element Books, 1989, 190 pp., illustrated.

Umanesimo e esoterismo. A collective work, Padova: Cedam, Dott A. Milani. 1960, 448 pp., illustrated. Archivio di Filosofia. Articles on M. Ficin, S. Champier, Vasari, G. Postel et al.

Umanesimo e simbolismo. A collective work. Same editor, same series as *supra.* 1958, 317 pp., illustrated.

Vasoli, Cesare. *Filosofia e religione nella cultura del Rinascimento.* Neaples: Guida, 1988, 377 pp. On Ficino, Postel, Giorgi of Venice, Giulo Camillo.

―――. *Magia e scienza nella civilta umanistica.* Collective work edited by C. Vasoli. Bologne: Il Mulino, 1976, 303 pp.

Walker, D. P. *Spiritual and Demonic Magic. From Ficino to Campanella.* London: University of Notre-Dame Press, 1975, 244 pp. (First edition: Warburg Institute, 1958). In addition to studies on Ficino and Campanella, some well-documented chapters on Pletho, Lazarelli, Trithemius, Agrippa, Paracelsus, J. Gohory, Pomponazzi, Giorgi, et al.

Wind, Edgar. *Pagan Mysteries in the Renaissance.* London: Peregrine Books, 1967, 345 pp., illustrated (first edition, 1958). Iconology, emblematics and esotericism.

Yates, Frances A. *The Art of Memory.* London: Routledge and Kegan Paul, 1966, and reprint, Univ. of Chicago, Phoenix Books, s.d., 400 pp. Already a classic. Any serious devotee should possess the works of this author, two others of which are cited in the following pages. One should see all of them in order to approach the history of esotericism in the Renaissance.

―――. *The Occult Philosophy in the Elizabethan Age.* London: Routledge, 1979, 217 pp. Studies on Lull, Pico della Mirandola, Reuchlin, Giorgi, Agrippa, Dürer, John Dee, the Rosicrucians, et al. Other studies by F. A. Yates are collected under the title:

―――. *Collected Essays.* 3 vols. London: Routledge and Kegan Paul. Vol. 1, *Lull and Bruno,* 1982, 279 pp., illustrated; vol. 2, *Renaissance and Reform: The Italian Contribution,* 1983, 273 pp., illustrated; vol. 3, *Ideas and Ideals in the North European Renaissance,* 1984, 356 pp., illustrated.

Zambelli, Paola. *L'Ambigua natura della magia.* Milan: Il Saggiatore (A. Mondadori). 1991, 345 pp.

B) Reception of Alexandrian Hermetism

Blanco, A. G. Cf. *supra,* From the Second to the Fifteenth Centuries.

Copenhaver, Brian P. *Symphorien Champier and the Reception of the Occultist Tradition in Renaissance France.* The Hague-Paris-New York: Mouton, 1978. 368 pp.

Dannenfeldt, K. H. *Hermetica Philosophica.* Op. cit. *supra,* From the Second to the Fifteenth Centuries. Cf. Alverny.

Faivre, Antoine. *The Eternal Hermes. From Greek God to Alchemical Magus.* Grand Rapids (Mich.): Phanes Press (forthcoming, ca. 200 pp.).

Garin, Eugenio. *Ermetismo del Rinascimento.* Siena: Riuniti (Biblioteca Minima), 1988. 79 pp.

Hermes Trismegistus, Pater Philosophorum. Cf. *supra,* From the Second to the Fifteenth Centuries.

(De) Hermetische Gnosis in de loop der eeuwen . . . Cf. *supra,* General Works.

McGuire, J. E. Cf. Westman, Robert S.

Shumaker, Wayne. *The Occult Sciences.* Op. cit. *supra, A) Varia.* Cf. pp. 211–250.

Présence d'Hermès Trismégiste. A collective work presented by A. Faivre in the series "Cahiers de l'Hermétisme." Paris: A. Michel, 1988. 235 pp. On the reception of the *Corpus Hermeticum* in modern times and the role of the mythical Hermes Trismegistus.

Sladek, Mirko. *Fragmente der hermetischen Philosophie.* Op. cit. *supra,* General works.

Testi Umanistici su l'Ermetismo. (Collective work.) Archivo di Filosofia. Rome: Fratelli Bocca, 1955. 161 pp. Articles on Lazarelli, Giorgi and Agrippa.

Tuveson, Ernest Lee. *The Avatars of Thrice Great Hermes.* Op. cit. *supra,* General Works.

Walker, D. P. *The Ancient Theology: Studies in Christian Platonism from the Fiftenth to the Eighteenth Century.* Old Working (G.B.): The Gresham Press, s.d. (first edition) London: Duckworth, 1972.

Westman, Robert S. and McGuire, J. E. *Hermeticism and Scientific Revolution.* Los Angeles: William Andrews, Clark Memorial Library, Univ. of California, 1977. 150 pp., illustrated.

Yates, Frances A. *Giordano Bruno and the Hermetic Tradition.* Chicago-London: The Univ. of Chicago Press, Midway Reprints, 1979. First edition: London: Routledge and Kegan Paul, 1964. 466 pp. Although now disputed on several matters of interpretation, this remains a masterpiece and an indispensable work tool.

C) Christian Kabbalah

Guillaume Postel (1581–1981). Collective work presented by Jean-Claude Margolin. Conference proceedings of Avranches, April 1981. Paris: G. Trédaniel (La Maisnie), 1985. 391 pp., illustrated.

Javary, Geneviève. *Recherches sur l'utilisation du thème de la Sekina dans l'apologétique chrétienne.* Univ. of Lille III: Reproduction of theses; distribution Paris: Champion, 1977. 598 pp.

Kabbalistes chrétiens. Collective work. Series "Cahiers de l'Hermétisme." Paris: Albin Michel, 1979. 314 pp., illustrated. Articles by G. Scholem, G. Javary, E. Benz, H. Grieve, C. Wirszubski, et al.

Postello, Venezia e il suo Mondo. Collective work presented by Marion L. Kuntz. Florence: L.S. Olschki, 1988. 376 pp.

Secret, François. *Les Kabbalistes chrétiens de la Renaissance.* Paris: Arma Artis and Milan: Arché, 1985. 395 pp., illustrated (new expanded edition). First edition, Paris: Dunod, 1964. Still the most thoroughly documented work on this subject.

Swietlicki, Catherine. *Spanish Christian Cabala (The works of Luis de Leon, Santa Teresa de Jesus, and San Juan de la Cruz).* Columbia: Univ. of Missouri Press, 1986. 227 pp.

D) Paracelsianism and Nature Philosophy

Bianchi, Massimo Luigi. *Signatura Rerum. Segni, magia e conoscenza, di Paracelso a Leibniz.* Rome: Ed. dell'Ateneo, 1987. 199 pp.

Debus, Allen G. *Man and Nature in the Renaissance.* Cambridge: Univ. Press, 1978. 159 pp., illustrated.

———. *The Chemical Philosophy: Paracelsian Science and Medicine in the Sixteenth and Seventeenth Centuries.* New York: Science History Publications, 1977. Vol. I, 293 pp., vol. II, 606 pp., illustrated. Paracelsus, Fludd, F. M. Van Helmont, etc. An impressive collection of a very high quality. A good work tool and reference.

Kaiser, Ernst. *Paracelsus in Selbstzeugnissen und Dokumenten.* Reinbek bei Hamburg: Rowohlts Monographien, 1969. 158 pp. One of the best introductions to Paracelsianism.

Koyré, Alexandre. *Mystiques, Spirituels, Alchimistes, du XVIe siècle allemand.* From the "Cahiers des Annales". No. 10. Paris: Arm. Colin, 1955. 116 pp. On Schwenkfeld, Sebastian Frank, Weigel, Paracelsus.

Kreatur und Kosmos: Internationale Beiträge zur Paracelsusforschung. Ed. Rosemarie Dilg-Frank. Stuttgart-New York: G. Fischer, 1981. 206 pp. Articles by W. Pagel, J. Telle, A. Miller-Ginsburg, L. Braun, et al.

Occult and Scientific Mentalities in the Renaissance. Ed. Brian Vickers, Center for Renaissance Studies, E.T.H. Zurich-London-New York: Cambridge Univ. Press, 1984. 408 pp. On Kepler, Bacon, Newton. One of the most important works on this question.

Pagel, Walter. *Paracelsus: an Introduction to Philosophical Medicine in the Era of the Renaissance* (first edition). Basel and New York: S. Karger, 1958, 368 pp., illustrated. New edition 1982, 399 pp., illustrated. An excellent synthetic exposition on Paracelsus.

Paracelse. Collective work, series "Cahiers de l'Hermétisme." Paris: Albin Michel, 1980. 280 pp. Texts of L. Braun, K. Goldammer, P. Deghaye, E. W. Kämmerer, B. Gorceix, and bibliography by R. Dilg-Frank.

Parerga Paracelsica. Paracelsus in Vergangenheit und Gegenwart. Collective work presented by Joachim Telle. Stuttgart: F. Steiner, 1992. 426 pp., illustrated.

Reason, Experiment, Mysticism in the Scientific Revolution. Collective work presented by M. L. Righini Bonelli and William R. Shea. New York: Science History Publications, 1975. 320 pp. On Fludd, alchemy, Newton, Hermetism, etc.

Scienze, credenze occulte, livelli di cultura. Proceedings of the Florence conference, June 1980. Florence: L. S. Olschki, 1982. 562 pp., illustrated.

E) Rosicrucianism

Arnold, Paul. *Histoire des Rose-Croix et les origines de la Franc-Maçonnerie.* Paris: Mercure de France, 1955. 343 pp. The first important work on this topic in French. Based on documentation assembled by H. Schick. It remains interesting, especially for its bibliography.

———. *La Rose-Croix et ses rapports avec la Franc-Maçonnerie. Essai de synthèse historique.* Paris: Maisonneuve, 1970. 259 pp.

Edighoffer, Roland. *Rose-Croix et société idéale selon Johan Valentin Andreae.* Paris: Arma Artis, 1982. Vol. I, 1982, 461 pp., vol. II, 1987, pp. 463–840, illustrated. By far the most up-to-date volume on Rosicrucianism of the seventeenth century. High-priority reading after his "Que sais-je?" (*infra*).

————. *Les Rose-Croix.* From the collection "Que sais-je?". Paris: PUF, 1982, 126 pp., and 1992 (revised). A reliable exposition and the best synthesis of this topic.

Das Erbe des Christian Rosenkreutz (Johann Valentin Andreae 1586–1986 und die Manifeste der Rosenkreuzerbruderschaft 1614–1616). Proceedings from the conference of the Bibliotheca Philosophica Hermetica, Amsterdam, November 1986. Collective work presented by Franz Janssen. Amsterdam: In den Pelikaan (Bibliotheca Philosophica Hermetica), 1988. 288 pp.

Gorceix, Bernard. *La Bible des Rose-Croix.* Paris: PUF, 1970. 125 pp. After an introduction of 64 pages, one of the best initiations to the original Rosicrucian corpus. B. Gorceix gives an excellent French translation of those works (*Fama, Confessio,* and *Chemical Wedding*).

McIntosh, Christopher. *The Rosicrucians (The History and Mythology of an Occult Order).* "Crucible" series. 1980. Revised and expanded edition: Wellingborough (England): n.p., 1987. 160 pp., illustrated.

Montgomery, John Warwick. *Cross and Crucible: Johan Valentin Andreae (1586–1654) Phoenix of the Theologians.* "Archives Internationales d'histoire des idées," No. 55. The Hague: Nijhoff, 1973. Vol. I, *Andreae's Life, World-view and Relations with Rosicrucianism and Alchemy.* 255 pp., illustrated; vol II, *The Chymische Hochzeit, with Notes and Commentary.* 257–577 pp., illustrated.

Peuckert, Will-Erich. *Die Rosenkreutzer. Zur Geschichte einer Reformation.* Jena: Diederichs, 1928. Rpt. *Das Rosenkreutz.* Introduced and presented by Rolf Christian Zimmermann. Berlin: E. Schmidt, 1973. 408 pp.

Schick, Hans. *Das ältere Rosenkreuzertum. Zur Geschichte einer Reformation.* Jena: Diederichs, 1928. Rpt.: *Die Geheime Geschichte der Rosenkreutzer.* Introduction by Alain Godet. Schwarzenburg (Switzerland): Ansata, 1980. 338 pp.

Yates, Frances A. *The Rosicrucian Enlightenment.* London: Routledge and Kegan Paul, 1972. 269 pp., illustrated. A classic that does not duplicate the other good works.

F) Theosophy

Boehme, Jacob. *Mysterium Magnum.* Translated by S. Jankelevitch. Paris: Aubier-Montaigne, 1945. Two vols: vol. 1, 592 pp.; vol. 2, 516 pp. Mentioned here for the two studies on Boehme by Nicolas Berdiaeff presented at the beginning of vol. 1, pp. 5–45. These are essays that one must read. They are titled, respectively, "L'*Ungrund* et la liberté" and "La doctrine de la Sophia et de l'Androgyne. Jacob Boehme et les courants sophiologiques russes."

———. *Les Épîtres Théosophiques.* "Gnose" series. Paris: Éd. du Rocher, 1980. 407 pp. Mentioned here for the critical introduction of Gorceix (the first 110 pp.).

Deghaye, Pierre. *La Naissance de Dieu ou la doctrine de Jacob Boehme.* Series "Spiritualités Vivantes." Paris: Albin Michel, 1985. 302 pp. The best introduction written in French to the work of Jacob Boehme.

Gorceix, Bernard. *La Mystique de Valentin Weigel (1533–1588) et les origines de la théosophie allemande.* Univ. of Lille, thesis reproduction service, 1970. 500 pp.

———. *Flambée et agonie. Mystiques du XVIIe siècle allemand.* Series "Le Soleil dans le Coeur." Sisteron: Présence, 1977. 358 pp., illustrated. Very good introduction to D. Czepko, Fr. Spee, Catharina R. von Greiffenberg, Angelus Silesius, Quirinus Kuhlmann, J. G. Gichtel.

———. *Johann Georg Gichtel, théosophe d'Amsterdam.* Series "Delphica." Paris: L'Age d'Homme, 1974. 174 pp., illustrated. One of the best works by B. Gorceix. Important for understanding Bohemian theosophic thought and environment in the seventeenth century and early eighteenth century.

Hutin, Serge. *Henry More. Essai sur les doctrines théosophiques chez les platoniciens de Cambridge.* Hildesheim, G. Olms. "Studien und Materialien zur Geschichte der Philosophie; 2", 1966. 214 pp. Useful and well documented.

———. *Les Disciples anglais de Jacob Boehme.* Series "La Tour Saint-Jacques." Paris: Denoël, 1960. 332 pp. Reference work. A classic—one of Serge Hutin's best books.

Jacob Boehme. Collective work. Series "Cahiers de l'Hermétisme". Paris: Albin Michel, 1977. 236 pp. Texts by G. Wehr, P. Deghaye, and J. Boehme.

Jacob Boehme ou l'obscure lumière de la connaissance mystique. (Homage to Jacob Boehme from the staff of the Centre d'études et de recherches interdisciplinaires of Chantilly.) Paris: J. Vrin, 1979. 158 pp. Articles of H. Schmitz, P. Deghaye, J. L. Vieillard-Baron, J. F. Marquet, M. Vetö, M. de Gandillac, B. Rousset, A. Faivre, P. Trotignon.

Koyré, Alexandre. *La Philosophie de Jacob Boehme*. Paris: J. Vrin, 1980. 525 pp. (Facsimile of the first edition, 1929.) The classical work on Boehme (in French).

Weeks, Andrew. *Boehme. An Intellectual Biography of the Seventeenth Century Philosopher and Mystic*. Albany: SUNY Press, 1991, 268 pp. Illustrated. A brilliant and up-to-date study on the theosopher's thought.

Wehr, Gerhard. *Jakob Boehme in Selbstzeugnissen und Bilddokumenten*. Reinbek bei Hamburg: Rowohlts Monographien, 1971. 157 pp., illustrated. Rpt. in "Cahiers de l'Hermétisme", cited *supra* where it is presented in a French version.

EIGHTEENTH CENTURY

Amadou, Robert. *Trésor martiniste*. Paris: Villain et Belhomme, 1969. 240 pp., illustrated. Several studies on Illuminism in the eighteenth century. Includes a valuable bibliography of works by the author up to the date of publication.

Aspects de l'Illuminisme au XVIIIème siècle. Collective work edited by Robert Amadou. Nr. II-III-IV of *Les Cahiers de la Tour Saint-Jacques*. Paris: H. Roudil, 226 pp. Illustrated.

Benz, Ernst. *Les Sources mystiques de la philosophie romantique allemande*. Paris: J. Vrin, 1968. 155 pp. English edition: *The Mystical Sources of German Philosophy*. Allison Park (PA): Pickwick, 1983, 132 pp. On Saint-Martin in Germany, Mesmer, Baader, et al. A classic.

———. *Theologie der Elekrizität. Zur Begegnung und Auseinandersetzung von Theologie und Naturwissenschaft im 17. un 18. Jahrhundert*. Mainz: Ak. der Wissenschaften und der Literatur, 1970. 98 pp. English edition: *The Theology of Electricity*. Allison Park (PA): Pickwick, 1989, 104 pp. On Fricker, Divisch, Oetinger. About Illuminism in the eighteenth century to the romantic *Naturphilosophie*.

Cellier, Léon. *Fabre d'Olivet. Contribution à l'étude des aspects religieux du Romantisme*. Paris: Nizet, 1953. 448 pp. Broadly covers the period. Excellent synthesis.

Deghaye, Pierre. *La doctrine ésotérique de Zinzendorf (1700–1760)*. Paris: Klincksieck, 1969. 735 pp., illustrated.

Emmanuel Swedenborg, A Continuing Vision (A Pictorial Biography and Anthology of Essays and Poetry). Collective work. Presented by Robin Larsen. New York: Swedenborg Foundation, 1988. 558 pp.

Faivre, Antoine. *Kirchberger et l'Illuminisme du XVIIIe siècle.* Series "Archives internationales d'histoire des idées," No. 16. The Hague: Nijhoff, 1965. 284 pp., illustrated.

———. *Eckartshausen et la théosophie chrétienne.* Paris: Klincksieck, 1969. 788 pp., illustrated.

———. *L'Ésotérisme au XVIIIe siècle en France et en Allemagne.* Series "La Table d'Émeraude." Paris: Seghers, 1973. 224 pp., illustrated. Spanish edition, Madrid: EDAF, 1976.

———. *Mystiques, théosophes et illuminés au siècle des Lumières.* Hildesheim, G. Olms. "Studien und Materialien zur Geschichte der Philosophie, 20," 1976, 263 pp. On Saint-Martin, Baader, Lavater, Corberon, alchemy, etc.

Frick, Karl R. H. *Licht und Finsternis* and *Die Erleuchteten.* Op. cit. *supra*, General Works.

Geiger, Max. *Aufklärung und Erweckung. Beiträge zur Erforschung Johann Heinrich Jung-Stillings und der Erweckungstheologie.* Zurich: EVZ, 1963. 619 pp., illustrated. About Jung-Stilling, F. R. Salzmann, Karl von Hessen-Kassel, Julie de Krüdener, et al.

Jacques-Chaquin, Nicole. *Le théosophe et la sorcière: deux imaginaires du monde des signes* (Etudes sur l'illuminisme saint-martinien et sur la démonologie). 4 volumes. See volumes I (372 pp.) and II (309 pp.), on Saint-Martin. Ph.D. 1994, University of Paris VII, not yet published.

Joly, Alice. *Un mystique lyonnais et les secrets de la Franc-Maçonnerie (1730–1824).* Macon: Protat, 1938. 329 pp., illustrated. New edition: Paris : Demeter, 1986. Remains a basic work for the study of Illuminism in Lyons, although surpassed on several points by subsequent studies.

Keller, Jules. *Le Théosophe alsacien Friedrich Rudolf Salzmann et les milieux spirituels de son temps. Contribution à l'étude de l'Illuminisme et du mysticisme à la fin du XVIIIe et au début du XIXe siècle.* Bern/Frankfurt: P. Lang, 1985. Two vols. 211 and 620 pp. One of the best contributions to the study of Illuminism.

Le Forestier, René. *La Franc-Maçonnerie templière et occultiste.* Op cit. *supra*, Freemasonry.

Leventhal, Herbert. *In the Shadow of Enlightenment.* New York: New York University Press, 1976. 330 pp.

Lumières et Illuminisme. Collective work presented by Mario Matucci. Proceedings of the Cortona Conference (Italy), October 1983. Pisa: Pacini Editore, "Critica e Storia letteraria", 1984.

McIntosh, Christopher. *The Rose Cross and the Age of Reason: 18th Century Rosicrucianism in Central Europe and its Relationship to the Enlightenment.* Leyden: E. J. Brill, 1992. 200 pp. Illustrated.

Meillassoux -Le Cerf, Micheline. *Dom Pernety et les Illuminés d'Avignon. Suivi de la transcription intégrale de la Sainte Parole.* Milan: Archè-Edidit, 1992, 455 pp.

Oetinger, Friedrich Christoph. *Die Lehrtafel der Prinzessin Antonia. Hrsg. von Reinhard Breymayer und Friedrich Häusserman*, "Texte zur Geschichte des Pietismus". Abteilung vii. Berlin/New York: de Gruyter, 1977. Vol. 1 Text, 266 pp., illustrated. Vol. 2 Anmerkungen, 633 pp. Vol. 2 is of admirable scholarship. A wealth of irreplaceable information.

Présence de Louis-Claude de Saint-Martin. Collective work presented by J. F. Marquet and J. L. Vieillard-Baron. Tours: Société Ligérienne de Philosophie, series "L'Autre Rive", 1986, 319 pp.

Presenza di Cagliostro. Collective work presented by Daniela Gallingani. Proceedings of the San Leo Conference (Italy), 20–22. June 1991. Florence: Centro Editoriale Toscano, 1994, 688 pp. A rich documentation on the esoteric currents in the time of the Enlightenment.

Saint-Martin, Louis-Claude de. *Oeuvres Majeures.* Hildesheim: G. Olms. Edited by Robert Amadou since 1975. Five volumes have come out—mentioned here because of the introductions and presenter's notes.

Schuchard, Marsha Keith Manatt. *Freemasonry, Secret Societies, and the Continuity of the Occult Traditions in English Literature.* Diss. The University of Texas at Austin, 1975 (Xerox University Microfilms, Ann Arbor, Michigan 48106.) 698 pp. W. Blake, Swedenborgism, W. B. Yeats, etc.

Sekrecka, Mieczyslawa. *Louis-Claude de Saint-Martin, le Philosophe inconnu. L'homme et l'oeuvre.* Warsaw: Acta Universitatis Wratislaviensis, No. 65, 1968. 224 pp.

Swedenborg and his Influence. Conference Proceedings at Bryn Athyn, Penn., February 1988. Collective work. Bryn Athyn (Penn.): The Academy of the New Church, 1988. 492 pp.

Trautwein, Joachim. *Die Theosophie Michael Hahns und ihre Quellen.* From "Quellen und Forschungen zur württ. Kirchengeschichte". Bd. 2. Stuttgart: Calwer, 1969. 403 pp.

Van Rijnberk, Gérard. *Un Thaumaturge au XVIIIe siècle: Martinès de Pasqually. (Sa vie, son oeuvre, son ordre.)* Vol. 1, Paris: Alcan, 1935. 225 pp.; vol 2, Lyon: Derain-Radet, 1938. 185 pp. (Facsimile Plan de la Tour: Éd. d'Aujourd'hui, 1980).

Viatte, Auguste. *Les Sources occultes du Romantisme: Illuminisme-Théosophie (1770–1820).* Paris: Champion, 1928. (Many facsimile reprints, same editor.) Vol I, *Le Préromantisme*. 331 pp. Vol. 2, *La Génération de l'Empire.* 332 pp. Basic work on the issue, with which all researchers and amateurs in the study of eighteenth-century Illuminism should begin their work. It should be understood that the approach is literary, rather than philosophical.

Zimmermann, Rolf Christian. *Das Weltbild des Jungen Goethe.* Munich: W. Fink. Vol. 1, *Elemente und Fundamente*, 1969. 368 pp., illustrated; vol 2, *Interpretation und Dokumentation*, 1979. 447 pp., illustrated. Great study on hermetic literature in Germany in the Century of Enlightenment. A new approach to the genesis of Goethe's thought.

ROMANTICISM AND "NATURPHILOSOPHIE"

Ayrault, Roger. *La Genèse du Romantisme allemand.* Paris: Aubier. Vol. 1, 1961. 361 pp.; vol. 2, 1961. 782 pp.; vol. 3, 1969. 572 pp.; vol. 4, 1976. 573 pp. Each volume contains many explanations dealing directly with esoteric Romanticism..

Baader, Franz von. *Sämtliche Werke.* 16 vols. Leipzig: n.p., 1860. Rpt. Aalen: Scientia Verlag, 1963. Mentioned here because of the numerous notes from the editor, Franz Hoffmann, who was a student of Baader. Also noteworthy for the copious introductions and presentations to these volumes by other theosophers (Julius Hamberger, Anton Lutterbeck, E. A. von Schaden, Ch. Schlüter, Fr. von Ostensacken, et al).

Besset, Maurice. *Novalis et la pensée mystique.* Paris: Aubier, 1947. 197 pp. The best "esoteric" approach to the *Naturphilosophie* of Novalis.

Cellier, Léon. *Fabre d'Olivet*, op. cit. *supra*, Eighteenth Century. Cf. especially the sixth part.

(Les) Études Philosophiques. Paris: PUF, January and April 1983. These two issues are devoted to German romanticism. Articles about romantic medicine deal with J. W. Ritter, F. C. Oetinger, Novalis, etc.

Fabry, Jacques. *Le Bernois Friedrich Herbort et l'ésotérisme chrétien en Suisse à l'époque romantique.* Bern: P. Lang, Publications Universitaires Européennes, Series I, vol. 718, 1980. 280 pp. Good study of the environment and interesting contribution to the history of alchemy.

————. *Le Théosophe de Francfort Johann Friedrich von Meyer (1771–1849) et l'ésotérisme en Allemagne au XIXe siècle.* Two vols. Bern/Frankfurt: P. Lang, 1989. 1256 and 625 pp. A considerable amount of information and documentation.

Faivre, Antoine. *Physica Sacra (Etudes sur Franz von Baader et les Philosophes de la Nature).* Paris: A. Michel, "Bibliothèque Philosophique" series, 1994 (forthcoming, ca. 300 pp.)

Gode Van Aesch, Alexander G. F. *Natural Science in German Romanticism.* New York: Columbia Univ. Press, 1941. 302 pp.

Gusdorf, Georges. *Les Sciences humaines et la Pensée occidentale.* Paris: Payot. Vol. 9, *Fondements du savoir romantique*, 1982. 471 pp.; vol 10, *Du néant à Dieu dans le savoir romantique*, 1983. 430 pp.; vol. 11, *L'Homme romantique*, 1984. 368 pp. *Le Savoir romantique de la Nature*, 1985. 345 pp. These volumes represent a useful introduction to romantic *Naturphilosophie*.

Juden, Brian. *Traditions orphiques et tendances mystiques dans le Romantisme français (1800–1855).* Paris: Klincksieck, 1971. 805 pp.

(Die) Philosophie, Theologie und Gnosis Franz von Baader's (Spekulatives Denken zwischen Aufklärung, Restauration und Romantik). Ed. by Peter Koslowski. Vienna: Passagen Verlag, 1993. Proceedings of the symposium held in Munich 20.–23. May 1993. With contributions from Lidia Procesi, Pierre Deghaye, Ferdinand Schumacher, et *alia*.

Romantik in Deutschland. Ein Interdisziplinäres Symposion. Hrsg. von Richard Brinkman. Sonderband der "Deutschen Vierteljahresschrift für Literaturwissenschaft und Geistesgeschichte." Stuttgart: J. B. Metzler, 1978. 722 pp., illustrated. All interesting. On *Naturphilosophie*, cf. especially pp. 167–430. We would point out particularly the important bibliography by Dietrich von Engelhardt.

Romantische Naturphilosophie. (Texts selected by Christoph Bernoulli und Hans Kern) Jena: E. Diederich, 1926. 431 pp., illustrated. Notable and important names are missing; nevertheless there is a good presentation and choice of texts of L. Oken, Fr. Hufeland, J. von Kieser, G. H. von Kieser, J. B. Friedreich, W. Butte, G. Malfatti, I.P.V. Troxler, G. R. Treviranus, and C. G. Carus.

Schubert, Gotthilf Heinrich. *La symbolique du rêve.* Series "Cahiers de l'Hermétisme." Paris: Albin Michel, 1982. 217 pp. French translation of *Symbolik des Traums* (1814). Mentioned here as a critical work for the valuable introduction by the translator Patrick Valette, pp. 12–54.

Sladek, Mirko. *Fragmente der hermetischen Naturphilosophie.* op. cit. *supra,* General Works.

Susini, Eugène. *Franz von Baader et le Romantisme mystique.* Two vols., 519 and 595 pp. Paris: J. Vrin, 1942.

―――. *Lettres inédites de Franz von Baader,* Paris: J. Vrin, 1942. 515 pp.

―――. *(Commentaires aux) Lettres inédites de Franz von Baader.* Vienna: Herder, 1952. Two vols., 511 and 628 pp., illustrated.

―――. *Lettres inédites de Franz von Baader.* Paris: PUF, 1967. 623 pp., illustrated.

―――. *(Commentaires aux) Lettres inédites de Franz von Baader.* Frankfurt: P. Lang, 1983. 846 pp. in two vols., illustrated. In the notes and commentaries to the letters, there is a considerable information on preromantic and romantic esoteric circles.

Tuveson, Ernest Lee. *The Avatars of Thrice Great Hermes.* Op. cit. *supra,* General Works.

Viatte, Auguste. *Victor Hugo et les Illuminés de son temps.* Montreal: Éd. de l'Arbre, 1942. 284 pp. Magnetism, Swedenborgism, É. Lévi, l'abbé Châtel, L. de Tourreil, and V. Hugo.

END OF THE NINETEENTH CENTURY THROUGH THE TWENTIETH CENTURY

"Cults and New Religions." Collection edited by J. Gordon Melton. Each work (from 400 to 500 pp.) consists of a collection of facsimilie reprint texts. It is preceded by a general introduction. Many of these works touch on our subject. Regarding esotericism properly understood, the following titles have appeared (1990, New York/London: Garland Publishing): *Theosophy I (The Inner Life of Theosophy); Theosophy II (Controversial and Polemical Pamphlets); Rosicrucianism in America; The Beginnings of Astrology in America; Spiritualism I (Spiritualist Thought); Spiritualism II (The Movement); Neo-Pagan Witchcraft I; Neo-Pagan Witchcraft II.*

(Le) Défi magique. Cf. *supra,* General Works.

Ellwood, Robert S. *Alternative Altars: Unconventional and Eastern Spirituality in America.* The Univ. of Chicago Press, 1979. 192 pp. New religious movements, Zen in the West, and above all, a good historical exposition of the beginnings of the Theosophical Society.

Cellier, Léon. *Fabre d'Olivet.* Op. cit *supra*, Eighteenth Century. Cf. the last chapter: "Les Compagnons de la hiérophanie."

Frick, Karl R. H. *Die Erleuchteten.* Op. cit. *supra*, General Works.

Hemleben, Johannes. *Rudolf Steiner in Selbstzeugnissen und Bild-dokumenten.* Reinbek bei Hamburg: Rowohlts Monographien, 1963. 175 pp., illustrated. Good introduction to Steiner and anthroposophy.

Introvigne, Massimo. *Il Cappello del Mago (I nuovi movimenti magici, dallo Spiritismo al Satanismo).* Milan: SugarCo, 1990. 487 pp. Abridged French edition: *La Magie (Les Nouveaux Mouvements Magiques).* Paris: Droguet et Ardent, 1993. A clear, detailed, and probably complete panorama of movements, associations, and initiatory orders having to do with magic from the end of the nineteenth century to today. Copious, well chosen bibliography. An indispensable work.

James, Marie-France. *Ésotérisme, Occultisme, Franc-Maçonnerie et Christianisme aux XIXe et XXe siècles. Explorations bio-bibliographiques.* Paris: Nouvelles Éd. Latines, 1981. 268 pp. Missing a number of important names. Choice of entries very questionable; nevertheless what it does contain makes an interesting and practical catalogue.

Laurant, Jean-Pierre. *L'Ésotérisme chrétien en France au XIXe siècle.* Lausanne: L'Age d'Homme, 1992. 246 pp. an indispensable restatement and a wealth of information.

Melton, J. Gordon. *Witchcraft and Paganism in America.* New York/London: Garland Publishing, 1982. 231 pp. Very valuable bibliographical work.

———. *Biographical Dictionary of American and Sect Leaders.* New York/London: Garland Publishing, 1986. 364 pp. Many names presented in this dictionary actually have to do with esoterical currents of thought.

———. *Encyclopedic Handbook of Cults in America.* New York/London: Garland Publishing, 1986, 272 pp. Same remark as above. Revised and updated edition, 1992, 407 pp.

Mercier, Alain. *Les Sources ésotériques et occultes de la poésie symboliste (1870–1914).* Paris: Nizet. Vol. 1, Le *Symbolisme français,* 1969. 286 pp.; vol. 2, *Le Symbolisme européen,* 1974. 253 pp. This clear and serious study covers the period (end of the nineteenth and beginning of the twentieth centuries) and approaches the core issues through literature. Thus the focus is similar to that in Viatte's thesis on the eighteenth century—more literary than philosophical.

————*Édouard Schuré et le renouveau idéaliste en Europe.* Université de Lille, thesis reproduction, 1980. 748 pp. Through this presentation of the author of *Les Grands Initiés*, aspects of occultist thought of this period are better understood.

Möller, Helmut, and Howe, Ellic. *Merlin Peregrinus.* . . . Cf. *supra*, Esoteric Freemasonry.

(The) Occult in America: New Historical Perspectives. Ed. Howard Kerr and Charles L. Crow. NP Univ. of Illinois Press, 1983. 246 pp., illustrated. Occultism in the nineteenth century, theosophy, and contemporary occultism.

Roszak, Theodore. *Unfinished Animal: The Aquarian Frontier and the Evolution of Consciousness.* 1975. New York: Harper and Row, 1977. 271 pp. A valuable reflection on the avatars of contemporary occultism.

Saunier, Jean. *La Synarchie.* Paris: CAL, 1971. 287 pp. Interesting approach to certain forms of esoteric societies.

————. *Saint-Yves d'Alveydre ou une synarchie sans énigme.* Series "Histoire et Tradition." Paris: Dervy, 1981. 487 pp., illustrated. Saint-Yves and his Synarchy are discussed as well as several aspects of the occultist movement.

(The) Theosophical Movement (1875–1950). Anonymous. Los Angeles: The Cunningham Press, 1951. 351 pp. Probably one of the best works on the Theosophical Society.

Webb, James. *The Occult Underground.* LaSalle, Ill.: Open Court, 1974. 387 pp. Good approach on esoteric trends at the turn of the century.

————. *The Occult Establishment.* LaSalle, Ill.: Open Court, 1976. 535 pp. Webb's second work mainly deals with western esoteric trends during the first half of the twentieth century. Well documented.

————. *The Harmonious Circle (The Lives and Work of G. I. Gurdjieff, P.D. Ouspensky, and Their Followers).* G.P. Putman, 1980. Second edition. Boston: Shambhala, 1987. 608 pp. Gurdjeff and his circle are presented by Webb in the esoteric context of their times.

Finally, several of the works cited *supra* under "Freemasonry" could actually be placed here; these deal with the "fringe Masonry": Rosicrucianism, Golden Dawn, etc. (cf. also the note *supra*, p. 313, concerning the works published by The Aquarian Press).

CONCERNING TRADITION

Abellio, Raymond. *La Structure absolue. Essai de phénoménologie génétique.* Bibliothèque des Idées. Paris: Gallimard, 1965. 527 pp. Basic work by a philosopher on esotericism and tradition. His thoughts are very personal and original. See also by the same author:

————. *La Fin de l'ésotérisme.* Paris: Flammarion, 1973. 254 pp.

————. *Approches de la nouvelle gnose.* Paris: Gallimard, 1981. Series "Les Essais." 254 pp.

A.R.I.E.S. (Association for Research and Information on Esotericism). Paris: La Table d'Emeraude, No. xi (1990), xii–xiii and xiv (1990–1991). These volumes contain material on perennialism (pro and con). Articles by Leo Bowman, Sheldon R. Isenberg, Tyson Anderson, James Cutsinger.

Bonardel, Françoise. *Philosophie de l'Alchimie: Grand Oeuvre et Modernité.* Paris: PUF, 1993, 706 pp. After defining the notions of hermetism and alchemy, the author studies numerous philosophers, writers, and creative persons of the nineteenth and twentieth centuries, looking into their "alchemic" development (even when they themselves do not refer explicitly to esotericism). This is a work of considerable interest, in the spirit of what I have called here the "third path."

————. *L'Hermétisme.* op. cit. *supra*, General Works.

Durand, Gilbert. *Science de l'homme et Tradition: Le "Nouvel Esprit anthropologique."* Series "L'Isle Verte." Paris: Berg International, 1980. First edition: "Tête de feuille." Paris: Sirac, 1975. 243 pp. In the spirit of what I have called the "third path," this work and the following by the same author clearly represent some of the more important works written. See in particular the chapters "Hermetica ratio" and "Science de l'Homme."

————. *Figures mythiques et visages de l'Oeuvre: De la mythocritique à la mythanalyse.* Collection "L'Isle Verte." Paris: Berg International, 1979. 327 pp.

————. *L'Ame tigrée: Les pluriels de la psyché.* Collection "Méditations." Paris: Denoël-Gonthier, 1980. 210 pp.

————. *La Foi du cordonnier.* Paris: Denoël, 1984. 231 pp.

James, Marie-France. *Esotérisme et christianisme. Autour de René Guénon.* Preface by Jacques-Albert Cuttat. Paris: Nouvelles Editions Latines, 1981. 48 pp. A wealth of information concerning the esoteric circles with which Guénon was familiar.

Laurant, Jean-Pierre. *Le Sens caché dans l'oeuvre de René Guénon.* Lausanne: L'Age d'Homme, 1975. 277 pp. An indispensable work on Guénon's thought.

Nasr, Seyyed Hossein. *Knowledge and the Sacred.* New York: Crossroad, 1981. 341 pp. A good historical and philosophical work very much committed to the "traditional" approach.

Raymond Abellio. (Collective work) Ed. by Pierre Lombard. Paris: L'Herne, 1979. 428 pp. Y. Dauge, C. Hirsch, M. Beigbeder, et al. Numerous documents and much evidence.

René Guénon. (Collective work) Ed. by Jean-Pierre Laurant (with the assistance of Paul Barba-Negra). Paris: Cahiers de l'Herne, 1985. 459 pp., illustrated. J.P. Laurant, M. Michel, J. Borella, M. Eliade, F. Schuon, F. Tristan, et al.

René Guénon et l'actualité de la pensée traditionnelle. Proceedings of the international conference at Cerisy-la-Salle (July 13–20, 1973). Ed. by René Alleau and Marina Scriabine. Belgium (Braine-le-Comte), 1973. Republished Milan: Archè, 1981. 333 pp. R. Alleau, J. Tourniac, Ph. Lavastine, R. Amadou, B. Guillemain, M. de Gandillac, M. Scriabine, R.M. Burlet, J. Hani, A. Faivre, and G. Ferrand.

Roszak, Theodore. *Unfinished Animal.* Op.cit. *supra*, End of the 19th through the 20th century. The general inspiration for this work corresponds to our "third path."

Robin, Jean. *René Guénon témoin de la Tradition.* Paris: Tredaniel, 1978. 349 pp.

Schaya, Leo. Cf. *supra*, From the 2nd to the 15th century.

(The) Sword of Gnosis (Metaphysics, Cosmology, Tradition, Symbolism). Ed. by Jacob Needleman. Baltimore: Penguin Metaphysical Library, 1974. 464 pp. Contains essays of F. Schuon, R. Guénon, M. Pallis, A. Bakr Siraj Ad-Din, M. Lings, T. Burckhardt, S. Nasr, L. Schaya, and D.M. Deed. All the essays in this volume have appeared previously in the journal *Studies in Comparative Religion* (formerly *Tomorrow*). These texts are committed to a perennialist perspective. Nevertheless this work is cited here, on the one hand because of its usefulness for those who wish to get some understanding of this field, and on the other because of Jacob Needleman's illuminating introduction.

Tomberg, Valentin. Cf. *supra*, General Works.

Vallin, Georges. *La Perspective métaphysique.* Foreword by Paul Mus. Paris: Dervy, 1977. First edition, 1958. 253 pp.

————. *Voie de Gnose et Voie d'amour: Eléments de mystique comparée.* Sisteron: Présence, 1980. 178 pp.

Versluis, Arthur. *American Transcendentalism and Asian Religions.* New York/Oxford: Oxford Univ. Press, 1993, 353 pp.

Wehr, Gerhard. *Esoterisches Christentum.* Op.cit. *supra*, General Works.

Wissende, Verschwiegene, Eingeweihte. Hinführung zur Esoterik. Ed. Gerd-Klaus Kaltenbrunner (collective work). Munich: Herder, "Initiative 42," 1981, 192 pp. Articles of F. Schuon, H. Küry, Leo Schaya, R. Pietsch, T. Burckhardt, and H.J. von Baden.

ESOTERICISM AND ISLAM

We find *supra*, under "Alchemy," references to the works of Pierre Lory, Julius Ruska, and Monod-Herzen; under "Concerning Tradition," to a work by Seyyed H. Nasr. Let us limit ourselves, in a vast domain like Arab esotericism, to some other recent and prominent titles:

Amir-Moezzi, Mohammed Ali. *Le Guide Divin dans le shî'isme originel. Aux sources de l'ésotérisme en Islam.* Paris: Verdier, 1992, 379 pp.

Chittick, William C. *Ibn al-'Arabi's Metaphysics of Imagination: The Sufi Path of Knowledge.* Albany: SUNY Press, 1989, 478 pp. One of the major works on occidental research on Sufism, and a turning point in the study of Islamic esotericism in the West.

Corbin, Henry. *En Islam Iranien, aspects spirituels et philosophiques.* Bibliothèque des Idées Series: vol. 1, *Le Shî'isme duodécimain,* 332 pp.; vol. 2, *Sohrawardî et les platoniciens de Perse,* 384 pp.; vol. 3, *Les Fidèles d'Amour. Shî'isme et soufisme,* 358 pp.; vol. 5, *L'École Shaykhie, le Douzième Imam,* 567 pp. Paris: Gallimard, 1971–72. In this area H. Corbin is the principal reference author. Reading his works not only allows us to enter into Shiite esotericism, but also helps us to better understand Judeo-Christian esotericism, especially since the author himself never missed the opportunity to establish discerning connections. All of his work should be cited; let us limit ourselves to six other titles:

————. *L'Imagination créatrice dans le soufisme d'Ibn 'Arabi.* Idées et Recherches Series. Paris: Flammarion, 1977, 328 pp., illustrated. First edition, 1958. English edition: *Creative Imagination in the Sufism of Ibn' Arabi.* Princeton Univ. Press, 1969, 406 pp.

————. *Avicenne et le récit visionnaire.* L'Ile Verte series. Paris: Berg International, 1979, 316 pp. (First edition, Teheran, 1954); English edition: *Avicenna and the Visionary Recital.* New York: Pantheon, 1960, 423 pp. (new edition 1980).

————. *Terre céleste et corps de résurrection.* Paris: Buchet-Chastel, 1960. English edition: *Spiritual Body and Celestial Earth.* Princeton Univ. Press, 1977, 351 pp.

————. *Temple et contemplation, Essais sur l'Islam iranien.* Idées et Recherches Series. Paris: Flammarion, 1980, 447 pp.

————. *L'Homme et son ange, initiation et chevalerie spirituelle.* Paris: Fayard, 1983, 276 pp.

————. *Face de Dieu, face de l'homme.* Idées et Recherches Series. Paris: Flammarion, 1983, 282 pp.

Sezgin, Fuat. *Geschichte des arabischen Schrifttums.* Vol. IV, Leiden: E.J. Brill, 1971. Cf. section "Alchimie-Chimie", pp. 1–300.

Ullmann, Manfred. *Die Natur- und Geheimwissenschaften in Islam.* Leiden and Cologne: Brill, 1972.

ESOTERICISM, LITERATURE, AND ART

Does not our approach of esotericism allow the esoteric to be found in many creations of the imagination (the "imaginary")? Historians and critics have addressed the nature and specificity of this relationship. Since it appears to be more difficult to prepare a succinct bibliography on this subject than on those preceding, the following indications are limited to a simple *orientation,* i.e. a necessarily arbitrary choice. In the preceding rubrics, many works can be found which address this question (i.e., F. Bonardel, B. Juden, A. Mercier, M. Sladek, E.L. Tuveson, G. van Lennep, A. Viatte, F. Yates, R.C. Zimmerman). On the relationships between alchemy and literature, the Adepts have occasionally expressed themselves (i.e., Eugène Canseliet, *L'Hermétisme dans la vie de Swift et dans ses voyages.* Paris: Fata Morgana, 1983). Among critical works worthy of interest we note also:

Abraham, Lyndy. *Marvell and Alchemy.* Brookfield, Vermont: Solar Press, Gower Publishing, 1990, 364 pp., illustrated.

Knapp, Bettina. *Theater and Alchemy.* Detroit: Wayne University Press, 1980, 283 pp.

Nichol, Charles. *The Chemical Theater.* London: Routledge and Kegan Paul, 1980, 292 pp., illustrated.

Schmidt, Albert-Marie. *La Pensée scientifique au XVIè siècle.* Lausanne: Rencontres, 1970, 463 pp.

Certain great authors have been the object of diverse historio-critical approaches. Among them:

Arnold, Paul. *Esotérisme de Shakespeare.* Paris: Mercure de France, 1955, 280 pp.

Dauphiné, James. *Les Structures symboliques dans le théâtre de Shakespeare.* Paris: Les Belles Lettres, 1983, 255 pp.

Yates, Frances A. *Shakespeare's Last Plays. A New Approach.* London: Routledge and Kegan Paul, 1975, 140 pp., illustrated.

Faivre, A. and F. Tristan, eds. *Goethe.* Cahiers de l'Hermétisme series. Paris: A. Michel, 1980, 263 pp.

Centeno, Yvette K. *A alquimia e o Fausto de Goethe.* Artes e Letras series. Lisbon: Arcadai, 1983, 283 pp., illustrated.

Masters, G. Mallary. *Rabelaisian Dialectic and the Platonic-Hermetic Tradition.* Albany: SUNY Press, 1969, 152 pp.

Richer, Jean. *Gérard de Nerval et les doctrines ésotériques.* Paris: Le Griffon d'Or, 1947, 216 pp., illustrated. Greatly enlarged in *Nerval: Expérience vécue et tradition ésotérique.* Paris: Trédaniel, 1987, 399 pp.

————. *Prestiges de la lune et damnation par les étoiles dans le théâtre de Shakespeare.* Paris: Les Belles Lettres, 1982, 119 pp., illustrated.

————. *Lecture astrologique des pièces romaines de Shakespeare.* Paris: Trédaniel (La Maisnie), 1988, 94 pp., illustrated.

Among the critical works not limited to one author, also to be consulted:

Dauphiné, James, ed. *Création littéraire et traditions ésotériques (XVè–XXè siècles).* Proceedings of a colloquium of the Faculty of Pau. November 1989. Pau: J. et D., 1991, 374 pp.

————. *Esotérisme et Littérature: Etude de symbolique en littérature française et comparée du moyen âge à nos jours.* Nice: Centre d'Etudes Médiévales de Nice, 1992, 370 pp.

Mebane, John S. *Renaissance Magic and the Return of the Golden Age (The Occult Tradition and Marlowe, Jonson, and Shakespeare).* Lincoln (Nebr.): Univ. of Nebraska Press, 1989, 309 pp., illustrated.

Monneyron, Fédéric, ed. *L'Androgyne dans la Littérature.* Proceedings of the symposium in Cerisy-la-Salle (26. June 7, July 1986). Cahiers de l'Hermétisme Series (follows *L'Androgyne* edited by A. Faivre, same publisher, 1986). Paris: A. Michel, 1990, 157 pp.

Richer, Jean. *Aspects ésoteriques de l'oeuvre littéraire*. L'Oeuvre Secrète series. Paris: Dervy, 1980, 308 pp.

Riffaterre, Hermine, ed. *The Occult in Language and Literature*. New York: Literary Forum, 1980.

Roos, Jacques. *Aspects littéraires du mysticisme philosophique au début du Romantisme: W. Blake, Novalis, Ballanche*. Strasbourg: P.H. Heitz, 1951, 471 pp.

Senior, John. *The Way Down and Out: The Occult in Symbolist Literature*. Ithaca: Cornell Univ. Press, 1959, 217 pp.

Tatar, Maria M. *Spellbound, Studies on Mesmerism and Literature*. Princeton (N.J.): Princeton Univ. Press, 1978, 293 pp.

Vadé, Yves. *L'enchantement littéraire (Ecriture et Magie de Chateaubriand à Rimbaud)*. Paris: Gallimard, 1990, 489 pp.

Woodman, David. *White Magic and English Renaissance Drama*. Cranbury, New Jersey: Associated University Presses, 1973, 148 pp.

The relationships between esotericism and music have recently been the subject of excellent studies, among them:

Chailley, Jacques. *La Flûte Enchantée, Opéra Maçonnique*. Diapason series. Paris: R. Lafont, 1968, 367 pp., illustrated. English translation, *The Magic Flute, Masonic Opera*. New York: Alfred A. Knopf, 1971, 336 pp., illustrated (new edition 1982).

Eckelmeyer, Judith A. *The Cultural Context of Mozart's Magic Flute (Social, Aesthetic, Philological)*. 2 vols. Lewiston: Edwin Mellen Press, 1991, 329 pp. and 475 pp., illustrated.

Godwin Joscelyn. *Harmonies of Heaven and Earth (The Spiritual Dimension of Music from Antiquity to the Avant-Garde)*. London: Thames and Hudson, 1987, 208 pp.

———. *Music, Mysticism and Magic. A Sourcebook*. London/New York: Arkana/Routledge and Kegan Paul, 1987, 349 pp.

———. *L'Esotérisme musical en France (1750–1950)*. Bibliothèque de l'Hermétisme series. Paris: Albin Michel, 1991, 272 pp.

———. *The Harmony of the Spheres. A Sourcebook of the Pythagorean Tradition in Music*. Rochester, Vermont: Inner Traditions International, 1993, 495 pp., illustrated.

Irmen, Hans-Josef. *Mozart, Mitglied Geheimer Gesellschaften*. Germany: Prisca Verlag, 1988, 360 pp., Illustrated.

In the area of painting and architecture, esoteric style points of view have been expressed in diverse ways, notably by the defenders of perennialism (cf. for example *supra*, the authors of *The Sword of Gnosis*), or by the Adepts of alchemy such as the celebrated Eugène Canseliet and Fulcanelli. Here are several examples of particularly interesting historical works:

Chastel, André. *Marsile Ficin et l'art.* Geneva: Droz, 1954.

———. *Art et Humanisme à Florence au temps de Laurent le Magnifique. Etudes sur la Renaissance et l'humanisme platonicien.* Paris: Presses Universitaires de France, 1982, 580 pp.

Deswarte, Sylvie. *Le "De Aetatibus Mundi Imagines" de Francisco de Holanda.* Vol 66 of Monuments et Mémoires publiés par l'Académie des Inscriptions et Belles-Lettres. Paris: PUF, 1983, 190 pp.

Kaplan, Stuart R. *The Encyclopedia of Tarot.* Vol 1, 1978, 387 pp.; vol. 2, 1986, 552 pp.; vol. 3, 1990, 694 pp. Stamford, Connecticut: U.S. Games Systems.

Lima de Freitas. *515—Le Jeu du Miroir. Art et Numérologie.* Bibliothèque de l'Hermétisme series. Paris: A. Michel, 1993, 327 pp., illustrated.

Tuchman, Maurice, ed. *The Spiritual in Art: Abstract Painting 1890–1985.* New York: Abbeville Press, 1986, 435 pp., illustrated. Great exhibit catalogue.

JOURNALS AND SERIALS

In addition to journals (cited *supra*, Alchemy) devoted to alchemy, and among the most interesting periodicals and serials, the following can be mentioned:

Alexandria. The Journal of the Western Cosmological Traditions. Annual. David Fideler, ed. Grand Rapids (Mich.): Phanes Press. Two issues published (1991, 378 pp.; 1994, 429 pp.).

A.R.I.E.S. (Association for Research and Information on Esotericism). Biannual publication. Roland Edighoffer, Jacques Fabry, Antoine Faivre and Jean-Paul Corsetti, eds. Paris: La Table d'Emeraude. 17 issues, about 90 pp. each (1985–1994). The only publication dedicated chiefly to analyses, book reviews, compilations and explanations of recent publications, university theses and colloquia on the topic of western esotericism. Written in several languages (mostly English, French and German).

Atlantis (Archéologie scientifique et traditionnelle). Vincennes: Atlantis. Bimonthly. Jacques d'Ares, editor-in-chief. 390 issues, about 60 pp. each, since 1929. Very characteristic of the "second path" of Tradition (see *supra*, pp. 38–39).

Bibliotheca Hermetica (Alchemy-Astrology-Magic). A series. Paris: Denoël & Retz. René Alleau, ed. 15 volumes, about 300 pp. each (1971–77). Elegant presentation. Each volume is accompanied by critical commentary by a scholar (like Sylvain Matton, Bernard Husson, Maxime Préaud, et al.). This series includes works by Nicolas Flamel, Louis Figuier, Alfred Maury, Marcus Manilius, Limojon de Saint-Didier, Jean d'Espagnet, Dom Pernety, etc. Many of these texts deal with alchemy.

Cahiers du Groupe d'Etudes Spirituelles Comparées (G.E.S.C.). Takes up from U.S.J.J. (cf. *infra*). Since 1992. President, Gilbert Durand. Proceedings of the May 1992 colloquium (*Transmission culturelle et transmission spirituelle*) appeared in 1993 (Paris: Archè). Proceedings of the May 1993 colloquium (*Images et Valeurs*) in 1994 (same editor).

Cahiers de l'Hermétisme. A series. Paris: Albin Michel, Editor: Antoine Faivre. 18 vols, about 300 pp. each (1977–1994): *Faust, L'ange et l'Homme. Jacob Boehme. Alchimie. Kabbalistes chrétiens. Paracelse. Goethe. Lumière et Cosmos. Sophia et l'Ame du Monde. L'Androgyne. Astrologie. L'Androgyne dans la Littérature. Le Mythe et le Mythique. Présence d'Hermès Trismégiste. Magie et Littérature. La Littérature Fantastique. Les Vampires; La Bible, histoire et mythe.* These are collective works.

Cahiers de l'Université de Saint-Jean de Jérusalem (Centre International d'Etudes Spirituelles Comparées), series of Proceedings. Paris: Berg International. Center and series founded by Henry Corbin. 14 volumes (first volume published by A. Bonne), 150–200 pp. each (1975–1985): *Sciences traditionnelles et Sciences profanes. Jérusalem la Cité spirituelle. La Foi prophétique et le Sacré. Les Pèlerins de l'Orient et les Vagabonds de l'Occident. Les Yeux de chair et les Yeux de feu. Le Combat pour l'Ame du Monde. L'Herméneutique permanente. Le Désert et la Queste. Apocalypse et sens de l'Histoire. La Chevalerie spirituelle. Face de Dieu et théophanies. La Matière spirituelle. Temps et hiérohistoire.* The U.S.J.J. ceased operations in 1988 and was succeeded by the G.E.S.C. (cf. *supra*). Each of these collective works presents the papers of the corresponding annual session of the U.S.J.J. Included among the regular collaborators were G. Durand, P. Deghaye, A. Abécassis, C. Jambet, J. Brun, J. L. Vieillard-Baron, A. Faivre.

(Les) Cahiers de Saint-Martin. Annual but irregular publication. Nice: Belisane. Annie Becq, Antoine Faivre and Nicole Jacques-Chaquin, eds. Eight issues, 100–120 pp. each (1976–1993). Journal destined to contribute to a better understanding of the "unknown philosopher" (Saint-Martin) and eighteenth-century Illuminism. Reprintings of ancient presentation of previously published documents, original articles, etc.

Charis. Archives de l'Unicorne. Annual publication. Milan/Paris: Archè. 2 issues, 198 pp. (1988) and 318 pp. (1993). High-level scholarly texts, edited and published by Ladislau Toth.

Connaissance des Religions (métaphysique, cosmologie, anthropologie, symbolisme, science et arts traditionnels). Quarterly publication, since 1984. Nancy: "Connaissance des Religions" Association. Leo Schaya and Jean Borella, editors. About 50 pp. Well put together; similar to *Etudes traditionelles.*

Conoscenza Religiosa. Quarterly publication. Florence: La Nuova Italia. Elemire Zolla, editor. 400–500 pp. annually. Mentioned here on account of several remarkable issues on the topic of esotericism (for example, *La Linguistica e il Sacro,* 1–2, 1972; *Numeri e figure geometriche come base della Simbologia,* 1–2, 1979).

Eranos Jahrbücher. Series. Frankfurt: Insul Verlag, last publisher (after Rhein Verlag, Zurich). 57 volumes, about 500 pp. each (1933–1988). This series is composed of contributions in German, French, and English that were the object of presentations at the annual meeting ("Eranos Tagung") in Ascona, Switzerland. Among the most well-known participants and panelists were G. Durand, M. Eliade, H. Corbin, G. Scholem, and C.G. Jung.

Etudes traditionnelles. Bimonthly publication. Paris: Etudes traditionnelles. Leo Schaya, ed. Michael Valsan, original ed. 500 issues, about 50 pp. each (1900–1993). This well-known publication has included numerous texts that influenced the history of esotericism in the twentieth century. Long published under the direction of R. Guénon and later of F. Schuon, it was formerly entitled *Le Voile d'Isis.*

Gnosis. A Journal of the Western Inner Traditions. Quarterly publication. San Francisco: The Lumen Foundation. Jay Kinney and Richard Smoley, eds. 32 issues since 1985, 70–80 pp. each. Attractive, well-illustrated journal destined to reach a wide audience. Each issue offers a dossier on a specific esoteric or religious topic and contains several interesting reviews and reports.

Hermès (Recherches sur l'expérience spirituelle). New series. Paris: Les Deux Océans. Lilian Silburn, ed. 300–450 pp. Includes *Les voies de la mystique* (1981), *Le Vide* (1981), *Le Maître spirituel* (1983), *Tch'An Zen* (1985).

Hermetika. Zeitschrift fur christliche Hermetik. Quarterly publication. Kinsau (Lech, R.F.A.). Michael Frensch, ed. Since 1983. 30–40 pp. per issue. Alexandrian hermetism, Christian esotericism, philosophy of nature.

This publication is committed to spirituality rather than careful scholarship.

(L')Initiation (Cahiers de documentation ésotérique traditionnelle). Official publication of the Martinist order. Quarterly publication. Paris: Martinist Order. Michel Leger, ed. About 50 pp. per issue. This publication has always come out on a regular basis. It has followed in the footsteps of the journal that Papus founded and published from 1888–1914. Created in 1953, it was run by Papus's son, Philippe Encausse, until his death in 1984. While the quality of this publication is sometimes lower than might be expected, it nevertheless contains abundant information and occasionally remarkable articles.

Politica Hermetica. Annual scholarly publication. Lausanne: L'Age d'Homme. Jean-Pierre Brach and Jean-Pierre Laurant, eds. 7 issues since 1987, 130–200 pp. each. A large part of each issue is dedicated to the publication of works from the yearly colloquium "Politica Hermetica." Issues to date are as follows: *Métaphysique et Politique (René Guénon and Julius Evola); Doctrines de la Race et Tradition; Gnostiques et mystiques autour de la Révolution Francaise; Maçonnerie et anti-Maçonnisme; Secrets, initiations et sociétés modernes; Le complot; La postérité de la théosophie*. An excellent scholarly journal.

Spring. An Annual of Archetypal Psychology and Jungian Thought. Annual publication since 1941. Dallas (Texas): Spring Publications. James Hillman and Randolph Severson, eds. 20–250 pp. per issue. Often contains interesting contributions on esotericism.

Symbolos. Revista Internacional de Arte, Cultura, Gnosis. Bimonthly publication. Guatemala: Agartha. Federico Gonzalez, ed. 5 issues since 1990, about 180 pp. each. Eclectic with a predilection toward "traditional" symbolism.

Theosophical History. A Quarterly Journal of Research. Quarterly review founded by Leslie Price. California State Univ. Press. James S. Santucci, ed. Since 1985, 30–50 pages each. A well-documented critical-historical journal, independent of any ideological orientation. It is dedicated to the study of the history, the members and influence of the Theosophical Society. Also worth mentioning is a 10-volume series, also edited by James Santucci, entitled "Theosophical History Centre" (California Univ. Press): documents and excellent studies edited here include Joscelyn Godwin's *The Birth of Theosophy in France* (1989).

(La) Tour Saint-Jacques. Published on an irregular basis from 1955–58. Paris, Roudil. Robert Amadou, ed. 13 issues, 100 pp. each. This publication

covers a broad range of esoteric topics. It was followed in 1958 by a series of nine volumes, each of which was dedicated to a specific author or theme, such as: *L'Illuminisme au XVIII siècle, Saint Martin, Huysmans, Parapsychologie*. All s.d. A fine conception beautifully carried out by Robert Amadou.

Triades. Revue trimestrielle anthroposophique. Paris: Triades. Published quarterly since 1953, about 100 pp. each. An anthroposophic publication in the Rudolf Steiner tradition.

A WORD ABOUT LIBRARIES

Even in a restrictive sense, esotericism is a vast field, present in all large libraries and often even in the smaller ones. There is not enough space here to present all those which preserve interesting esoteric collections. We will only mention some of them, limiting ourselves to several western European countries and the United States.

In Paris recommended are the Bibliothèque Nationale and the Bibliothèque Mazarine for their printed matter and manuscripts; the Bibliothèque de l'Arsenal for its manuscripts; in Strasburg, the Bibliothèque de l'Université, for its large collection of German books. Also useful are general printed and classified catalogues, which are easily accessible in the French libraries. Several of these are particularly interesting, even those who do not specializing in esotericism; for example, the collections at the Paris Museum (Eugène Chevreul's alchemy collection), the Calvet Museum in Avignon (documents on the "Illuminés" of Avignon), the Inguibertine in Carpentras (Gaffarel, Peresc collections, etc.), the Bibliothèque Méjanes in Aix-en-Provence (Illuminism in the 18th century), and the Bibliothèque Municipale in Lyons (Willermoz Collection), the municipal libraries of Blois, Montluçon (Desbois collections), Auxerre (collections of Billaudot), and Grenoble (Prunelle de Lière papers). Several esoteric movements maintain collections that are partially open to the public, including the Paris Theosophical Society (located in the Square Rapp) and the A.M.O.R.C., located in the d'Omonville château in the Eure.

In Munich, the Bayerische Staatsbibliothek is full of treasures. But the most extensive collection in Germany is located in the Herzog August Bibliothek in Wolfenbüttel. For a long time, this country was the chief record keeper of European esotericism, and almost every large library, municipal or university, maintains an interesting alchemical or theosophical collection (the Universitätsbibliothek at Hamburg still has its beautiful collection of alchemical texts, although its esoteric and theosophical collections were destroyed during the war). The library in Greifswald merits special mention for its documents concerning religious variations or heterodoxy. The Frankesche Stiftung at Halle-an-der-Saale maintains an important Böhmian collection.

The Johann Friedrich von Meyer collection, located in Erlangen (Institut für Historische Theologie, Abteilung ältere Kirchengeschichte), is rich in Masonic texts, among others.

Among the Masonic libraries of Germany, the one at the Deutsches Freimaurer Museum in Bayreuth is one of the richest in esoteric documents of all kinds (see the two-volume catalog compiled by Herbert Schneider in 1976 and 1984). The Masonic and Illuminist collection of Prince Christian von Hessen Darmstadt is located in the public Hessisches Staatsarchiv in Darmstadt. Another similar collection, which once belonged to Georg Kloss, is found in The Hague at the Grand Orient of the Netherlands (see catalogue compiled in 1880). The collection at the National Grand Loge of Denmark, in Copenhagen, is of comparable importance. It is a well-known fact that, as a general rule, no matter what country you are in the libraries of the Masonic Obediences are not open to the public. However, it is not unheard of to obtain permission to work in them.

Amsterdam can be proud of its unique collection at the Biblioteca Philosophica Hermetica. This private collection belongs to Joost R. Ritman, who is continually adding to it and has opened a portion of it to the public. More than 15,000 titles, most dating from the late fifteenth to early nineteenth centuries, are listed under the following: Hermetism, Kabbalah, alchemy, Rosicrucianism, and mysticism (in the sense of traditional theosophy).

The rich grouping of eighteenth-century Illuminism (manuscripts and printed works) formerly held by the Free Faculty of Protestant Theology at Lausanne has been transferred to the Bibliothèque Cantonale et Universitaire in the same town. At the Zentralbibliothek in Zurich, the prolific correspondence of Johann Caspar Lavater still waits to be used systematically, as does that of Jacob Sarasin, at the Staatsarchiv in Basel (a precious resource of information about the Cagliostrians). The private library of Oscar Schlag (Zurich) contains considerable resources for the field in which we are interested. In 1993, after the death of its owner, this collection was incorporated into the Zentralbibliothek in Zurich and will henceforth be available to the public.

In Italy, in addition to the Vatican in Rome and the Ambrosian in Milan, three libraries in Florence merit more than passing mention—the Biblioteca Medicea Laurenziana, the Biblioteca Nazionale, and the library in the Museum of Sciences. The Biblioteca Casanatense in Rome and the University Library in Bologna (with its important collection of alchemical texts) are also worth mentioning. Even the smaller towns hold some great surprises. In Vigerano, near Pavia, the library in the cathedral holds the archives of G. Caramuel (numerous seventeenth-century steganographic and alchemical documents).

In London, the British Library (formerly the British Museum) holds what may be the richest collection of manuscripts and printed texts in the

United Kingdom (the collections of Sloane are found there, among other legacies). In the same city, the library at the Warburg Institute specializes in Renaissance esotericism and related fields (including legacies of A. Warburg, Frances Yates, etc.). The Wellcome Library (Institute of the History of Medicine) specializes in medical writings (especially Paracelsian); and the Dr. Williams Library, which belongs to the Church of England, contains documents pertaining to Comenius and his milieu—William Law, Andreas Freher, and Jacob Boehme (see five-volume catalog). The Saint Andrews University library contains the alchemical collections of John Read. At Oxford, the Bodleian Library, one of the most interesting in the world for our field of study, has, among others, the collections of Elias Ashmole and John Dee (see the printed catalogue of the old collection). But there are also, in Glasgow: a) the Glasgow University Library, which is the repository for John Ferguson's own very substantial library of alchemical and related works; and b) the Andersonian Library of the University of Strathclyde, in which the rich collection of James Young is preserved.

In Washington, D.C., in addition to the enormous Library of Congress, the Shakespearian library at the Folger Institute contains some surprises. In Los Angeles, the Philosophical Research Library, a private institution, is a gift from esoteric scholar Manly P. Hall. The Howard Library is found at the World University of Tucson (Arizona). The John Hay Library, at Brown University in Providence, Massachusetts, holds the collections of Harris and Geiger. The principal library of the A.M.O.R.C. is located in San Jose, California. The collection of Paul and Mary Mellon (see the 1969 catalog—four volumes, two for printed texts and two for manuscripts) now belongs to Yale University in New Haven, Connecticut. The Memorial Library at the University of Wisconsin at Madison contains the collection of Denis I. Duveen.

A systematic inventory ought to be accompanied by a well-thought-out list of private collections including those that have been, unfortunately, destroyed either accidentally or willfully by their owners. To find a specific old book or manuscript collection in a private dwelling, often after a lengthy search, is one of the greatest joys that the searcher can experience, even if this search sometimes entails myriad difficulties. In many cases private archives and official library cabinets are like the seven sleepers of Ephesus.

INDEX OF NAMES

Persons listed in the "Bibliographical Guide for Research" are not included in this index.

INDEX OF SUBJECTS AND TERMS
by Leesa Stanion

359

Printed in Great Britain
by Amazon

29983740R00212